Frommer's®

# Britain's Best
# Bed & Breakfasts
# and Country Inns

**IDG Books Worldwide, Inc.**
**An International Data Group Company**
Foster City, CA ■ Chicago, IL ■ Indianapolis, IN ■ New York, NY

Typeset by Anton Graphics, Andover

Printed and bound by Rotolito Lombarda SpA

Cover design by PPD, Basingstoke

Internal design by Nautilus Design UK Ltd & PPD, Basingstoke

Editorial contributors: Julia Hynard & Christopher Staines

Published in the United States by IDG Books Worldwide, Inc.

An International Data Group Company 919 E. Hillsdale Blvd; Suite 400 Foster City. CA 94401

Find us online at www.frommers.com

Frommer's is a registered trademark of Arthur Frommer; used under license.

ISBN 0-7645-6129-4

# CONTENTS

# *H*ow to use the guide

## Finding the REGION

The guide divides Britain into six regions:

**The West Country, South & South East England, Central England & East Anglia, Wales, Northern England, Scotland & Northern Ireland**

If you are looking for somewhere to stay within an area rather than a specific town, refer to the regional divisions shown on the key map on page 6. The name of the region appears at the top left and right hand side of each page. Each region is divided into counties. The county index is found on pages 8 and 9.

## Finding the TOWN

If you know which town you are looking for, refer to the index at the back of the book. Towns are listed in the index in alphabetical order showing their region, county, page number and names of the establishments in or closest to the town. To locate towns geographically within each county refer to the atlas.

## Finding a Top Place to Stay

Within each county through the guide, establishments are listed approximately alphabetically by town. The town name is shown in capitals in the establishment address.

## Map reference

The map reference for each establishment shows the atlas map page first. The rest of the map reference gives you the co-ordinates of the establishment on the map page. Maps locating establishments can also be found on the AA web site, www.theaa.co.uk

## Telephone, fax and e-mail

Telephone and fax numbers are given where available for the establishments. Please refer to page 13 for an explanation of telephone codes and international dialling. Where establishments have e-mail, the address is given after the telephone and fax numbers.

## AA Web site www.theaa.co.uk

The AA web site gives details of all AA recommended establishments including the places to stay listed in this guide. Many of the establishments have a hotlink direct from the AA web site to their own site so you can obtain further details before making a booking.

## Address and Directions

The full postal address of each establishment is given, followed by brief directions.

## Rooms

The number of rooms at the establishment is shown in the heading box after the directions. Further details of room facilities will appear in the main description, check when booking to ensure that all the facilities you require will be available.

## AA inspected accommodation

All bed & breakfast accommodation in the guide has been inspected by the AA and belonged to the AA guest accommodation scheme at the time of going to press, with the exception of a small number of

*Bettmans Oast, Biddenden*

'restaurants with rooms' (see explanation under restaurants, below).

## Prices

The price range (£) for rooms is shown in the heading. This represents the average price for a double room for one night including breakfast. Prices may vary for different rooms or at peak times. Do check exactly what is included in the price when booking.

*Sawrey House Country Hotel, Near Sawrey*

Price Range:
   £ = up to £50 / $80
  ££ = £51-90 / $81-144
 £££ = £91 and over / $145 and over
based on £1 = US$1.6)

## Smoking Restriction

Restrictions for smokers are given in the heading box. See also booking information on page 11.

## Description

The description of the establishment includes information about the range and type of facilities and special features.

## Recommended in the area

These recommendations are made by the AA and not by the bed and breakfast establishment.

## Restaurants

Restaurants are inspected and recommended through the AA Rosette Award scheme. This scheme awards from one to five rosettes for quality of cuisine. Where places to stay have their own AA recommended restaurant this will be mentioned in the description and not in the 'Recommended in the area' section.

## Restaurants with Rooms

A small number of entries in the guide are for 'restaurants with rooms'. The restaurants will be part of the AA rosette scheme, but the rooms are not listed by the AA as recommended places to stay and have therefore not been inspected to the same quality standards as all the other accommodation in the guide. The description for these entries will include the words 'restaurant with rooms' to identify this separate category of accommodation.

## Pubs & Inns

Where possible, a traditional pub will be recommended in the area. This will be selected from the AA's recommended pubs & inns. Some bed & breakfast establishments will be pubs or inns themselves, in which case no further recommendation is made.

## Visits

Recommended visits will typically include popular attractions, museums or historic sights taken from the AA database.

# KEY TO REGIONS

Scotland and Northern Ireland

Northern England

Wales

Central England and East Anglia

South and South East England

The West Country

Shetland Islands

Orkney Islands

Inverness
Aberdeen
Fort William
Perth
Edinburgh
Glasgow

Londonderry
Larne
Belfast
Stranraer
Newcastle
Carlisle
Middlesbrough
Kendal
York
Leeds
Hull
Galway
Dublin
Liverpool
Manchester
Holyhead
Sheffield
Lincoln
Limerick
Nottingham
Norwich
Rosslare
Aberystwyth
Birmingham
Cambridge
Cork
Carmarthen
Gloucester
Colchester
Cardiff
Bristol
Oxford
LONDON
Guildford
Maidstone
Dover
Barnstaple
Taunton
Southampton
Brighton
Exeter
Dorchester
Plymouth
Penzance

Isles of Scilly
Channel Islands

The map opposite shows how Britain is divided into six separate regions for this guide. The regions are listed below with just a few of the highlights to be found in each area.

# The West Country

This area includes Britain's most southerly point, Land's End; stunning coastal scenery; the wild expanse of Dartmoor and Exmoor; and the historic towns of Bristol, Salisbury, Bath and Plymouth. Stonehenge, in Wiltshire, is one of the world's best known prehistoric sites.

# South & South East England

This region offers the picturesque wilderness of the New Forest, the coastal resorts of Brighton, Eastbourne and Hastings, the peaceful Channel Islands and the dreaming spires of Oxford. Major centres include Southampton, Portsmouth, Guildford, Reading, Canterbury, Milton Keynes, and, of course, London.

# Central England & East Anglia

Covering an enormous expanse, this region is the 'Heart of England' and includes Stratford-upon-Avon, birthplace of William Shakespeare. Among the highlights are the Suffolk and Norfolk Broads, the magnificence of Cambridge and a number of historic towns including Lincoln, Norwich and Birmingham.

# Wales

Wales is sparsely populated and enjoys some of Britain's most breathtaking countryside and glorious coastline. The country is rich in history and has more than its fair share of castles and ancient sites. Carmarthen, Bangor, Merthyr Tydfil, Swansea and Cardiff are its best known towns and cities.

# Northern England

Including North Yorkshire, Britain's largest county, this region contains the lively industrial centres of Liverpool, Hull, Leeds, Newcastle and Manchester. It also covers the stunning mountain scenery of the Lake District, the beauty of the Yorkshire Dales and the popular seaside resorts of Blackpool, Morecambe and Whitby.

# Scotland & Northern Ireland

Scotland's beauty is world famous. Its islands, lochs, mountains, and windswept moors are the stuff of legend. The cities and major towns are as vibrant as the country is majestic. Edinburgh, Glasgow, Aberdeen, Dundee and Inverness all offer plenty for visitors. The beautiful countryside of Northern Ireland includes the huge expanse of Lough Neagh, and the Sperrin Mountains. Belfast and Londonderry are the major centres.

# County Index

## Region 1

### The West Country

Cornwall, Bristol, Devon, Dorset, Gloucestershire, Somerset, Wiltshire

## Region 2

### South and South East England

Berkshire, Buckinghamshire, Hampshire, Isle of Wight, Kent, Greater London, London, Oxfordshire, Sussex East, Sussex West, Surrey, The Channel Islands

## Region 3

### Central England and East Anglia

Bedfordshire, Cambridgeshire, Essex, Herefordshire, Hertfordshire, Leicestershire, Lincolnshire, Norfolk, Northamptonshire, Rutland, Shropshire, Suffolk, Warwickshire, West Midlands, Worcestershire

## Region 4

### Wales

Blaenau Gwent, Bridgend, Caerphilly, Cardiff, Carmarthenshire, Ceredigion, Conwy, Denbighshire, Flintshire, Gwynedd, Isle of Anglesey, Merthyr Tydfil, Monmouthshire, Neath Port Talbot, Newport, Pembrokeshire, Powys, Rhondda Cynon Taff, Swansea, Torfaen, Vale of Glamorgan, Wrexham

## Region 5

### Northern England

Cheshire, Cumbria, Derbyshire, County Durham, Greater Manchester, Isle of Man, Lancashire, Merseyside, Northumberland, Nottinghamshire, Staffordshire, Tyne & Wear, Yorkshire (North, South, East Riding and West)

## Region 6

### Scotland and Northern Ireland

Aberdeenshire, Aberdeen City, Angus, Argyll & Bute, City of Edinburgh, City of Glasgow, Clackmannanshire, East Ayrshire, East Dunbartonshire, East Lothian, East Renfrewshire, Dundee City, Dumfries & Galloway, Falkirk, Fife, Highland, Inverclyde, Mid Lothian, Moray, North Ayrshire, North Lanarkshire, Perth & Kinross, Renfrewshire, Scottish Borders, South Ayrshire, South Lanarkshire, Stirling, Western Isles, West Dunbartonshire, West Lothian

Northern Ireland: Antrim, Armagh, County Down, Tyrone, Londonderry

*Augill Castle, Brough*

*Dannah Farm Country
Guest House, Belper*

# AA Recommended Places to Stay

The AA inspects and classifies small private hotels, guest houses, farmhouses and inns. Establishments applying for AA quality assessment are visited on a 'mystery guest' basis by one of the AA's team of qualified accommodation inspectors. Inspectors stay overnight to make a thorough test of the accommodation, food and hospitality offered. On settling the bill the following morning they identify themselves and ask to be shown round the premises. The inspector completes a full report, making a recommendation for the appropriate level of quality. The establishments in this guide have been recommended by AA inspectors for their excellent hospitality, accommodation and food.

## Guest houses

Many guest houses include the word 'hotel' in their name, which can lead to confusion. For AA purposes, small and private hotels are included in the guest accommodation category when they cannot offer all the services required for the AA hotel star scheme (for example evening meals). The establishments selected for this guide represent top of the range accommodation with many of the services and facilities you might expect of a hotel; however, there may be restricted guest access to the house, particularly in the late morning and during the afternoon, so do ask about this when booking.

## Farmhouses

Farmhouse accommodation generally represents good value for money and excellent home-cooking. Many farmhouses listed are on working farms, and while some farmers are happy to allow visitors to look around, or even to help feed the animals, others may discourage visitors from exploring the working land. Please note that modern farms are potentially dangerous places, especially where machinery and chemicals are concerned. Visitors should exercise care, in particular when accompanying children, and should never leave children unsupervised around the farm. Farmhouses may also be in remote locations so do ask for directions when booking to supplement the information provided in the guide.

## Inns

Traditional inns provide a cosy bar, convivial atmosphere, good beer and pub food. Inns with accommodation entries in the guide will provide breakfast in a suitable room and should also serve light meals during licensing hours. Some small, fully licensed hotels may be classified as inns, and the character of the properties will vary according to whether they are traditional country inns or larger town establishments. Check details before you book, including arrival times as these may be restricted to the opening hours.

## Breakfast and evening meals

Guest houses usually offer a full, cooked breakfast in the British or Irish tradition. Where this is advertised as not available, a substantial continental breakfast will be provided. Some guest houses offer bed and breakfast only, so guests must go out for the evening meal. Many guest houses do provide evening meals, ranging from a set meal to a full menu; some have their own restaurants. You may have to arrange dinner in advance, at breakfast or on the previous day, so ask about this when booking. If you book on bed, breakfast and evening meal terms, you may find that the tariff includes only the set menu. If there is a carte you may be able to order from this and pay a supplement. On Sundays, many establishments serve the main meal at midday, and provide only a cold supper in the evening. In some parts of Britain, particularly in Scotland, high tea (a savoury dish followed by bread and butter, scones, cake etc.) is sometimes served instead of dinner. Dinner may be available as an alternative.

*King Charles II Guest House, Rye*

*Ballifeary House Hotel,
Inverness*

*Martins Restaurant
with rooms, Llandudno*

The AA's Recommended Places to Stay listed in this guide may be particularly popular, so advance booking is strongly recommended to avoid disappointment. The peak holiday period in Great Britain is from the beginning of June to the end of September. Easter and public holidays are also busy times so bear this in mind when planning your stay. In some parts of Scotland the skiing season is a peak holiday period. Some establishments may only accept weekly bookings from Saturday. Some establishments will require a deposit on booking.

## Further Details

We have tried to provide sufficient information about establishments in the guide but if you require more information you can contact the establishment directly. Address, telephone, fax and e-mail details are given where known. Do remember to enclose a stamped addressed envelope, or an international reply coupon, and please quote this publication in any enquiry. Although we try to publish accurate information, please bear in mind that all details may be subject to change without notice during the currency of the guide. If in any doubt, confirm details with the establishment at the time of booking.

## Cancellation

If you find that you must cancel a booking, let the proprietor know immediately. If the room you booked cannot be re-let you may be held legally responsible for partial payment. This may mean losing your deposit or being liable for compensation. You should consider taking out cancellation insurance.

## Payment

Most proprietors will accept only UK cheques in payment of accounts if notice is given and identification produced (preferably a cheque guarantee card). Guest houses may not accept credit cards, so do check when booking. VAT (Value Added Tax at 17·5%) is payable in the UK and in the Isle of Man, on both basic prices and any service. VAT does not apply in the Channel Islands. You should always confirm the current prices before making a booking. The price ranges in this guide must be accepted as indications of the price range rather than firm quotations. It is a good idea to confirm exactly what is included in the price when booking.

## Smoking Regulations

No Smoking appears in the heading box when there is a total ban on smoking throughout all main areas of the premises. If only certain areas are restricted, this will appear, for example, as "No smoking in bedrooms". Although we have tried to get accurate information about smoking restrictions, please be aware that the situation may change during the currency of the guide. If smoking regulations are of importance to you please make sure that you check the exact details with the establishment when booking.

# *U*seful Information

## Licensed Premises

All inns hold a full licence but not all guest houses are licensed to sell alcohol. Some may have a full liquor licence, others may have a table licence and wine list so check when booking. Licensed premises are not obliged to remain open throughout the permitted hours, and they may do so only when they expect reasonable trade.

## London

AA guest accommodation in London includes small hotels which may not be privately owned. London prices tend to be higher than outside the capital and usually only include bed and breakfast, check when booking.

## Fire Precautions and safety

Many of the establishments listed in the guide are subject to the requirements of the Fire Precautions Act of 1971. The Fire Precautions Act does not apply to the Channel Islands or the Isle of Man where their own rules are exercised. All establishments should display details of how to summon assistance in the event of an emergency at night.

## Codes of Practice

The AA encourages the use of The Hotel Industry Voluntary Code of Booking Practice in appropriate establishments. Its prime objective is to ensure that the customer is clear about the price and the exact services and facilities being purchased, before entering into a contractually binding agreement. If the price has not been previously confirmed in writing, the guest should be handed a card at the time of registration, stipulating the total obligatory charge.

The Tourism (Sleeping Accommodation Price Display) Order 1977 compels hotels, motels, guest houses, farmhouses, inns and self-catering accommodation with four or more letting bedrooms to display in entrance halls the minimum and maximum prices charged for each category of room. This order complements the Voluntary Code of Booking Practice.

## Dogs

Some establishments which do not normally accept dogs may accept guide dogs. Some establishments that accept dogs may restrict the size and breed of dogs permitted and the rooms into which they may be taken. Generally, dogs are not allowed in the dining room. Check the conditions when booking.

## Children

Restrictions for children may be mentioned in the B&B description. Some establishments may offer free accommodation to children when they share their parents' room. Please note that this information may be subject to change without notice and it is essential to check when booking.

## Complaints

Readers who have any cause to complain are urged to do so on the spot. This should provide an opportunity for the proprietor to correct matters. If a personal approach fails, readers should inform AA Hotel Services, Fanum House, Basingstoke, Hants RG21 4EA. The AA does not however undertake to obtain compensation for complaints.

*Magnolia House,*
*Canterbury*

# Telephone Codes & international dialling

## Telephones

Many guest houses have direct dial telephones in the rooms or guests may have use of a telephone by arrangement with the proprietor, check the rate that you will be charged before calling. Payphones may be available, these usually take cash or phonecards. Phonecards can generally be purchased from newsagents and post offices. Some payphones, usually in large cities, will also take credit cards. Some cell phones may be adaptable for use in Britain, check with your service provider.

## Dialling the UK from Abroad

The telephone and fax numbers given for establishments in this guide are made up of a four or five digit area code followed by a local number. When dialling from abroad first dial the international network access code - 00- from Europe, -011- from the US. Next dial the country code (44 for the UK). Omit the first digit of the area code then dial the rest of the local number.

### For example

0111 121212 becomes:
00 44 111 121212 from Europe, or
011 44 111 121212 from the US.

## Dialling Abroad from the UK

When dialling abroad from the UK the same principles apply. First dial the international network access code, then the country code. Country codes are listed at the back of UK telephone directories. The first digit of the area code should be omitted (with the exception of calls to Russia). Further information can be obtained from International Directory Enquiries by dialling 153 from the UK, calls are charged.

Telephone and fax numbers given in the guide are believed correct at the time of going to press but changes may occur during the currency of the guide. The AA web site is regularly updated, establishment details can be found on the accommodation pages at www.theaa.uk/hotels

*At the Sign of the Angel, Lacock*

# *I*nternational
# Information

## Money

Establishments may not accept travellers cheques or credit cards so ask about payment methods when you book. Make sure you have enough currency for your everyday needs, particularly in rural areas, as there may be little opportunity to exchange currency. There are exchange offices at airports and usually at high street banks where the current exchange rates will be displayed. Some European and American credit and debit cards will allow you to withdraw cash from British ATMs, check with your bank before travelling.

## Medical Treatment and Health Insurance

Travellers who normally take certain medicines should ensure that they have sufficient supply for their stay before travelling. Travellers who for health reasons carry drugs or appliances eg a hypodermic syringe, may experience difficulties in entering the UK without a letter from their doctor describing the condition and treatment required. Before travelling to the UK from abroad make sure that you are covered by insurance for emergency medical and dental treatment as a minimum. Before taking out additional insurance check whether your homeowner or health insurance policy covers you for travel abroad. Many European countries have reciprocal agreements for medical treatment and will

require EU citizens to obtain a validated E111 certificate of entitlement before travel. You should not rely exclusively on these arrangements and are strongly advised to take out personal travel insurance.

## Electrical appliances

These may require an adapter for the plug, as well as an electrical voltage converter that will allow for example a normal 110-volt American appliance to take 220-240-volt British current. Two-in-one adapter/converters are available at some hardware stores.

## Trains

There is an extensive rail network in Britain. Check with a travel agent before travelling to find out about special offers or passes. It may be advisable to book more popular routes (e.g. London to Edinburgh) well in advance. When booking accommodation check that it is accessible by train if this is your main method of transport.

*The Gallery Hotel,
London*

## Ferries

Ferries operate regularly between the Isle of Wight, Isle of Man, Scottish Islands, Ireland and mainland Britain. Services operate for foot passengers as well as cars and it may be necessary to book in advance. Ferry services are subject to seasonal variations so check with a travel agent in advance.

## Air

Heathrow, Gatwick, Birmingham, Manchester and Glasgow are the major international airports in the UK. There are airports in many cities and internal flights can be a relatively cheap option for longer distances. Ask your travel agent or browse the internet, often the best prices are limited to a small number of seats available only through advance booking.

## Car Rental

You will need your drivers licence and preferably an International Driving Permit (a document with a photograph which confirms you as the holder of a valid driving licence in your own country), you may also be asked to show your passport. You may be required to produce an additional credit card or further proof of identity when renting more expensive cars. It is advisable to book in advance and check that you have the appropriate insurance coverage, mileage allowance and transmission (you'll pay more for an automatic). When collecting your car check whether it takes diesel, unleaded or leaded petrol.

## Driving

Drive on the left and overtake on the right in the UK. Ensure that seatbelts are worn by every occupant of your car, whether they sit in the front or the rear. Observe the speed limits, displayed in miles per hour.

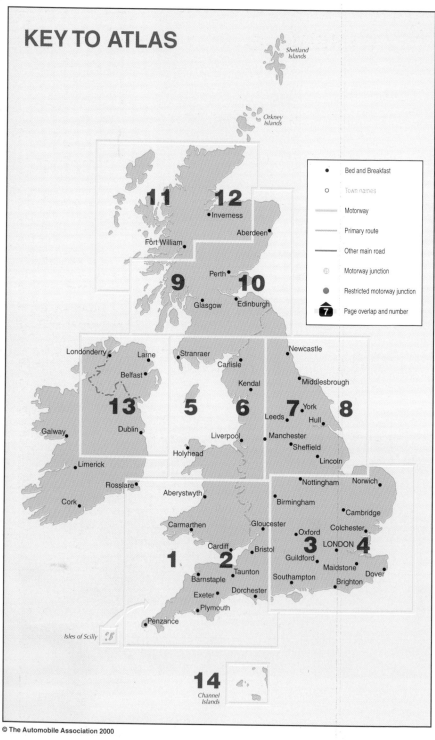

# KEY TO ATLAS

*Shetland Islands*

*Orkney Islands*

**11**
**12**
• Inverness
Aberdeen •
Fort William •

**9**
Perth •
**10**
Glasgow • Edinburgh •

Londonderry •
Larne •
**13**
Belfast •
Galway •
Dublin •
Limerick •
Rosslare •
Cork •

Stranraer •
Carlisle •
**5**
Kendal •
**6**
Liverpool •
Holyhead •

Newcastle •
Middlesbrough •
**7** York •
**8**
Leeds • Hull •
Manchester •
Sheffield •
Lincoln •

Nottingham • Norwich •
Birmingham •
Cambridge •
Aberystwyth •
Gloucester • Colchester •
Carmarthen •
Oxford • **3** LONDON **4**
**1**
Cardiff •
**2** Bristol • Guildford • Maidstone •
Taunton • Southampton • Brighton • Dover •
Barnstaple •
Dorchester •
Exeter •
Plymouth •
Penzance •
*Isles of Scilly*

**14**
*Channel Islands*

|  |  |
|---|---|
| • | Bed and Breakfast |
| ○ | Town names |
| ——— | Motorway |
| ——— | Primary route |
| ——— | Other main road |
| ⑮ | Motorway junction |
| ● | Restricted motorway junction |
| 🞂7 | Page overlap and number |

# KEY TO REGIONS

Shetland Islands

Orkney Islands

| | Scotland and Northern Ireland |
| | Northern England |
| | Wales |
| | Central England and East Anglia |
| | South and South East England |
| | The West Country |

Inverness
Aberdeen
Fort William
Perth
Edinburgh
Glasgow

Newcastle
Stranraer
Carlisle
Middlesbrough
Londonderry
Larne
Belfast
Kendal
York
Leeds
Hull
Galway
Dublin
Liverpool
Manchester
Holyhead
Sheffield
Limerick
Lincoln
Rosslare
Nottingham
Norwich
Aberystwyth
Cork
Birmingham
Cambridge
Carmarthen
Gloucester
Colchester
Cardiff
Oxford
LONDON
Bristol
Guildford
Barnstaple
Taunton
Maidstone
Dover
Southampton
Exeter
Brighton
Plymouth
Dorchester
Penzance
Isles of Scilly

Channel Islands

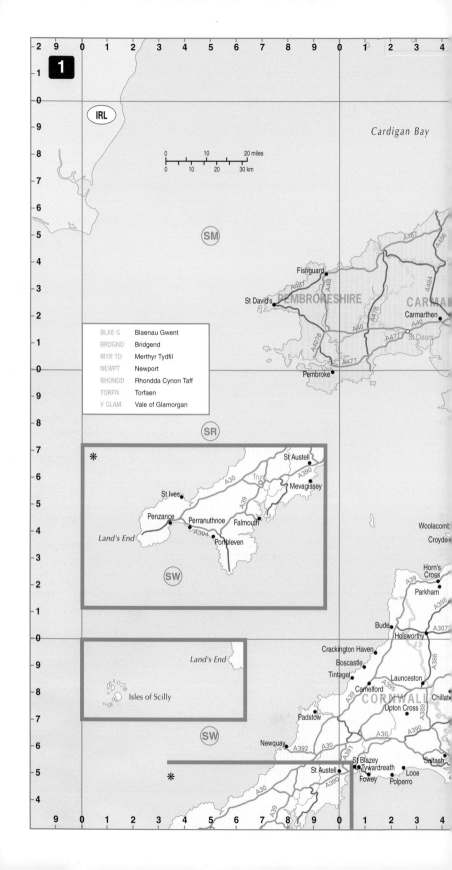

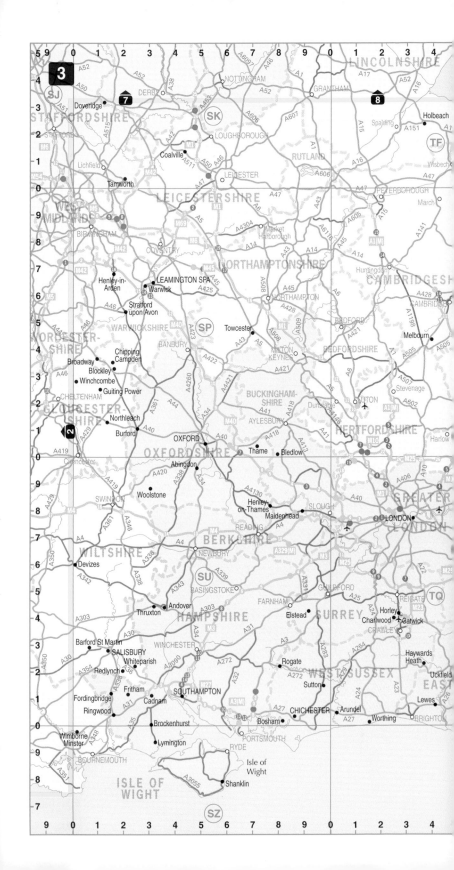

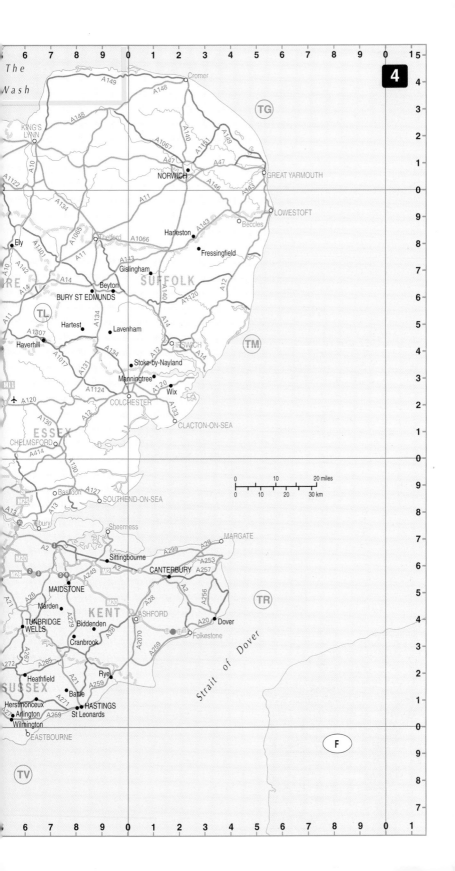

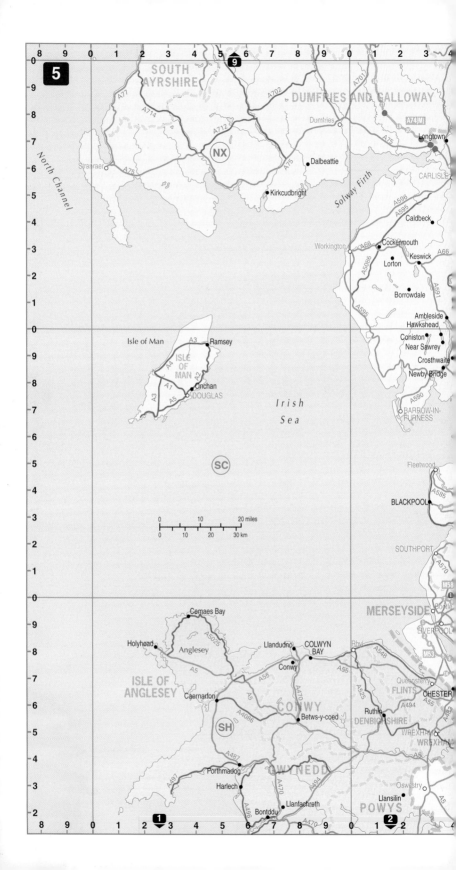

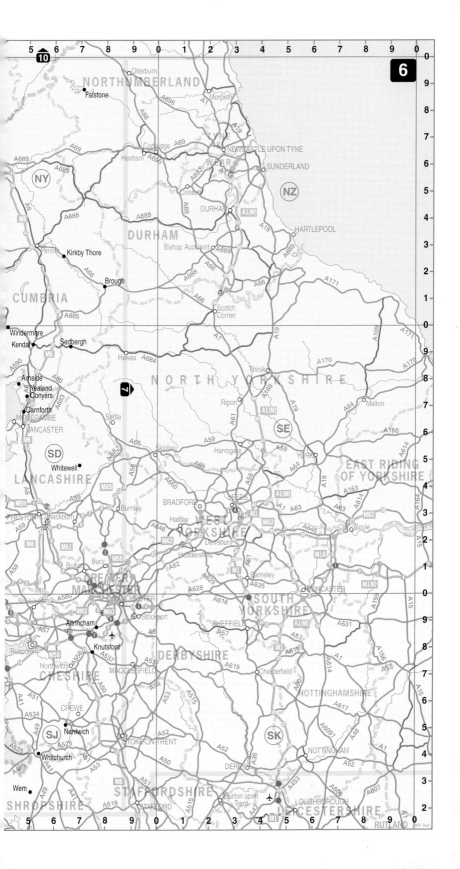

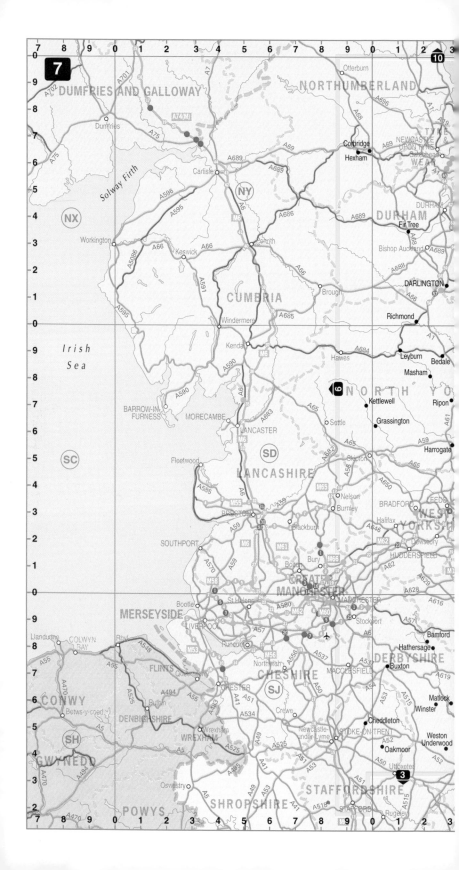

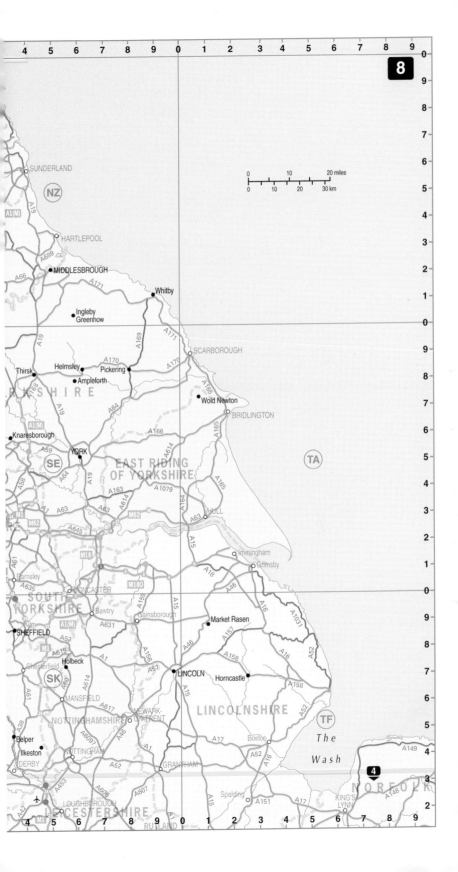

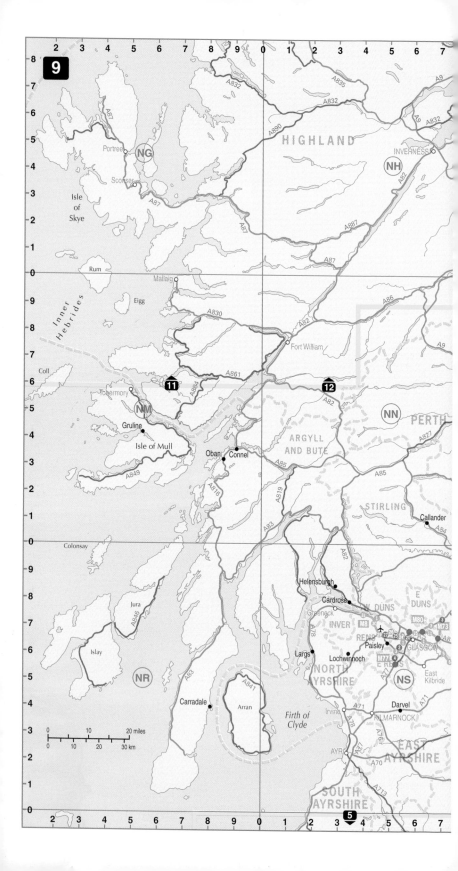

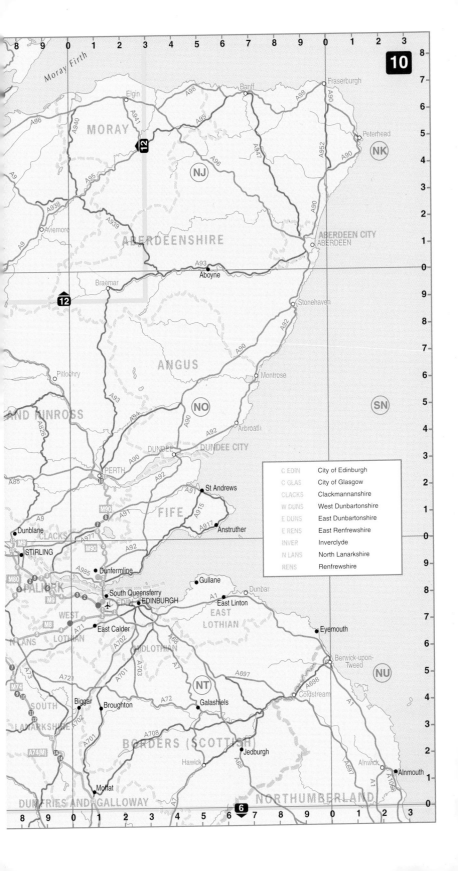

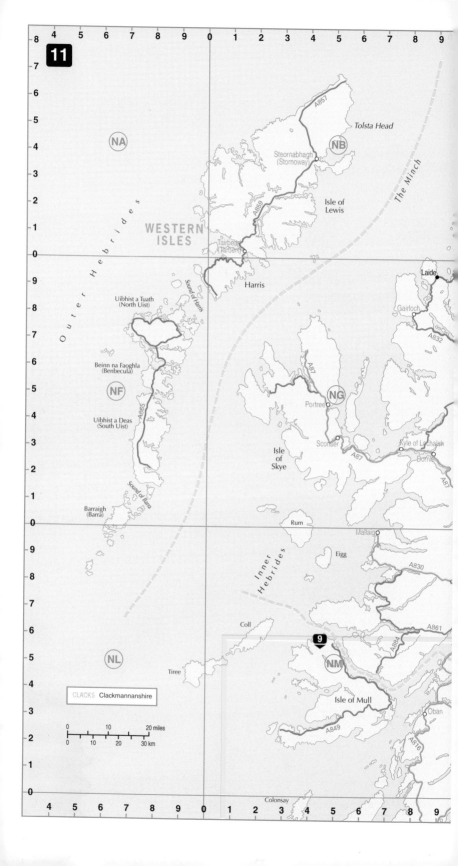

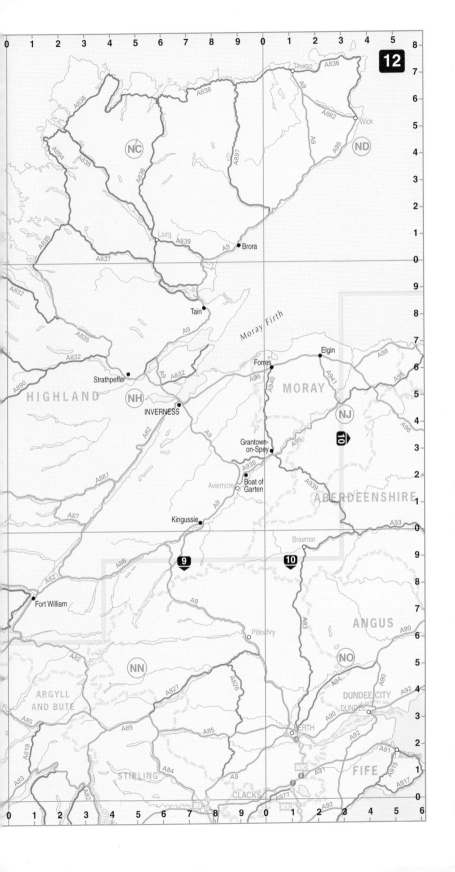

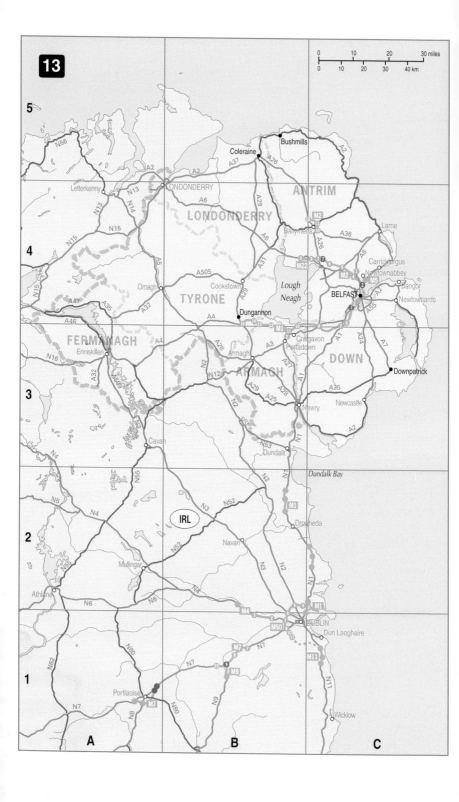

# Guernsey

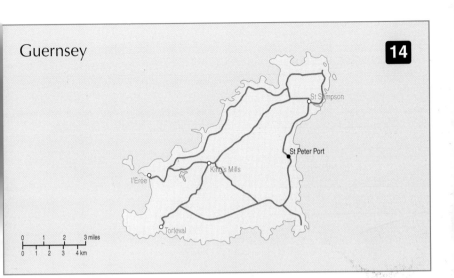

**14**

St Sampson

St Peter Port

King's Mills

l'Erée

Torteval

0 1 2 3 miles
0 1 2 3 4 km

---

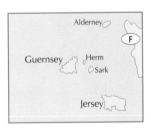

Alderney

F

Guernsey · Herm

Sark

Jersey

---

# Jersey

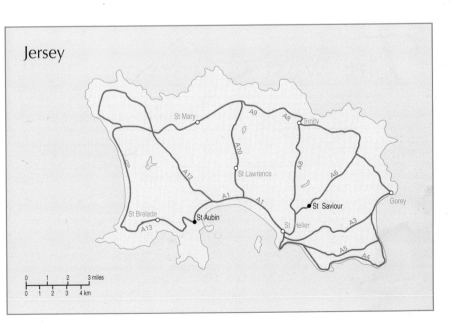

St Mary

A9 A8 Trinity

A10

A8

St Lawrence

A6

A12

A1

A1

St Saviour

Gorey

St Brelade

St Aubin

St Helier

A3

A13

A5

A4

0 1 2 3 miles
0 1 2 3 4 km

# The West Country

This region in the guide covers the area of England from Land's End in Cornwall through Devon and Dorset to Somerset, Wiltshire, and Gloucestershire. Each county has its own speciality such as the Cornish Pasty, Devon cream teas with clotted cream or Somerset cider. Dairy farming and fishing were the main traditional industries, tourism is certainly one of the major industries today.

The mild climate and sunny coastline make this area popular with holidaymakers and there is plenty to do. For keen walkers, the South West Coast Path runs 800 km along the coast from Minehead in Somerset to Poole in Dorset. Bodmin Moor, Dartmoor National Park and Exmoor National Park, all found in the West Country, provide a contrast from the coastal scenery and a quite different challenge on foot or on horseback for the more adventurous.

One of the most popular towns for visitors to Somerset is the elegant spa resort of Bath in the Avon Valley. The Roman Baths were built nearly 2000 years ago next to Britain's only hot spring. The Roman Baths and Pump Room are open to visitors and you can taste the famous water here, renowned for its curative properties. Other sights include The

*Barge on the River Thames, Lechlade, Gloucestershire*

*Exmoor National Park, Devon*

*Beach and Cliffs, Burton Bradstock*

Museum of Costume, Bath Industrial Heritage Centre, The Building of Bath Museum and the Holburne Museum and Craft Study Centre. Accommodation should be booked well in advance for this popular city, there are a number of AA recommended places to stay in Bath and the surrounding area.

The medieval city of Salisbury is well-known for its magnificent cathedral, the largest in England, with the tallest spire at 123 metres. The Chapter House has a frieze of Genesis and the finest surviving Magna Carta. Around 750 years ago, the cathedral choir began performing at daily services and continue to do so to this day. The surrounding cathedral close contains two museums and two small stately homes.

Cheltenham in Gloucestershire offers a number of interesting places to visit. The Art Gallery and Museum close to the town centre has a continuous programme of exhibitions as well a permanent collections. One of these is a display about Edward Wilson, one of Cheltenham's famous sons, who journeyed with Captain Scott on the ill-fated Antartic Expedition of 1911-1912. Another famous son was Gustav Holst, his Birthplace Museum contains unique displays of his life.

# $\mathcal{W}$estbury Park Hotel

*Ideal* accommodation for tourists or business guests is offered at this attractive hotel, conveniently situated on the edge of the Durdham Downs, with easy access to the motorways, city centre and shopping mall. The atmosphere is relaxed and staff are friendly.

*Lovely Victorian house close to the Durdham Downs*

☎ 0117 962 0465  📠 0117 962 8607
**Map ref 2 - ST57**

37 Westbury Road, Westbury-on-Trym,
BRISTOL, Bristol, BS9 3AU
M5 junct 17, follow A4018 for 4.5m
8 Rooms, ££

The bedrooms have been decorated with taste and style and modern comforts are provided, including en suite facilities, colour televisions, direct dial telephones, hair dryers and hospitality trays in every room.

There is a comfortable lounge bar area where guests can relax. Breakfast is served in the spacious dining room. Parking is easy and there is also limited private parking available.

## Recommended in the area

**RESTAURANT:**
*Glass Boat Restaurant, Bristol*

**TRADITIONAL PUB:**
*Highbury Vaults, Bristol*

**VISIT:**
*SS Great Britain, Bristol*

---

# $\mathcal{T}$olcarne House Hotel & Restaurant

*Late Victorian country house with glorious views*

☎ 01840 250654  📠 01840 250654
✉ crown@tolhouse.eclipse.co.uk
**Map ref 1 - SX09**

Tintagel Road, BOSCASTLE, Cornwall,
PL35 0AS
at junct of B3266/B3263 in Boscastle
8 Rooms, ££

and relaxing atmosphere prevails. The individually furnished bedrooms all have en suite facilities. Colour televisions, hospitality trays, radio alarms and hairdryers are provided. All the rooms have pleasant views and some overlook the National Trust Headland and the Atlantic Ocean. There is a cosy bar and an elegant lounge. Dinner is available, with an emphasis on English home cooking, both fixed price and à la carte menus are available.

## Recommended in the area

**RESTAURANT:**
*Blagdon Manor, Ashwater*

**TRADITIONAL PUB:**
*The Napoleon Inn, Boscastle*

**VISIT:**
*Old Post Office, Tintagel*

*Tolcarne* House is set in extensive grounds including a croquet lawn and mature trees. From its elevated position there are splendid views over the wooded Jordan Valley and the National Trust owned cliff tops. The hotel is just 10 minutes walk from the historic harbour, through the old village. The South West Coast Path is close by, and Willapark promontory a 317ft view-point, which was an Iron Age fort.

Margaret and Graham Crown have long experience of welcoming guests into their home, and a peaceful

# Downlands

*Chalet-style bungalow overlooking the golf course*

☎ 01288 355545

**Map ref 1 - SS20**

1 Flexbury Avenue, BUDE, Cornwall,
EX23 8RE
right off A39 to Bude, thro' one-way system,
past P.O., right fork but left lane. Downlands
approx 200yds
7 Rooms, £, Closed Jan

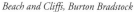

A warm welcome awaits guests at Yvonne Phillip's delightful detached property. The comfortably furnished bedrooms include two on the ground floor, all have en suite facilities, colour televisions and hospitality trays. Family suites, double, twin and single rooms are available.

A spacious guests' lounge is provided, and a dining room with a polished wooden floor. Breakfast is a feast beginning with fresh fruits, yoghurts and fruit juices. There follows a choice of freshly cooked breakfasts, including traditional English choices such as smoked salmon and scrambled eggs, or warm croissants and pain au chocolat, served with fresh coffee or one of a range of teas. For your evening meal there are plenty of restaurants within easy reach.

Downlands overlooks the golf course and is within walking distance of the lovely sandy beaches and the town centre. The house has its own large private car park.

## RECOMMENDED IN THE AREA

**RESTAURANT:**
*Blagdon Manor, Ashwater*

**TRADITIONAL PUB:**
*The Bush Inn, Morwenstow*

**VISIT:**
*Old Post Office, Tintagel*

*Beach and Cliffs, Burton Bradstock*

# *M*anor Farm

*Historically interesting manor house on a non-working farm*

☎ 01840 230304

**Map ref 1 - SX19**

CRACKINGTON HAVEN, Cornwall,
EX23 0JW
4 Rooms, ££, No smoking

## RECOMMENDED IN THE AREA

**RESTAURANT:**
*Blagdon Manor, Ashwater*

**TRADITIONAL PUB:**
*Wellington Hotel, Boscastle*

**VISIT:**
*Old Post Office, Tintagel*

*W*illiam the Conqueror's half-brother, the Earl of Mortin, is recorded as holding this manor in the Doomsday book of 1086. He chose well, as the house enjoys a magnificent setting about a mile from the sea, with panoramic views of the surrounding countryside. The house has beautiful gardens and thirty acres of land.

All the bedrooms are individually furnished and beautifully decorated. Children under 18 are not accommodated and dogs are not permitted, making this a peaceful place to stay. An honesty bar is available and the house is licensed so guests can enjoy a drink in one of the comfortable lounges. Guests should note that the house is completely non smoking. Breakfast is served in a sunny room at the front of the house. Dinner is available by prior arrangement, served dinner-party style round one table. Guests meet for introductions before dinner. The baby grand is a new addition and pianists are most welcome.

# *T*revigue

*Authentic farmhouse atmosphere with home comforts*

☎ 01840 230418  ☏ 01840 230418

**Map ref 1 - SX19**

CRACKINGTON HAVEN, Cornwall,
EX23 0LQ
6 Rooms, ££, No smoking
Closed Xmas 3 days

## RECOMMENDED IN THE AREA

**RESTAURANT:**
*Blagdon Manor, Ashwater*

**TRADITIONAL PUB:**
*Wellington Hotel, Boscastle*

**VISIT:**
*Tintagel Castle, Tintagel*

*T*his is a large 16th-century National Trust farmhouse built of local stone. It is set in open countryside with panoramic views of the surrounding area and 500 acres of mixed dairy farmland. The guest bedrooms retain many original features but have modern en suite facilities and lovely furnishings. Tea and coffee making facilities are provided and there is colour television in two of the bedrooms. The comfortable lounges have traditional flagstone floors covered with rugs, and the log burning fires enhance the warm and cosy atmosphere.

Children over 12 can be accommodated but dogs are not permitted. The farmhouse is licensed and excellent evening meals are available, served in an elegant converted barn. Memorable breakfasts include home produced bacon, sausages and many other choices. There is plenty of parking space and some credit cards are taken.

# Dolvean Hotel

*Traditional Victorian hotel retaining its original character while offering modern facilities*

☎ 01326 313658
🖷 01326 313995
✉ reservations@dolvean.freeserve.co.uk

**Map ref 1 - SW83**

50 Melvill Road,
FALMOUTH, Cornwall,
TR11 4DQ
on main road to
Pendennis Castle &
Docks, 11 Rooms,
£, No smoking
Closed Xmas

*T*he Dolvean is ideally situated between the beach and Falmouth's internationally renowned harbour, where everything from tall ships to cruise liners can be seen. The welcome from Paul and Carol Crocker is warm and friendly, and there is a particular emphasis on good service and quality food. Guests can enjoy early morning tea in their rooms while watching the sun come up over the bay and the Lizard beyond. Breakfast is served in the elegant dining room, and local books and guides are provided in the comfortable parlour, where guests can plan their itineraries. The bedrooms are all en suite and welcoming extras include complimentary biscuits, bottled water and chocolates. The rooms are equipped with remote control televisions, hospitality trays, and radio and room intercom. An enclosed private car park is provided.

## RECOMMENDED IN THE AREA

**RESTAURANT:**
*Powell's Cellar, Falmouth*

**TRADITIONAL PUB:**
*Trengilly Wartha Inn, Constantine*

**VISIT:**
*Pendennis Castle, Falmouth*

# Prospect House

*Historically interesting property offering smartly presented accommodation*

☎ 01326 373198 📠 01326 373198

**Map ref 1 - SW83**

1 Church Road, Penryn, FALMOUTH, Cornwall, TR10 8DA
off A39 at Treluswell rndbt, B3292 past pub & thro' lights, after 1.5m right thro' white gates next to phone box
3 Rooms, ££, No smoking in bedrooms

*P*rospect House is a Grade II listed Packet Ship Captain's house, situated at the top of the Penryn River and set in a traditional Cornish walled plantsman's garden with Victorian conservatory.

Spacious and beautifully appointed accommodation is offered in three en suite bedrooms (twin, King and Queen size beds).

An elegant and comfortable drawing room is provided, with a log fire on cold evenings, and a traditional English breakfast is served in the dining room around a large antique Flemish dining table.

### RECOMMENDED IN THE AREA

**RESTAURANT:**
*Penmere Manor, Falmouth*

**TRADITIONAL PUB:**
*Pandora Inn, Mylor Bridge*

**VISIT:**
*Pendennis Castle, Falmouth*

# Carnethic House

*Regency family home and beautiful gardens with excellent facilities*

☎ 01726 833336 📠 01726 833296
✉ carnethic@btinternet.com

**Map ref 1 - SX15**

Lambs Barn, FOWEY, Cornwall, PL23 1HQ
off A3082, directly opposite 'Welcome to Fowey' sign
8 Rooms, £££, Closed Dec-Jan

*T*he warmth and exuberance of David and Trish Hogg's hospitality makes guests feel very welcome. Their home, with its covered veranda and large windows, looks across an award-winning garden with well tended lawns, mature trees and shrubs, as well as an outdoor heated swimming pool, putting green, golf practice net and a grass tennis court. At the end of the garden, there is a leafy lane leading to the beach. There is ample parking for cars and boats.

The bedrooms are light, with a clean, modern look and very good beds; five rooms are en suite. Traditional breakfast is served in the dining room, where you can also choose to have dinner from the changing menu, fresh local fish is a speciality. There is a licensed lounge bar.

### RECOMMENDED IN THE AREA

**RESTAURANT:**
*Food for Thought, Fowey*

**TRADITIONAL PUB:**
*The Ship Inn, Fowey*

**VISIT:**
*St Catherine's Castle, Fowey*

# *T*revanion Guest House

*Character property in the heart of Daphne du Maurier country*

☎ 01726 832602 📠 01726 832602
✉ trefoy@globalnet.co.uk
**Map ref 1 - SX15**

70 Lostwithiel Street, FOWEY, Cornwall,
PL23 1BQ
exit A390 onto B3269 signposted for Fowey,
on descending the hill premises situated
200mtrs past turning for main car park
5 Rooms, £, No smoking

*T*revanion is a Grade II listed building, dating in part from the 16th century, conveniently situated for exploring the whole of the historic town on foot. It offers comfortable accommodation, with colour televisions and tea and coffee making equipment. Two of the five bedrooms have en suite facilities and all the rooms are attractively decorated with co-ordinated fabrics.

The charming dining room retains many original features, and in addition to the hearty cooked breakfast, a good selection of alternatives is offered. Car parking is provided, and the house is the ideal base from which to visit the Lost Gardens of Heligan, the Eden Project, and many National Trust houses and gardens. Children under four cannot be accommodated, and neither can dogs (except guide dogs).

### RECOMMENDED IN THE AREA

**RESTAURANT:**
*Food for Thought, Fowey*

**TRADITIONAL PUB:**
*Rashleigh Inn, Polkerris*

**VISIT:**
*St Catherine's Castle, Fowey*

# *H*arescombe Lodge

*18th-century lodge in an idyllic riverside location*

☎ 01503 263158
✉ harescombe@dial.pipex.com
**Map ref 1 - SX25**

Watergate, LOOE, Cornwall, PL13 2NE
from Looe A387 Polperro, 1m from Looe is
an isolated house on right, after 300yds turn
right, 1m on left
3 Rooms, £, No smoking
Closed 1 Nov 2000 - 14 Jan 2001

*H*arescombe Lodge is one of the four dwellings which constitute the hamlet of Watergate. Sheltered by the wooded valley and looking out across the West Looe River, a more peaceful or delightful setting would be hard to imagine.

The comfortable bedrooms are divided between the main house and the adjacent cottage and all have en suite facilities. Televisions, hairdryers and tea and coffee making equipment are provided in each room. Television reception in the valley is poor but there is a video library for guests' use. Full English or vegetarian breakfast is served, and there is a good choice of restaurants in Looe and Polperro (3 miles). The Lodge's situation, with a stream passing through the gardens, makes it unsuitable for children. A large private car park is located 100 yards from the house, but luggage may be unloaded at the door on arrival.

### RECOMMENDED IN THE AREA

**RESTAURANT:**
*The Kitchen, Polperro*

**TRADITIONAL PUB:**
*Jubilee Inn, Pelynt*

**VISIT:**
*Fowey Castle, Fowey*

For LISKEARD see Darley House, Upton Cross on page 53

# St Aubyn's Guest House

*Late Victorian house with veranda, balconies, and superb sea views*

☎ 01503 264351   ✆ 01503 263670
✉ staubyns@westlooe.freeserve.co.uk

**Map ref 1 - SX25**

Marine Drive, Hannafore, WEST LOOE,
Cornwall, PL13 2DH
from Looe Bridge, West Quay Rd (Hannafore)
0.75m, onto Marine Drive, house on right
facing sea
8 Rooms, ££, No smoking

The house stands in attractive gardens at the headland of Hannafore, which has a small beach and rock pools. It looks across the coastal path and straight out to sea, towards Rame Head and Looe Island. There are recreational facilities of all kinds, shark fishing and diving for the more adventurous. There are no facilities for children under five, and pets are not allowed.

Built in the late 1890s, the house retains architectural features and has spacious rooms typical of the Victorian style, all tastefully and sympathetically decorated, with some fine pieces of furniture, tapestries and paintings. The bedrooms, six en suite, are named after villages and towns in the Chilterns. Most have sea views and all have colour TV; 'Whiteleaf', 'Kimble' and 'Chesham' have balconies. The resident proprietors, Peter and Di Bishop, make St Aubyn's a relaxed, friendly place to stay.

## RECOMMENDED IN THE AREA

**RESTAURANT:**
*Fowey Hotel, Fowey*

**TRADITIONAL PUB:**
*Ye Olde Plough House Inn, Duloe*

**VISIT:**
*Fowey Castle, Fowey*

*Dunster Castle, Somerset*

# *K*erryanna Country House

*Peacefully located house, close to Mevagissey, serving home-made fare*

☎ 01726 843558  📠 01726 843558

**Map ref 1 - SX04**

Treleaven Farm, Valley Road, MEVAGISSEY, Cornwall, PL26 6SA
off B3273 on entrance to village, turn right by tennis courts
6 Rooms, £, No smoking in bedrooms

*K*erryanna is a quietly situated house with views over the town and out to sea. It is well placed for relaxing in peace or as a base for touring the area. Heligan Gardens are located close by.

The attractively furnished and decorated bedrooms all have modern en suite facilities and there are comfortable public rooms in which to sit and enjoy the view. Outside there are well-kept gardens, an open air swimming pool and a putting green. A games room is also provided for guests' use.

An evening meal is available by prior arrangement, served in the cosy dining room. The food is all home-made using fresh local produce.

## RECOMMENDED IN THE AREA

**RESTAURANT:**
*Nare Hotel, Veryan*

**TRADITIONAL PUB:**
*Rising Sun Inn, St Mawes*

**VISIT:**
*The Lost Gardens of Heligan, Peutewen*

# *T*releaven Farmhouse

*Farmhouse with its own restaurant overlooking Mevagissey*

☎ 01726 842413  📠 01726 842413

**Map ref 1 - SX04**

Valley Road, MEVAGISSEY, Cornwall, PL26 6SA
turn right at foot of hill when entering Mevagissey
6 Rooms, £
Closed 15 Dec-7 Jan

*L*ocated in an elevated position with spectacular views over the fishing village of Mevagissey, the farmhouse is ideally located for leisure guests. A warm welcome is assured from Anne and Colin Hennah, who offer good food and comfortable accommodation.

All the bedrooms have en suite showers, colour televisions, and tea and coffee making equipment. There is a relaxing lounge and a large dining room, also open to non-residents, where a range of freshly prepared dishes is offered.

The house is set on a working farm of 200 acres, and is surrounded by well tended gardens, which include an open air heated swimming pool, 18-hole putting green, croquet lawn and a games barn.

## RECOMMENDED IN THE AREA

**RESTAURANT:**
*Nare Hotel, Veryan*

**TRADITIONAL PUB:**
*Rising Sun Inn, Mevagissey*

**VISIT:**
*The Lost Gardens of Heligan, Peutewen*

# Degembris Farmhouse

*18th-century farmhouse overlooking a wooded valley and arable farmland*

☎ 01872 510555
📠 01872 510230
📧 kathy@tally-connect.co.uk

**Map ref 1 - SW86**

St Newlyn East,
NEWQUAY, Cornwall,
TR8 5HY
from A30 turn right for
Summercourt village,
right at x-rd (Newquay
A3058), 3rd left St
Newlyn East, 2nd left)
5 Rooms, £, No smoking
Closed Xmas

## RECOMMENDED IN THE AREA

**RESTAURANT:**
*Trengilly Wartha Inn,
Constantine Bay*

**TRADITIONAL PUB:**
*Falcon Inn, St Mawgan*

**VISIT:**
*Trerice, Newquay*

*D*egembris is a period farmhouse retaining much of its original character. It is set in 165 acres of arable farmland overlooking a lovely valley. The bedrooms are tastefully decorated and furnished in pine with attractively co-ordinated soft furnishings. The rooms vary in size; three have en suite facilities and the majority have southerly views. Colour televisions and tea and coffee making equipment are provided. In the evening a delightful four-course meal is served in the beamed dining room, using fresh locally produced ingredients. Guests can relax in the comfortable lounge which has a television and a selection of books and games. There is a pleasant garden with views of the surrounding countryside, and an interesting farm trail.

# Cross House Hotel

*Pretty Georgian house within easy walking distance from the harbour*

☎ **01841 532391**  📠 **01841 533633**

**Map ref 1 - SW97**

Church Street, PADSTOW, Cornwall, PL28 8BG

off A30 onto B3274. Follow signs to Padstow, on reaching town take 3rd right. Follow one way street past church 50 yds, take sharp left

9 Rooms, £££, No smoking in bedrooms

*A* path leads up through a colourful little garden to the door of Cross House, a charming property with shutters on the windows, situated in the centre of the town. The hotel was recently refurbished, and the furnishings and decor are of the highest quality throughout. Each of the bedrooms has been individually designed, and they all have en suite bathrooms, as well as many pleasing extras.

There is a cosy dining room where you can choose between a full English breakfast or a continental breakfast with a variety of tasty pastries. The service is always friendly and efficient. Guests are free to make use of the bar while relaxing in the two very comfortable lounges, one of which is a smoking lounge.

## RECOMMENDED IN THE AREA

**RESTAURANT:**
*St Petroc's House, Padstow*

**TRADITIONAL PUB:**
*The Maltsters Arms, Chapel Amble*

**VISIT:**
*The Lost Gardens of Heligan, Peutewen*

*Boscastle, Cornwall*

# *C*hy-an-Mor Hotel

## RECOMMENDED IN THE AREA

**RESTAURANT:**
*Cornish Range,*
*Mousehole*

**TRADITIONAL PUB:**
*Turks Inn, Penzance*

**VISIT:**
*St Michael's Mount,*
*Marazion*

*A Grade II listed Georgian building in a prime seafront position*

☎ 01736 363441
🖷 01736 363441

**Map ref 1 - SW43**

15 Regent Terrace,
PENZANCE, Cornwall,
TR18 4DW
A30-Penzance. Follow
rd to rlwy stn, left lane
(Newlyn). Pass harbour
& Jubilee Pool on left,
right at Stanley Hotel
10 Rooms, £
No smoking
Closed Dec-Jan

*O*wners Mike and Jan Russell have sympathetically restored this lovely seaside property to its former glory. The bedrooms, most of which have sea views, are individually styled and beautifully decorated, with quality co-ordinated fabrics and furnishings. Rooms come in a variety of sizes and some are located on the ground floor. Each has an en suite shower room, colour television, radio alarm, hairdryer, central heating and tea and coffee making facilities. The smart dining room has an art deco theme, and breakfast is served at separate tables. Guests can relax in the elegant ground floor lounge which offers fine views over Mounts Bay. The town centre, harbour, promenade and gardens are just a short walk away, and there are plenty of places to eat in the locality. Ample private parking is provided.

# Ennys Farm

*Complete tranquillity at a beautiful
Cornish manor house*

☎ 01736 740262 ▪ 01736 740055
✉ ennys@zetnet.co.uk

**Map ref 1 - SW43**

St Hilary, PENZANCE, Cornwall, TR20 9BZ
1m N of B3280, Leedstown to Goldsithney
road
5 Rooms, ££, No smoking in bedrooms
Closed Nov-13 Feb

Guests return time after time to soak up the comfortable country house atmosphere on this small farm, an ideal spot for a peaceful holiday. The house dates back to the 17th century, with clematis and wisteria clinging to its old stone walls. It has large, sheltered, landscaped gardens, with beautiful lawns and beds of colourful flowers and shrubs, and there is an outdoor heated swimming pool and a grass tennis court within the grounds.

The bedrooms are tastefully furnished in the style of a traditional country house, three in the main house, all with en suite bathroom facilities, one with a four-poster bed. The family suite is in a converted barn adjoining the house. Children under two years and dogs cannot be accommodated.

## RECOMMENDED IN THE AREA

**RESTAURANT:**
*Old Coastguard Inn, Mousehole*

**TRADITIONAL PUB:**
*Turks Head Inn*

**VISIT:**
*Tate Gallery, St Ives*

# Landaviddy Manor

*An impressive manor house in two acres
of mature gardens*

☎ 01503 272210

**Map ref 1 - SX25**

Landaviddy Lane, POLPERRO, Cornwall,
PL13 2RT
right at mini rdbt at Polperro main car park,
1m to T-junct. Landaviddy signposted to the
left
7 Rooms, ££, No smoking

Landaviddy Manor is a former magistrate's house, built in 1785. It is peacefully located just ten minutes walk from Polperro harbour and restaurants.

The bedrooms are individually designed and have beautiful four poster and Victorian beds. Most of the bedrooms have en suite shower rooms, two have their own private shower rooms. All are equipped with colour televisions and tea and coffee making facilities. Some of the rooms have sea views and all are very comfortably furnished.

There is a cosy bar, spacious dining room and a comfortable lounge for guests to relax in. The house is licensed and fully centrally heated, parking is available for guests. Children under 14 and dogs cannot be accommodated.

## RECOMMENDED IN THE AREA

**RESTAURANT:**
*Old Rectory House Hotel, St Keyne*

**TRADITIONAL PUB:**
*Jubilee Inn, Pelynt*

**VISIT:**
*Dobwells Family Adventure Park, Dobwells*

# Trenderway Farm

*16th-century farmhouse set on the gentle slopes at the head of the Polperro valley*

☎ 01503 272214
🖷 01503 272991
📧 trenderwayfarm
@hotmail.com

**Map ref 1 - SX25**

Pelynt, POLPERRO, Cornwall, PL13 2LY
Looe A387 to Polperro, farm is signposted on main rd
4 Rooms, ££
No smoking
Closed Xmas

## RECOMMENDED IN THE AREA

**RESTAURANT:**
*The Kitchen, Polperro*

**TRADITIONAL PUB:**
*The Jubilee Inn, Pelynt*

**VISIT:**
*Llanhydrock House, Bodmin*

The farm comprises a group of local stone buildings set on a working mixed farm surrounded by stunning Cornish countryside. The perfect situation for a relaxed and peaceful stay. Talland Bay beach is just a mile away and there are miles of National Trust cliff paths to explore. The accommodation is stylishly presented, and includes a twin or king-size double room in the main house, or a king-size or four-poster room in the adjacent converted barn. All the rooms have en suite facilities with a bath and shower, central heating, colour television, and tea and coffee making equipment. Electric blankets are also provided in cooler weather. The four-course breakfast sets guests up for the day, though a lighter continental option is available. For dinner, the proprietors are happy to advise on local restaurants, and in the evening guests can relax by the open fire in the large sitting room.

# *E*dnovean Farm

*17th-century granite barn restored to provide charming bed and breakfast accommodation*

☎ 01736 711883
🖷 01736 710480

**Map ref 1 - SW52**

PERRANUTHNOE,
Cornwall, TR20 9LZ
off A394 Penzance
towards Perranuthnoe,
drive on left by
post box
3 Rooms, ££
No smoking

### RECOMMENDED IN THE AREA

**RESTAURANT:**
*Old Coastguard Inn, Mousehole*

**TRADITIONAL PUB:**
*Halzephron Inn, Gunwalloe*

**VISIT:**
*St Michael's Mount, Marazion*

*C*harles and Christine Taylor welcome guests to their delightful home, a 17th-century barn which they have lovingly restored and converted in recent years. The small farm is located above the village, and there are stunning views over St Michael's Mount and Mount's Bay from the gardens.

The ground floor bedrooms are furnished and decorated in a country style, with chintz fabrics and many thoughtful extras such as fresh flowers, fruit and magazines. In addition to the attractive sitting room, a former dairy provides a candlelit retreat in the evening. This, known as the garden room, opens onto a sheltered terrace overlooking the bay. Breakfast is served at an oak refectory table, almost nine-foot long, in the impressive family dining room which runs the length of the building. Alternatively, continental breakfast can be served in the bedrooms, on the terrace or in the garden room. Children cannot be accommodated.

# Critchards Seafood Restaurant

*Renowned harbour-side restaurant in a quaint Cornish fishing village*

☎ 01326 562407  📠 01326 564444

**Map ref 1 - SW62**

PORTHLEVEN, Cornwall, TR13 9JA
A394 to Helston, B3304 to Porthleven, harbour is at village centre, Critchards at harbour head.
2 Rooms, ££, No smoking

The main building of this restaurant with rooms is a former granary mill, you can still see the original crane arm used for hoisting the sacks of flour. Today the white exterior and charming bay windows on the ground floor add to its appeal. The dining room overlooks the harbour and the menu naturally specialises in fresh seafood and fish. Superb full breakfasts are served to residents in the restaurant, run by Steve and Jo Critchard.

The accommodation comprises two bedrooms, both with en suite shower rooms and TV. The larger bedroom, with views of the harbour and the sea, has a double and a single bed. Tea and coffee making facilities are provided in the rooms. The Cornish coastal footpaths and beach are nearby, while Truro, Helford, Falmouth and Penzance are within easy reach by car.

## RECOMMENDED IN THE AREA

**RESTAURANT:**
*Critchards Seafood Restaurant*

**TRADITIONAL PUB:**
*The Ship Inn*

**VISIT:**
*National Seal Sanctuary, Gweek*

---

# Anchorage House Guest Lodge

*Wonderful hospitality and superb cooking in the centre of Cornwall*

☎ 01726 814071

**Map ref 1 - SX05**

Nettles Corner, Tregrehan, ST AUSTELL, Cornwall, PL25 3RH
2m E of St Austell on A390, follow rd signed Tregrehan (opp Garden Centre) 50 metres, turn left into drive leading to courtyard
3 Rooms, ££, No smoking

This Georgian style house is in a prime location for discovering Cornwall's treasures. It takes no more than an hour to drive anywhere in the county, and the Lost Gardens of Heligan and Eden Project are minutes away. There is ample parking space in the courtyard. The Eppersons make a fine team, Steve is American and Jane is English, making sure your stay is relaxed and comfortable.

The bedrooms are furnished with antiques and kept sparkling clean; they all have en suite bathrooms with power showers and large baths; they are supremely comfortable with king-size beds, satellite TV and many extras. In the morning, you can enjoy an unhurried breakfast in the luxury conservatory overlooking the heated swimming pool. Jane loves to cook, as is evident in her popular, candlelit four-course dinners (available by arrangement).

## RECOMMENDED IN THE AREA

**RESTAURANT:**
*Food for Thought, Fowey*

**TRADITIONAL PUB:**
*Rashleigh Inn, Polkerris*

**VISIT:**
*Charlestown Shipwreck & Heritage Centre, St Austell*

# *T*he Wheal Lodge

*Superbly located just above the sea at Carlyon Bay, opposite the Golf Club*

☎ 01726 815543  📠 01726 815543

**Map ref 1 - SX05**

91 Sea Road, Carlyon Bay, ST AUSTELL,
Cornwall, PL25 3SH
6 Rooms, ££, No smoking in bedrooms
Closed 23 Dec-2 Jan

The Wheal Lodge offers excellent accommodation, most rooms are on the ground floor, overlooking beautiful gardens and lawns. All the bedrooms have good modern en suite facilities, remote control colour televisions, radio alarms, hospitality trays and electric blankets. The public rooms include a comfortable lounge and a well-spaced, bright and airy dining room, with a licensed bar. There is ample safe car parking space in the grounds.

The warm hospitality at this charming guest house has guests returning time after time to enjoy the wonderful care and comfort. Jeanne Martin (runner-up in the AA Landlady of the Year Awards for 1998) is an excellent home cook, who delights in spoiling her guests.

## RECOMMENDED IN THE AREA

**RESTAURANT:**
*Boscundle Manor Hotel, St Austell*

**TRADITIONAL PUB:**
*Crown Inn, Lanlivery*

**VISIT:**
*Wheal Martin China Clay Heritage Centre, St Austell*

# *N*anscawen Manor House

*Elegant Georgian manor house in a glorious country setting*

☎ 01726 814488  📠 01726 814488

✉ keithmartin@tesco.net

**Map ref 1 - SX05**

Prideaux Road, ST BLAZEY, Cornwall,
PL24 2SR
A38 from Plymouth, turn left at Dobwalls to
A390-St Austell, in St Blazey turn right after
railway, opposite garage, Nanscawen is
0.75m on right
3 Rooms, ££, No smoking
Closed 25-26 Dec

Nanscawen Manor House offers lavish hospitality in lovely surroundings. There is a choice of luxuriously appointed bedrooms with four-poster and six-foot double beds. All the rooms have en suite facilities, colour televisions, hairdryers, direct dial telephones, and tea and coffee making equipment. Breakfast is cooked to order and options might include the traditional English breakfast or locally smoked salmon with scrambled eggs. For dinner there is a varied choice of good restaurants in the area and the proprietor is happy to assist guests with their selection. Guests can relax in the drawing room which has its own well stocked bar. Alternatively, there is a large outdoor swimming pool with a hot spa tub beside it. Children over 12 are welcome, but younger children and pets cannot be accommodated.

## RECOMMENDED IN THE AREA

**RESTAURANT:**
*Well House Hotel, Liskeard*

**TRADITIONAL PUB:**
*Rashleigh Inn, Polkerris*

**VISIT:**
*Charlestown Shipwreck & Heritage Centre, St Austell*

**49**

# Kynance Guest House

*19th-century tin miner's cottage in a conservation area*

☏ **01736 796636**

**Map ref 1 - SX54**

The Warren, ST IVES, Cornwall, TR26 2EA
take A3074 town centre, sharp right before
bus/coach terminus, into rail station
approach rd. Kynance 20yds on left
6 Rooms, £, No smoking

The Kynance is a charming old property in the heart of the village, a short level walk from the picturesque harbour and sandy Porthminster beach. The bedrooms have either private or en suite facilities and are equipped with colour televisions and hospitality trays. Some have stunning views of the harbour and bay. The lounge and dining room have been cleverly altered, and the decor reflects the St Ives' heritage, featuring work by local artists. Guests are offered a choice at breakfast, including a vegetarian option. There is a south facing patio garden from where a short flight of steps takes you to within 50 yards of the coach terminus and railway station car park.

Dawn and Simon Norris are welcoming hosts, happy to advise guests on the local attractions and restaurants for evening meals. Children under seven and pets cannot be accommodated.

## RECOMMENDED IN THE AREA

**RESTAURANT:**
*Garrack Hotel, St Ives*

**TRADITIONAL PUB:**
*White Hart, Ludgvan*

**VISIT:**
*Tate Gallery, St Ives*

*The Grand Western Canal, Tiverton, Devon*

# Crooked Inn

*Attractive stone-built inn deep in the countryside but only fifteen minutes from Plymouth*

☎ 01752 848177
🖷 01752 843203

**Map ref 1 - SX45**

Stoketon, SALTASH, Cornwall, PL12 4RZ
A38 Tamar Bridge, cross & thro' tunnel. Over rdbt towards Liskeard. 2nd left (Trematon), Inn at bottom
19 Rooms, ££

You are assured of a warm welcome from the Arnold family and staff at this well run inn. The grounds are home to various friendly farm animals, 'MiMi' the sheep, Misty the goat and the pigs Daisy and Penny. The bedrooms, located around the courtyard from the Inn, are furnished to a high standard, with modern en suite facilities. One room has a fine four-poster bed and all have remote control colour televisions, radio alarms, and tea and coffee making equipment. Hairdryers and heated tongs are also provided. The menu offers an interesting choice of freshly cooked dishes using local produce, and meals are served in the beamed bar by the log fire. Children and pets are made welcome, and guests with young children can take their meals in the comfortable family room. Outside, there is a heated pool, a beer garden and a children's playground.

## RECOMMENDED IN THE AREA

**RESTAURANT:**
*Duke of Cornwall, Plymouth*

**VISIT:**
*Cotehele House, Calstock*

# Polkerr Guest House

*Conveniently placed for Tintagel village and coastal walks*

☎ 01840 770382

**Map ref 1 - SX08**

TINTAGEL, Cornwall, PL34 0BY
Off A30 just S of Launceston, A395
(Camelford), A3314 Tintagel. Hotel on right
just after Tintagel village sign
7 Rooms, £, No smoking

Robert and June Fry offer a very warm welcome to their guests. The large detached house just inside the village of Tintagel is surrounded by well tended gardens and parking is available. The ground floor public areas are well presented, they include a spacious, well appointed dining room and a sunny conservatory where guests can relax.

Six of the bedrooms have en suite shower facilities and one has a separate bathroom. All the bedrooms are decorated to a high standard and thoughtfully furnished. The room facilities include colour televisions and tea and coffee making equipment for guests. Evening meals are available by prior arrangement. Dogs are not accepted at the guest house.

## RECOMMENDED IN THE AREA

**RESTAURANT:**
*Cornish Cottage Hotel, Polzeath*

**TRADITIONAL PUB:**
*The Port William, Tintagel*

**VISIT:**
*Tintagel Castle, Tintagel*

# Elmswood House Hotel

*Fine gabled house in a peaceful village setting*

☎ 01726 814221  📠 01726 814399

**Map ref 1 - SX05**

Tehidy Road, TYWARDREATH, Cornwall,
PL24 2QD
off A390 at junct for Fowey, for 3m B3269.
left at junct Tywardreath & Par Hotel opp St
Andrews Church
7 Rooms, £

Richard and Pam Warren offer a warm welcome to guests and are justifiably proud of their clean and comfortable establishment. The house is in a quiet rural situation convenient for St Austell and Fowey. Bedrooms are individually decorated with co-ordinated fabrics and quality furnishings. All the rooms have colour television and tea and coffee making equipment, and most have modern en suite facilities. A ground floor room is available for family occupation.

There is a licensed bar and a relaxing sitting room. The attractive dining room overlooks the beautifully kept garden. In the evening a set dinner is offered comprising home-cooked dishes based on good local produce. Children are welcome, and cots, high chairs and a baby-sitting service can all be arranged.

## RECOMMENDED IN THE AREA

**RESTAURANT:**
*Food for Thought, Fowey*

**TRADITIONAL PUB:**
*Ship Inn, Fowey*

**VISIT:**
*The Lost Gardens of Heligan, Peutewen*

# Darley House

*Rural seclusion and extensive grounds*

☎ 01579 362766  ☎ 01579 363636

**Map ref 1 - SX27**

North Darley, UPTON CROSS, Liskeard,
Cornwall, PL14 5AS
from Plymouth A38 Liskeard, then B3254
Launceston. After Upton Cross continue
1mile, house on L.
3 Rooms, £, No smoking,
Closed 21 Dec-1 Jan

Darley House is set in extensive grounds, including a 3.5 acre woodland walk with cut grass paths. A tennis court/croquet lawn is available for guests' use. There is also an indoor barbeque house, which can be used by prior arrangement.

You can expect the highest quality of home-cooked food here, prepared using fresh local produce. The English breakfast menu is extensive, fresh fruit is always available, along with fish, cold meats and cheeses. Meals are served in the dining room, where a wood-burning stove adds warmth and atmosphere. There is also a comfortable lounge with a television, stereo unit and a grand piano. The spacious bedrooms are individually and tastefully furnished to a high standard, two have en suite bathrooms, the other has a private bathroom. All rooms have television, radio alarm, hairdryer and tea and coffee making facilities. The hosts give personal attention to the individual needs of all their guests.

## Recommended in the Area

**Restaurant:**
*Thyme & Plaice, Callington*

**Traditional Pub:**
*Springer Spaniel, Treburley*

**Visit:**
*Launceston Castle, Launceston*

# Greencott

*Attractive house with a secluded location amid beautiful countryside*

☎ 01803 762649

**Map ref 2 - SX77**

Landscove, ASHBURTON, Devon, TQ13 7LZ
A38 to Plymouth, 2nd exit Landscove. At top
of slip rd left, 2m, village green on left,
opposite village hall
2 Rooms, £, No smoking in bedrooms
Closed 25-26 Dec

Modern facilities in an old world atmosphere are offered at this totally renovated house in the village of Landscove, which is just two and a half miles from Ashburton. Greencott is set in its own garden with lovely country views.

The guest bedrooms are carefully furnished and well equipped with en suite baths and showers, central heating and tea and coffee making amenities. Television, books, maps, and information about the area are provided in the comfortable guests' sitting room, and traditional country cooking is served around the oak dining table. The full English breakfast includes home-made bread, and dinner is available on request. Older children are welcome, but pets cannot be accommodated, with the exception of guide dogs. Tarmac off-road parking is provided. The cider press at Dartington and the steam railway at Staverton are nearby attractions.

## Recommended in the Area

**Restaurant:**
*Sea Trout Inn, Staverton*

**Traditional Pub:**
*Dartbridge Inn, Buckfastleigh*

**Visit:**
*Buckfast Abbey, Buckfastleigh*

# East Burne Farm

*Grade II listed medieval hall house with a cobbled courtyard*

☎ 01626 821496  📠 01626 821105

**Map ref 2 - SX87**

BICKINGTON, Devon, TQ12 6PA
1.5m from A38 off A383
2 Rooms, £, No smoking
Closed Xmas & New Year

## RECOMMENDED IN THE AREA

**RESTAURANT:**
*Holne Chase Hotel, Ashburton*

**TRADITIONAL PUB:**
*The Rising Sun, Ashburton*

**VISIT:**
*Buckfast Abbey, Buckfastleigh*

A warm welcome is assured at this lovely old farmhouse from owners Mike and Emma Pallett. The house is very well kept and superbly located along a narrow winding lane in a quiet valley just a mile from the A38. Two guest bedrooms are provided, a twin with en suite facilities and a double with four-poster bed and a private bathroom. The rooms have electric night storage heating, electric blankets and tea and coffee making facilities. There is a beamed sitting room where an open fire burns in cooler weather. In the morning a full English breakfast is served.

Guests are free to explore the open farmland, which is rich in flora and fauna. There is a heated swimming pool in the garden with gentle steps at the shallow end. Some of the farm buildings around the cobbled yard have been converted into self-catering holiday accommodation.

# Front House Lodge

*Pretty 16th-century house with a sense of the past*

☎ 01626 832202  📠 01626 832202
✉ fronthouselodge@yahoo.co.uk

**Map ref 2 - SX87**

East Street, BOVEY TRACEY, Devon,
TQ13 9EL
turn off A38 onto A382 into Bovey Tracey,
through town centre, Front House Lodge is
past the Town Hall on right
6 Rooms, £, No smoking

Front House Lodge is a charming property dating back to 1540 with interesting connections to the Civil War. Bovey Tracey is a little Dartmoor town featuring the River Bovey, Devon Guild of Crafts, with small shops, restaurants, pubs and tea shops. Three miles from Haytor rocks, on the edge of Dartmoor National Park it makes an ideal location for touring the South West.

The interior is enchanting throughout in English country style with a varied collection of antiques and china. The bedrooms are traditionally furnished, pretty beds with cushions and canopies all with shower or bath en-suite, CTV and many thoughtful extras.

Breakfasts are a delicious treat beautifully presented using lovely china and served in the beamed dining room. A relaxed friendly atmosphere plus secluded garden and private parking.

## RECOMMENDED IN THE AREA

**RESTAURANT:**
*Edgemoor Hotel, Bovey Tracey*

**TRADITIONAL PUB:**
*Claycutters Arms, Chudleigh Knighton*

**VISIT:**
*Canonteign Falls, Chudleigh*

# $\mathcal{B}$racken House

*A country house on Exmoor, with grounds teeming with wildlife*

☎ 01598 710320

**Map ref 2 - SS63**

BRATTON FLEMING, Devon, EX31 4TG
off A399, signposted Bratton Fleming, on left
just after Post Office
8 Rooms, ££

*O*riginally a rectory dating from 1840, Bracken House stands in 8 acres of garden, woodland and paddocks, with a small lake on which mallards usually breed. An aviary in the garden houses injured and convalescent owls. There are magnificent views out over rolling hills and wooded valleys to the Taw Estuary in the distance. Although only a few minutes' walk from the village, the house is in a peaceful world of its own.

All of the bedrooms have en suite bathrooms, colour TV, push-button radios and hot drink facilities. The drawing room has a well stocked bar, and there is a library with a range of books, including information on the local area - both rooms have open fires. You can enjoy traditional food cooked on the Aga. A daily-changing dinner menu is available, with a vegetarian option, and there is a good wine list.

## Recommended in the area

**Restaurant:**
*Halmpstone Manor, Barnstaple*

**Traditional Pub:**
*62 The Bank, Barnstaple*

**Visit:**
*Arlington Court, Arlington*

*Thatchers at work,
Colebrook, Devon*

# Week Farm

*17th-century farmhouse set in beautiful countryside within walking distance of Dartmoor*

☎ 01837 861221
🖷 01837 861221
✉ weekfarm@
biscuits.win-uknet.
**Map ref 2 - SX58**

BRIDESTOWE, Devon,
EX20 4HZ
exit A30 at Sourton
junct, right then left
(Bridestowe), 2nd right,
cross dual carriageway,
left at x-d, house 0.5m
on right.
5 Rooms, £, No
smoking, Closed Xmas

## RECOMMENDED IN THE AREA

**RESTAURANT:**
*Horn of Plenty,
Gulworthy*

**TRADITIONAL PUB:**
*Castle Inn, Lydford*

**VISIT:**
*Okehampton Castle,
Okehampton*

*J*ohn and Margaret Hockridge have been welcoming guests for thirty years into what has been their family home for three generations. Guests are greeted with a complimentary cream tea, as a foretaste of the traditional values and delicious home cooking that are synonymous with Week Farm. The comfortable bedrooms come in a variety of sizes and styles, all with modern en suite facilities. Log fires burn in the lounge in cooler weather, and between May and September guests can make use of the outdoor heated swimming pool or relax on the patio. The cosy dining room is the setting for a hearty English breakfast. Dinner is also available as a four-course meal featuring the best of local produce. The house is not licensed but guests are invited to bring their own wine. The granary and barns have been converted to provide self-catering accommodation. Dogs can be accommodated by arrangement.

# Parford Well

*Comfortable house and walled garden within Dartmoor National Park*

☎ 01647 433353

**Map ref 2 - SX78**

Sandy Park, CHAGFORD, Devon, TQ13 8JW
A30 onto A382, after 3m turn left at Sandy Park towards Drewsteignton, house 50yds on left
3 Rooms, ££, No smoking

Named after the village well in the lovingly tended garden, Parford Well is only five minutes from the A30 and less than two miles from the Stannary town of Chagford, with wonderful walks right on the doorstep, both in the wooded valley of the River Teign and on the open moor.

Tim Daniel provides guests with personal, attentive service. He has decorated and furnished his house with care and taste. The attractive bedrooms, two of which are en suite, are equipped with thoughtful little extras like fresh flowers and magazines. The sitting room has lovely paintings and sculpture, and French windows onto the garden; it is warmed by the wood-burning stove when the weather turns colder, and there are candles in long wooden candlesticks on the mantlepiece. Top quality English breakfast is served around an antique table, dishes include a range of local produce.

## Recommended in the Area

**Restaurant:**
*22 Mill Street, Chagford*

**Traditional Pub:**
*Drewe Arms, Drewsteignton*

**Visit:**
*Castle Drogo, Drewsteignton*

# Tor Cottage

*An attractive cottage set in its own private valley*

☎ 01822 860248  📠 01822 860126
✉ info@torcottage.demon.co.uk

**Map ref 1 - SX48**

CHILLATON, Devon, PL16 0JE
from A30 exit Lewdown thro' Chillaton towards Tavistock. Right 300mtrs after P.O. signed 'Bridlepath No Public Vehicular access' to end
4 Rooms, £££, No smoking
Closed 6 Dec-Jan

## Recommended in the Area

**Restaurant:**
*Lewtrenchard Manor, Lewdown*

**Traditional Pub:**
*Peter Tavy Inn, Peter Tavy*

**Visit:**
*Buckland Abbey*

Maureen Rowlatt's charming home is a luxurious and tranquil retreat set in 18 acres of grounds with a profusion of wildlife. It offers privacy and seclusion in a cosy and relaxed atmosphere. The gardens are a feature in their own right, with many quiet corners where you can sit in the sun or cool off in the shade. The bedrooms offer en suite facilities, log fires and private gardens. The Cottage Wing is in the main house, comprising a bedroom and separate sitting room overlooking the valley. The three other rooms are a few steps from Tor Cottage and have recently been carefully restored, with individual themes, including an art deco room. Mrs Rowlatt is an accomplished vegetarian cook, but is also happy to cater for meat eaters at breakfast. The heated outdoor pool is available for guest use. Cheques cannot be accepted. No pets.

# The Old Bakehouse

## Listed 16th-century building set around a delightful courtyard

☎ 01769 580074 📠 01769 580074

**Map ref 2 - SS61**

South Molton Street, CHULMLEIGH, Devon, EX18 7BW
off A377, onto B3096, proceed 2m to village, turn left into S Molton St, guest house is 100yds on left
4 Rooms, £, No smoking

Charming hosts Colin and Holly Burls take great delight in welcoming guests to their historic home. Four immaculately presented bedrooms are available. One in the thatched former merchant's house, which now doubles as a tea room, and the others across the flower-bedecked courtyard in the old village bakehouse. The accommodation has full central heating and all the rooms have en suite baths or showers, colour televisions, radios and hospitality trays. A guest telephone and laundry/drying facilities are also provided. The complex includes a licensed

restaurant serving excellent home-cooked dishes including local specialities. Special diets can be catered for by arrangement. There is a guest sitting room with a log fire in cooler weather. Children are welcome, and a cot and high chair are available, however pets cannot be accommodated.

## RECOMMENDED IN THE AREA

**RESTAURANT:**
*Marsh Hall Hotel, South Molton*

**TRADITIONAL PUB:**
*The New Inn, Coleford*

**VISIT:**
*Arlington Court, Arlington*

# Ashelford

## 17th-century farmhouse facing south across its own valley

☎ 01271 850469 📠 01271 850862
✉ ashelford@ashelford.co.uk

**Map ref 2 - SS54**

East Down, COMBE MARTIN, Devon, EX31 4LU
in Barnstaple follow signs for Lynton A39, take 2nd left after Shirwell. Follow signs to Churchill, property on right
3 Rooms, £££, No smoking

Ashelford sits in over 70 acres of pasture and woodland, with views across to Exmoor. The grey stone exterior, and the oak beams and open log fires inside give the house its rural charm, and the atmosphere is friendly. Well behaved dogs are welcome, there is even a bath for use after muddy walks. The accommodation is not suitable for children. The bedrooms, named 'Okewill', 'Churchill' and 'Exmoor', are neat and cosy, with pretty co-ordinated curtains and bedspreads; they all have en suite bathrooms; and each one has a fridge with fresh milk, orange juice and spring water; 'Okewill' has a four-poster bed.

Breakfast is leisurely, with a wide choice, and more good cuisine is available for dinner, by prior arrangement. Meals are taken either in the elegant dining room or in the large bright farmhouse kitchen. There are two sitting rooms.

## RECOMMENDED IN THE AREA

**RESTAURANT:**
*Rising Sun, Lynmouth*

**TRADITIONAL PUB:**
*Rising Sun Hotel, Lynmouth*

**VISIT:**
*Arlington Court, Arlington*

# Croyde Bay House Hotel

*Small hotel with stunning views across the sea*

☎ **01271 890270**

**Map ref 1 - SS43**

CROYDE, Devon, EX33 1PA
Take N. Devon link to Barnstaple, follow signs to Braunton, left in Braunton to Croyde, left (Moor Lane) to slipway.
7 Rooms, £

The beach can be seen from every window, and the highest tides wash against the garden wall. This comfortable, clean hotel commands a superb position on the edge of the bay. You do not have to go far to play tennis, or golf, or go horse riding, and you could try some surfing, but with the high standard of service from the friendly owners and staff, you will be very happy to get back to the hotel.

Beautifully cooked big breakfasts, and light evening meals are served in the spacious dining room, and you can relax in the sun lounge or the panelled lounge, or the bar. Outside there is a sun deck, a south facing garden and a conservatory.

The bedrooms are tastefully decorated, with soft lighting; all have en suite bathrooms or shower rooms. There is a laundry room with coin operated machines. Dogs are accepted at the management's discretion.

## RECOMMENDED IN THE AREA

**RESTAURANT:**
*Halmpstone Manor, Barnstaple*

**TRADITIONAL PUB:**
*62 The Bank, Barnstaple*

**VISIT:**
*Arlington Court, Arlington*

*Paignton and Dartmouth Railway, Devon*

# Broome Court

**RECOMMENDED IN THE AREA**

**RESTAURANT:**
*The Carved Angel, Dartmouth*

**TRADITIONAL PUB:**
*Hunters Lodge Inn, Cornworthy*

**VISIT:**
*Bayard's Cove Fort, Dartmouth*

*An attractive stone-built property set in an area of outstanding natural beauty*

☎ 01803 834275
🖷 01803 833260

**Map ref 2 - SX85**

Broomhill,
DARTMOUTH, Devon,
TQ6 0LD
A38 to A384, Totnes,
right onto A381, left at
Halwell onto A3122
(Dartmouth). Right at
Sportsman Arms, then
3rd right
3 Rooms, ££, No
smoking in bedrooms

*B*roome Court is situated at the end of a long winding lane, deep in glorious countryside. The atmosphere is that of a country house, friendly, relaxed and inclusive, with a warm welcome from owners Jan Bird and Tom Boughton. There is a charming paved courtyard, abundant with plants and shrubs, with a fountain at its centre. The bedrooms, including twins and doubles, are beautifully decorated and three have en suite facilities. All the rooms have tea making equipment and colour television. Breakfast is served in the old farmhouse kitchen, and guests also have the option of dinner. For relaxation guests have the use of the terrace, summer lounge and conservatory, and the winter lounge in cooler weather. Self-catering accommodation is also available in the Granary and 'Eeyore's Tail'.

# Ford House

*Listed Regency town house a short walk from the quayside*

☎ 01803 834047
📠 01803 834047
📧 richard@ford-house.freeserve.co.uk

**Map ref 2 - SX85**

44 Victoria Road,
DARTMOUTH, Devon,
TQ6 9DX
right off A3122,
Townstal Rd to Victoria
Rd, last house, bottom
of hill
3 Rooms, ££

*C*onveniently situated for the town centre and the quay, this handsome town house is personally run by Richard and Jayne Turner. The individually decorated bedrooms come equipped with a choice of king/queen-size double beds or twins, a fridge with a pint of fresh milk, direct dial telephones, an iron and ironing board, hairdryer, colour television, radio alarm, and tea and coffee making equipment. The en suites have a full size bath and shower, plus a range of toiletries. Breakfast, served from 8.30am till 12 noon, offers the full English using free range eggs and dry cured bacon, or specials, such as kippers, smoked haddock, scrambled egg with smoked salmon, or devilled kidneys. Coffee is freshly ground and orange juice freshly squeezed. For dinner, the town centre restaurants are within easy walking distance. Private off-street parking is provided, and pets are most welcome.

## RECOMMENDED IN THE AREA

**RESTAURANT:**
*The Carved Angel, Dartmouth*

**TRADITIONAL PUB:**
*The Cherub Inn, Dartmouth*

**VISIT:**
*Dartmouth Castle*

# Nonsuch House

*Superbly located Edwardian house with breathtaking sea views*

☎ 01803 752829  📠 01803 752357

**Map ref 2 - SX85**

Church Hill, Kingswear, DARTMOUTH,
Devon, TQ6 0BX
A3022/A379 left onto B3205. 2m, left up
Higher Contour Rd. House 0.75m on
seaward side of hairpin bend
3 Rooms, ££, No smoking in bedrooms

Nonsuch House is located on a south-facing hill affording wonderful views over the port of Dartmouth and the sea. You can step outside for bracing coastal walks, and the ferry across to Dartmouth is a five-minute walk away.

Bedrooms are beautifully presented and all have en suite facilities, but again the most striking feature is the view from the rooms, all of which look out to sea. There is a conservatory and terrace where guests can enjoy the fine weather, and in winter log fires are lit in the saloon and dining room. Whatever the weather, the atmosphere is warm and welcoming. A generous breakfast is served, and evening meals are also available. The house is not licensed but guests are welcome to bring their own drinks. Animals are not accommodated.

## RECOMMENDED IN THE AREA

**RESTAURANT:**
*Soar Mill Cove, Salcombe*

**TRADITIONAL PUB:**
*Royal Castle Hotel, Dartmouth*

**VISIT:**
*Woodlands Leisure Park, Blackawton*

---

# The Edwardian

*Edwardian residence five minutes walk from the city centre*

☎ 01392 276102  📠 01392 253393
✉ edwardex@globalnet.co.uk

**Map ref 2 - SX99**

30/32 Heavitree Road, EXETER, Devon,
EX1 2LQ
M5 J30 to Middlemoor rndbt, 2nd exit to
Heavitree. Edwardian on Heavitree Rd after
Exeter Uni Schl of Education (St Lukes)
12 Rooms, ££
Closed Xmas

## RECOMMENDED IN THE AREA

**RESTAURANT:**
*Buckerell Lodge, Exeter*

**VISIT:**
*Underground Passages, Exeter*

Michael and Kay Rattenbury's families have lived in rural Devon for generations, and the couple take pleasure in inviting guests into their home and helping them to enjoy their stay in this lovely part of the world. The Edwardian residents' lounge is supplied with plenty of maps and guide books to aid the planning of itineraries. The house has been beautifully refurbished, and features china and antique pieces lovingly collected over the years. A good choice is offered at breakfast, which is served in one of the attractive dining rooms. All the bedrooms have en suite facilities, including one room on the ground floor. The rooms are equipped with remote control televisions, individual heating thermostats, double glazing, direct dial telephones, hairdryers and hospitality trays. Four-poster, antique brass, wrought iron or period wooden bedsteads are a feature. There is a large car park opposite the house.

# Clawford Vineyard

*Comfortable accommodation uniquely located on a working vineyard*

☎ 01409 254177 ☏ 01409 254177

**Map ref 1 - SS30**

Clawton, HOLSWORTHY, Devon, EX22 6PN
A388 Holsworth to Launceston road, turn left
at Clawton crossroads, 1.5m to T-junct, turn
left, then in 0.5m left again
11 Rooms, £, No smoking in bedrooms

Situated in the peaceful Claw Valley, Clawford Vineyard, as its name suggests, is a working vineyard. It also has a cider orchard, and guests can enjoy sampling the produce. Extensive course fishing is also available, with some monster carp awaiting anglers in several well stocked lakes.

The spacious en suite bedrooms are a recent addition, all of them are exceedingly well furnished and equipped. Public areas, overlooking the lakes, include a comfortable lounge, spacious bar and games room. Meals are served in the conservatory, which allows each party to enjoy the views and observe the abundant wildlife.

The vineyard is centrally situated for the southwest tourist attractions and golf courses.

## RECOMMENDED IN THE AREA

**RESTAURANT:**
*Blagdon Manor, Ashwater*

**VISIT:**
*Underground Passages, Exeter*

# The Old Forge

*17th-century thatched cottage in a village setting*

☎ 01404 831297
✉ oldforge.wilmington@tesco.net

**Map ref 2 - ST10**

Wilmington, HONITON, Devon, EX14 9JR
from Honiton A35 Dorchester. Wilmington
approx 3m from Honiton. Old Forge near
Wilmington sign
3 Rooms, £, No smoking

Located in the village of Wilmington on the main Axminster to Honiton road, this charming old property is home to Carole and Jim Hudson. The hospitality is every bit as warm and friendly as the character of the building, which still offers a wealth of beams and other original features.

Around the house are three quarters of an acre of gardens and wooded grounds with a walk through the woods to lovely countryside beyond. The nearest seaside resort is Seaton, just six miles away.

The pretty cottage-style bedrooms are equipped with many personal touches, including fresh flowers, books and magazines. Hearty breakfasts and imaginative dinners are served in the intimate dining room, adjacent to the attractive and comfortable sitting room. The house is not licensed but diners are invited to bring their own wine.

## RECOMMENDED IN THE AREA

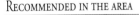

**RESTAURANT:**
*Old Steam Bakery, Beer*

**TRADITIONAL PUB:**
*The Otter Inn, Honiton*

**VISIT:**
*Cadhay, Ottery St Mary*

# Lower Waytown

*A converted barn and roundhouse with ponds in the garden*

☎ 01237 451787  📠 01237 451787

**Map ref 1 - SS32**

HORN'S CROSS, Devon, EX39 5DN
A39 from Bideford through Horns Cross,
0.5m past Hoops Inn, Roundhouse on left
3 Rooms, ££, No smoking
Closed Xmas & New Year

There are five acres of grounds, and 17th-century thatched cottages next door for self-catering. You can sit in the pretty courtyard garden and watch the black swans and waterfowl in the stream-fed ponds. The spectacular North Devon coastline is only half a mile away, and it is just five miles to the famous village of Clovelly.

The original structure of the roundhouse is clearly visible in the round shape of the sitting room, with its beams and inglenook fireplace. Adjoining this is the spacious dining room furnished with antiques, where a delicious home cooked breakfast, traditional or continental, is served.

The comfortable bedrooms, one of which is round, have en suite bathrooms, tea and coffee facilities, colour TV and hairdryers. Children over the age of 12 are welcome, no pets are allowed.

## RECOMMENDED IN THE AREA

**RESTAURANT:**
*Halmpstone Manor, Barnstaple*

**TRADITIONAL PUB:**
*Hoops Inn, Horn Cross*

**VISIT:**
*Dartington Crystal, Great Torrington*

# Higher Cadham Farm

*Farmhouse accommodation with a riverside setting in rural Devon*

☎ 01837 851647  📠 01837 851410

**Map ref 2 - SS50**

JACOBSTOWE, Devon, EX20 3RB
from Jacobstowe A3072 (Hatherleigh/Bude),
a few yards after church sharp right in front of
Cottage Farm, 0.5m
9 Rooms, £
Closed Dec

John and Jenny King have been welcoming guests to their lovely farmhouse for more than 20 years. The bedrooms are divided between rooms in the original farmhouse and those in converted farm buildings. Each is thoughtfully equipped, neatly decorated and furnished in modern pine. Five rooms have en suite facilities and one has a four-poster bed. The restaurant is open to the public for morning coffees, lunches and cream teas. For residents, there is a choice between continental and full English breakfast, and a set evening meal of Jenny's traditional home cooking is available.

The Kings raise cattle and sheep on 139 acres, and as supporters of green tourism, they are proud of the wildlife on their land, including a family of otters (the farm is located on the Tarka Trail). There are also farm trails identifying the plants, birds and animals to be seen. Well behaved dogs are welcome.

## RECOMMENDED IN THE AREA

**RESTAURANT:**
*Pophams, Winkleigh*

**TRADITIONAL PUB:**
*Tally Ho, Hatherleigh*

**VISIT:**
*Okehampton Castle, Okehampton*

# Waterloo House Hotel

*A listed Georgian building right in the heart of old Ilfracombe*

☎ 01271 863060
📠 01271 863060

Map ref 2 - SS54

Waterloo Terrace, Fore Street, ILFRACOMBE, Devon, EX34 9DJ
exit M5 J27, to A361 to Ilfracombe, along High St, after Cinema, filter left (Fore St), thro' no entry signs, 1st terrace on right
9 Rooms, ££, No smoking in bedrooms

## RECOMMENDED IN THE AREA

**RESTAURANT:**
*Little Beach Hotel, Woolacombe*

**TRADITIONAL PUB:**
*Rising Sun, Lynmouth*

**VISIT:**
*Arlington Court, Arlington*

*T*his charming period property is within easy walking distance of the harbour and all the amenities of the town. Originally three cottages, the building has retained many of its original features, providing accommodation of character. Each of the rooms is themed after someone from the period; most have en suite facilities, and some have harbour views. All the rooms are equipped with hospitality trays, remote control colour televisions, individually controlled central heating and many other individual touches. Guests can relax in either the Wellington lounge bar or the elegant tented lounge based on Napoleons campaign tent. Smoking is only permitted in these two rooms. A good choice is available at breakfast, served up to 11 am. Gourmet meals are served in the evening in Bonapartes restaurant, which is also open to the public. Bar meals are also available. Children under 12 cannot be accommodated, making the hotel ideal for romantic breaks, weddings or group bookings. Special rates apply for house parties of 12 or more.

# Moor View House

*Small country house facing Dartmoor, a comfortable and elegant place for guests since 1869, with fine English food*

☎ 01822 820220
📠 01822 820220

**Map ref 2 - SX58**

Vale Down, LYDFORD, Devon, EX20 4BB
off A30 Sourton Cross to A386 Tavistock rd, hotel drive 4m on right
4 Rooms, ££
No smoking

## RECOMMENDED IN THE AREA

**RESTAURANT:**
Lewtrenchard Manor, Lewdown

**TRADITIONAL PUB:**
Castle Inn & Hotel, Lydford

**VISIT:**
Lydford Castle, Lydford

*I*n Victorian times, the writer Eden Phillpots was a regular visitor and found inspiration here to write 'A Farmer's Wife' and 'Widdicombe Fair'. The views across the Devon and Cornwall countryside are fantastic, especially in the light of the setting sun. It is a particularly good base for touring these beautiful parts of the country.

The daily four-course dinner menu uses traditional country recipes and the finest local meat, fish and game to create delicious dishes, beautifully presented on bone china, with gleaming silver and sparkling crystal, in the dining room. The bedrooms are decorated in Victorian style, and all have en suite bathrooms. The house is decorated with panache throughout. The sitting room is lovely and bright, with an open fire in winter; there is a grand piano in the corner, with photos of the friendly owners, the Sharples family, on top.

# Victoria Lodge

*Victorian house ideally located for exploring the glories of Exmoor and North Devon*

☎ 01598 753203
📠 01598 753203
✉ info@victoria lodge.co.uk
**Map ref 2 - SS74**

Lee Road, LYNTON, Devon, EX35 6BS
off A39 opposite Post Office
9 Rooms ££
No smoking

## RECOMMENDED IN THE AREA

**RESTAURANT:**
*Chough's Nest Hotel, Lynton*

**TRADITIONAL PUB:**
*Rising Sun, Lynmouth*

**VISIT:**
*Arlington Castle, Arlington*

Victoria Lodge, dating from the 1880s, has been carefully restored by Ben and Jane Bennett to retain its original features. The house has a remarkable collection of over 800 Victorian prints and photographs, along with antique clocks and other pieces which help recreate the period atmosphere. High quality fabrics, furniture and fittings have been used to good effect and no detail has been missed to ensure guests' comfort. There are two stylish lounges and an elegant dining room.

Justifiably proud of her cooking, Jane offers imaginative menus with a variety of traditional puddings, everything is homemade. A three course dinner is served on certain evenings, usually Thursday to Sunday inclusive. There is a sunny terrace at the front of the house overlooking a beautiful water garden. With their intimate knowledge of the area, Ben and Jane are able to help guests' make the most of their stay.

**67**

# *L*ongmead House Hotel

*A fine country home set in pretty gardens*

☎ 01598 752523   📠 01598 752523

**Map ref 2 - SS74**

9 Longmead, LYNTON, Devon, EX35 6DQ
follow signs for 'Valley of Rocks'
7 Rooms, £
No smoking

*J*ohn and Carol Pluck extend a warm welcome to guests at their lovely home. Longmead House is set in large gardens just a short walk from the beautiful Valley of the Rocks, and the centre of the village.

Bedrooms, which vary in size, are meticulously kept and very well equipped, to include colour televisions and hospitality trays. All the rooms have en suite facilities.

A spacious lounge with a well stocked bar is available for guests' use. Breakfast is served in the panelled dining room which has a magnificent oak fireplace. Evening meals are also available by prior arrangement. Dogs cannot be accommodated.

## RECOMMENDED IN THE AREA

**RESTAURANT:**
*Rising Sun Hotel, Lynmouth*

**TRADITIONAL PUB:**
*The Ship Inn, Porlock*

**VISIT:**
*Arlington Castle, Arlington*

# *B*lackaller Hotel & Restaurant

*17th-century woollen mill on the Bovey River*

☎ 01647 440322   📠 01647 441131
📧 blackaller@dartmoor.co.uk

**Map ref 2 - SX78**

North Bovey, MORETONHAMPSTEAD,
Devon, TQ13 8QY
A38, A382 to Moretonhampstead, on entering Moretonhampstead take 1st left by newsagents to North Bovey
6 Rooms, ££, No smoking in bedrooms
Closed Jan & Feb

*B*lackaller is the West Country name for the Black Alder tree which grows along the river banks by this lovely former mill. Peter Hunt and Hazel Phillips run the hotel on very relaxed and friendly lines. Bedrooms are pleasing for their simplicity - comfortable and understated. All the rooms have en suite facilities, colour television, and tea and coffee making equipment. Public areas include a charming old sitting room, a well stocked bar, and an attractive dining room with an inglenook fireplace and exposed granite walls.

A four-course dinner is served to residents and visitors, except on Sunday and Monday nights, and vegetarian meals can be provided on request. Fresh produce is a feature of the menus, all sourced from within the county, including organic Jacobs' lamb and fish from Brixham. Home-produced bread, honey and muesli are a real treat at breakfast.

## RECOMMENDED IN THE AREA

**RESTAURANT:**
*(own restaurant)*

**TRADITIONAL PUB:**
*The Cleave, Lustleigh*

**VISIT:**
*Castle Drogo, Drewsteignton*

# Gate House

*Thatched medieval hall house, Grade II listed, in a conservation village setting*

☎ 01647 440479
📠 01647 440479

**Map ref 2 - SX78**

North Bovey,
MORETONHAMPSTEAD,
Devon, TQ13 8RB
A30, A382
Moretonhampstead,
B3212 to North Bovey
3 Rooms, ££
No smoking

A pot of tea and a slice of scrumptious home-made cake, what better way to welcome guests to this idyllic 15th-century hideaway? Hospitable hosts, John and Sheila Williams, are justly proud of their home, which is full of charm and character. Guests can relax beside the wood-burning stove, framed in the huge granite fireplace, and contemplate all that has taken place beneath this thatch during the last five centuries. Bedrooms are tastefully decorated in a country style and offer views of the garden or the moors. A hearty breakfast is served featuring local produce, and candlelit dinners are available by prior arrangement, providing the opportunity for Sheila to indulge her culinary skills.

There is a large garden with an outdoor swimming pool in a sheltered corner, where guests may like to relax in fine weather. Nearby, there are beautiful walks, historic houses and lovely gardens to visit.

## RECOMMENDED IN THE AREA

**RESTAURANT:**
*Mill End Hotel, Chagford*

**TRADITIONAL PUB:**
*Rock Inn, Haytor Vale*

**VISIT:**
*Castle Drogo, Drewsteignton*

# Heathfield House

*High above Okehampton with views of Dartmoor*

☎ 01837 54211
🖷 01837 54211

**Map ref 2 - SX59**

Klondyke Road,
OKEHAMPTON, Devon,
EX20 1EW
Okehampton Stn-under
bridge 300yds up steep
hill, thro' woods then
straight up drive into
hotel car park
4 Rooms, £
No smoking
Closed 12 Dec-11 Jan

## RECOMMENDED IN THE AREA

**RESTAURANT:**
*Castle Hotel, Taunton*

**TRADITIONAL PUB:**
*Rising Sun, Knapp*

**VISIT:**
*Combe Sydenham
Country Park, Monksilver*

Once the Station Master's House, Heathfield overlooks the town, with a vast expanse of Dartmoor National Park stretching into the distance behind. It is in an area known as the centre for walking and cycling in Devon. Guests wishing to swim can use the heated outdoor pool at the house, believed to be the only upstairs open-air swimming pool in the county. Heathfield House is also famed for its food. Scrumptious home-cooked meals are served in the Victorian dining room. The freshest produce is carefully cooked and prepared to create splendid dishes. A bright conservatory looks out over the pool, providing an alternative to the comfortable residents' lounge, for after dinner relaxation. The guest bedrooms are thoughtfully equipped and individually designed around a particular colour. All the bedrooms offer excellent standards of comfort and en suite bathroom facilities.

# *P*ercy's at Coombeshead

*A converted barn offering superb food and peaceful surroundings*

☎ 01409 211236
🖷 01409 211275
✉ info@percys.co.uk

**Map ref 2 - SX59**

OKEHAMPTON, Devon, EX21 5EA
approx 3m N of Launceston, off A388
8 Rooms, ££
No smoking

Situated on a 130 acre estate, north of the A30 between Okehampton and Launceston, this converted barn offers spacious, well appointed en suite accommodation. The bedrooms are all elegantly decorated and have large comfortable beds. The facilities are modern and include colour television, telephones, tea and coffee making facilities, shortbread, fruit bowl, mineral water and quality toiletries. Superb country views can be enjoyed from the bedroom windows. Many guests return here to enjoy the exceptional food, including fresh salads and herbs and vegetables from the garden. The sausages are homemade and fresh local dairy produce and organic vegetables feature on the menus. Percy's is also a restaurant, serving dinner, with two AA rosettes awarded for quality of cuisine. Children over 10 are welcome in the main dining room. Supper for younger children can be provided between 5 and 6.30 pm by prior arrangement.

## RECOMMENDED IN THE AREA

**TRADITIONAL PUB:**
*Eliot Arms, Tregadillet*

**VISIT:**
*Launceston Castle*

# The Old Rectory

*Peaceful, small country house with superb cuisine*

☎ 01237 451443

**Map ref 1 - SS32**

PARKHAM, Devon, EX39 5PL
take A39 from Bideford towards Bude, at Horns Cross left to Parkham, thro' village to Bell Pub, left onto Rectory Ln, 3rd house on right
3 Rooms, ££, No smoking

Jean and Jack Langton manage to make their home an extremely comfortable place for guests to stay. This applies as much to their hospitality as it does to the appearance and easy atmosphere of their house. A beautiful front lawn enhances the entrance. Log fires, fresh fruit and flowers in the bedrooms complement the simple, elegant furnishings, comfortable armchairs and elegant wooden furniture. Two of the bedrooms have en suite facilities. In the evening guests can meet up in the drawing room for an aperitif before taking dinner together in the charming dining room. There are four courses, and there is also a vegetarian menu. Jean, an Elizabeth David devotee, cooks everything herself, using organically grown fresh vegetables and locally produced meat and fish, and the results are magnificent.

## RECOMMENDED IN THE AREA

**RESTAURANT:**
*Halmpstone Manor, Barnstaple*

**TRADITIONAL PUB:**
*Hoops Inn, Horn Cross*

**VISIT:**
*Dartington Crystal, Great Torrington*

*Maverdine House, Gloucester*

# Beach End Guest House

*Attractive Edwardian guest house set between the sea and the sheltering cliffs*

☎ 01297 23388
📠 01297 625604

**Map ref 2 - SX29**

8 Trevelyan Road,
SEATON, Devon,
EX12 2NL
at eastern end of
seafront near yacht
club and harbour
4 Rooms, £

## RECOMMENDED IN THE AREA

**RESTAURANT:**
*Old Steam Bakery, Beer*

**TRADITIONAL PUB:**
*Masons Arms, Branscombe*

**VISIT:**
*Otterton Mill Centre, Otterton*

Resident proprietors Philip and Joan Millard extend a warm welcome to guests at this quietly located guest house on Seaton esplanade. The freshly prepared food is a highlight. Dishes are based on local produce whenever possible, and at dinner there is a choice of starters and a set main course. An omelette or salad is offered as an alternative. Vegetarian, diabetic and other special diets can be catered for. There is a residential licence so wine is also available. A full English breakfast is served complete with freshly squeezed orange juice and home-made marmalade. All the bedrooms have lovely sea views and are equipped with en suite facilities and colour televisions. Tea and coffee are available at any time and hospitality trays can be requested. There is also a colour television in the cosy lounge, along with a collection of board games. Seaton has a clean pebble beach and fine walks along the cliff tops, the guest house makes a great base for guests exploring the Axe valley and the wonderful Devon coastline. Seaton tramway is a local attraction.

# *T*he Old Farmhouse

*Thatched 16th-century farmhouse, close to the sea and town centre*

☎ **01395 512284**

**Map ref 2 - SY18**

Hillside Road,
SIDMOUTH, Devon,
EX10 8JG
Exeter, A3052 to
Sidmouth, right at
Bowd x-rds 2m, left at
rdbt, left at mini-rdbt,
right over bridge,
bear right on corner
7 Rooms, £
No smoking
Closed Dec-Jan

*T*his charming farmhouse, in a quiet residential area, dates back to 1569, it gets a mention in the Doomsday Book. Some of the bedrooms are in the cottage across the patio which once housed the local cider mill. All of them have en suite bathrooms and they are decorated with pretty floral wallpaper. Beams, curtained alcoves and twisty hallways are enhanced by prints and dried flowers to give the place a traditional look.

The dining room has an inglenook fireplace and old china plates decorate the walls, the tables are set with royal blue cloths with lace, and linen napkins. Food is freshly prepared from the best local produce, with old-fashioned recipes forming the base of the varied menus. There is a TV lounge and an intimate Inglenook bar.

## RECOMMENDED IN THE AREA

**RESTAURANT:**
*Barton Cross Hotel, Exeter*

**TRADITIONAL PUB:**
*Jack in the Green Inn, Rockbeare*

**VISIT:**
*Bicton Park, Bicton*

# *C*otfordbridge Hotel & Restaurant

*Small family owned hotel in an acre of lovely gardens*

☎ 01395 597351  📠 01395 597351

**Map ref 2 - SY18**

Cotford Road, Sidbury, SIDMOUTH, Devon, EX10 0SQ

N end of Sidbury on A375

5 Rooms, £, No smoking

*O*wners Bob and Sally Bustyan offer their guests a warm and friendly welcome at the Cotfordbridge Hotel. It is an attractive property, set well back from the road which runs through Sidbury; a small village just three miles from Sidmouth's seafront.

The bedrooms, located at first floor and ground floor levels, are comfortable and attractively decorated. All have en suite facilities and colour televisions.

The smart Ocharside Restaurant, popular with locals and residents alike, presents interesting menus including many traditional dishes. Local farm fresh produce is a feature of the cooking. There is a comfortable lounge bar and patio with views over the well tended gardens. A large private car park is provided.

## RECOMMENDED IN THE AREA

**RESTAURANT:**
*River House Restaurant, Lympstone*

**TRADITIONAL PUB:**
*The Masons Arms, Branscombe*

**VISIT:**
*Otterton Mill Centre, Otterton*

# *C*oombe House

*Georgian farmhouse in a lovely secluded valley*

☎ 01548 821277  📠 01548 821277

**Map ref 2 - SX66**

North Huish, SOUTH BRENT, Devon, TQ10 9NJ

A38 from Exeter, exit at Ermington/Modbury/Yealmpton, A3210, at x-rds B3196 (Loddiswell). 2nd left & 2nd lane left

4 Rooms, £, No smoking

*C*oombe House is set in four acres of grounds with a large pond and two streams attracting an abundance of wildlife. It stands at the head of a broad valley surrounded by fields and woodlands. From the house there are uninterrupted views of beautiful countryside, and guests have their own elegant sitting room overlooking the gardens and valley.

Breakfast is served in the dining room, dinner is available by prior arrangement. Food is freshly prepared using as much local produce as possible. The individually styled bedrooms are fully en suite with a bath and shower to each room. The rooms are also equipped with televisions, hairdryers, and hospitality trays.

Traditional stone farm buildings around the courtyard have been converted to provide four self-catering cottages. Dartmoor is close by and the coast is just half an hour away.

## RECOMMENDED IN THE AREA

**RESTAURANT:**
*Chez Nous, Plymouth*

**TRADITIONAL PUB:**
*Avon Inn, Avonwick*

**VISIT:**
*Buckfast Abbey, Buckfastleigh*

# Kerscott Farm

*Peacefully located traditional farmhouse serving wholesome cooking*

☎ **01769 550262**

**Map ref 2 - SS72**

Ash Mill, SOUTH MOLTON, Devon,
EX36 4QG
6m east of South Molton on B3227. Sign
1.5m from A361 at bottom of lane
3 Rooms, £, No smoking
Closed Nov-Jan

Kerscott is a working farm of 140 acres, situated 700ft up, opposite the first hills of Exmoor, providing wonderful views all around. Exposed beams, flagstone floors and two impressive inglenook fireplaces are features of the lovely old farmhouse, and there are many interesting pictures and antiques to admire. Attractive bedrooms are fitted with en suite facilities, colour televisions, central heating, and tea and coffee making equipment. The friendly hospitality of Theresa and John Sampson is a major attribute, and in 1999 Theresa was an AA Landlady of the Year finalist. Home farm produced meat and locally grown vegetables are used wherever possible in Theresa's honest award-winning West Country cooking. There

is a choice of a hearty or lighter breakfast, and dinner is available by arrangement.

Breads, soups and puddings are all home-made, and meals are served in the charming dining room at one large table.

## RECOMMENDED IN THE AREA

**RESTAURANT:**
*Whitechapel Manor, South Molton*

**TRADITIONAL PUB:**
*Masons Arms, Knowstone*

**VISIT:**
*Quince Honey Farm, South Molton*

# Thomas Luny House

*Georgian house quietly situated in the old quarter*

☎ **01626 772976**

**Map ref 2 - SX97**

Teign Street, TEIGNMOUTH, Devon,
TQ14 8EG
A381 to Teignmouth, at 3rd lights right to
quay, 50yds left into Teign St, 60yds right
through white archway
4 Rooms, ££

Alison and John Allan's delightful home was built in the late 18th century by the marine artist Thomas Luny. It is situated in the old part of town not far from the fish quay. The house is approached through an impressive archway leading into the courtyard, which provides ample parking space.

The bedrooms vary in size and are individually designed, though all have either a bath or shower en suite. Direct dial telephones and remote control colour televisions are provided in the rooms along with welcoming extras such as fresh flowers, bottled water and toiletries. Public rooms include a large drawing room and dining room, beautifully furnished and both with open fires. French doors open onto a lovely walled garden. A selection of home-made dishes and a full cooked breakfast are served, attentive but unobtrusive service is assured.

## RECOMMENDED IN THE AREA

**RESTAURANT:**
*Orestone Manor, Torquay*

**TRADITIONAL PUB:**
*Anchor Inn, Cockwood*

**VISIT:**
*Bradley Manor, Newton Abbot*

# Hornhill Farmhouse

*18th-century former coaching inn in peaceful rural surroundings*

☎ 01884 253352  📠 01884 253352

**Map ref 2 - SS91**

Exeter Hill, TIVERTON, Devon, EX16 4PL
follow signs to Grand Western Canal, take
right fork up Exeter Hill. Farmhouse on left at
top of hill
3 Rooms, £, No smoking

The house is situated on the top of a hill with wonderful views over the Exe valley. It is set in its own mature gardens and 75 acres of farmland. Hornhill was originally a coaching inn for the wool traders of Exmoor taking fleeces to Exeter for onward shipment to Europe.

For the last 100 years it has been home to the Pugsley family. The atmosphere is happy and relaxed, there is lovely countryside to explore, including the coast and moors.

Good home cooking is served in the elegant dining room, using home-grown or local produce. There is a comfortable drawing room with a good supply of books and a log fire on cooler evenings. The ground floor bedroom is en suite, the Victorian four-poster room and twin rooms each have a private bathroom with bath and shower. Televisions and tea/coffee facilities are provided in all the rooms.

RECOMMENDED IN THE AREA

**RESTAURANT:**
*Ebford House, Exeter*

**TRADITIONAL PUB:**
*Butterleigh Inn, Butterleigh*

**VISIT:**
*Tiverton Castle, Tiverton*

# Lower Collipriest Farm

*Thatched farmhouse, meadows and woods in the Exe Valley*

☎ 01884 252321  📠 01884 252321

**Map ref 2 - SS91**

TIVERTON, Devon, EX16 4PT
off Great Western Way, approx 1m
3 Rooms, £, No smoking

From the lounge, there are views over the farm and down the valley. You can take a walk in the grounds of the dairy farm and see as far as Dartmoor and Exmoor, or you can relax in the garden, where visitors can enjoy their drinks in summer. There is a pond and a conservation area with deer, herons and ducks; and private fishing on the River Exe which borders the meadow in front of the house.

Inside, the bedrooms are spacious and comfortable, all with en suite bath and shower. The lounge has a colour TV and a huge inglenook fireplace where a log fire glows on colder evenings. Mrs Olive provides for her guests with outstanding hospitality, and serves delicious fresh cooking at a large communal table in the dining room. She uses local produce, featuring prize winning cheeses and cream.

RECOMMENDED IN THE AREA

**RESTAURANT:**
*St Olaves Court, Exeter*

**TRADITIONAL PUB:**
*Butterleigh Inn, Butterleigh*

**VISIT:**
*Knightshayes Court, nr Tiverton*

# Mulberry House

*Charming Victorian terraced hotel renowned for its good food*

☎ **01803 213639**

**Map ref 2 - SX96**

1 Scarborough Road, TORQUAY, Devon,
TQ2 5UJ
from Torquay seafront turn up Belgrave Rd,
then 1st right up Scarborough Rd, premises
on left
3 Rooms, ££, No smoking

*A* small restaurant and hotel, Mulberry House has been personally run by the chef owner, Lesley Cooper, for the last 15 years. Food is a major focus, with an eclectic menu based on quality fresh local produce. Customer cooking demonstrations are an interesting extra, and guests love the delicious home made preserves. Lesley's creativity extends beyond her cooking and is reflected in the stylish decor and effective use of colour throughout, set off by attractive flower arrangements.

The bedrooms have either twin or double beds. All are en suite or have a private bathroom, and colour televisions are provided. Tea, coffee and wine are available on a self-service basis in the Upper Gallery hallway. Cookery demonstrations are held on a Friday morning starting with coffee, followed by the demonstration and ending with a three-course lunch with a glass of wine.

RECOMMENDED IN THE AREA

**TRADITIONAL PUB:**
*Barn Owl, Kingsteignton*

**VISIT:**
*Torre Abbey Historic House & Gallery*

# Norwood Hotel

*Family-run hotel conveniently located for the town and beach*

☎ **01803 294236**  🖷 **01803 294236**
✉ **enquiries@norwood-hotel.co.uk**

**Map ref 2 - SX96**

60 Belgrave Road, TORQUAY, Devon,
TQ2 5HY
11 Rooms, £
Closed Xmas

*T* he Norwood is an attractively presented hotel offering quality accommodation with a warm and welcoming atmosphere. The spacious bedrooms are comfortably furnished and equipped with central heating, remote control televisions, radios, hairdryers, hospitality trays and a baby-listening service. All the rooms have en suite facilities and there is one particularly luxurious room ideal for honeymoons or anniversaries. Traditional home cooking is served in the recently refurbished dining room, and meals include a full English breakfast and a four-course evening meal. A selection of wines is also available to accompany your meal. At the end of the day guests can relax in the pleasant lounge. Car parking is provided, and the hotel is just a few minutes' walk from the town centre, the beach, the Riviera Centre and bowling greens.

RECOMMENDED IN THE AREA

**RESTAURANT:**
*The Osborne Hotel, Torquay*

**TRADITIONAL PUB:**
*Barn Owl Inn, Kingkerswell*

**VISIT:**
*Paignton Zoo Environmental Park*

# The Durant Arms

*An 18th-century inn set in the centre of a picturesque village*

☎ 01803 732240
🖷 01803 732470

**Map ref 2 - SX86**

Ashprington, TOTNES,
Devon, TQ9 7UP
from A38 take A384 or
A385 to Totnes, at
traffic lights take A381
Kingsbridge. 1m turn
left for Ashprington
3 Rooms, £, No smoking
in bedrooms, Closed
Xmas/Boxing Day

The Durant Arms is a charming feature of the quiet village of Ashprington. The inn embodies traditional standards with fine ales, selected wines (including some from the nearby Sharpham Estate), and excellent food prepared by the creative kitchen team. The blackboard menu offers a good choice ranging from light lunches to full meals with delicious home-made soups and desserts. The beautifully furnished en suite bedrooms have their own private entrance. The views from the rooms are of the village and the countryside beyond, which invites exploration. This is the valley of the River Dart, with its rolling hills and enchanting lanes. The old town of Totnes, a centre of art and craft, is just three miles away. Proprietors Graham and Eileen Ellis extend a warm welcome to guests and make every effort to make their stay a memorable one. Self-catering accommodation is also available in a separate cottage.

## RECOMMENDED IN THE AREA

**RESTAURANT:**
*Sea Trout Inn, Staverton*

**VISIT:**
*Totnes Castle*

# Down House

Down House

*Edwardian style country house in six acres of peaceful gardens*

☎ 01404 822860

**Map ref 2 - SY09**

WHIMPLE, Devon, EX5 2QR
leave A30 signed Whimple, right at 30mph
sign by Woodhayes Hotel. Continue 0.75m &
house is up hill on left behind 5-bar gate
6 Rooms, £, No smoking

## RECOMMENDED IN THE AREA

**RESTAURANT:**
*Home Farm Hotel, Honiton*

**TRADITIONAL PUB:**
*The Otter Inn, Weston*

**VISIT:**
*Cadhay, Ottery St Mary*
*Killerton House & Garden, Killerton*

Michael and Joanne Sanders welcome guests to their elegant home set in beautiful grounds including an orchard and paddocks. There are many activities to enjoy within the gardens, such as croquet, boules, skittles and badminton.

Inside, the house offers 21st-century comforts with traditional hospitality. The attractive bedroom decor is enhanced with fresh flowers, guests will find useful extras in the rooms, such as a trouser press, tea/coffee tray, hairdryer, colour television and clock radio. Four bedrooms have en suite facilities and there is a suite of rooms suitable for families. An excellent breakfast is served in the dining room, and a spacious sitting room is also provided. There is ample parking.

# Woodhayes Country House Hotel

*Elegant Georgian house in four acres of grounds*

☎ 01404 822237 ℻ 01404 822337
✉ info@woodhayes-hotel.co.uk

**Map ref 2 - SY09**

WHIMPLE, Devon, EX5 2TD
0.5m from A30, Honiton to Exeter road
6 Rooms, ££, No smoking in bedrooms

## RECOMMENDED IN THE AREA

**TRADITIONAL PUB:**
*Five Bells Inn, Clyst Honiton*

**VISIT:**
*Underground Passages, Exeter*

Woodhayes is located on the edge of the picturesque village of Whimple, originally famous for its cider industry, hence the apple orchards which surround the grounds. The house gives easy access to the M5 and major roads, ideal for touring Devon and visiting the ancient cathedral city of Exeter. Lynda and Eddie Katz warmly welcome guests into their gracious home. There are many thoughtful touches such as fresh flowers and a large bowl of fresh fruit in the imposing entrance hall. Lynda's modern home cooking, using local fresh produce, is served in the sunny dining room, with views across the gardens. There are two well-presented sitting rooms with open fires; and a snug bar, where the original flag stone floor and reclaimed haberdashers counter create a relaxed, informal ambience. The bedrooms are large and airy with attractive views. Modern comforts are provided with en suite facilities, direct dial telephone, television, hairdryer, refreshment tray and many extras.

# The Cleeve House Hotel

*Friendly hotel with coastal walks from the doorstep*

☎ 01271 870719  📠 01271 870719
✉ cleevehouse@mcmail.com

**Map ref 1 - SS44**

Mortehoe, WOOLACOMBE, Devon,
EX34 7ED
from A361 onto B3343 at Mullacott Cross,
right towards Mortehoe, right at post office,
hotel 300yds on left
7 Rooms, ££, No smoking in bedrooms

Cleeve House, in the historic village of Mortehoe, is run with a very personal touch by owners David and Anne Strobel. It perches on the hillside that leads down to the dramatic cliffs of the coastline.

Some rooms boast a sea view, while others look over the village and surrounding countryside. The bedrooms are clean and modern in style, all with en suite bathrooms, colour TV and other comforts, one bedroom on the ground floor is designed for the less able.

Full English breakfasts are served in the elegant dining room. Evening meals are also on offer, with a daily changing menu that includes a wide variety of freshly prepared local cuisine. After dinner you can retire to the bar or to the sitting room. In addition there is a tea room where morning coffees, light lunches and cream teas are served during the summer months.

## RECOMMENDED IN THE AREA

**RESTAURANT:**
*Rising Sun Hotel, Lynmouth*

**TRADITIONAL PUB:**
*Rising Sun, Lynmouth*

**VISIT:**
*Underground Passages, Exeter*

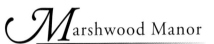

# Marshwood Manor

*Victorian manor house set in lovely Dorset countryside*

☎ 01308 868442

**Map ref 2 - ST30**

BETTISCOMBE, Dorset, DT6 5NS
off B3164 between Broadwindsor and
Marshwood
6 Rooms, ££
Closed Dec-Jan

This fine property, dating from 1853, is the home of Terry and Tricia Shakeshaft, who offer a warm and friendly welcome to guests. The house is set in 10 acres of woodland and gardens surrounded by beautiful countryside and just five miles from the coast. The nearest beaches are at Charmouth and Lyme Regis.

Bedrooms are spacious and comfortable, all with en suite facilities, colour televisions and tea making equipment. Guests can relax in the large lounge, which has its own bar, or in the grounds where you will find a croquet lawn, putting green and outdoor swimming pool. Good home-cooked meals are served in the dining room. The bread, preserves, soups and puddings are all home made, and much of the fresh fruit and vegetables comes from the garden. Dogs can be accommodated by prior arrangement only.

## RECOMMENDED IN THE AREA

**RESTAURANT:**
*Riverside Restaurant, Bridport*

**TRADITIONAL PUB:**
*Bottle Inn, Marshwood*

**VISIT:**
*Parnham, Beaminster*

# Thatch Lodge
## Hotel & Restaurant

*14th-century picture-postcard thatched hotel, with acclaimed restaurant*

☎ 01297 560407
🖷 01297 560407

**Map ref 2 - SY39**

The Street,
CHARMOUTH, Nr Lyme
Regis, Dorset, DT6 6PQ
Charmouth - off A35,
2m E of Lyme Regis.
Hotel half way along
high street
6 Rooms, £££
No smoking
Closed mid Jan-mid
Mar

Once a monks' retreat for nearby Forde Abbey, the 'Thatch' has many features, besides its roof, making it a beautiful and peaceful place to stay. There are pink walls with hanging baskets outside, walled gardens and a conservatory with a 200-year-old vine; oak beams and unusual artefacts inside.

Charmouth is world renowned for its fossil strewn beach, and Lyme Regis nearby has the famous Cobb, used in 'The French Lieutenant's Woman'.

The Inglenook Restaurant in the hotel (awarded two AA rosettes) serves the freshest local cuisine. Grapes from the ancient vine are served with Stilton in season. There is a full English breakfast, cereals and juices, with a selection of bread which you can toast with your own table toaster. The six en suite bedrooms are unique in character with many thoughtful extras; some rooms have four-poster beds, others have half-tester antique beds. The new Garden View suite has its own private lounge.

### RECOMMENDED IN THE AREA

**TRADITIONAL PUB:**
*George Inn, Chideock*

**VISIT:**
*Parnham, Beaminster*

# The Casterbridge Hotel

*An elegant Georgian residence in the town centre of Dorchester*

☎ 01305 264043  📠 01305 260884
✉ reception@casterbridgehotel.co.uk

**Map ref 2 - SY69**

49 High East Street, DORCHESTER, Dorset,
DT1 1HU
in town centre 75mtrs from town clock
14 Rooms, ££
Closed 25-26 Dec

This well run hotel maintains high standards of accommodation, enhanced with antiques and tasteful furnishings. The hotel provides a traditional English welcome with cheerful attentive staff. The public rooms include an elegant dining room, gracious drawing room and an intimate bar/library. Breakfast is served in the conservatory, providing an extensive buffet as well as individually cooked breakfasts.

All bedrooms are ensuite with either bath or shower, one room is suitable for families and three are suitable for the less able. Children are welcome, cots and high chairs are available. All rooms have colour television, tea and coffee making facilities and direct dial telephones.

The hotel offers special short breaks. Major credit and debit cards are taken and small groups are accepted.

## RECOMMENDED IN THE AREA

**RESTAURANT:**
*Moonfleet Manor, Weymouth*

**TRADITIONAL PUB:**
*New Inn, West Knighton*

**VISIT:**
*Dorchester County Museum, Dorchester*

---

# Yalbury Cottage Hotel & Restaurant

*Thatched cottage offering excellent food and comfortable accommodation*

☎ 01305 262382  📠 01305 266412
✉ yalbury.cottage@virgin.net

**Map ref 2 - SY69**

Lower Bockhampton, DORCHESTER,
Dorset, DT2 8PZ
off A35 past Thomas Hardy's cottage, over
x-rds, 400yds on left, just past red tel box
and opp village pump
8 Rooms, ££, No smoking in bedrooms
Closed 28 Dec-3 Feb

Nestling amid winding rivers and peaceful fields, Yalbury Cottage was originally the home of the local shepherd and keeper of the water meadows. It is a thatched property dating from the 17th century with attractive gardens, where teas and pre-dinner drinks are served in the summer.

The pretty restaurant offers Head Chef Russell Brown's award winning food, earning two AA rosettes, in an atmosphere enhanced by oak beams and inglenook fireplaces. The cosy lounge, the only part of the building where smoking is permitted, is also in the old part of the building.

The spacious cottage-style bedrooms all have en suite bathrooms, remote control television, hairdryers and tea and coffee making equipment. Ample parking is provided in the grounds.

## RECOMMENDED IN THE AREA

**TRADITIONAL PUB:**
*Wise Man Inn, West Stafford*

**VISIT:**
*Hardy's Cottage, Dorchester*

# *R*ectory House

*Charming 18th-century country guest house in a quiet village*

☎ 01935 83273  ✆ 01935 83273

**Map ref 2 - ST50**

Fore Street, EVERSHOT, Dorset, DT2 0JW
1.5m off A37 Yeovil to Dorchester road
5 Rooms, ££
No smoking

*E*vershot is in the heart of Thomas Hardy's beautiful Wessex countryside. The bedrooms are named after towns familiar from his novels. All are en suite, each with its own very individual character. They are furnished and decorated with antiques, paintings and home-made quilts; there are some king-size beds and half-tester beds. Three of the bedrooms are in the converted stable block with views over the green lawns and colourful flower beds, a small patio and a 200 year old copper beech tree.

A wonderful breakfast, served at individual tables

with crisp linen and fresh flowers, is made with local produce. There is twelve fruit compote and freshly squeezed orange juice. You can expect a friendly welcome from all the helpful, understanding staff, and from Flossie the resident dog (with her frisbee).

## RECOMMENDED IN THE AREA

**RESTAURANT:**
*Summer Lodge, Evershot*

**TRADITIONAL PUB:**
*The Acorn Inn, Evershot*

**VISIT:**
*Sherborne Castle, Sherborne*

# *H*untsbridge Farm

*L*ocated on the edge of the village of Leigh, the farm enjoys a country setting but is still only a short drive from Dorchester, Sherborne and many other places of interest.

*Delightful farm in a peaceful rural location*

☎ 01935 872150  ✆ 01935 872150

**Map ref 2 - ST60**

Batcombe Road, LEIGH, Dorset, DT9 6JA
A352 Dorchester. 1.5m right Lewiston/Leigh.
4m to Give Way sign, right to Leigh. Left before bridge, on right
3 Rooms, ££, No smoking
Closed Xmas & Jan

The bedrooms are stylishly decorated and furnished to a high standard, and each one is fitted with modern en suite facilities. One of the rooms has a double four-poster bed, ideal for a special occasion. Thoughtful extras such as fresh flowers make for a welcoming atmosphere.

Breakfast is a highlight of a stay at Huntsbridge Farm, served in the bright and airy conservatory overlooking the pretty garden. In the evening guests may wish to relax in the smartly appointed lounge.

## RECOMMENDED IN THE AREA

**RESTAURANT:**
*Castleman Hotel, Blandford Forum*

**TRADITIONAL PUB:**
*Three Elms, North Wootton*

**VISIT:**
*Sherborne Castle, Sherborne*

# The Marquis of Lorne

*A 16th-century country inn with good food*

☎ 01308 485236  📠 01308 485666
📧 ian@marquis-of-lorne.co.uk

**Map ref 2 - SY59**

NETTLECOMBE, Bridport, Dorset, DT6 3SY
N from Bridport on A3066, after 1.5m after
mini-rdbt turn right, through West Milton,
straight over at junct, premises up hill
6 Rooms, ££

This hostelry is found in the unspoilt Dorset hills, in the shadow of Eggardon hill, the ancient earth fort, and close to Powerstock common, with its ancient oaks, fallow deer and rare butterflies, making it great for country walks. It has a large car park and well kept gardens. Children under 10, and pets are not accepted in the rooms.

The inn maintains its original character with exposed stone walls and wooden beams. It has two bars, a non-smoking area and a small games room, and has earned a fine reputation for its food, serving a menu that changes regularly, with home cooked favourites, some foreign dishes, vegetarian options and excellent fresh fish from the nearby coast. The menu is supported by an extensive wine list, a range of lagers and local Real Ales. The bedrooms are comfortable and simply furnished, all with en suite showers and colour TV.

## RECOMMENDED IN THE AREA

**RESTAURANT:**
*Riverside Restaurant, Bridport*

**VISIT:**
*Parnham House, Beaminster*

# The Old Vicarage Hotel

*Listed Victorian property in a charming village setting*

☎ 01963 251117  📠 01963 251515

**Map ref 2 - ST61**

Sherborne Road, Milborne Port,
SHERBORNE, Dorset, DT9 5AT
off A30
7 Rooms, ££, No smoking in bedrooms
Closed Jan

Dating from 1870, this imposing former vicarage is set in three and a half acres of wooded grounds overlooking rolling Dorset countryside. The hotel is owned by Jörgen Kunath and Anthony Ma, who come from the renowned Noughts & Crosses Restaurant in West London. As you might expect, the food is rather special, and evening meals are served in the conservatory on a Friday and Saturday. There are three large en suite bedrooms in the main house, all stylishly presented and affording lovely country views. Four smaller en suite rooms are offered in the coach house. These have rustic appeal and the added benefit of a sun terrace overlooking the garden. The spacious lounge, beautifully furnished with antique pieces, is available to guests throughout the day. Chinese, German, French and Spanish are all spoken. Children under five cannot be accommodated, and dogs are accepted in the Coach House by special arrangement only.

## RECOMMENDED IN THE AREA

**RESTAURANT:**
*Plumber Manor, Sturminster Newton*

**TRADITIONAL PUB:**
*The White Hart, Sherborne*

**VISIT:**
*Sherborne Museum, Sherborne*

# The Pheasants

*Attractive small hotel in a delightful country town*

☎ 01935 815252 📠 01935 815252
**Map ref 2 - ST61**

24 Greenhill, SHERBORNE, Dorset, DT9 4EW
centre of town on A30
6 Rooms, ££
Closed 2 wks mid-Jan

At the top of the high street in Sherborne, this handsome Georgian property enjoys an excellent location. The surrounding countryside offers many attractions including Hardy's Wessex, the National Trust's Stourhead and the unspoilt Dorset coastline forty minutes away. The Pheasants has been decorated and furnished to a high standard, the comfortable accommodation includes well equipped modern bathrooms. Single, double, twin and family rooms are available, all have direct dial telephones. Ample car parking is provided at the rear. The restaurant, which has a two AA rosette award, produces modern English cooking based on prime quality ingredients. It is open for lunch at weekends and for dinner from Tuesday to Saturday. A wide ranging fixed price dinner is offered throughout the week and at weekend lunch times.

## RECOMMENDED IN THE AREA

**TRADITIONAL PUB:**
*Skippers Inn, Sherborne*

**VISIT:**
*Sherborne Old Castle, Sherborne*

---

# Stourcastle Lodge

*Cosy cottage atmosphere and tasty traditional food from the Aga*

☎ 01258 472320 📠 01258 473381
✉ enquiries@stourcastle-lodge.co.uk
**Map ref 2 - ST71**

Goughs Close, STURMINSTER NEWTON, Dorset, DT10 1BU
small lane off Town Square opposite Cross
5 Rooms, ££
No smoking in bedrooms

Originally a thatched farmhouse, Stourcastle Lodge is tucked away behind high walls just off the market square. It has a south facing terrace, a sitting room with a log fire, and a quiet cottage garden with some sculptures. The Hookham-Bassetts lend the Lodge a very personal touch. Jill is an inspired cook, and provides four-course dinners using herbs and vegetables grown in the garden, as well as farmhouse breakfasts with crusty homemade bread and local preserves. The house is decorated with pictures by local artists and with Ken's collection of antique kitchen utensils. The bedrooms are named after the Dashwood family who owned the Lodge in the 19th century. They have antique pine furniture and brass bedsteads, and the air is charged with the fragrance of dried flowers and spices; bedrooms all have modern en suite bathrooms, some with whirlpool tubs.

## RECOMMENDED IN THE AREA

**RESTAURANT:**
*Plumber Manor, Sturminster Newton*

**TRADITIONAL PUB:**
*The Cricketers, Blandford Forum*

**VISIT:**
*Royal Signals Museum, Blandford Forum*

# Esplanade Hotel

*Seafront hotel in an elegant Georgian terrace*

☎ 01305 783129

**Map ref 2 - SY67**

141 The Esplanade, WEYMOUTH, Dorset, DT4 7NJ
E end of Esplanade, opposite pier bandstand
11 Rooms, £, No smoking

Caring hospitality is assured from owners Kathy and Len Paul at this attractive seafront hotel, where guests are welcomed with homemade cake, tea and coffee on arrival.

The comfortably appointed first floor lounge has views over Weymouth Bay, and some of the bedrooms also enjoy sea views. Guest rooms, located on the ground, first, second and third floors of the hotel, vary in size but are particularly well furnished. All have en suite facilities, cooling fans, central heating, colour television, hospitality tray, easy chair, hairdryer, iron, and radio.

Kathy's good home cooking is served at breakfast, using only the best fresh ingredients. Private car parking is provided for guests at the rear of the hotel.

## RECOMMENDED IN THE AREA

**RESTAURANT:**
*Perry's Restaurant, Weymouth*

**TRADITIONAL PUB:**
*Manor Hotel, West Bexington*

**VISIT:**
*Portland Castle, Portland*

---

# Ashton Lodge

*A spacious family house with a pretty garden*

☎ 01202 883423  ℻ 01202 886180
✉ ashtonlodge@ukgateway.net

**Map ref 3 - SZ09**

10 Oakley Hill, WIMBORNE MINSTER, Dorset, BH21 1QH
from A31 S of Wimborne A349 Poole, left at next roundabout Wimborne/Canford Magna. House on right after 200yds
4 Rooms, £, No smoking

Ashton Lodge is a smart, modern brick house with big bay windows, decorated with boxes of flowers. The owners give their guests a warm welcome, and they are very happy for you to enjoy their garden, which has two ponds. There is plenty of parking space.

The bedrooms are very comfortable, with attractive co-ordinated decor and fabrics, equipped with colour TV, clock radio, tea and coffee facilities, and hair dryer; two have en suite bathrooms. With your own key, you have free access to your room.

There is a delicious freshly cooked full English breakfast, with a vegetarian option, and local marmalades and jams, which you can enjoy in the spacious dining room that overlooks the garden. The residents' lounge has satellite TV.

## RECOMMENDED IN THE AREA

**RESTAURANT:**
*Beechleas Hotel, Wimborne Minster*

**TRADITIONAL PUB:**
*Cock & Bottle, East Morden*

**VISIT:**
*Kingston Lacy House, Garden & Park*

# Bay Lodge

*Superb sea views from a family-run hotel set in tranquil grounds at the centre of Weymouth Bay*

☎ 01305 782419  📠 01305 782828  📧 barbara@baylodge.co.uk

**Map ref 2 - SY67**

27 Greenhill, WEYMOUTH, Dorset, DT4 7SW
brown tourist signs to Lodmoor Country Park. Hotel 200yds on
town centre side of entrance (A353)
12 Rooms, ££

*A*n elegant seaside establishment, Bay Lodge is quietly located on the edge of town in its own grounds, which include a large private car park. The attractions of the town and harbour are only a few minutes' walk along the esplanade to the right.

Just opposite are the award-winning Greenhill Gardens, with the tennis courts, bowling green, putting green and flower clock. To the left is Lodmoor Country Park, the Sea Life Centre, tropical jungle, nature reserve, and nine-hole golf course. Both the dining room and lounge bar overlook the sea, and here guests can relax and view the yachts in the bay. Public rooms also include an oak-panelled lounge. The Lodge is open all year round and crackling log fires provide a warm welcome in the cooler months. The food is English in style, and dishes are cooked to order using quality local produce. There is a daily fresh fish choice, and options such as noisettes of lamb with minted gravy, or duck breast with cranberry and red wine jus. To follow, steamed puddings are a speciality of the house.

## RECOMMENDED IN THE AREA

**RESTAURANT:**
*Perry's Restaurant,
Weymouth*

**TRADITIONAL PUB:**
*Sailors Return, East
Chaldon*

**VISIT:**
*RSPB Nature Reserve,
Radipole Lake, Weymouth*

The bedrooms are split between the main house and an adjacent annexe, and are located on the ground and first floors only. They have full en suite bathrooms, with bath, shower and courtesy tray. Each bedroom is individually themed and equipped with a complimentary drinks tray, direct dial telephone, remote controlled colour television, security safe, and two easy chairs. The luxury Bay View room, ideal for honeymoons and other special occasions, has sea views, a balcony, open log fire, mini bar, Jacuzzi and king-size bed. Well behaved pets are accepted by prior arrangement.

# Lower Brook House

*A 17th-century Cotswold stone house with an award-winning restaurant*

☎ 01386 700286
🅕 01386 700286
🅔 lowerbrookhouse
@compuserve.com

**Map ref 3 - SP13**

Lower Street,
BLOCKLEY,
Gloucestershire,
GL56 9DS
from Moreton-in-Marsh
A44 (Broadway) thro'
Bourton-on-Hill, past
garage on left. 1st right
Blockley Rd leading to
car park
7 Rooms, ££, No
smoking in bedrooms

Lower Brook House is located in pretty gardens at the edge of the renowned Cotswold village. It dates from the 17th century and retains much of its original character, with features such as polished flagstone floors, a large inglenook fireplace and exposed beams. The building has been enhanced by the use of quality fabrics, antique furniture and an interesting collection of bric-a-brac. Imaginative dinners and comprehensive English breakfasts are taken in the cosy, elegant dining room. The dinner menu changes daily, offering the best of fresh local produce supported by a cellar of around thirty fine wines. Bedrooms, though compact, are equipped with lots of thoughtful extras to ensure guests' comfort; including fresh fruit, flowers and towelling bathrobes. Marie Mosedale-Cooper is a charming and caring hostess, justifiably proud to welcome guests to her lovely home.

## RECOMMENDED IN THE AREA

**RESTAURANT:**
*Manor House Hotel, Moreton-in-Marsh*

**TRADITIONAL PUB:**
*The Plough Inn, Ford*

**VISIT:**
*Snowshill Manor, Snowshill*

# Cleeve Hill Hotel

*An elegant residence in the heart of the Cotswolds*

☎ 01242 672052  📠 679969

**Map ref 2 - SO92**

Cleeve Hill, CHELTENHAM, Gloucestershire, GL52 3PR
on B4632 2.5m from Cheltenham between Prestbury and Winchcombe
10 Rooms, ££, No smoking

Cleeve Hill Hotel is in a superb location, overlooking the Malvern Hills in an area of outstanding natural beauty. There are spectacular views from all the bedrooms, either across the valley to the hills or to Cleeve Common and the golf course. The rooms are beautifully decorated and very well equipped, with en suite facilities, direct dial telephones, television with a movie channel, tea and coffee, radio alarms, toiletries and hairdryers. A trouser press is available on request.

Spacious public rooms include a conservatory dining room where guests are served an excellent breakfast, and an elegant lounge where guests can relax and enjoy a drink from the licensed bar. Hosts John and Marion Enstone provide friendly and attentive service.

The hotel makes a good base for visiting the tourist attractions of the Cotswolds, and there is a good range of places to eat in the locality.

## RECOMMENDED IN THE AREA

**RESTAURANT:**
*Daffodil, Cheltenham*

**TRADITIONAL PUB:**
*The Little Owl, Cheltenham*

**VISIT:**
*Art Gallery & Museum, Cheltenham*

---

# Georgian House

*Georgian Grade II listed property in elegant Montpellier*

☎ 01242 515577  📠 01242 545929

**Map ref 2 - SO92**

77 Montpellier Terrace, CHELTENHAM, Gloucestershire, GL50 1XA
3 Rooms, ££, No smoking
Closed Xmas/New Year

Dating from 1807, Georgian House is one of the earliest terraced houses built in Cheltenham. The accommodation has been designed with guests' comfort as a priority while retaining the period character and charming original features, enhanced by antique furniture.

The bedrooms are all en suite and each one has remote-control television with satellite channels, direct dial telephones with modem sockets, trouser presses and mini fridges. Garage parking is provided to the rear of the house and street parking to the front. While smoking is not permitted inside, one of the rooms has a balcony where guests are free to smoke; there is also a convenient bench in the front garden!

The house is within easy walking distance of the town centre, shops, parks and many restaurants.

## RECOMMENDED IN THE AREA

**RESTAURANT:**
*Le Petit Blanc, Cheltenham*

**TRADITIONAL PUB:**
*Harvest Home, Greet*

**VISIT:**
*Art Gallery & Museum, Cheltenham*

# Lypiatt House Hotel

*Restored Victorian house in the exclusive Montpelier district*

☎ 01242 224994  📠 01242 224996
✉ lypiatthouse@gofornet.co.uk

**Map ref 2 - SO92**

Lypiatt Road, CHELTENHAM,
Gloucestershire, GL50 2QW
on A40 from London, 3 miles from M5
Junction 11, towards Cheltenham
10 Rooms, ££

Sympathetically restored to its original splendour, this early Victorian property offers quality accommodation. Bedrooms are spacious and all have modern en suite bath or shower rooms, direct dial telephones, radios and televisions. Public areas retain many original features, and the comfortable sitting room has a conservatory extension with an honesty bar.

The house is located in one of the most attractive areas of Cheltenham, and makes a good base for touring the Cotswolds. Ample parking space is provided in the hotel's own grounds.

A full English breakfast is served, and for dinner there are plenty of restaurants within easy walking distance. Resident proprietors Jane and Michael Medforth assure guests of a warm welcome and friendly personal service.

## RECOMMENDED IN THE AREA

**RESTAURANT:**
*The Greenway, Cheltenham*

**TRADITIONAL PUB:**
*Royal Oak, Winchcombe*

**VISIT:**
*Pittville Pump Room & Museum, Cheltenham*

# Stretton Lodge Hotel

*Friendly, elegant Victorian house in the heart of Cheltenham*

☎ 01242 570771  📠 01242 528724
✉ info@strettonlodge.demon.co.uk

**Map ref 2 - SO92**

Western Road, CHELTENHAM,
Gloucestershire, GL50 3RN
M5 J11 over 2 rdbts Landsdown Rd, left at lights, Christchurch Rd, at end into Malvern Rd, then Western Rd, 2nd on right
4 Rooms, ££, No smoking

The hotel is situated in a quiet area yet only a six minute walk from the centre of town. There is a mature garden and private parking area. Traditional home cooked English food is served at breakfast, and a daily changing carte is available for dinner (by arrangement) with main courses such as roasts or fresh salmon with hollandaise sauce, all with fresh vegetables, as well as a range of vegetarian dishes.

The house is kept spotlessly clean and tidy, and enticing pink and rosy colours feature in the decor throughout. The public rooms are spacious, lit by chandeliers. The lounge has original ceiling mouldings and a marble fireplace.

All of the bedrooms are individually designed with stylish drapes and canopies; all have en suite bathrooms.

## RECOMMENDED IN THE AREA

**RESTAURANT:**
*Hotel Kandinsky, Cheltenham*

**TRADITIONAL PUB:**
*Kilkenny Inn, Andoversford*

**VISIT:**
*Art Gallery & Museum, Cheltenham*

# *T*he Malt House

*Charming service and relaxed atmosphere in an immaculate 16th-century home of local Cotswold limestone*

☎ 01386 840295
🖷 01386 841334
✉ nick@the-malt-house.freeserve.co.uk

**Map ref 3 - SP13**

Broad Campden,
CHIPPING CAMPDEN,
Gloucestershire,
GL55 6UU
1m S, signposted
from B4081
8 Rooms, ££
Closed 25-26 Dec

RECOMMENDED
IN THE AREA

TRADITIONAL PUB:
*The Bakers Arms,
Chipping Campden*

VISIT:
*Snowshill Manor,
Snowshill*

Still retaining its original beams, stone fireplaces and leaded windows, this former malting house lies in the heart of the quiet village of Broad Campden. Its sweeping lawns lead down to the brook, there is an orchard beyond, and the kitchen garden supplies flowers for displays in the house, and fresh vegetables, herbs and fruit for the chef. In summer, guests can enjoy a drink by the croquet lawn.

The bedrooms all have en suite bath or shower, tea and coffee making facilities and colour TV, and all look across the gardens. There is a four-poster room, and a suite with its own sitting room and private access to the gardens. The house is decorated with a light stylish touch, with some fine pieces of Georgian furniture. The food has received high acclaim: a three course set menu, modern British in style, is available in the evening, accompanied by an excellent wine list.

**93**

# Marnic House

*Family home with country views and colourful garden*

☎ 01386 840014  📠 01386 840441
✉ marnic@zoom.co.uk

**Map ref 3 - SP13**

Broad Campden, CHIPPING CAMPDEN,
Gloucestershire, GL55 6UR
off A44, B4081 Chipping Campden over T-
junct for Broad Campden. 0.75m, Marnic on
left as entering village
3 Rooms, £, No smoking,
Closed 21 Dec-1 Jan

## RECOMMENDED IN THE AREA

**RESTAURANT:**
*Cotswold House, Chipping Campden*

**TRADITIONAL PUB:**
*Eight Bells Inn, Chipping Campden*

**VISIT:**
*Snowshill Manor, Snowshill*

On the outskirts of the small historic market town of Chipping Campden, looking out over open Cotswold countryside, Marnic is a comfortable, well-furnished family home where you can expect a friendly welcome. Private parking is available. There is a neat garden, which guests are encouraged to use, looked after with the utmost care. The same care has been devoted to restoring and maintaining the house, all the original woodwork has been stripped and waxed.

The bedrooms are furnished with antique pine, have excellent beds and all have both bath and shower en suite, as well as remote control colour TV. Mrs Rawlings provides her guests with a traditional hearty English breakfast, which she cooks on an Aga, and serves in the dining room on a large oak table. Next to the dining room is the sitting room which overlooks the garden.

*The fountain on the promenade, Cheltenham, Gloucestershire*

# Guiting Guest House

*16th-century former farmhouse in a village setting*

☎ 01451 850470  📠 01451 850034
✉ guiting.guest_house@virgin.net

**Map ref 3 - SP02**

GUITING POWER, Gloucestershire,
GL54 5TZ
A40, Andoversford lights R, Stow-on-the-
Wold, 4m L Lower Swell B4068, 1m L Guiting
Power. L into village, house in centre
4 Rooms, ££, No smoking in bedrooms

A lovely old building of mellow Cotswold stone, this guest house retains many original features including exposed beams, inglenook fireplaces and polished wooden floors. Public areas have a warm, comfortable and cosy atmosphere, enhanced by open fires, decorative pottery and family memorabilia. Fresh flowers, fruit and a teddy to cuddle at night are among the thoughtful extras in the welcoming bedrooms. Four-poster beds are a feature of the rooms, along with generously filled hospitality trays, quality toiletries and bathrobes. Two of the rooms are en suite and the third has private facilities.

Food is imaginative, cooked on the family Aga and well worth experiencing. Yvonne and Bernie Sylvester are warm and attentive hosts who greet arriving guests with a cup of tea and a slice of home-made cake.

## RECOMMENDED IN THE AREA

**RESTAURANT:**
*Restaurant on the Park, Cheltenham*

**TRADITIONAL PUB:**
*Plough Inn, Ford*

**VISIT:**
*Pittville Pump Room & Museum, Cheltenham*

# Cotteswold House

*400-year-old Cotswold stone wool merchant's house*

☎ 01451 860493  📠 01451 860493

**Map ref 3 - SP11**

Market Place, NORTHLEACH,
Gloucestershire, GL54 3EG
between Oxford and Cheltenham, off junction
of A40/A429
3 Rooms, ££, No smoking
Closed 24 Dec-1 Jan

Situated on the edge of the market square of this historic town, Cotteswold House retains much of its original character with oak beams, Tudor archway and rich panelling.

Bedrooms are spacious and well equipped with modern en suite baths and/or showers, colour television, central heating and tea and coffee making facilities. A ground floor double room is available and a private suite featuring a draped king size bed and a canopied corner bath. Full English breakfast is served in the 16th-century dining room, and traditional three-course dinners are also available (pre-booking essential), to which guests are welcome to bring their own wine.

Elaine and Graham Whent are friendly and caring hosts who enjoy welcoming guests into their home. The house is right in the middle of the Cotswolds, well placed for those exploring the region.

## RECOMMENDED IN THE AREA

**RESTAURANT:**
*Bibury Court, Bibury*

**TRADITIONAL PUB:**
*New Inn, Coln St Aldwyns*

**VISIT:**
*Cotswold Heritage Centre, Northleach*

# *T*he Grey Cottage

*Warm welcoming grey Cotswold stone cottage*

☎ 01453 822515  ℱ 01453 822515

**Map ref 2 - SO80**

Bath Road, Leonard Stanley, STONEHOUSE, Gloucestershire, GL10 3LU
leave M5 junct 13 onto A419. After lights right - Leonard Stanley, at T-junct turn left, Grey Cottage on right
3 Rooms, ££, No smoking in bedrooms

Constructed of local Selsley stone over 170 years ago, this immaculate cottage and garden have been extensively restored, retaining many original features. The cottage garden is dominated by a magnificent Cedar Wellingtonia and still has its original yew hedge. It is overlooked by the sitting and dining room, both with log fires, and the conservatory, where meals are served in warm weather.

The bedrooms are all individual in their decoration, with views of the garden, field, or hills. Two have en suite facilities, one has a private bathroom. The rooms have a range of items to ensure guests' comfort, from colour TV to bathrobes, books and local information. Food is presented very attractively, with an excellent choice of home cooking for breakfast. Dinner is also available, preferences are discussed when you book.

## RECOMMENDED IN THE AREA

**RESTAURANT:**
*Stonehouse Court, Stonehouse*

**TRADITIONAL PUB:**
*The Ram Inn, Stroud*

**VISIT:**
*Owlpen Manor, Owlpen*

# *H*unters Lodge

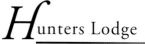

*A large beautifully furnished Cotswold stone house*

☎ 01453 883588  ℱ 01453 731449

**Map ref 2 - SO80**

Dr Browns Road, Minchinhampton, STROUD, Gloucestershire, GL6 9BT
from Cirencester A419 Stroud. Left to Aston Down, over cattle grid 3rd turn left, Lodge on right
3 Rooms, £, No smoking, Closed Xmas

Conveniently located for the towns of Stroud and Cirencester, this impressive Victorian house is set on the edge of Minchinhampton Common. Margaret and Peter Helm are the friendly and caring hosts, justifiably proud of their home, which is centrally heated throughout. There are some nice period pieces in the spacious public rooms. The good-sized bedrooms offer plenty of welcoming extras, including dressing gowns, remote control colour TV, radio/alarm clock and hair dryer. All bedrooms have a hospitality tray, shaving point, and private or en suite facilities. There is a large, well-maintained garden, which can be enjoyed from the comfort of the conservatory.

Peter is a Gloucestershire Green Badge Tourist Guide, so he is well placed to advise on places of interest. There is a good choice of local restaurants and inns, and menus from several of these are available to study.

## RECOMMENDED IN THE AREA

**RESTAURANT:**
*Bear of Rodborough, Stroud*

**TRADITIONAL PUB:**
*The Ram Inn, Stroud*

**VISIT:**
*Painswick Rococo Garden, Painswick*

# Tavern House

*17th-century former Cotswold inn and staging post with secluded walled gardens*

☎ **01666 880444**
📠 **01666 880254**
✉ **tavernhousehotel
@ukbusiness.com**

**Map ref 2 - ST89**

Willesley, TETBURY,
Gloucestershire, GL8 8QU
M4 to A46, at Petty
France right fork to
Tetbury/Didmarton,
A433, 4m to Willesley,
tavern on right
4 Rooms, ££, No
smoking in bedrooms

On the outskirts of the hamlet of Willesely and close to the Westonbirt Arboretum, one of the finest and largest collections of trees and shrubs in the world, is Tavern House, once a coach house for weary travellers on the road between Cheltenham and Bath. It stands within a very English country garden overlooking Silk Wood, in a handy location for local sights, recreational facilities and sports.

Original beams and open fireplaces are plain to see, particularly in the sitting room, where there is also a chaise longue, and lamps giving a warm glow throughout. The bedrooms are furnished with antique country furniture; all have a bathroom en suite, with both bath and shower, most with bidet and all with hairdryer. Breakfast is taken in the dining room, where selected hunting prints decorate the walls, or in the garden when it is warm enough.

## RECOMMENDED IN THE AREA

**RESTAURANT:**
*The Close Hotel, Tetbury*

**TRADITIONAL PUB:**
*Gumstool Inn, Tetbury*

**VISIT:**
*Westonbirt Arbetoreum, Westonbirt*

# Wesley House
## Restaurant

*A renowned restaurant with rooms housed in a 15th-century half-timbered building in the main street of this pretty Cotswold town*

☎ 01242 602366 ✆ 01242 602405

**Map ref 3 - SP02**

High Street, WINCHCOMBE, Gloucestershire, GL54 5LJ
5 Rooms, ££, No smoking in bedrooms, Closed 14 Jan-10 Feb

*T*his former merchant's house, dating from around 1435, is named in commemoration of the Methodist John Wesley, who is believed to have stayed here in 1779. The house is well known to a discerning clientele who come to enjoy the fine food served at lunch and dinner in the restaurant, which has been awarded two AA rosettes.

*T*he restaurant is central to the establishment, but the house also offers excellent accommodation in individually styled rooms. Every modern convenience is provided where it is possible without detrimental effect to the medieval structure. There are five cosy double or twin bedded rooms, and the superior Terrace Room offers superb views across the North Cotswold Edge.

Guests can expect to be pampered by Matthew Brown and his staff, help and advice is willingly given with the booking of theatre tickets and the planning of places to visit. The lounge is full of old world charm, and guests can relax in comfortable settees by a lovely log fire.

The restaurant offers a fixed price two or three course lunch; an attractively priced early-bird menu

### RECOMMENDED
### IN THE AREA

**RESTAURANT:**
*Wesley House,
Winchcombe*

**TRADITIONAL PUB:**
*Harvest Home, Greet*

**VISIT:**
*Hailes Abbey, Hailes
Highland Mysteryworld,
Glencoe*

of two or three courses between 6.45pm and 7.45pm Monday to Friday, and a two or three course dinner menu. Typical dishes are salmon marinated in lime, chilli, honey and coriander with salad leaves and charred polenta, as a starter. This might be followed by roast chump of lamb on a confit of shallots with pan-fried flageolet beans. Tempting desserts include English lemon tart with chantilly cream, and ginger and plum sponge pudding with crème anglaise. On a Saturday night a minimum of three courses will be charged.

# Sudeley Hill Farm

*Old, rustic farmhouse on large mixed arable and sheep rearing farm*

☎ 01242 602344  📠 01242 602344

**Map ref 3 - SP02**

WINCHCOMBE, Gloucestershire, GL54 5JB
off B4632 in Winchcombe into Castle St,
White Hart Inn on corner. Farm 0.75m on
right
3 Rooms, £, No smoking in bedrooms
Closed Xmas

The 15th-century farmhouse is situated above
Sudeley Castle, one mile from the old town of
Winchcombe. There is a large garden, where guests
are welcome to relax and use the barbecue, as well
as 800 acres of farmland. There is golf and horse
riding, and plenty of good walks locally. Dogs are not
accepted.

The house is built of mellow stone, and it has a
wealth of charm and character, with features such
as the large inglenook fireplace in the sitting room.
The dining room, which overlooks the garden, has
some fine period furniture, and wonderful farmhouse
breakfasts are served around one big table. The
atmosphere is especially friendly.

The bedrooms all have en suite bathrooms with bath
and shower; one is suitable as a family room (cot
available). They all have outstanding, panoramic
views across the Sudeley Valley.

## RECOMMENDED IN THE AREA

**RESTAURANT:**
*Wesley House, Winchcombe*

**TRADITIONAL PUB:**
*Royal Oak, Winchcombe*

**VISIT:**
*Sudeley Castle & Gardens, Winchcombe*

*The Royal Crescent from Royal Victoria Park, Bath, Somerset*

# Apsley House

*Attractive Georgian property on the outskirts of the city*

☎ 01225 336966
🖷 01225 425462
📧 info@
apsley-house.co.uk

**Map ref 2 - ST76**

Newbridge Hill, BATH,
Somerset, BA1 3PT
on A431 1m west of city
9 Rooms, ££
Closed 1 wk Xmas

This elegant house, located about a mile from the city centre, was built for the Duke of Wellington. Hospitality is warm, friendly and enthusiastic from proprietors and staff alike. The spacious public areas are delightfully decorated and furnished and the lounge is full of period charm.

The bedrooms are individually styled, well maintained, and equipped with en suite bathrooms, colour televisions, direct dial telephones, and tea and coffee making facilities. A delicious variety of breakfast items is offered. Children under five and dogs cannot be accommodated (except for guide dogs).

## RECOMMENDED IN THE AREA

**RESTAURANT:**
*Homewood Park, Hinton Charterhouse*

**TRADITIONAL PUB:**
*George Inn, Norton St Philip*

**VISIT:**
*Roman Baths & Pump Room, Bath*

# *H*aydon House

*Elegant Edwardian house located in a quiet residential area of Bath*

☎ 01225 444919
📠 01225 427351
✉ stay@
haydonhouse.co.uk

**Map ref 2 - ST76**

9 Bloomfield Park, BATH,
Somerset, BA2 2BY
follow signs A367
Exeter. Left at rdbt,
right at shop centre,
60yds on fork right,
2nd right 200yds
5 Rooms, ££
No smoking

## RECOMMENDED IN THE AREA

**RESTAURANT:**
*The Olive Tree, Bath*

**TRADITIONAL PUB:**
*The Olde Green Tree, Bath*

**VISIT:**
*Bath Abbey, Bath*

*H*aydon House, located half a mile south of the city centre, offers comfort, elegance and hospitality of the highest standard. In addition to the welcome extended by the helpful hosts, guests can expect an equally friendly reception from their two golden retrievers Cloud and Cobweb.

The reception rooms are delightfully furnished with antique pieces, and the sumptuous sitting room is the place to relax, with its fine period furniture and comfortable seating. The spacious bedrooms have been individually designed and appointed. Soft, pleasing colour schemes have been chosen and there are many thoughtful extras, including a decanter of sherry, mineral water and fresh flowers. An extensive breakfast menu is offered, with innovative choices such as Scottish whisky or rum porridge. Breakfast is served in the Edwardian splendour of the dining room, guests sharing one large table in true family style. Pets are not accommodated, and children may stay by prior arrangement only.

# $\mathcal{B}$adminton Villa

*Large Victorian house with wonderful city views*

☎ 01225 426347   📠 01225 420393
✉ badmintonvilla@cableinet.co.uk

### Map ref 2 - ST76

10 Upper Oldfield Park, BATH, Somerset, BA2 3JZ
from city centre A367 then A37 (Radstock). 1st right 600yds up hill into Upper Oldfield Park. 300yds on right
4 Rooms, ££, No smoking
Closed 24 Dec-1 Jan

---

### RECOMMENDED IN THE AREA

**TRADITIONAL PUB:**
*George Inn, Norton St Philip*

**VISIT:**
*No 1 Royal Crescent, Bath*

$\mathcal{J}$ohn and Sue Burton are the friendly owners of this fine Victorian villa, which is situated in a wide tree-lined road just ten minutes walk from the city centre.

The house has been extensively refurbished, and the accommodation includes central heating, colour television, radio alarms, hairdryers and generous hospitality trays. All the rooms have en suite facilities with either a shower or bath.

At breakfast guests have a choice between the full English option or something a little lighter. Guests can relax in the comfortable lounge, where there is plenty of tourist information to help you plan your itinerary. Parking is provided, and with all the sights of the city as well as pubs and restaurants close to hand, you can happily venture forth without the need for a car.

---

# $\mathcal{H}$ighways House

*Elegant Victorian villa, 10 minutes from the city centre*

☎ 01225 421238   📠 01225 481169
✉ highways@toscar.clara.co.uk

### Map ref 2 - ST76

143 Wells Road, BATH, Somerset, BA2 3AL
on A367
7 Rooms, ££, No smoking

$\mathcal{G}$uests can be sure of a warm welcome at Highways House from owners Tony and Sarah Carter. The house is located on the southern side of the city, convenient for the city centre, and an ideal base from which to explore the Georgian splendour of Bath.

The bedrooms are attractively decorated and comfortably furnished with good quality beds. The rooms are also well equipped; six of them have en suite facilities and the remaining room has use of a separate bathroom.

A spacious lounge is available for rest and relaxation, and generous breakfasts are served in the bright and cheerful dining room. Free off-street car parking is provided.

---

### RECOMMENDED IN THE AREA

**RESTAURANT:**
*No 5 Bistro, Bath*

**TRADITIONAL PUB:**
*Wheatsheaf Inn, Combe Hay*

**VISIT:**
*American Museum, Bath*

# Holly Lodge

*Victorian town house with glorious views across the heritage city of Bath*

☎ 01225 424042
🖷 01225 481138
📧 george.h.hall@
btinternet.com

**Map ref 2 - ST76**

8 Upper Oldfield Park,
BATH, Somerset,
BA2 3JZ
0.5m SW of city centre
off A367
7 Rooms, ££
No smoking

## RECOMMENDED IN THE AREA

**RESTAURANT:**
*Restaurant Lettonie, Bath*

**TRADITIONAL PUB:**
*George Inn, Bathampton*

**VISIT:**
*Bath Industrial Heritage Centre, Bath*

*H*olly Lodge is an opulent establishment in an elevated situation affording spectacular views. The house is luxuriously comfortable and richly decorated with sumptuous fabrics. Attention to detail is evident in the personal touches that ensure guests' comfort.

The bedrooms are individually designed, with queen-size or four-poster beds, en suite bathrooms, satellite television, direct dial telephones, and hospitality trays. There is a gracious lounge, and breakfast is served in the attractive conservatory. The owner is justifiably proud of the fine terraced garden, a feature of which is the floodlit gazebo, the perfect place to relax in the evening. Ample parking is provided, but guests should note that pets are not permitted.

# Kennard Hotel

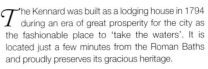

*The* Kennard was built as a lodging house in 1794 during an era of great prosperity for the city as the fashionable place to 'take the waters'. It is located just a few minutes from the Roman Baths and proudly preserves its gracious heritage.

With views over the city, the bedrooms are beautifully decorated, their modern facilities include satellite televisions, direct dial telephones with modem points, hairdryers and hospitality trays. The en suite bathrooms are stylishly fitted and make good use of space.

A choice of full English or continental breakfast is offered, prepared with quality fresh produce and the finest teas and coffees. The meal is served in the original Georgian kitchen. Proprietors Malcolm Wright and Richard Ambler assure guests of a warm welcome with attention to detail.

*Elegant Georgian town house just over Pulteney Bridge*

☎ 01225 310472  **F** 01225 460054
**E** kennard@dircon.co.uk

**Map ref 2 - ST76**

11 Henrietta Street, BATH, Somerset,
BA2 6LL
from A4 London Road turn left onto A36 over
river past fire station
13 Rooms, £££, No smoking

## RECOMMENDED IN THE AREA

**RESTAURANT:**
*The Olive Tree at the Queensberry, Bath*

**TRADITIONAL PUB:**
*Inn at Freshford, Freshford*

**VISIT:**
*The Building of Bath Museum, Bath*

# Leighton House

*By* staying here, leaving your car in the private car park and taking a 10 minute walk into the centre of Bath, you discover the ideal way to explore this city (pedestrian zones, one-way streets and parking make it difficult for cars otherwise).

The house, brought to life by a colourful assortment of flowers, overlooks the city and the surrounding hills. The bedrooms, with period wooden furniture, have both bath and shower en suite, direct dial telephone, colour TV, radio alarm and hairdryers, and the double beds are luxurious king or queen size.

You can relax and take a look at some local information in the drawing room, restored and decorated in burgundy and shades of cream, with a gilt mirror over the fireplace. There is a carte with choices for breakfast, served in the dining room which overlooks the neat gardens.

*Victorian residence, close to city centre, with splendid bedrooms*

☎ 01225 314769  **F** 01225 443079
**E** welcome@leighton-house.co.uk

**Map ref 2 - ST76**

139 Wells Road, BATH, Somerset, BA2 3AL
leave A36 at Churchill Bridge in town centre,
take A367, 600mtrs, house on left, at junction
with Hayesfield Park
8 Rooms, ££, No smoking

## RECOMMENDED IN THE AREA

**RESTAURANT:**
*The Royal Crescent, Bath*

**TRADITIONAL PUB:**
*Globe Inn, Newton St Loe*

**VISIT:**
*Holborne Museum & Craft Study Centre*

# Meadowland

*Elegant property close to the city centre*

☎ 01225 311079
🖷 01225 311079
✉ meadowland@
bath92.freeserve.
co.uk

**Map ref 2 - ST76**

36 Bloomfield Park,
BATH, Somerset,
BA2 2BX
take A367 signed
Exeter/Wells, past
Bear pub, right fork
Bloomfield Rd. 2nd
right Bloomfield Park
3 Rooms, ££
No smoking

*M*eadowland is an award winning Guest House, peacefully set in a conservation area a 15 minute stroll from the centre of Bath. John and Catherine Andrew take delight in sharing their beautiful home with guests and have created 3 beautiful well equipped, tastefully decorated bedrooms of real quality, all with en-suite facilities and with sumptuous luxurious beds, fluffy pillows and cushions. The house is a peaceful retreat and a great place to relax and unwind, perhaps with a book in the elegant drawing room or, alternatively, in the attractive secluded gardens where ample car parking is available. Recommendations are available on where to go what to see, and where to dine in Bath and surrounding areas.

## RECOMMENDED IN THE AREA

**RESTAURANT:**
*The Moody Goose, Bath*

**TRADITIONAL PUB:**
*The Olde Green Tree, Bath*

**VISIT:**
*Museum of Costume*

# *M*onkshill Guest House

*Edwardian property peacefully set in extensive gardens*

☎ 01225 833028  📠 01225 833028

**Map ref 2 - ST76**

Shaft Road, Monkton Combe, BATH,
Somerset, BA2 7HL
A36, A3062 (Prior Park Rd), left at top of hill
(North Rd), right (Shaft Rd). Monkshill 100yds
on right past playing fields
3 Rooms, ££, No smoking
Closed 2 wks over Xmas and New Year

*T*his delightful house is set in attractive gardens, including a croquet lawn, and offers superb views across the Limpley Stoke Valley.

The bedrooms are spacious, comfortably furnished and fully in keeping with the character of the building. Two of the rooms have en suite facilities and the third has a private bathroom. Plenty of thoughtful extras are provided, and each room has a colour television and tea and coffee making equipment. The attractive sitting room with its many personal touches has a real homely feel and is the perfect place in which to relax.

A choice of dishes is offered at breakfast, which is served in the elegant dining room. Guests sit down together, family style, at one large table.

## RECOMMENDED IN THE AREA

**RESTAURANT:**
*The Moody Goose, Bath*

**TRADITIONAL PUB:**
*Wheatsheaf Inn, Combe Hay*

**VISIT:**
*Royal Photographic Society, Bath*

# *O*akleigh House

*Elegant Victorian house 10 minutes from the city centre*

☎ 01225 315698  📠 01225 448223
✉ oakleigh@which.net

**Map ref 2 - ST76**

19 Upper Oldfield Park, BATH, Somerset,
BA2 3JX
off A367
3 Rooms, ££

*O*akleigh Guest House offers a well kept, comfortable and relaxing environment in a quiet residential area. It is a large property offering four attractively presented bedrooms with a good range of facilities, including en suite baths or showers, colour televisions, radio alarms, tea and coffee, hairdryers and central heating.

The lounge, complete with books, newspapers and games, is available for guests' enjoyment, and is also home to an authentic 1950s wireless in full working order, the pride and joy of proprietor Jenny King.

Delicious freshly cooked breakfasts, from an extensive menu, are served in the pleasant dining room. Excellent levels of hospitality are assured, and private car parking is provided.

## RECOMMENDED IN THE AREA

**RESTAURANT:**
*Bath Spa, Bath*

**TRADITIONAL PUB:**
*George Inn, Bathampton*

**VISIT:**
*Sally Lunn's Refreshment House & Museum, Bath*

**107**

# Paradise House Hotel

*Classic, dignified Bath house with beautiful gardens overlooking the city*

☎ **01225 317723** 🖶 **01225 482005**
✉ **info@paradise-house.co.uk**

**Map ref 2 - ST76**

Holloway, BATH, Somerset, BA2 4PX
from A36 (Bristol/Warminster rd) at Churchill
Bridge rdbt A367, 3rd left, down hill into cul-
de-sac, house 200yds on left
10 Rooms, ££, No smoking in bedrooms
Closed 3 days Xmas

Paradise House was built in the 1720s, on the ancient Roman Fosse Way where it descends Beechen Cliff to enter Bath. It is now one of the quietest streets in Bath, providing safe and easy access to the city by foot, with only a seven minute walk to the city centre. Parking is provided.

At the back of the house are secluded, walled gardens, with trim lawns and rose-covered pergolas, and probably some of the finest views of Bath, looking down to the Royal Crescent and the Abbey. The bedrooms, all en suite, are decorated with an air of opulence; one has a four poster bed and two have grand bay windows. The lounge is very comfortable, and the dining room, where a lovely breakfast is served, is especially smart.

## RECOMMENDED IN THE AREA

**RESTAURANT:**
*Bath Spa, Bath*

**TRADITIONAL PUB:**
*Inn at Freshford, Freshford*

**VISIT:**
*Roman Baths & Pump Room, Bath*

# Sarnia

*Large Victorian house on the western side of the city*

☎ **01225 424159** 🖶 **01225 337689**

**Map ref 2 - ST76**

19 Combe Park, BATH, Somerset, BA1 3NR
A4 from city centre, 1m fork right at lights,
A431, right at rdbt Combe Pk (in same road
as Royal United Hospital)
3 Rooms, ££, No smoking
Closed 24 Dec-2 Jan

Sarnia is an attractive property situated near the Royal United Hospital about a mile and a half from the centre of the city. The private parking is a huge asset in Bath and guests are advised to use the regular bus service for their sight-seeing in the city. Children are made particularly welcome, and a playroom, high chair and cot are provided.

Bedrooms are individually styled and include televisions, tea and coffee making facilities, alarm clocks and central heating. Rooms are either en suite or have a private bathroom. A hairdryer, iron and ironing board are available on request.

Guests can relax in the comfortable lounge or the secluded garden, and a four-course breakfast with a vegetarian option is served in the sunny dining room.

## RECOMMENDED IN THE AREA

**RESTAURANT:**
*Clos du Roy, Bath*

**TRADITIONAL PUB:**
*Wheatsheaf Inn, Combe Hay*

**VISIT:**
*No 1 Royal Crescent, Bath*

# $\mathcal{V}$illa Magdala

*Victorian villa in a tranquil setting just five minutes walk from the city centre*

☎ 01225 466329
📠 01225 483207
📧 office@
VillaMagdala.co.uk

**Map ref 2 - ST76**

Henrietta Road, BATH,
Somerset, BA2 6LX
off A4 follow signs for
A36 Warminster.
Henrietta Rd is 2nd on
right, opp Henrietta
Park
17 Rooms, £££
No smoking

## RECOMMENDED IN THE AREA

**RESTAURANT:**
*The Moody Goose, Bath*

**TRADITIONAL PUB:**
*Inn at Freshford, Freshford*

**VISIT:**
*Bath Abbey, Bath*

*A* gracious period property, Villa Magdala is conveniently located a short level walk from the many and varied sights of Bath. It is set in its own pleasant grounds overlooking Henrietta Park. Fine views can be enjoyed from the spacious and attractively presented bedrooms, all of which are equipped to meet the needs of both business and leisure visitors. There are family rooms, twins and doubles, and superior double rooms with canopy or four-poster beds. All have en suite facilities, mostly with a bath and shower, colour television, direct dial telephones, and hospitality trays. Public rooms include a charming lounge and dining room overlooking the park, and in the latter a full English breakfast is served. The hotel has its own private parking, which is a great advantage in the city. Mr and Mrs Thwaites are the welcoming hosts.

# The Plaine

*16th-century Grade II listed building in a conservation village*

☎ 01373 834723 📠 01373 834101
✉ theplaine@easynet.co.uk

## Map ref 2 - ST75

Bell Hill, NORTON ST PHILIP, Somerset,
BA3 6LT
from A36 Bath to Warminster rd, right onto
A366 signed Radstock, house at x-rds in
village
3 Rooms, ££, No smoking
Closed 24-26 Dec

## RECOMMENDED IN THE AREA

**RESTAURANT:**
*Homewood Park, Hinton Charterhouse*

**TRADITIONAL PUB:**
*George Inn, Norton St Philip*

**VISIT:**
*Farleigh Hungerford Castle, Farleigh Hungerford*

The Plaine is a charming family home in a delightful village setting, first recorded in the Doomsday Book of 1086, and surrounded by the beautiful rolling Mendip countryside. It provides an excellent base from which to explore the city of Bath, with its wealth of Georgian architecture, just 7 miles away, and the picturesque villages of Bradford-on-Avon, Lacock and Castle Combe. Other local places of interest include Glastonbury and Wells, Longleat House, Stonehenge and Wookey Hole. The accommodation is beautifully presented and well equipped. The bedrooms all have four-poster beds and en suite facilities with radio alarms, television, hairdryers, hospitality trays and complimentary toiletries. There is a comfortable guest lounge and plenty of local information. Generous breakfasts include juice, yoghurt, fresh fruit, homemade jams and full English breakfast using free-range eggs and local produce. Excellent meals can be booked for you at the nearby medieval George Inn.

# Saltmoor House

*Luxurious decor in a Georgian countryside property, near the M5*

☎ 01823 698092

## Map ref 2 - ST33

Saltmoor, BURROWBRIDGE, Somerset,
TA7 0RL
from M5 J24 through Huntworth Moorland
towards Burrowbridge
3 Rooms, ££, No smoking
Closed 22 Dec-5 Jan

## RECOMMENDED IN THE AREA

**RESTAURANT:**
*The Castle, Taunton*

**TRADITIONAL PUB:**
*Rose and Crown, Stoke St Gregory*

**VISIT:**
*Coleridge Cottage, Nether Stowey*

Saltmoor House is a listed building in the heart of Somerset's wetland, an area as rich in myth and legend as it is in wading birds, wildfowl and willow, and now protected as an environmentally sensitive area. It is conveniently situated about four miles from the M5 motorway.

The front of the house overlooks the River Parrett; at the rear there is a walled garden, old farm buildings and twelve acres of pasture with views of unspoilt countryside all around. The house is furnished with stylish simplicity, black and white bathrooms and white bedspreads complement traditional features such as antique pictures and furniture, log fires and flagstone floors. One bedroom has en suite facilities and the others have private bathrooms. Guests are served a delicious breakfast in the garden room, which has French windows onto the terrace and lawns. Dinner is served by prior arrangement.

# Clanville Manor

*Georgian farmhouse and family home
with wonderful breakfasts*

☎ 01963 350124  📠 01963 350313
📱 07966 512732
✉ clanville@aol.com

**Map ref 2 - ST63**

CASTLE CARY, Somerset, BA7 7PJ
off A371 onto B3153, entrance via white gate
& cattle grid under bridge 0.75m along B3153
3 Rooms, £, No smoking

Clanville Manor has been a working dairy farm since the Snook family bought it in 1898. It is in a beautiful position, with the River Brue running through the fields behind the house. The dining room overlooks the farm drive; so in summer, at breakfast time, while you enjoy eggs produced by the farm's own hens and cooked on the farmhouse Aga, you can watch the cows as they wander down after morning milking.

The house is built of local, honey-coloured stone. In the entrance hall there is an oak staircase that leads up to the bedrooms - two of which have en suite bathrooms, and all of which have colour TV, hairdryers, clock radios and modern beds. There is a drawing room for reading and relaxing, with a blazing open fire in winter; and a swimming pool outside in the walled garden, which can be used in summer.

## RECOMMENDED IN THE AREA

**RESTAURANT:**
*Truffles Restaurant, Bruton*

**TRADITIONAL PUB:**
*The George Hotel, Castle Cary*

**VISIT:**
*Hadspen Garden & Nursery, Castle Cary*

*The fountain on the promenade, Cheltenham, Gloucestershire*

# Manor Farm

*Peacefully situated farmhouse with wonderful country views*

☎ 01460 78865  📠 01460 78865

**Map ref 2 - ST40**

Wayford, CREWKERNE, Somerset, TA18 8QL
from Crewkerne take B3165 to Lyme Regis,
after 3m in Clapton village, turn right into
Dunsham Lane, 0.5m up hill Manor Farm on
right
4 Rooms, £, No smoking

## RECOMMENDED IN THE AREA

**RESTAURANT:**
*Bridge House Hotel, Beaminster*

**TRADITIONAL PUB:**
*Lord Poulett Arms, Hinton St George*

**VISIT:**
*Tintinhull House, Tintinhull*

Manor Farm is a fine Victorian house located off the beaten track with extensive views over Clapton towards the Axe Valley. It is a working farm set in 20 acres including stocked ponds where guests can do some fishing.

The bedrooms are comfortably furnished and equipped with remote control televisions, hospitality trays and ironing facilities. All of the rooms have en suite showers. A spacious, well appointed lounge is available for guests' use and breakfast is served in the cosy dining room.

The farm is located on the Liberty Trail, an ancient footpath, and close to several National Trust houses and gardens. Lyme Regis on the south coast is just 12 miles away. A self-catering apartment is also available.

# Higher Langridge Farm

*17th-century farmhouse on a traditional working farm*

☎ 01398 323999  📠 01398 323999
📧 gill.langridge@ukf.net

**Map ref 2 - SS92**

Exbridge, DULVERTON, Somerset, TA22 9RR
off A396 between Exbridge & Oldways End
3 Rooms, £, No smoking

Peace, hospitality and delightful countryside are just some of the qualities that make a stay at Higher Langridge Farm so relaxing. This is the home of the Summers family, who farm 400 acres on the edge of Exmoor, and it has been in the family for over 100 years, and six generations.

The bedrooms are tastefully furnished in traditional style, offering both comfort and lovely views. The spacious lounge overlooks the valley and is warmed by a log-burning fire. A hearty breakfast is served, and you might glimpse an Exmoor Red Deer while you are sitting at the table. Freshly prepared evening meals are available by prior arrangement, using local and home grown produce from the farm's cottage garden. Guests are welcome to bring their own wine. The Exmoor National Park provides plenty of scope for exploring and enjoying the wildlife.

## RECOMMENDED IN THE AREA

**RESTAURANT:**
*Bark House Hotel, Bampton*

**TRADITIONAL PUB:**
*Anchor Inn, Exbridge*

**VISIT:**
*Knightshayes Court, Knightshayes*

▲ *Cheddar Gorge,
Somerset*

*Willow Figure,
Stoke St Gregory,
Somerset*

113

# The Old Rectory

*Thatched rectory in a rural location with easy access to the South West of England*

☎ 01460 54364  📠 01460 57374
✉ theoldrectory@
malherbie.freeserve.co.uk

**Map ref 2 - ST31**

Cricket Malherbie, ILMINSTER, Somerset,
TA19 0PW
from rdbt junct A358/A303, A358 S (Chard).
After Donyatt left towards Ilminster, right to
Cricket Malherbie, Old Rectory on left
5 Rooms, ££, No smoking

This grade II listed house has been beautifully restored and makes a delightful place to stay, with its thatched roof, sandstone walls and grand windows overlooking green lawns.

Your charming hosts Michael and Patricia Fry-Foley take particular trouble to offer fine local produce at breakfast and dinner, cooked with flair and imagination. The comfortable bedrooms are well equipped, all are en suite and have tea and coffee making facilities and colour television. The house is licensed and children over 16 can be accommodated, no dogs are allowed except for guide dogs.

There is plenty of guest parking space and most credit cards are accepted. Yeovil, Taunton and the South coast are within easy reach by car.

## RECOMMENDED IN THE AREA

**RESTAURANT:**
*Bindon House, Wellington*

**TRADITIONAL PUB:**
*Square & Compass, Ashill*

**VISIT:**
*East Lambrook Manor Garden, East Lambrook*

---

# Wychwood

*Comfortable accommodation in a welcoming home*

☎ 01935 825601  📠 01935 825601
✉ wychwoodmartock@yahoo.co.uk

**Map ref 2 - ST41**

7 Bearley Road, MARTOCK, Somerset,
TA12 6PG
exit A303 to centre of Martock, up East St
from P.O., Bearley Rd on left opposite Nags
Head
3 Rooms, £, No smoking in bedrooms

Helen Turton has been a top twenty finalist for the AA landlady of the Year award, and that speaks volumes for the levels of hospitality provided at this lovely home.

Three guest bedrooms are available, all with comfortable beds. Two have en suite showers and the third has a private bathroom. Colour television and tea and coffee making facilities are provided in the rooms. Good home cooking is served, and there is a delightful conservatory where guests can relax and enjoy afternoon tea and homemade cake. The conservatory opens onto a pretty garden with a fish pond.

Detailed directions and advice can be given to guests for visiting the ten 'Classic Gardens of South Somerset'. Children and pets cannot be accommodated. Credit cards accepted.

## RECOMMENDED IN THE AREA

**RESTAURANT:**
*Little Barwick House, Yeovil*

**TRADITIONAL PUB:**
*Royal Oak, Over Stratton*

**VISIT:**
*Montacute House & Gardens*

# Glendower Hotel

*Small and friendly family-run hotel in an attractive residential terrace*

☎ 01643 707144
📠 01643 708719

**Map ref 2 - SS94**

32 Tregonwell Rd,
MINEHEAD, Somerset,
TA24 5DU
A39 into Minehead,
last exit at mini-rdbt,
200yds then right,
hotel on left
14 Rooms, £

Glendower is a Victorian building, only a few minutes away from the town centre and seafront. Proprietors Ute and Herbert Lauben have recently restored the property, which now offers modern creature comforts combined with the elegance and charm of the Victorian architecture.

Bedrooms are spacious with gleaming en suite shower rooms, and a choice of double, twin, single and family rooms is offered. Amenities include colour television, tea and coffee making equipment, clock radios and hairdryers. An à la carte breakfast is served in the two cosy dining rooms.

The house is licensed, and an abundance of reading material is provided for guests to look at in the bar and lounge. Plenty of parking space is available at the rear, and there is a pretty garden and patio where cream teas can be enjoyed in fine weather.

## RECOMMENDED IN THE AREA

**RESTAURANT:**
*White House Hotel, Williton*

**TRADITIONAL PUB:**
*Royal Oak, Luxborough*

**VISIT:**
*Dunster Castle, Dunster*

# Barkham

*Peace and privacy in a traditional 18th-century farmhouse in Exmoor National Park*

☎ 01643 831370
📠 01643 831370
✉ adie.exmoor@btinternet.com

Map ref 2 - SS73

Sandyway,
SIMONSBATH,
Somerset, EX36 3LU
exit A361 to N Molton,
thro' village, signs to
Sandyway, left at x-rd
(Simonsbath), 400m
turn right
3 Rooms, ££
No smoking

This was one of the first farmhouses built in the Old Royal Park on Exmoor, the extensive grounds include a valley of steep woodland, pasture with a stream running through it, and a large treehouse. Walks, riding, trout and salmon fishing in season, are all close at hand.

The drawing room has an inglenook fireplace and French windows opening onto the croquet lawn.

Bedrooms are attractive and satisfyingly simple, one has an en suite bathroom and king-sized double bed. An excellent dinner is available by arrangement, served by candlelight around a long central table in the oak-panelled dining room. The premises are licensed. One of the barns has been converted into an art gallery where concerts take place. A number of courses are run at Barkham and it is a lovely setting for weddings and functions.

## RECOMMENDED IN THE AREA

**RESTAURANT:**
*Crown Hotel, Exford*

**TRADITIONAL PUB:**
*Crown Hotel, Exford*

**VISIT:**
*Arlington Court, Arlington*

# Lydford House

*A treasure trove of antiques in a former vicarage*

☎ 01963 240217  🖷 01963 240413
✉ lynn@jamesribbons.demon.co.uk

**Map ref 2 - ST42**

Lydford-on-Fosse, SOMERTON, Somerset, TA11 7BU
A303 to Podimore rdbt, A37 Bath/Bristol after 3m x-rds B3153. Lydford House on left after traffic lights
4 Rooms, ££

*R*ight on the crossroads in the centre of the village, the house was built in 1860 as a vicarage. Now it is a family home with owners who really enjoy having guests. Their other passion is antiques and they deal mainly in their export. This means that the house is full, though by no means cluttered, with beautiful furniture and ornaments: you are welcome to browse, and buy if you see something that takes your fancy.

There is a particularly fine reception hall and a polished wooden staircase. The bedrooms are spacious with showers en suite and colour TV. Traditional English breakfast is served in the panelled dining room around a large table. Although evening meals are not served, the 'local' pub is just a few minutes' walk away.

The owners have a thorough knowledge of the area, and can direct you to roads and places off the beaten track, the sort of locations you would never find otherwise.

## RECOMMENDED IN THE AREA

**RESTAURANT:**
*Holbrook House Hotel, Wincanton*

**TRADITIONAL PUB:**
*The Globe, Somerton*

**VISIT:**
*Lytes Cary Manor, Kingsdon*

# Creechbarn Bed & Breakfast

*Converted Somerset longbarn in a beautiful rural location*

☎ 01823 443955  🖷 01823 443509
✉ mick@somersite.co.uk

**Map ref 2 - ST22**

Vicarage Lane, Creech-St-Michael, TAUNTON, Somerset, TA3 5PP
exit M5 J25 onto A358. Turn to Creech St Michael via Ruishton. Follow canal boat signs to end of Vicarage Lane
3 Rooms, £, No smoking in bedrooms
Closed 15 Dec-15 Jan

## RECOMMENDED IN THE AREA

**RESTAURANT:**
*Langley House, Wiveliscombe*

**TRADITIONAL PUB:**
*Rising Sun, Knapp*

**VISIT:**
*Hestercombe Gardens, Taunton*

*V*isitors are assured of a warm welcome from Hope and Mick Humphreys at this charming country home, a lovingly converted stone-built Somerset longbarn. It is peacefully situated at the end of a private drive, and surrounded by nearly an acre of well tended gardens with access to the Taunton/Bridgwater Canal. There is a golf course just a mile and a half away, and junction 25 of the M5 is only a few minutes' by car.

The bedrooms are comfortably furnished, one double room has an en suite shower and the other has a separate private bathroom. A further twin room is available. There is a studio sitting room where a host of books, table tennis equipment and a television are provided for guests. Good home cooked dinners and hearty breakfasts are served at one large table in the dining room. Guests should be sure to ask about the unique revolving log fire.

# Heathfield Lodge

*Regency house set in landscaped gardens in the beautiful Vale of Taunton*

☎ 01823 432286
🖷 01823 432286
✉ heathfieldlodge@tinyworld.co.uk

**Map ref 2 - ST22**

Heathfield, Nr
Hillcommon, TAUNTON,
Somerset, TA4 1DN
Taunton, B3227 W
(Wiveliscombe),
thro' Norton Fitzwarren,
approx 2.5m, on right
3 Rooms, ££
No Smoking
Closed 20 Dec-2 Jan

### RECOMMENDED IN THE AREA

**RESTAURANT:**
*Castle Hotel, Taunton*

**TRADITIONAL PUB:**
*Rising Sun, Knapp*

**VISIT:**
*Combe Sydenham Country Park, Monksilver*

The family home of Sue and Phil Thornton, this delightful Regency house has been refurbished to retain all the charm and elegance of the period while providing comfortable accommodation for guests. The house is set in five acres of lovely landscaped gardens, surrounded by beautiful countryside falling between three ranges of hills, the Quantocks, the Brendons and the Blackdowns. The coast and Exmoor National Park are also within easy driving distance.

The attractive en suite bedrooms are thoughtfully equipped with tea and coffee making facilities, Teletext colour television, and radio alarms. Other rooms available for guests' use are the dining room, billiard room, and peaceful guests' sitting room, which is ideal for reading or catching up on your paperwork. Home-cooked suppers are available and special diets can be catered for with adequate notice. Children and pets are not permitted.

# *H*igher Dipford Farm

*Heavily beamed Somerset longhouse on a working dairy farm convenient for Taunton*

☎ 01823 275770
🖷 01823 257916

**Map ref 2 - ST22**

Trull, TAUNTON, Somerset, TA3 7NU
pass Queens College on Honiton/Trull Rd, right to Dipford Rd, before fork farm on left
3 Rooms, ££
No Smoking in bedrooms

*W*ell situated for both business and leisure guests, this Grade II listed, 600-year-old longhouse, is only three miles from the county town of Taunton and just a few miles from the M5. It is the family home of Maureen and Chris Fewings, who extend a warm welcome to their guests.

The comfortable en suite bedrooms are spacious and airy. Each one is equipped with a large remote control television, including Sky as an option, a hairdryer, and electric blankets. The selection of teas and biscuits in the rooms is a nice additional touch. There is a large lounge with an inglenook fireplace where log fires burn in cooler weather, and a cosy honesty bar is provided for guests' use. Meals are served at one large table in the attractive dining room, and Maureen Fewings serves freshly cooked food using quality local produce.

## RECOMMENDED IN THE AREA

**RESTAURANT:**
*Bindon House, Taunton*

**TRADITIONAL PUB:**
*White Horse Inn, Bradford on Tone*

**VISIT:**
*Willow & Wetlands Visitor Centre, Stoke St Gregory*

**119**

# Meryan House

*A charming period residence with its own restaurant*

☎ 01823 337445
🖷 01823 322355
✉ nickclark<anglo@dircon.co.uk

**Map ref 2 - ST22**

Bishop's Hull,
TAUNTON, Somerset,
TA1 5EG
from Taunton take A38
Wellington. After
crematorium on left
take 1st right, house
approx 600yds
12 Rooms, ££

## RECOMMENDED IN THE AREA

**RESTAURANT:**
*Mount Somerset Hotel, Taunton*

**TRADITIONAL PUB:**
*Brazz, Taunton*

**VISIT:**
*Hestercombe Gardens, Taunton*

*G*uests receive individual attention and unrivalled hospitality when visiting this fascinating house. Over 300 years old, and set in delightful grounds only one mile from the centre of Taunton. The owners have opened up three of the original inglenook fireplaces and a complete working well over 30 feet deep which was uncovered in the kitchen. The bedrooms are individually decorated with antique furniture and the luxurious honeymoon room has a Half Tester Bed. All rooms are en suite and have a hospitality tray, radio/baby alarms, direct dial telephones and remote control colour television with video and satellite channels. Extra touches include luxury toiletries, sweets and paper handkerchiefs. Meryan House has its own rosette awarded restaurant where local seasonal produce and vegetables from the garden are used as much as possible. There is a balanced à la carte menu as well as daily specials.

# The Spinney

*Detached modern house on the slopes of the Blackdown Hills*

☎ 01460 234362  📠 01460 234362
✉ bartlett.spinney@zetnet.co.uk

**Map ref 2 - ST22**

Curland, TAUNTON, Somerset, TA3 5SE
off A358, Taunton to Ilminster road
3 Rooms, £, No smoking

Ann and John Bartlett are the welcoming owners of this well appointed property. The house is set in a lovely garden, with panoramic views towards the Quantock and Mendip Hills, in a designated area of outstanding natural beauty.

Two of the bedrooms are on the ground floor, and some are suitable for family occupation. All of them have en suite facilities, remote control colour television, hairdryer and hospitality tray. There is a comfortable guest lounge with a log fire and colour television, and a large dining room overlooking the patio and garden.

Ann's two-course evening meals of traditional English fare have proved very popular, particularly the wonderful puddings. The house is not licensed, but guests are welcome to bring their own wine. Packed lunches and light suppers are available, and special diets can be catered for. Ann was a finalist in the AA's Landlady of the Year Award for 1999.

## RECOMMENDED IN THE AREA

**RESTAURANT:**
*The Castle, Taunton*

**TRADITIONAL PUB:**
*Greyhound, Staple Fitzpaine*

**VISIT:**
*Hestercombe Gardens, Taunton*

# Bekynton House

*Stone-built house three minutes' walk from the cathedral*

☎ 01749 672222  📠 01749 672222
✉ reservations@bekynton.freeserve.co.uk

**Map ref 2 - ST54**

7 St Thomas Street, WELLS, Somerset, BA5 2UU
St Thomas St(B3139 from Wells to Radstock)
signed The Horringtons
6 Rooms, £, No smoking
Closed 24-26 Dec

Bekynton House has an interesting history, beginning as a cottage with an old barn, once a chapel and perhaps a school, which is now part of the guest house. There is a Victorian addition to the property, where the lounge is now located.

The house provides comfortable accommodation with a family room, doubles and twins. All rooms have either en suite or private facilities, colour televisions, radio alarms, tea and coffee making equipment, central heating and a full length mirror.

A guests' lounge and a pay phone are available, and breakfast is served in the attractive dining room. There is a private car park, and plenty of pubs and restaurants within easy walking distance.

## RECOMMENDED IN THE AREA

**RESTAURANT:**
*The Market Place Hotel, Wells*

**TRADITIONAL PUB:**
*Who'd a Thought It Inn, Glastonbury*

**VISIT:**
*The Bishop's Palace, Wells*

# Double-Gate Farm

*Lovely old farmhouse with good food and a friendly atmosphere.*

☎ 01458 832217  📠 01458 835612
✉ hilary@doublegate.demon.co.uk

**Map ref 2 - ST54**

Godney, WELLS, Somerset, BA5 1RX
from Wells A39 Glastonbury, at Polsham right
(Godney/Polsham), approx 2m to x-roads,
farmhouse on left after Inn
8 Rooms, £, No smoking
Closed Xmas & New Year

The farm is situated on the Somerset Levels and is conveniently located for visitors to Wells and Glastonbury. Guests receive a warm welcome and individual attention from the owners Hilary and Terry Millard.

A variety of options are offered at breakfast, freshly prepared in the farmhouse kitchen, and served at two traditional 'long' tables. Two en suite bedrooms, and one family room with private facilities, are in the main house. Two adjoining barn conversions house a further 5 bedrooms, all en suite (one is specifically adapted for wheelchair users. All are delightfully decorated and well equipped with modern comforts. Pets are not accommodated (with the exception of guide dogs). Extensive leisure equipment is provided, including table tennis and traditional English games. Most credit cards are accepted.

## RECOMMENDED IN THE AREA

**RESTAURANT:**
*Bowlish House, Shepton Mallet*

**TRADITIONAL PUB:**
*Apple Tree Inn, West Pennard*

**VISIT:**
*Glastonbury Abbey, Glastonbury*

---

# Hollow Tree Farm

*A 32-year-old bungalow overlooking Wells and Glastonbury Tor*

☎ 01749 673715

**Map ref 2 - ST54**

Launcherley, WELLS, Somerset, BA5 1QJ
from Wells A39 Glastonbury rd, 1st left at
Brownes Garden Centre & farm approx
0.75m on right
3 Rooms, £, No smoking

Warm hospitality, good home cooking and immaculately kept accommodation are offered at this comfortable home. Cheerful colour schemes and polished wooden floors combine to create a welcoming environment, and every effort is made to put guests at their ease.

The views are superb, with the magnificent cathedral at Wells to the north and the striking silhouette of Glastonbury Tor to the south. Many hours of dedication are reflected in the lovely flower-filled garden, which is the perfect place to relax.

Home-made bread, jams and marmalades are a speciality of the house, and a highlight of the delicious breakfasts served at the communal table in the dining room.

## RECOMMENDED IN THE AREA

**RESTAURANT:**
*Charlton House Hotel, Shepton Mallet*

**TRADITIONAL PUB:**
*The Fountain Inn, Wells*

**VISIT:**
*Wookey Hole Caves & Papermill, Wookey Hole*

# Littlewell Farm

*A 200-year old farmhouse with extensive country views*

☎ **01749 677914**

**Map ref 2 - ST54**

Coxley, WELLS, Somerset, BA5 1QP
1m from centre on A39 towards Glastonbury
5 Rooms, £
No smoking

This sturdy stone farmhouse sits in the hamlet of Coxley, looking far across the beautiful countryside and the Mendip Hills. It is just one mile from the centre of Wells, making it an ideal base for touring, walking, and visiting the picturesque villages, towns and cities in the area.

The bedrooms have been lovingly restored, decorated, and furnished to give guests quality accommodation, and all rooms have their own bathroom or shower, as well as a colour TV, and a guest tray with tea and coffee making facilities.

The farm offers excellent cuisine for dinner, serving traditional and original dishes using fresh local produce. Gerry and Di Gnoyke make sure your stay is easy and relaxing.

## RECOMMENDED IN THE AREA

**RESTAURANT:**
*Ston Easton Park, Ston Easton*

**TRADITIONAL PUB:**
*The Pheasant Inn, Wells*

**VISIT:**
*King John's Hunting Lodge, Axbridge*

# Riverside Grange

*Converted tannery in a quiet position on the river edge*

☎ **01749 890761**

**Map ref 2 - ST54**

Tanyard Lane, North Wootton, WELLS, Somerset, BA4 4AE
A39 towards Glastonbury. On leaving Wells 1st left (North Wootton), thro' village to T-junct, left & 2nd left
2 Rooms, £, No smoking

The tannery was built in 1853 to supply leather to Clarks the shoemakers. Its foundations are actually laid in the bed of the River Redlake which flows gently past. As well as the river, Riverside Grange overlooks a cider orchard, and the peaceful surroundings have been designated an area of outstanding natural beauty. It is a convenient location for visiting Wells and Glastonbury, parking is available.

Both bedrooms have been tastefully decorated with comfortable furnishings, tea and coffee and TV in the rooms. One room has an en suite bathroom with shower.

Breakfast is served around one large table. Mrs English, an AA Landlady of the Year finalist, and her family greet their guests with a warm welcome.

## RECOMMENDED IN THE AREA

**RESTAURANT:**
*Bowlish House, Shepton Mallet*

**TRADITIONAL PUB:**
*Apple Tree Inn, West Pennard*

**VISIT:**
*Glastonbury Abbey, Glastonbury*

# Southway Farm

*Beautiful Georgian farmhouse close to Glastonbury and Wells*

☎ 01749 673396　📠 01749 670373

**Map ref 2 - ST54**

Polsham, WELLS, Somerset, BA5 1RW
between Wells/Glastonbury, off A39
3 Rooms, £
No smoking

Southway is a Grade II listed farmhouse set on a working farm, which is easy to locate and ideally situated between the towns of Glastonbury and Wells.

Bedrooms are spacious and well furnished in country style to include impressive linen. All the rooms have televisions, radios, and tea and coffee making equipment and access to a private bathroom. Downstairs there is a comfortable lounge in which to relax after a day exploring the delights of the area.

Breakfast is served at separate tables in the pleasant dining room. Special diets can be catered for on request. There is a large garden surrounding the house, with parking space provided.

## RECOMMENDED IN THE AREA

**RESTAURANT:**
*The Market Place Hotel, Wells*

**TRADITIONAL PUB:**
*New Inn, Priddy*

**VISIT:**
*The Shoe Museum, Street*

---

# The Old Farmhouse

*A fine 17th-century farmhouse in the heart of Wells*

☎ 01749 675058　📠 01749 675058

**Map ref 2 - ST54**

62 Chamberlain Street, WELLS, Somerset,
BA5 2PT
from Bath or Bristol A39, signs for city centre,
fork right at lights (Chamberlain St). Old
Farmhouse on right before petrol station
2 Rooms, £, No smoking
Closed 24 Dec-2 Jan

Only in Wells, England's smallest cathedral city, would you expect to find an old farmhouse within a pretty walled garden, so well preserved and right in the centre. It only takes a short stroll to reach the Gothic cathedral, the 13th-century marketplace or the oldest medieval street in Europe. With Bath, Glastonbury and the unique Somerset Levels within easy driving distance, and secure private parking, this is the perfect base for exploring the city on foot, or the surrounding area by car. It is well worth coming back for dinner, available by prior arrangement. Felicity is a Cordon Bleu chef, and the food is truly delicious. Breakfast is either traditional or continental, with homemade bread and preserves. Colours throughout the home are subtle and warm. Both bedrooms have en suite bathrooms, as well as colour TV, radio and tea and coffee. There is a payphone available to guests. The beds are extremely comfortable.

## RECOMMENDED IN THE AREA

**RESTAURANT:**
*Ancient Gate House Hotel, Wells*

**TRADITIONAL PUB:**
*New Inn, Priddy*

**VISIT:**
*Cheddar Gorge*

# Tilbury Farm

*Peacefully located farmhouse with fine country views*

☎ 01823 432391

**Map ref 2 - ST13**

Cothelstone, WEST BAGBOROUGH,
Somerset, TA4 3DY
A358 Minehead, 0.75m after 2nd railway
bridge sharp right (W Bagborough). Thro'
village, on left up steep hill
3 Rooms, £, No smoking

*P*amela and Mike Smith offer a hospitable
welcome to guests at Tilbury Farm, which is said
to be the highest dwelling on the Quantocks. From
this elevated and very peaceful position, the house
affords spectacular views over the vale of Taunton.

The Smiths have taken enormous care in the
renovation of their wonderful home, which retains
impressive original features such as flagstone floors,
oak beams and inglenook fireplaces.

Bedrooms, decorated in individual style, have been
tastefully furnished and equipped with modern en
suite facilities. Dinner is available by arrangement
and served around a splendid 17th-century table.
Pam is an innovative cook and prepares dishes from
the best of fresh ingredients. No pets or children
under eight can be accommodated.

## RECOMMENDED IN THE AREA

**RESTAURANT:**
*Langley House, Wiveliscombe*

**TRADITIONAL PUB:**
*Fitzhead Inn, Fitzhead*

**VISIT:**
*Hestercombe Gardens, Taunton*

# Little Brendon Hill Farm

*Family-run farmhouse in the centre of Exmoor*

☎ 01643 841556   🖷 01643 841556
✉ larry.maxwell@btinternet.com

**Map ref 2 - SS93**

WHEDDON CROSS, Somerset, TA24 7BG
from Wheddon Cross B3224 towards
Taunton, farm on left after 1m
3 Rooms, £, No smoking
Closed Xmas

*S*ituated in the centre of the beautiful Exmoor
National Park, this charming farmhouse offers
high standards of accommodation with a Victorian
ambience.

The bedrooms (all en suite) are comfortably
appointed, each of the rooms has colour television,
central heating and tea and coffee making
equipment. Good quality food is served, and guests
can enjoy a well prepared candlelit dinner, by a
crackling log fire, in colder weather. At breakfast you
can expect free range eggs from the farm.

Owners Shelagh and Larry Maxwell create an
informal atmosphere and provide a delightfully
relaxing style of hospitality. Dogs and children under
seven cannot be accommodated.

## RECOMMENDED IN THE AREA

**RESTAURANT:**
*Savery's at Karslake House, Winsford*

**TRADITIONAL PUB:**
*The Notley Arms, Monksilver*

**VISIT:**
*Cleeve Abbey, Washford*

# $\mathcal{T}$he Rest & Be Thankful Inn

*Former coaching inn surrounded by lovely countryside*

☎ 01643 841222  📠 01643 841222
✉ enquiries@restandbethankful.co.uk

**Map ref 2 - SS93**

Wheddon Cross, WHEDDON CROSS, Somerset, TA24 7DR
on crossroads of A396 & B3224, 5m S of Dunster
5 Rooms, ££, No smoking in bedrooms
Closed 24-26 Dec

## RECOMMENDED IN THE AREA

VISIT:
*Dunster Castle, Dunster*

$\mathcal{T}$he inn is beautifully located in a moorland village overlooking Dunkery Beacon, the highest point in Exmoor. A warm welcome is extended by the resident proprietors, who go out of their way to make guests feel at home.

The comfortable bedrooms all have en suite facilities. Colour televisions, direct dial telephones, and tea and coffee making equipment are provided for guests' comfort.

The restaurant, popular with residents and non-residents alike, offers a good selection of dishes, ranging from bar snacks to more substantial house specialities. There is a comfortable guest lounge. Additional amenities include darts, pool and a skittle alley. No pets or children under the age of 11 can be accommodated. Parking is available.

# $\mathcal{H}$olywell House

*Beautiful 18th-century Hamstone house in a small village setting*

☎ 01935 862612  📠 01935 863035
✉ b&b@holywellhouse.freeserve.co.uk

**Map ref 2 - ST51**

Holywell, East Coker, YEOVIL, Somerset, BA22 9NQ
leave Yeovil on A30 Crewkerne rd, 2m left past Yeovil Court Hotel (East Coker), down lane, house on right opposite Foresters Arms
3 Rooms, ££
Closed Xmas & New Year

## RECOMMENDED IN THE AREA

RESTAURANT:
*Little Barwick House, Yeovil*

TRADITIONAL PUB:
*The Haselbury Inn, Haselbury Plucknett*

VISIT:
*Tintinill House Garden, Tintinhill*

$\mathcal{B}$uilt of mellow local stone, this former miller's house has been carefully restored and elegantly furnished with many antiques. Each of the bedrooms is individual in style. There is the 'Pine Suite', themed around the fitted pine wardrobe that was built with the house; the 'Cottage Suite' with its own galleried sitting room; and the luxurious 'Master Suite', featuring a mahogany panelled bathroom and antique furnishings. Television, clock radios, hairdryers, trouser presses, bathrobes and hospitality trays are provided in every room, along with extras such as fresh flowers, fruit, mineral water, and even hot water bottles. There are three acres of wonderful gardens with a tennis court and croquet lawn. Bog gardens are cultivated on the banks of the two streams that run through the grounds, and there are large herbaceous borders, two wild flower meadows, a herb garden, organic vegetable and fruit gardens, and a large fish pond.

# Cheney Cottage

*An idyllic thatched cottage in beautiful gardens*

☎ 01225 742346  📠 01225 742346
✉ cheneycottage@btinternet.com

**Map ref 2 - ST86**

Ditteridge, BOX, Wiltshire, SN13 8QF
A4 Bath-Chippenham rd, just before Box turn left signed Ditteridge. Next T-junct turn left, house 0.5m on left
6 Rooms, £, No smoking
Closed 21 Dec-Jan

*T*he house is in a peaceful rural location, set back from the road in four acres of well tended grounds, with views across the Box Valley. It is five miles from Bath, handy for exploring the countryside, but you might just want to enjoy the garden, or play tennis on the all weather court.

Five of the immaculate bedrooms are en suite, one twin room has a separate private bathroom. Tea and coffee facilities, clock radio, hairdryers, biscuits, magazines and fresh flowers are provided. Three rooms are in the cottage, three more, with colour TV, are in the former stable block. A wonderful full English breakfast is served, with a wide choice of menu.

Joan (AA Landlady of the Year Finalist) and Arthur Evans give guests a warm welcome and look after them with gentle care. Children are welcome (cot available), not pets, special diets by prior arrangement, packed lunch on request.

## RECOMMENDED IN THE AREA

**RESTAURANT:**
*White Hart Inn, Ford*

**TRADITIONAL PUB:**
*The Quarrymans Arms, Box*

**VISIT:**
*Romans Baths & Pump Room, Bath*

---

# Owl House

*Attractive property set in lovely gardens close to Bath*

☎ 01225 743883  📠 01225 744450
✉ venus@zetnet.co.uk

**Map ref 2 - ST86**

Lower Kingsdown Road, Kingsdown, nr BOX, Wiltshire, SN13 8BB
3 Rooms, ££
No smoking

*O*nly five miles from the city centre with views over the valleys to Bath, Owl House has an idyllic location for those looking for peace and quiet. The house is set in its own well kept gardens surrounded by lovely countryside. Beautiful interior decor with an Asian influence is another feature of the appealing property.

Comfortable accommodation is provided in three well furnished, en suite bedrooms, all of which provide central heating, colour televisions, and tea and coffee making equipment. Dogs cannot be accommodated (with the exception of guide dogs). Car parking space is available.

## RECOMMENDED IN THE AREA

**RESTAURANT:**
*Lucknam Park, Colerne*

**TRADITIONAL PUB:**
*The Quarrymans Arms, Box*

**VISIT:**
*Corsham Court, Corsham*

# *B*urghope Manor

*13th-century manor house set in lovely countryside*

☎ 01225 723557  📠 01225 723113
✉ burghope.manor@virgin.net

## Map ref 2 - ST86

Winsley, BRADFORD-ON-AVON, Wiltshire,
BA15 2LA
from A36 Bath-Warminster rd, B3108 Winsley
rd, in Winsley 1st right off by-pass, 1st left at
x-rd, gates at top of lane
6 Rooms, ££, No smoking
Closed Xmas/New Year

## RECOMMENDED IN THE AREA

**RESTAURANT:**
*Georgian Lodge, Bradford-on-Avon*

**TRADITIONAL PUB:**
*The Canal Tavern, Bradford-on-Avon*

**VISIT:**
*Great Chalfield Manor, Bradford-on-Avon*

*B*urghope is a beautiful old manor house in a country setting just five miles from the city of Bath. Much of the property's historic character has been retained, and a particular feature is the Cranmer Room (the house has associations with Henry VIII's prelate Archbishop Cranmer). Here an enormous fireplace takes up almost the whole of one wall.

Modern comforts have not been neglected, as can be seen in the attractively presented and centrally heated bedrooms. Those in the manor itself are all en suite. Two rooms in the Dower House are en suite, one with adjoining bathroom.

A full English breakfast is served in the elegant dining room. There are plenty of pubs and restaurants within easy reach, by car or on foot, and an immense range of places to visit.

# *F*ern Cottage

*Historic building in a lovely village setting*

☎ 01225 859412  📠 01225 859018

## Map ref 2 - ST86

Monkton Farleigh, BRADFORD-ON-AVON,
Wiltshire, BA15 2QJ
off A363 at sign for Monkton Farleigh.1m
right at T-junct by Manor House gates, 1st
cottage on left
3 Rooms, ££, No smoking in bedrooms

## RECOMMENDED IN THE AREA

**RESTAURANT:**
*Woolley Grange, Bradford-on-Avon*

**TRADITIONAL PUB:**
*Inn at Freshford, Freshford*

**VISIT:**
*The Courts, Holt*

*T*his 17th-century stone cottage lies in a pretty conservation between Bath and Bradford-on-Avon. The warm, friendly atmosphere created by the proprietors, Christopher and Jenny Valentine, adds to its appeal.

There are three delightful bedrooms, one of which is in the adjacent Coach House and is available for self-catering holidays. Two rooms have en suite facilities, one of the rooms in the main house has a private bathroom. All the bedrooms are beautifully decorated and furnished with quality pieces. Colour televisions and tea and coffee making equipment are provided.

Delicious home-cooked breakfasts are served at one large table in the dining room. Car parking is available for guests, dogs cannot be accommodated (except for guide dogs)

# Hillcrest

*Splendid property with magnificent views over Limpley Stoke Valley*

☎ 01225 868677 📠 01225 868655
**Map ref 2 - ST86**

Bradford Road, Winsley, BRADFORD-ON-AVON, Wiltshire, BA15 2HN
from Bath, A36 Warminster 4m, left at lights (B3108), up hill (ignore Winsley sign) at island turn right, Hillcrest on left at bend
2 Rooms, ££, No smoking
Closed Xmas & New Year

Barbara Litherland is a real 'people person' with a talent for doing several things at once, or so it seems! Her aim is to please, so guests can be sure of an enjoyable stay. Hillcrest is situated only six miles from Bath and two miles from Bradford on Avon, and is surrounded by old dry stone walls. High quality accommodation is offered in stylishly decorated en suite bedrooms, with dark wood furniture and classic fabrics. The rooms are equipped with thoughtful extras such as fresh fruit, sweets and good toiletries. There is an elegant sitting room for guests' use. Hillcrest offers an extensive a la carte breakfast with a variety of traditional and continental choices, served in the attractive dining room at a large communal table.

## RECOMMENDED IN THE AREA

**RESTAURANT:**
*Georgian Lodge, Bradford-on-Avon*

**TRADITIONAL PUB:**
*Pear Tree, Whitley*

**VISIT:**
*Iford Manor, Bradford-on-Avon*

*Cheddar Gorge, Somerset*

**129**

# Chilvester Hill House

*Large rooms in a Victorian house of local Bath stone*

☎ 01249 813981 📠 01249 814217

**Map ref 2 - ST97**

CALNE, Wiltshire, SN11 0LP
A4 Calne to Chippenham, after 0.5m right turn marked Bremhill, drive of house immediately on right
3 Rooms, ££

The house stands well back from the A4 in well kept gardens and extensive grounds, complete with cattle. There is plenty to do in the area, whether you want to visit the countryside or local gardens, play golf or go to the races, and Dr and Mrs Dilley are happy to help you plan your itinerary.

The bedrooms are airy, with en suite bathrooms, colour TV, clock radio, guide books and maps. Breakfast is particularly fine, and dinner is available by arrangement - most of the fruit and vegetables used are home grown. Meals are served around one large table in the dining room.

The house has a drawing room, as well as a sitting room with papers and magazines. It retains all the style and elegance of the Victorian period, and the owners welcome you as they would their friends.

## RECOMMENDED IN THE AREA

**RESTAURANT:**
*George & Dragon, Rowde*

**TRADITIONAL PUB:**
*Lansdowne Arms, Calne*

**VISIT:**
*Lacock Abbey, Lacock*

# Fenwicks

*Peaceful house and secluded gardens in the Wiltshire countryside*

☎ 01249 760645 📠 01249 760645

**Map ref 2 - ST97**

Lower Goatacre, CALNE, Wiltshire, SN11 9HY
from Lyneham A3102 (Calne),0.75m left at bus shelter, Goatacre Lane, bear right at Harts Close, fork right at hill bottom
3 Rooms, £, No smoking

Fenwicks is tucked away in the quiet hamlet of Goatacre, with two and a half acres of gardens, lawns and meadow, and views across the open valley. Tea may be taken in the garden in summer, and there is a play area for children. A golf course, fitness and leisure centre, water sports, fishing and riding can all be found nearby. There is ample parking.

The bedrooms are decorated in light and simple style, with showers en suite or a private bathroom. Fresh fruit, flowers and electric blankets, as well as colour TV, clock radio and tea and coffee, demonstrate the care taken to guarantee guests a comfortable stay.

Breakfasts are served around one large table in the guest sitting room, where there is a warming fire in winter. Whether you go for traditional English or choose from the carte, the food is recommended for its quality.

## RECOMMENDED IN THE AREA

**RESTAURANT:**
*Pear Tree at Purton*

**TRADITIONAL PUB:**
*George & Dragon, Rowde*

**VISIT:**
*Avebury Museum, Avebury*

# *B*lounts Court Farm

*Farmhouse with country views, on top of a wooded hillside*

☎ 01380 727180

**Map ref 3 - SU06**

Coxhill Lane, Potterne, DEVIZES, Wiltshire, SN10 5PH
A360 to Potterne turn into Coxhill Lane opp George & Dragon, left at fork and follow drive to farmhouse
2 Rooms, £, No smoking in bedrooms

*T*his lovely, old farmhouse sits in a perfectly quiet position with views across the gardens and the Wiltshire countryside - it is definitely an environment to relax in. The Cary family make charming hosts and treat their guests to exceptional hospitality.

The old barn and cider press have been converted into two beautiful bedrooms, with their original beams still clear to see. They have been decorated with style and elegance, and both have smart en suite bathrooms. There is also a private sitting room for guests.

Breakfast is served in the farmhouse dining room: there is wide choice of hot dishes, cooked there and then for you, using only the freshest produce - the owners care is once again evident in their delicious food.

## RECOMMENDED IN THE AREA

**RESTAURANT:**
*George & Dragon, Rowde*

**TRADITIONAL PUB:**
*The Elm Tree, Devizes*

**VISIT:**
*Ludgershall Castle, Ludgershall*

# *A*t the Sign of the Angel

*16th-century wool merchant's house with excellent restaurant*

☎ 01249 730230   ✆ 01249 730527

**Map ref 2 - ST96**

6 Church Street, LACOCK, Wiltshire, SN15 2LB
exit M4 junct 17, follow Chippenham signs, 3m S of Chippenham on A350 Lacock signed left, follow 'local traffic' sign
9 Rooms, £££
Closed 23 Dec-30 Dec

*T*he log fires and oak panelling, low beams and squeaky floors create all the atmosphere of an old English Inn; the house is situated in the National Trust village of Lacock, a history lesson in itself, and a perfect base for seeing the sights and the countryside of Wiltshire, Somerset and Gloucestershire.

All of the bedrooms are en suite; four are in the cottage over the footbridge, across the stream. They are all furnished with antique wooden furniture - one has an enormous bed that was owned by the Victorian engineer, Isambard Kingdom Brunel. The restaurant is internationally renowned for its traditional English cooking, with herbs and vegetables (asparagus is a speciality) fresh from the garden. The Angel's own hens provide eggs for breakfast; lunch is available every day except Monday; and there is a daily changing menu and a full carte, by candlelight, in the evening.

## RECOMMENDED IN THE AREA

**RESTAURANT:**
*Toxique, Melksham*

**TRADITIONAL PUB:**
*The George Inn, Lacock*

**VISIT:**
*Lacock Abbey, Lacock*

# Langley Wood Restaurant

*Comfortable rooms, fine food and wine, in wooded grounds*

☎ 01794 390348

**Map ref 2 - ST73**

REDLYNCH, Wiltshire, SP5 2PB
A338 from Salisbury to Downton, left onto
B3080, on entering Redlynch turn left at
garage, 2.5m on left.
3 Rooms

Traditional breakfast is prepared to the same high standards as all the cuisine, with homemade bread. The lounge and the rooms all overlook the garden. In the summer, drinks and even Sunday lunch may be served on the lawns; in the winter there are log fires.

Originally built in the 17th century as a cottage in the woods, the house had been greatly enlarged by the end of the Victorian era. It still stands surrounded by five acres of informal wooded grounds with lovely walks and roaming deer. It is now a restaurant with rooms, serving a short, unpretentious carte which changes frequently according to what is good and what is in season. There is a well chosen list of some 75 wines.

## RECOMMENDED IN THE AREA

**TRADITIONAL PUB:**
*The Kings Head, Redlynch*

**VISIT:**
*Stourhead House & Garden*

# Clovelly Hotel

*Friendly family hotel close to the city centre*

☎ 01722 322055  📠 01722 327677
✉ clovelly.hotel@virgin.net

**Map ref 2 - SU12**

17-19 Mill Road, SALISBURY, Wiltshire,
SP2 7RT
approx 5 mins from Market Square &
Cathedral, & 2 mins from station
12 Rooms, ££, No smoking

Professionally run by Rowena and Haydn Ingram, the Clovelly offers lovely accommodation suitable for business and leisure guests alike. A friendly atmosphere prevails and staff are always available to give advice on where to dine and what to see. Rowena is a Blue Badge Guide and also offers personalised tours around Wessex. The house is just five minutes' level walk from the city centre, close to the railway station.

Bedrooms are smartly decorated with co-ordinating soft furnishings, comfortable beds and modern facilities. All the rooms have fresh, bright en suite bathrooms, television and tea and coffee making equipment. Some rooms are located on the ground floor, including accommodation for disabled guests. There is a cosy lounge and a super dining room where a good cooked breakfast is served. Car parking is provided for residents.

## RECOMMENDED IN THE AREA

**RESTAURANT:**
*Howard's House Hotel, Salisbury*

**TRADITIONAL PUB:**
*The Old Mill at Harnham, Nr Salisbury*

**VISIT:**
*Salisbury Cathedral, Salisbury*

# *C*ricket Field House

*Game keeper's cottage overlooking the South Wilts Cricket Ground*

☎ 01722 322595
🖷 01722 322595
🄴 information@
cricketfieldhouse
hotel.com

**Map ref 2 - SU12**

Skew Bridge, Wilton
Road, SALISBURY,
Wiltshire, SP2 7NS
off A36 Warminster
road, between
Salisbury & Wilton on S.
Wilts Cricket Ground
14 Rooms, ££
No smoking
Closed 24-25 Dec

*C*ricket Field House is a 19th-century game keeper's cottage modernised to provide comfortable guest accommodation. It stands in its own extensive gardens overlooking the village church and the South Wiltshire Cricket Ground. There is a large private car park, and a well equipped meeting room. The bedrooms are divided between the main house and the pavilion annexe. They are individually decorated and furnished, all have en suite showers. Remote control television, tea making equipment and hairdryers are provided. One room is located on the ground floor and is suitable for disabled guests. Lunches and evening meals are available in the restaurant, which takes full advantage of the lovely views. The hotel is conveniently located for trips to Stonehenge, and the historic cities of Salisbury, Bath and Winchester.

## RECOMMENDED IN THE AREA

**RESTAURANT:**
*The Three Lions,
Fordingbridge*

**TRADITIONAL PUB:**
*Augustus John,
Fordingbridge*

**VISIT:**
*Mompesson House,
Salisbury*

# Glen Lyn House

*An elegant house in a quiet tree-lined lane, offering traditional hospitality*

☎ 01722 327880
🖷 01722 327880
📧 glen.lyn@
btinternet.com

**Map ref 2 - SU12**

6 Bellamy Lane, Milford Hill, SALISBURY, Wiltshire, SP1 2SP
from A36 take Tollgate Rd, at traffic lights turn right up Milford Hill. Bellamy Lane at top on left
7 Rooms, £,
No smoking
Closed Xmas/New Year

## RECOMMENDED IN THE AREA

**RESTAURANT:**
*Howard's House Hotel, Salisbury*

**TRADITIONAL PUB:**
*The Wheatsheaf, Lower Woodford*

This turn of the century house enjoys a quiet situation in a beautiful mature garden. There is parking at the front and the house is just eight minutes from the city centre. Inside, antique furniture is complemented by some fine original fireplaces. A superb traditional English or vegetarian breakfast is served in the dining room, a three-course dinner is available by arrangement. The spacious lounge has deep comfortable sofas, log fires in winter, books, magazines and games. The house is entirely non smoking. The bedrooms are individually decorated, with co-ordinating curtains and covers. Four have en suite bathroom facilities and there is a deluxe double for the ultimate in luxury. The whole house can be let out to groups and the owners can cater for special events with a barbecue or a celebration meal. Patrick Fairbrother was a top twenty finalist in the AA Landlady of the Year Awards for 1999. Children over 12 are welcome, dogs only by prior arrangement.

# Stratford Lodge

*Attractive Victorian house enjoying a peaceful location within walking distance of the city centre*

☎ 01722 325177
📠 01722 325177
✉ enquiries@
stratfordlodge.co.uk
**Map ref 2 - SU12**

4 Park Lane, off Castle Road, SALISBURY, Wiltshire, SP1 3NP
A345 Castle Rd past St Francis Church & Victoria Park. Park Lane between park & Alldays
8 Rooms, ££
No smoking
Closed 23 Dec-1 Jan

Stratford Lodge, a detached red brick property, is quietly situated in a lane overlooking Victoria Park, with all the attractions and amenities of Salisbury close by. The bedrooms have en suite facilities and are decorated in relaxing soft shades with pretty co-ordinating fabrics. There is an emphasis on quality food, and the meals are carefully prepared using local produce and fresh vegetables, fruit and herbs. As well as the traditional British fry-up, you might have kedgeree, mushrooms on toast, or scrambled egg for breakfast. Muesli, fresh fruit, compotes and local honey are also a feature, with a choice of beverages including tea, coffee, herbal infusions and hot chocolate. There is a daily dinner menu, with vegetarian dishes always available. Other diets can also be catered for. For relaxation, there is a sheltered and secluded garden.

## RECOMMENDED IN THE AREA

**RESTAURANT:**
*Fifehead Manor, Middle Wallop*

**TRADITIONAL PUB:**
*Radnor Arms, Nunton*

**VISIT:**
*Royal Gloucestershire, Berkshire & Wiltshire Regiment Museum*

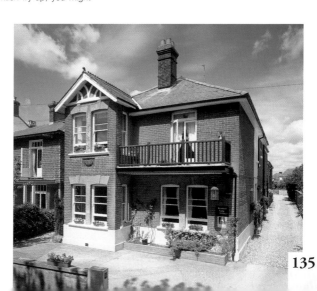

# *W*ebsters

*Fully en suite accommodation in a peaceful cul-de-sac*

☎ 01722 339779  📠 01722 339779
✉ websters.salis@eclipse.co.uk

**Map ref 2 - SU12**

11 Hartington Road, SALISBURY, Wiltshire, SP2 7LG
from city centre A360 Devizes Rd. Hartington Rd is 500yds from St Pauls rdb on left
5 Rooms, £, No smoking in bedrooms

Generous breakfasts are served on bright and cheerful crockery in the attractive dining room, the perfect start to the day. Children under 12 years old cannot be accommodated, neither can dogs (with the exception of guide dogs).

*T*he fascinating sights of Salisbury are just a short stroll away from this quietly located house, where guests are assured of a warm welcome from amiable hosts Mary and Peter Webb.

The bedrooms are well equipped with colour televisions and tea and coffee making facilities, and immaculately presented with co-ordinating fabrics and some lovely pieces of furniture. A ground floor room has been designed specifically for guests with disabilities.

## RECOMMENDED IN THE AREA

**RESTAURANT:**
*Bertie's, Romsey*

**TRADITIONAL PUB:**
*The Old Mill at Harnham, Salisbury*

**VISIT:**
*Salisbury & South Wiltshire Museum, Salisbury*

---

# *B*riden House

*18th-century house ideally located for 'the cradle of Britain'*

☎ 01722 743471  📠 01722 743471
✉ bridenhouse@barford25.freeserve.co.uk

**Map ref 2 - SU03**

West Street, Barford St Martin, SALISBURY, Wiltshire, SP3 4AH
close to village church on B3089
4 Rooms, £, No smoking in dining room

*B*riden House is a typical 18th-century Wiltshire village house situated between the church and village inn. The house is set in rolling countryside just 10 miles from Stonehenge, 5 miles from Salisbury and 2 miles from Wilton, the ancient capital of Wessex. Dogs are accepted by arrangement and there is private parking.

Guests enjoy a good night's rest in comfortable, well-equipped en suite bedrooms, and a traditional English breakfast in the large beamed dining room. Your hosts Patsy and Tim Barter are keen to share their extensive knowledge of all the tourist attractions in this historic area. Mystical Stonehenge, the splendour of Salisbury Cathedral, the history of Wardour Castle and the profusion of stately homes, besides many lesser known secrets of this enchanting region of Wessex.

## RECOMMENDED IN THE AREA

**RESTAURANT:**
*Howard's House Hotel, Salisbury*

**TRADITIONAL PUB:**
*Barford Inn, Barford St Martin*

**VISIT:**
*Stonehenge*

# $\mathcal{T}$he Barn

*Converted milking parlour in a quiet country situation*

☎ 01985 841138  📠 01985 841138

**Map ref 2 - ST84**

The Marsh, Longbridge, WARMINSTER, Wiltshire, BA12 7EA
A36 Salisbury/Bath, A350 into Longbridge Deverill, turn 300yds past BP garage on left, house 1st right
2 Rooms, £, No smoking in bedrooms

*O*riginally built in the mid 19th century, The Barn has been sympathetically extended and converted into a family residence with on-site parking, guests are welcomed with warm hospitality. It is in an idyllic rural position with a stream running by.

All rooms have en suite facilities; colour TV, radio alarm, hairdryers, tea and coffee are provided. One room has French windows leading out onto the lawn in the back garden. There is a spacious lounge with oak beams and a gallery, and plenty of books and magazines to look at.

A generous breakfast, English or continental, with home baked bread and fresh pastries, is served around a large pine table in the kitchen, or even out in the garden on warm sunny days.

## RECOMMENDED IN THE AREA

**RESTAURANT:**
*Bishopstrow House, Warminster*

**TRADITIONAL PUB:**
*The Angel, Heytesbury*

**VISIT:**
*Longleat*

---

# $\mathcal{G}$lenmore Farm

*Farmhouse accommodation close to the famous White Horse*

☎ 01373 865022

**Map ref 2 - ST85**

Ham Road, WESTBURY, Wiltshire, BA13 4HQ
A350 N from Westbury, at Heywood left into village and left at end of village. Farm on right after West Wilts Trading Estate
3 Rooms, £
No smoking

## RECOMMENDED IN THE AREA

**RESTAURANT:**
*Woolpack Inn, Beckington*

**TRADITIONAL PUB:**
*The Owl, Little Cheverell*

**VISIT:**
*Stonehenge*

*G*lenmore Farmhouse is set in 145 acres of farmland, surrounded by a lovely garden. Owners Stan and Rosemary Painter offer warm hospitality and are keen to ensure that your stay will be comfortable and enjoyable.

The bedrooms are very well furnished and equipped, two have four-poster beds and all have en suite facilities. Full English breakfast is served and a smart lounge and a sunny conservatory are available for guests' use.

Many interesting places to visit are within easy reach of the farm, such as Longleat Safari Park, Cheddar Gorge, Wookey Hole Caves and the Georgian splendour of Bath.

# Newton Farmhouse

*Characterful accommodation in a country setting*

**☎** 01794 884416 **ⓕ** 01794 884416
**ⓔ** newton.farmhouse.b-b@
lineone.net

**Map ref 3 - SU22**

Southampton Road, WHITEPARISH,
Wiltshire, SP5 2QL
on A36 1m S of junct with A27
8 Rooms, £, No smoking

preserves are a feature of the breakfasts. Dinner is also served, using home grown produce from the extensive garden. A swimming pool is available in the grounds.

Once part of the Trafalgar Estate owned by the Nelson family, this 16th-century farmhouse is situated on the borders of the New Forest, eight miles south of Salisbury. It offers eight delightfully decorated guest rooms, all with en suite facilities, including six with period four-poster beds. Central heating, colour television and tea and coffee making equipment are provided in all the rooms.

The beamed dining room houses a collection of Nelson memorabilia, and has a flagstone floor and an inglenook fireplace. Home made breads and

## RECOMMENDED IN THE AREA

**RESTAURANT:**
*Old Manor House, Romsey*

**TRADITIONAL PUB:**
*Hatchet Inn, Sherfield English*

**VISIT:**
*Mottisfont Abbey Garden, Mottisfont*

*The River Medway at Tonbridge, Kent*

# South & South East England

This area embraces Greater London and the surrounding 'Home Counties'. Although the population continues to increase in this area, there is still much unspoilt countryside to enjoy. The New Forest in Hampshire has been preserved to provide plenty of scope for walking, cycling and riding. The chalk hills of the North and South Downs cross the South of England from West Sussex to Kent.

Kent is known as the Garden of England and the climate is excellent for fruit farming. There are many orchards and some vineyards producing English wine. The traditional oast houses, where hops were stored, can still be seen here and in other parts of the South of England. Some have been converted into private houses and a handful feature in this guide as AA recommended places to stay.

The channel ports of Dover, Ramsgate and Folkestone are the gateway to France from Kent. The channel tunnel and Eurostar trains from London Waterloo and Ashford in Kent make Paris an easy day trip. Another popular channel crossing is the ferry to Jersey or Guernsey in the Channel Islands. AA recommended places to stay are featured for St Peter Port, Guernsey and St Aubin or St Saviour, Jersey.

Visitors to Hampshire may like to visit Winchester, a city which has played a major role in English history. The Domesday Book was compiled here, King Alfred united England under Wessex with Winchester as his capital, Henry III was born at the castle, Mary Tudor married Philip of Spain here, and some believe that the city was the fabled Camelot. Winchester College, founded in 1832, is one of the oldest schools in England. The chapel, and (during term time) the cloisters and Fromond's Chantry are open to the public. The Great Hall is the only surviving part of Winchester Castle. The round table, closely associated with the legendary King Arthur, has hung here for over 600 years.

North West of London, Berkshire, Oxfordshire and Buckinghamshire share ancient cities and rural countryside. Windsor Castle and town has historical tours as well as riverside walks along the Thames. Oxford has many museums, university colleges and historic buildings open to the public as well as sightseeing tours by bus or on foot. Marlow and Henley on the borders of Buckinghamshire and Oxfordshire are delightful small towns on the River Thames which come alive each summer for their annual regattas.

London itself is easily accessed from Heathrow Airport by underground or bus into the centre; or from Gatwick Airport on the Gatwick Express train or by bus. There is so much to see and do in London that we recommend you use a guide such as AA All-in-One London to make the most of your trip.

*Winchester High Street, Hampshire*

# Woodpecker Cottage

*Peacefully located cottage surrounded by woods and lovely countryside*

☎ 01628 822772  📠 01628 822125
✉ power@woodpecker.co.uk
**Map ref 3 - SU88**

Warren Row, MAIDENHEAD, Berkshire,
RG10 8QS
4m W of Maidenhead, N off A4 at Knowl Hill,
after 1m turn left up track, left fork into
woods, house 100yds 2nd on left
3 Rooms, £, No smoking
Closed Xmas/New Year

## RECOMMENDED IN THE AREA

**RESTAURANT:**
*Fredrick's Hotel, Maidenhead*

**TRADITIONAL PUB:**
*The Fish, Bray*

**VISIT:**
*Courage Shire Horse Centre, Maidenhead*

*T*his charming cottage, between Maidenhead and Reading, stands in an acre of well kept gardens in a small village setting. The nearby woods are carpeted with bluebells in the spring, and there is an abundance of wildlife in the surrounding countryside. So tranquil is the location that it is hard to believe that Heathrow Airport is within half an hour's drive.

The bedrooms are well equipped and comfortable. There is a large double room with an en suite shower, a twin room with a private bathroom opposite, and a spacious en suite single. All are on the ground floor and have individually controlled heating, televisions, tea and coffee making facilities and hairdryers. An excellent breakfast is served in the elegant dining room, with home-laid eggs, home made bread, and jam made from fruits grown in the garden. Guests can relax in the cosy sitting room with its wood burning stove, or out on the terrace in summer.

# Cross Lanes

*16th-century cottage in a beautiful English country garden*

☎ 01844 345339
**Map ref 3 - SP70**

Cross Lanes Cottage, BLEDLOW,
Buckinghamshire, HP27 9PF
leave M40 J6, B4009, after passing Bledlow
village sign, Cross Lanes 1st property on
right, behind gates
3 Rooms, £, No smoking

## RECOMMENDED IN THE AREA

**RESTAURANT:**
*Sir Charles Napier, Chinnor*

**TRADITIONAL PUB:**
*The Lions of Bledlow*

**VISIT:**
*Waddesdon Manor, Waddesdon*

*C*ross Lanes is a listed building with delightful character, with pretty hanging baskets decorating the outside. It is in an ideal position for trips to Oxford, Waddesdon, the Chiltern Hills and the Ridgeway Path; you can park your car on the premises. The owners are charming, they look after their guests with a warm concern for their comfort, and their home with a sharp attention to detail.

The bedrooms, all with showers, are in the newer part of the cottage. They are decorated with soothing colour schemes and matching fabrics, the crisp white sheets are edged with lace, and all those little things that you might have forgotten are provided. Breakfast is served in a cosy dining room.

# $\mathcal{B}$ates Green

## 18th-century gamekeeper's cottage on a quiet country village lane

☎ 01323 482039 📠 01323 482039

**Map ref 4 - TQ50**

ARLINGTON, East Sussex, BN26 6SH
2m W of A22 towards Arlington turn right
Old Oak Inn
3 Rooms, ££, No smoking
Closed 22-27 Dec

$\mathcal{B}$ates Green is an idyllic rural retreat. There is an oak-panelled sitting room, with an open log fire. The bedrooms are decorated in cottage style, brightened by fresh flowers, with en suite bathrooms and colour TV. Children and pets cannot be accommodated.

There is an impressive two-acre plantsman's garden: a rockery with pond; an enclosed garden with colourful borders; and a shaded, foliage garden. There is usually a selection of plants for sale, and garden chat is always welcome. Bates Green also has pasture with 300 sheep, as well as deciduous woodland, with spectacular vistas of bluebells towards the end of April and beginning of May.

On arrival guests are welcomed with tea and home made cakes. A substantial English breakfast is served that includes freshly squeezed orange juice, dried fruit compote, oak-smoked Sussex bacon and home made preserves.

## RECOMMENDED IN THE AREA

**RESTAURANT:**
*Hungry Monk, Jevington*

**TRADITIONAL PUB:**
*Old Oak Inn, Arlington*

**VISIT:**
*Michelham Priory, Upper Dicker*

---

# $\mathcal{F}$ox Hole Farm

## An 18th-century woodcutter's cottage

☎ 01424 772053 📠 01424 773771

**Map ref 4 - TQ71**

Kane Hythe Road, BATTLE, East Sussex,
TN33 9QU
off A271 onto B2096 farm 0.75m from
junction on right
3 Rooms, ££, No smoking

$\mathcal{H}$idden away in over 40 acres of rolling countryside and farmland, the cottage has a large garden with a pond and is surrounded by another one thousand acres of forest. You can expect complete peace and quiet here, with birds, deer and foxes to keep you company. There are plenty of walks, and many gardens, houses and castles within easy reach. Well-behaved dogs are welcome providing they get on with the farm dogs and other animals.

The farmhouse retains many of its original features, with heavy beams, and a large inglenook fireplace with wood-burning stove. The bedrooms are traditionally furnished, all with TV and en suite bathrooms. There is a cosy room for planning your day, relaxing and dining. Generous three-course cooked breakfasts are served, and simple dishes are available in the evening by arrangement.

## RECOMMENDED IN THE AREA

**RESTAURANT:**
*Netherfield Place, Battle*

**TRADITIONAL PUB:**
*Ashtree Inn, Ashburnham Place*

**VISIT:**
*Battle Abbey, Battle*

# Lionsdown House

*Historic house, dating back to medieval times, in an elevated position in the picturesque High Street*

☎ ✆ 01424 420802

**Map ref 4 - TQ80**

116 High Street,
HASTINGS &
ST LEONARDS,
East Sussex,
TN34 3ET
in town centre
3 Rooms, £

### RECOMMENDED IN THE AREA

**RESTAURANT:**
*Röser's Restaurant, Hastings*

**TRADITIONAL PUB:**
*Queen's Head, Icklesham*

**VISIT:**
*Battle Abbey, Battle*

The house was originally constructed in the middle of the 15th century. Renovated and restored, you can still trace its history in the old beams, Tudor fireplaces and antique furnishings. The Georgian façade was added around 1790. It is in an ideal location for exploring the lanes, browsing the antique shops, and enjoying other attractions of the old town of Hastings, and other places in Sussex and Kent. A tasty choice of breakfasts are on offer, with traditional English, continental and vegetarian options, cooked fresh to order and served in the oak beamed dining room. Bedrooms are individually furnished and decorated, with luxury en suite facilities or a private bathroom, as well as colour TV, bathrobes, tea and coffee, hairdryer and radio alarm. There is a sense of easy luxury throughout.

# *B*ryn-y-mor

*Extensive gardens and a swimming pool enhance this Victorian property*

☎ 01424 722744  📠 01424 445933

**Map ref 4 - TQ80**

12 Godwin Road, HASTINGS &
ST LEONARDS, East Sussex, TN35 5JR
A259 coast rd keep sea on right, bear left at
Old Town, follow rd up hill, right at Convent
(Ashburham Rd) then 2nd right
4 Rooms, ££, No smoking in bedrooms

Originally built as the private residence of a Victorian gentleman, the interior retains many original features including light fittings, stained glass windows and ornate wall coverings. Pictures, ornaments and rich fabrics contribute to the period elegance and many objects d'art are displayed in the spacious day room. There is a licensed bar area, comfortable lounge and a breakfast room leading to the extensive terraced gardens. The landscaping includes Koi lily ponds with cascading waterfalls and a fountain, there is also a swimming pool and views over Old Hastings to the sea.

All the bedrooms are beautifully decorated and have four poster beds and antique furniture. Four of the bedrooms have spacious en suite shower rooms with modern fittings.

## RECOMMENDED IN THE AREA

**RESTAURANT:**
*Röser's Restaurant, Hastings & St Leonards*

**TRADITIONAL PUB:**
*Queens Head, Icklesham*

**VISIT:**
*1066 Story of Hastings, Hastings*

# *O*ld Corner Cottage

*Extended period cottage in a village setting*

☎ 01435 863787

**Map ref 4 - TQ52**

Little London Road, HEATHFIELD,
East Sussex, TN21 0LT
A267 towards Heathfield, 1st right past
Cross in Hand pub, signposted Horam &
Eastbourne into Little London Rd
3 Rooms, £, No smoking

## RECOMMENDED IN THE AREA

**RESTAURANT:**
*Buxted Park, Uckfield*

**TRADITIONAL PUB:**
*Star Inn, Old Heathfield*

**VISIT:**
*Bateman's, Burwash*

A warm welcome is assured at this pretty cottage from Cynthia Brown, who offers hospitality of the highest standard. Corner Cottage is located close to the village centre, and makes a convenient base from which to visit Eastbourne, Beachy Head, Hastings and Brighton. There are also several notable houses and gardens within a short drive. Half a mile distant is the start of the Cuckoo Trail cycle track, on the old railway line, which runs from Heathfield to Polegate through pretty countryside.

The bedrooms are spacious and comfortably appointed with many thoughtful extras. All of the rooms have modern en suite facilities. A generous breakfast is served in the charming dining room, including a variety of cereals, fruit and yoghurt as well the traditional English breakfast with toast and preserves. Guests can relax in the well furnished conservatory lounge overlooking the attractive garden.

# Wartling Place

*A Georgian country house, formerly a rectory, set in two acres of mature secluded gardens*

☎ 01323 832590
📠 01323 832590
✉ accom@wartling place.prestel.co.uk

**Map ref 4 - TQ61**

Wartling Place, Wartling, HERSTMONCEUX, East Sussex, BN27 1RY
A271 signed Herstmonceux, after Windmill Hill turn right, follow signs Wartling village, Wartling Pl is on right
3 Rooms, ££
No smoking

Formerly the rectory for the Parish of Wartling, this listed period property has been carefully refurbished to provide accommodation of the highest quality. The standard of the furnishings and décor are matched by equally high levels of hospitality and service. Two of the bedrooms have four-poster beds and have a bath and shower en suite, tea and coffee making facilities, remote control colour televisions and hairdryers. Guests can relax in the stylish comfort of the drawing room and a fine breakfast is served in the elegant dining area. Wartling Place is set in extensive mature gardens, with some impressive trees, and private parking is provided within the grounds. The house is ideally situated for visiting many historic towns, castles, and National Trust houses and gardens in the South East. Golf, tennis, riding, walking, cycling and watersports can all be enjoyed in the immediate vicinity and the town of Eastbourne is just five miles away.

## RECOMMENDED IN THE AREA

**RESTAURANT:**
*Sundial Restaurant, Herstmonceux*

**TRADITIONAL PUB:**
*The Merrie Harriers, Cowbeech*

**VISIT:**
*The Truggery, Herstmonceux*

# Nightingales

*Fantastic gardens at the foot of the South Downs*

☎ 01273 475673  📠 01273 475673

**Map ref 3 - TQ41**

The Avenue, Kingston, LEWES, East Sussex, BN7 3LL
2.5m SW of Lewes, off A27 signed Kingston, right after 30mph sign
2 Rooms, ££, No smoking

Nightingales is situated in a quiet country road, surrounded by beautifully kept gardens that are part of the National Garden Scheme. Guests are free to explore the grounds, perhaps in the company of Geoff and Jean's black labrador, Ben, and to admire the exotic plants in the conservatory, where tea can be served.

The bedrooms are comfortably furnished, both with en suite facilities, and have colour television and tea and coffee making facilities for guests. The range of thoughtful extras in the rooms includes fresh fruit, flowers, chocolate and sherry.

Dinner is not available but Geoff and Jean are happy to recommend local restaurants and a 15th-century real ale pub nearby.

### RECOMMENDED IN THE AREA

**RESTAURANT:**
*Whytes, Brighton*

**TRADITIONAL PUB:**
*The Juggs, Kingston near Lewes*

**VISIT:**
*Anne of Cleves House Museum, Lewes*

# Cadborough Farm

*Spacious farmhouse with stunning views across Rye to the sea*

☎ 01797 225426  📠 01797 224097
📧 apperly@zoom.co.uk

**Map ref 4 - TQ92**

Udimore Road, RYE, East Sussex, TN31 6AA
on B2089
5 Rooms, ££, No smoking
Closed 24-26, 31 Dec-1 Jan

Cadborough Farm, first built in the 18th century, stands in an excellent position above the Brede Valley, with a south-facing patio to enjoy the panoramic view. There is ample parking.

The bedrooms are sunny and comfortable, with fresh flowers, sweets, home-made biscuits, books and magazines: three are in the main house; one has a private shower room, the others have sparkling en suite bathrooms with lovely, big bath sheets. Self-catering accommodation is also available in a converted dairy and stables.

There is a beamed sitting room, with family photos on the grand piano, and a separate breakfast room, where you can start your day with a delicious spread which includes fresh eggs from the farm's own free range hens. The house is warmed by central heating, and open fires in winter, and the atmosphere is cosy and relaxed all the year long.

### RECOMMENDED IN THE AREA

**RESTAURANT:**
*Netherfield Place, Battle*

**TRADITIONAL PUB:**
*The Ypres Castle, Rye*

**VISIT:**
*Lamb House, Rye*

# Jeake's House

*17th-century former wool store situated on one of Rye's ancient cobbled streets*

☎ 01797 222828
📠 01797 222623
📧 jeakeshouse@
btinternet.com

**Map ref 4 - TQ92**

Mermaid Street, RYE, East Sussex, TN31 7ET within cobbled medieval town centre, approach from High St or The Strand Quay

12 Rooms, ££

*A* fine old building in one of the most beautiful parts of Rye, Jeake's House dates from 1689 and during its colourful history it has been both a wool store and a Baptist school. In the early 20th century it was the home of American poet and author Conrad Potter Aiken and was the setting for many a literary get-together. The house is owned and run by Jenny Hadfield who offers guest accommodation of a high standard. The comfortable public rooms include an oak beamed lounge and a book lined bar where guests can relax over a drink. The original galleried chapel has been converted into a dining room where a traditional country breakfast is served. A vegetarian option is also available. The bedrooms are individually styled with sumptuous furnishings. Nine rooms have en suite facilities, and all offer telephones, televisions and hospitality trays. There is the added advantage of a private car park nearby.

## RECOMMENDED IN THE AREA

**RESTAURANT:**
*Netherfield Place, Battle*

**TRADITIONAL PUB:**
*The Ypres Castle, Rye*

**VISIT:**
*Rye Castle, Rye*

# King Charles II Guest House

*This unique medieval house was once a refuge of King Charles II*

☎ **01797 224954**

**Map ref 4 - TQ92**

4 High Street, RYE,
East Sussex, TN31 7JE
centrally located in Rye
High St
3 Rooms, ££
No smoking

## RECOMMENDED IN THE AREA

**RESTAURANT:**
*Rosers Restaurant, Hastings & St Leonards*

**TRADITIONAL PUB:**
*Queens Head, Icklesham*

**VISIT:**
*Rye Castle, Rye*

Known locally as the Black Boy because of its association with King Charles II, this listed, half-timbered building dates back to 1420. In the 1930s it was home to the writer Radclyffe Hall. The house has been sensitively restored by Margrit Berger and Nicola Fischbach, with antique furniture and fine quality fabrics and furnishings. Old black beams and ancient brick fireplaces are a feature of the day rooms, and fresh flowers are always arranged throughout the house. The three comfortable bedrooms combine historic charm with modern convenience. Comforting extras include mineral water and magazines. There is a small walled patio garden displaying an abundance of flowers in the summer. Dinner is not available here, but Nicola and Margrit are happy to recommend local restaurants to suit all tastes. They are also able to advise guests on local history and places of interest. There is restricted on road parking opposite the guest house and a public car park nearby.

# Manor Farm Oast

*Rest and excellent food with orchards all around*

☎ 01424 813787  📠 01424 813787
✉ manor.farmoast@lineone.net
**Map ref 4 - TQ92**

Windmill Orchard, Workhouse Lane, RYE,
East Sussex, TN36 4AJ
A259 from Rye (Hastings rd), in Icklesham
pass church on left, left into Workhouse
Lane. After sharp left bend turn left
3 Rooms, ££, No smoking
Closed 28 Dec-31 Jan

## RECOMMENDED IN THE AREA

**RESTAURANT:**
*Mermaid Inn, Rye*

**TRADITIONAL PUB:**
*Queens Head, Icklesham*

**VISIT:**
*Lamb House, Rye*

*B*uilt in 1860, and still surrounded by a working orchard, on the edge of the village, Manor Farm Oast is ideally situated for rest and relaxation, quiet breaks and country walks. It has been carefully converted keeping the unusual original features both inside and out, the double bedroom inside one of the oast towers is completely round.

Owner Kate Mylrea provides a very friendly welcome. Guests can enjoy tea and home made cake in one of the two lounges. Kate is passionate about food and as well as a traditional English breakfast or a healthier alternative, she will prepare a top quality five-course dinner by arrangement, all exquisitely presented.

Two of the rooms are en suite; all have colour TV and lots of thoughtful extras, such as bathrobes, home made biscuits, bottled water and fresh flowers.

# Playden Cottage Guesthouse

*Peaceful setting on the edge of a medieval town*

☎ 01797 222234
**Map ref 4 - TQ92**

Military Road, RYE, East Sussex, TN31 7NY
leave Rye in direction of Appledore, Playden Cottage is last house on left, at the de-limit sign
3 Rooms, ££
Nov-Mar, every 3rd night free

## RECOMMENDED IN THE AREA

**RESTAURANT:**
*Landgate Bistro, Rye*

**TRADITIONAL PUB:**
*The Ypres Castle, Rye*

**VISIT:**
*Rye Castle, Rye*

*T*he cottage stands on the old Saxon shore, where there was once a busy fishing harbour, the sea has since receded. Two bedrooms, 'Wysteria' and 'Hornbeam', look across the River Rother, towards the sheep on the Romney Marsh; the other, 'Badger', looks towards woodland. All the bedrooms have en suite shower rooms with hand-painted Rye tiles.

Breakfasts are wholesome, served in healthy portions, English or continental, with local soft fruits and home made preserves. Dinner, or a lighter supper menu, is available by arrangement. The sitting room has plenty of books and a piano. The garden door leads to a patio in the rose garden, with a barbecue you can hire on summer evenings. There is also a writing room and log fires in the Long Room in winter. The house is furnished with antiques in country cottage style, and you can expect a warm welcome.

# The Old Vicarage Guest House

*Outstanding breakfasts in a Georgian house on a cobbled square*

☎ 01797 222119  📠 01797 227466

**Map ref 4 - TQ92**

66 Church Square, RYE, East Sussex, TN31 7HF
from A259 follow town, enter at Landgate Arch, 3rd left in High St (West St), by St Mary's Church footpath to Vicarage
5 Rooms, ££, No smoking in bedrooms
Closed 24-26 Dec

The Old Vicarage is an elegant detached property surrounded by glorious pink roses and overlooked by the Church of St Mary's; it is right in the town centre, but free from traffic and noise. The rooms have wonderful views of the medieval houses and cobbled streets.

Breakfast is a leisurely, gastronomic extravaganza, with home made jams and marmalade, scones and crusty caraway bread hot from the oven, along with wholesome local produce. This is served in the dining room, looking out over the pretty walled garden. In the bedrooms, Laura Ashley prints and fabrics in country style set off the Georgian architecture. All bedrooms have en suite bathroom facilities, colour TV, books and information packs, and a hot drinks tray with homemade fudge and biscuits. In the evening you can sip a glass of sherry in the guest lounge. There is a blazing log fire in winter.

## RECOMMENDED IN THE AREA

**RESTAURANT:**
*Landgate Bistro, Rye*

**TRADITIONAL PUB:**
*Queens Head, Icklesham*

**VISIT:**
*Great Dixter, Northiam*

# Highlands

*Georgian country house with extensive grounds and fine views*

☎ 01825 890788  📠 01825 890803

**Map ref 3 - TQ42**

Framfield, UCKFIELD, East Sussex, TN22 5SA
A22 to Uckfield, signs to B2102. Just before Framfield, left at Hammonds Green, lane signed Buxted, house 500yds on right
2 Rooms, ££, No smoking
Closed 20 Dec-7 Jan

Reached by a winding country lane, this lovely old house is Georgian in appearance though some parts date back 400 years. The guest bedrooms are located in the 17th-century section, and these are both fully en suite. Tea and coffee making facilities are provided and television can be put in the rooms if required.

In addition to the full cooked breakfast, home-made scones and home-produced honey are served. Dinner and children's high teas are available by prior arrangement, and for dinner guests are asked to bring their own wine. There is a guest living room with an open fire and a grand piano.

The nine acres of grounds include attractive gardens, woodland, an arboretum and a paddock. Pets cannot be accommodated, but children of all ages are welcome.

## RECOMMENDED IN THE AREA

**RESTAURANT:**
*Horsted Place, Uckfield*

**TRADITIONAL PUB:**
*Blackboys Inn, Blackboys*

**VISIT:**
*Sheffield Park Garden, Sheffield Park*

# Hooke Hall

*Elegant, recently restored Queen Anne town house*

☎ 01825 761578  📠 01825 768025

**Map ref 3 - TQ42**

250 High Street UCKFIELD, East Sussex,
TN22 1EN
N end of Uckfield High St
10 Rooms, ££
Closed 25 Dec-1 Jan

Built in the early 18th century, this classic Queen Anne property is situated at the north end of the town. It has been carefully restored to provide comfortable accommodation in stylishly decorated bedrooms, which are named after celebrated lovers and mistresses. All of the rooms are fitted with en suite facilities and are equipped with televisions and direct dial telephones.

The public rooms feature panelled walls, antique furnishings, and welcoming open fires in winter. A fine array of paintings and other interesting pieces add to the effect. The study is a particularly inviting retreat, with its well stocked bar featuring a range of malt whiskies. Breakfast is served in an attractive room, from where french windows open onto a delightful terrace and garden. A good choice of restaurants is available within easy reach of Hooke Hall.

## RECOMMENDED IN THE AREA

**RESTAURANT:**
*Buxted Park, Uckfield*

**TRADITIONAL PUB:**
*Griffin Inn, Fletching*

**VISIT:**
*Bluebell Railway at Sheffield Park Station*

---

# The Old Oast Bed and Breakfast

*Converted oast house serving organic food at breakfast*

☎ 01825 766668  📠 01825 766669
✉ stay@oldoast.demon.co.uk

**Map ref 3 - TQ42**

Underhill, Maresfield, UCKFIELD,
East Sussex, TN22 3AY
from centre of Maresfield at mini-rdbt, north
200yds, right into steep bend, right into
Underhill. Past lake, house left
3 Rooms, ££, No smoking

## RECOMMENDED IN THE AREA

**RESTAURANT:**
*Winston Manor, Crowborough*

**VISIT:**
*Bluebell Railway at Sheffield Park Station*

John and Julie Belham-Payne have carefully restored this beautiful old oast house, which is set in four acres of secluded gardens and woodland in an area of outstanding natural beauty.

John has a keen eye for interior design and this is reflected in the charming bedrooms. All the rooms are exceptionally well equipped with lots of thoughtful extras. One room is located in the roundel of the oast, and another is suitable for family occupation and offers en suite facilities. There is a comfortable sitting room with luxurious sofas, an inglenook fireplace, satellite television and a huge collection of videos and music. The heated swimming pool is available to guests in the summer

Levels of hospitality are really special, and organic breakfasts are a special feature. All tastes are catered for, including vegetarian and special diets. Children under five cannot be accommodated.

# Crossways

*Fabulous food in a Georgian House in the heart of the glorious Cuckmere Valley*

☎ 01323 482455
📠 01323 487811
✉ crossways@
fastnet.co.uk
**Map ref 4 - TQ50**

Lewes Road,
WILMINGTON, East
Sussex, BN26 5SG
A27 between Lewes
and Polegate,
2m E of Alfriston rdbt
7 Rooms, ££
Closed 24 Dec-23 Jan

## RECOMMENDED IN THE AREA

**TRADITIONAL PUB:**
*Cricketers Arms, Berwick*

**VISIT:**
*Michelham Priory,
Hailsham*

Carved into the chalk of the South Downs, the famous Neolithic 'Long Man of Wilmington' gazes down at the pretty white front and blue shutters of Crossways. The house is set back from the road in two acres of neat informal gardens, complete with a small pond and resident ducks - with a bit of luck they will greet you on arrival. Even if the ducks fail to oblige, the resident proprietors always provide a friendly welcome to this restaurant with rooms. The elegant dining room serves food to a high standard - there is plenty to choose from on the fixed-price four course menu, and it changes every month. The rooms are well worth the stay; they all have en suite bathrooms and are equipped with a host of thoughtful extras including mini-bars, direct-dial phones and even a TV programme guide.

**151**

# Lains Cottage

*A pretty lime-washed thatched house in a large cottage garden*

☎ 01264 889697 📠 01264 889227
✉ lains-cott-hols@dial.pipex.com
**Map ref 3 - SU34**

Quarley, ANDOVER, Hampshire, SP11 8PX
from Andover A303 W, after 5m exit for
Quarley, left at T-junct. Right after 200yds
(Cholderton Ln), cottage on right
3 Rooms, £, No smoking
Closed 22 Dec-6 Jan

Parts of this delightful cottage date back to the 17th century. It is situated in the quiet village of Quarley, a convenient location in central southern England. The building has been carefully restored to combine modern comforts with traditional style. Mrs Angela Hicks, the resident owner, welcomes guests with the warmth and hospitality you can expect from an AA Landlady of the Year Finalist.

The cottage is pleasantly uncluttered and painted in light, warm pastel shades, with the finest wooden antique furniture. A polished wooden staircase leads up from the large hall, where there is a comfortable sofa and fireplace; to a gallery and bedrooms, all with en suite facilities.

Mrs Hicks prepares a choice of breakfasts, served around one table in the beamed dining room. From the dining room, French windows look onto the picturesque garden, with its enchanting lily pond.

## RECOMMENDED IN THE AREA

**RESTAURANT:**
*Fifehead Manor, Middle Wallop*

**TRADITIONAL PUB:**
*Red Lion Hotel, Clanville*

**VISIT:**
*Museum of Army Flying, Middle Wallop*

---

# Thatched Cottage Hotel & Restaurant

*400 year old cottage, old-fashioned charm and top cuisine*

☎ 01590 623090 📠 01590 623479
✉ thatchedcottagehotel@email.msn.com
**Map ref 3 - SU30**

16 Brookley Road, BROCKENHURST,
Hampshire, SO42 7RR
from M27 J1, S on A337 thro' Lyndhurst to
Brockenhurst, right just before level crossing
5 Rooms, £££
Closed 4-31 Jan

This timber-framed cottage is located in the village, within easy walking distance of the open heathland and woods of the New Forest. The bedrooms have antiques, lace bed linen, fresh and dried flowers. Some lack size, but each one is expertly designed, with features such as an open-hearth gas fireplace, four-poster bed or Turkish steam shower, all have luxury bathrooms and amenities. There is a snug rustic lounge with open fire. The vaulted restaurant has an open country kitchen, lace tablecloths and canaries warbling to classical music.

Breakfast, with an array of goodies, including American pancakes and eggs benedictine, is served until 11am, in bed if you wish. Lunches and cream teas can be taken under parasols in the garden. A range of fine cuisine is available for dinner from Tuesday to Saturday. You can also have a hamper packed for a picnic in the forest.

## RECOMMENDED IN THE AREA

**TRADITIONAL PUB:**
*Fleur de Lys, Pilley*

**VISIT:**
*Beaulieu National Motor Museum, Beaulieu*

# The Cottage Hotel

*350 year old forester's cottage in the New Forest*

☎ 01590 622296 🖷 01590 623014

**Map ref 3 - SU30**

Sway Road, BROCKENHURST, Hampshire,
SO42 7SH
from Lyndhurst on A337, right at Careys
Manor (Grigg Lane). 0.5m to x-rds, straight
over, cottage by war memorial
7 Rooms, ££, No smoking in bedrooms
Closed Dec-Jan

This small hotel, with its own charming garden and patio, and residents' car park, is just 200 yards from open forest and the centre of Brockenhurst. This is one of the few New Forest villages where ponies and cattle still have right of way as they roam and graze the land.

The Cottage Hotel is open from February to November. The owners have a dog, so check with them if you want to bring yours. There are no facilities for children under ten. Low ceilings, oak beams, and the open fire in the snug lounge with bar, give the place all the character of a traditional cottage.

The bedrooms are fresh and cosy, all with en suite bathrooms. The owners are happy to lend you binoculars, books, and boules for the garden. A hearty English breakfast is served, as well as afternoon tea (on the patio in summer), and dinner by appointment.

## RECOMMENDED IN THE AREA

**RESTAURANT:**
*Le Poussin, Brockenhurst*

**TRADITIONAL PUB:**
*Master Builders Hotel, Bucklers Hard*

**VISIT:**
*New Forest Museum & Visitor Centre, Lyndhurst*

# Walnut Cottage

*Victorian forester's cottage on the edge of the New Forest*

☎ 023 8081 2275 🖷 023 8081 2275

**Map ref 3 - SU31**

Old Romsey Road, CADNAM, Hampshire,
SO40 2NP
at Cadnam rdbt take A3090, Old Romsey Rd
is first on left
3 Rooms, £, No smoking
Closed 24-26 Dec

Eric and Charlotte Osgood extend a really warm and friendly welcome to guests at this charming cottage. It is an ideal base from which to explore the New Forest and the many places of interest in the area. Maps, guide books and even bicycles are available for guests' use. A comfortable lounge is provided, and a cosy dining room where hearty breakfasts are served. There are several pubs nearby where good meals are available for lunch or dinner.

The bedrooms are comfortable and well equipped, all of them have modern en suite facilities, colour televisions and hospitality trays. A twin bedded room is located on the ground floor and has direct access to the lovely garden. Children under the age of 14 cannot be accommodated, and neither can dogs, (with the exception of guide dogs).

## RECOMMENDED IN THE AREA

**RESTAURANT:**
*Les Mirabelles, Nomansland*

**TRADITIONAL PUB:**
*The White Hart, Cadnam*

**VISIT:**
*Furzey Gardens, Minstead*

# *A*lderholt Mill

## *Working water mill convenient for the New Forest*

☎ 01425 653130  📠 01425 652868
✉ alderholtmill@zetnet.co.uk

**Map ref 3 - SU11**

Sandleheath Road, FORDINGBRIDGE, Hampshire, SP6 1PU
M27 J1, B3078 thro' Fordingbridge towards Damerham/Sandleheath. Left at x-rds in Sandleheath, 0.5m over bridge, on right
4 Rooms, £, No smoking

*O*ne of the many pleasures of staying at Alderholt Mill is the home-baked bread, made from wholemeal flour stone ground in the water mill that forms part of this delightful property. All the machinery is still intact and guests can watch milling demonstrations.

Bedrooms are individually decorated and furnished and all have en suite facilities. A comfortable lounge is also provided. The dining room is decorated in lovely bold colours, and a super breakfast is served around one large table. Dinner is available by prior arrangement.

This is the ideal spot from which to discover the New Forest with its wonderful walks and cycle paths. The Wiltshire Downs and Dorset coast are also within easy reach. Resident proprietors Sandra and Richard Harte will be there at the end of the day to make sure that guests are relaxed and well taken care of.

## RECOMMENDED IN THE AREA

**TRADITIONAL PUB:**
*The Augustus John, Fordingbridge*

**VISIT:**
*Roman Villa, Rockbourne*

---

# *T*he Three Lions

## *Restaurant with rooms set in extensive gardens*

☎ 01425 652489  📠 01425 656144

**Map ref 3 - SU11**

Stuckton, FORDINGBRIDGE, Hampshire, SP6 2HF
0.5m E of Fordingbridge from A338 or B3078. At Q8 garage follow Three Lions tourist signs
3 Rooms, ££, No smoking in bedrooms
Closed 18 Jan-12 Feb

*T*he Three Lions began life as a farmhouse in 1863, it later became a pub and in the 1980s a restaurant of some repute. These days it is widely known and celebrated for the excellent cuisine of chef Michael Womersley. The establishment, owned and run by Michael and his wife Jayne, is quietly located in the hamlet of Stuckton, near Fordingbridge, on the edge of the New Forest.

A cosy bar area leads into the restaurant, where a log fire is lit in cooler weather. Michael creates outstanding dishes using the freshest ingredients. His menu reflects international influences and is supported by a selection of fine wines from his cellar of some 150 bins. Accommodation in the Lions' Den comprises light and airy double rooms with modern furniture and bold fabrics. The house is surrounded by two and a half acres of gardens, including a hot tub, ideal for an hour's relaxation.

## RECOMMENDED IN THE AREA

**VISIT:**
*Moors Valley Country Park, Ringwood*

# Fritham Farm

*18th-century farmhouse in the heart of the New Forest*

☎ 023 8081 2333  📠 023 8081 2333

**Map ref 3 - SU21**

FRITHAM, Hampshire, SO43 7HH
leave M27 junct 1 and follow signs to
Fritham
3 Rooms, £, No smoking
Closed Nov-Mid Feb

Mrs Hankinson welcomes guests to this delightful and ideally located farmhouse. It is a working farm with 51 acres of grassland where guests will see ponies, cows and sheep, and their young in season. This is a lovely area of the New Forest, rich in wildlife, where the famous forest ponies wander freely. Maps and guide books are available at the farm for guests to use.

The attractive bedrooms are traditionally furnished with en suite facilities and particularly comfortable beds. The rooms all have tea and coffee making equipment, hairdryers and radio alarms. Guests sit down to freshly prepared farmhouse breakfasts at one large table in the cosy dining room. There is also a spacious lounge with a television. Ample parking space is provided and bikes can be safely stored in one of the stables. Good food is available at a number of places in the vicinity.

## RECOMMENDED IN THE AREA

**RESTAURANT:**
*Parkhill Hotel, Lyndhurst*

**TRADITIONAL PUB:**
*Bell Inn, Brook*

**VISIT:**
*Furzey Gardens, Minstead*

*Beauclette Marina, Guernsey*

# Efford Cottage

*Georgian property in a village close to the New Forest*

☎ 01590 642315
🖷 01590 641030/642315
📧 effcottage@aol.com
**Map ref 3 - SZ39**

Milford Road, Everton, LYMINGTON,
Hampshire, SO41 0JD
on A337, 2m W of Lymington
3 Rooms, £, No smoking in bedrooms

*T*his charming, spacious, Georgian cottage offers high class, luxury en suite accommodation for the discerning guest. The large, well-equipped bedrooms contain many extra luxuries such as a fridge and hairdryer.

Patricia, the proprietor, is a qualified chef. She prepares fresh four course breakfasts from an extensive standard menu, as well as specialities including such delights as Kedgeree, cheese, herb, and mushroom egg cocotte, and pancakes with fresh seasonal fruit. All this is accompanied by home made bread and preserves, using home grown produce when available.

Guests may relax in the large Georgian drawing room, or in the garden which covers an acre. There is ample parking. You are assured of a warm welcome and a friendly stay, the motto of Efford Cottage is 'your comfort is our concern'.

## RECOMMENDED IN THE AREA

**RESTAURANT:**
*Gordleton Mill, Lymington*

**TRADITIONAL PUB:**
*The Chequers Inn, Lower Woodside*

**VISIT:**
*Exbury Gardens, Exbury*

# Jevington

*Attractive property in a quiet residential area of Lymington*

☎ 01590 672148  🖷 01590 672148
**Map ref 3 - SZ39**

47 Waterford Lane, LYMINGTON, Hampshire,
SO41 3PT
from High St, right at St Thomas Church into Church Lane. Take left fork into Waterford Lane
3 Rooms, £, No smoking

## RECOMMENDED IN THE AREA

**RESTAURANT:**
*Stanwell House Hotel, Lymington*

**TRADITIONAL PUB:**
*East End Arms, East End*

**VISIT:**
*National Motor Museum, Beaulieu*

*D*uring the summer months, guests will be enticed into this pretty house by the colourful display of climbing roses and hanging baskets. The house is ideally placed for walking to all parts of Lymington, including the town centre and the marinas. There are plenty of good places to eat nearby, and friendly resident proprietors Mr and Mrs Carruthers are happy to make suggestions as to where to go.

The peaceful bedrooms are decorated in a pleasant and engaging style, with co-ordinating fabrics adding to the pleasing effect. The rooms also have smart en suite bathrooms with quality fittings. An appetising breakfast is served in the attractive open plan dining room and lounge.

# *T*he Old Barn

*Beautiful barn conversion close to Lymington and the New Forest*

📞 01590 644939   📠 01590 644939

**Map ref 3 - SZ39**

Christchurch Road, Downton, LYMINGTON, Hampshire, SO41 0LA
on A337 approx 3m from Lymington, approx 1m after Everton Nurseries on right near Royal Oak Pub
2 Rooms, £, No smoking

*J*ulie and Simon Benford warmly welcome guests to their beautiful home, which is a carefully converted 17th-century barn.

The bedrooms are stylishly decorated, thoughtfully appointed and feature spacious en suite bathrooms equipped with power showers. Televisions are also provided in the rooms.

Breakfast is served around the farmhouse table in the attractive dining room, with a choice between the traditional full cooked English meal or a lighter continental alternative.

At the end of the day guests can relax in the comfortable lounge. A good choice of places to eat is available in the area, particularly in nearby Lymington.

## RECOMMENDED IN THE AREA

**RESTAURANT:**
*Master Builders House, Bucklers Hard*

**TRADITIONAL PUB:**
*East End Arms, East End*

**VISIT:**
*Exbury Gardens, Exbury*

# *A*mberwood

*Detached Victorian house in a peaceful residential setting*

📞 01425 476615   📠 01425 476615

**Map ref 3 - SU10**

3/5 Top Lane, RINGWOOD, Hampshire, BH24 1LF
2 Rooms, £
No smoking in bedrooms

*A*nne and Graham Maynard warmly welcome guests to their comfortable home, which is quietly but conveniently located three minutes' walk from the centre of Ringwood and all its amenities. The town itself is on the periphery of the New Forest, and within easy reach of Bournemouth and the south coast.

Each of the bedrooms is attractively furnished and decorated, one has an en suite shower room, while the other has its own bathroom next door. High standards of cooking are maintained, and breakfast is served in the lovely conservatory, which overlooks a beautiful garden. A choice of inviting sitting rooms is also available to guests.

## RECOMMENDED IN THE AREA

**RESTAURANT:**
*Les Bouviers, Wimborne Minster*

**TRADITIONAL PUB:**
*The Struan Country Inn, Ringwood*

**VISIT:**
*Moors Valley Country Park, Ringwood*

# Little Forest Lodge

*Hospitable hotel conveniently located in the New Forest*

☎ 01425 478848  📠 01425 473564

**Map ref 3 - SU10**

Poulner Hill, RINGWOOD, Hampshire,
BH24 3HS
1.5m E on A31
6 Rooms, ££, No smoking in bedrooms

Little **Forest Lodge**

where guests can enjoy a drink in summer. Judith offers a choice of honest home-cooked food in the beautiful panelled dining room, including delicious home-baked bread and fresh fish, organic meat, New Forest sausages and free range eggs from good local suppliers. Vegetarian and other dietary requirements can be met. Children are welcome, and dogs by prior arrangement.

*T*he Lodge is a charming small hotel in a quiet situation just off the east bound carriageway of the A31, ideal for exploring the New Forest. Judith Harrison extends a warm welcome to her guests, and makes sure that they are well cared for.

The attractively decorated bedrooms are all en suite and have colour television, tea, coffee and biscuits, toiletries and shoe cleaning materials. The garden room opens out onto the two-acre garden and can be let on a self-catering basis. There is a comfortable bar-lounge leading onto a terrace,

### RECOMMENDED IN THE AREA

**RESTAURANT:**
*Moortown Lodge, Ringwood*

**TRADITIONAL PUB:**
*Old Beams, Ibsley*

**VISIT:**
*Roman Villa, Rockbourne*

# The Old Cottage

*Thatched and beamed cottage in a rural setting*

☎ 01425 477956  📠 01425 477956

**Map ref 3 - SU10**

Cowpitts Lane, North Poulner, RINGWOOD,
Hampshire, BH24 3JX
3 Rooms, ££, No smoking
Closed Dec

*D*ating from the 17th century, this character cottage is set in one acre of attractive gardens, with excellent views of the New Forest. It provides a peaceful and relaxing base from which to visit the cities of Winchester, Salisbury and Southampton, and is convenient for Bournemouth and the south coast, all of which are within half an hour's reach. Activities such as riding, cycling, walking, swimming, and bird and animal watching are all easily accessible.

The house has been thoughtfully decorated and furnished in keeping with the architectural style. The charming bedrooms are comfortably appointed and well equipped with modern amenities, including an en suite bath and shower room in each. A freshly cooked breakfast is served in the elegant lounge/dining room.

### RECOMMENDED IN THE AREA

**RESTAURANT:**
*Royal Bath, Bournemouth*

**TRADITIONAL PUB:**
*Red Shoot Inn, Linwood*

**VISIT:**
*Moors Valley Country Park, Ringwood*

# The Nurse's Cottage

*Former District Nurse's Cottage offering delightful accommodation and an intimate restaurant*

☎ 01590 683402
🖷 01590 683402
✉ nurses.cottage @lineone.net

**Map ref 3 - SZ29**

Station Road, SWAY, Nr Lymington, Hampshire, SO41 6BA off B3055 in village next to post office
3 Rooms, ££
No smoking
Closed 15 Nov-15 Dec

*T*ony Barnfield, a former BBC radio presenter, the resident chef and owner, leads his young team of staff to provide warm, attentive service. His achievements have been recognised by a place among the top twenty finalists in the AA Landlady of the Year Awards for 1998 and 1999. The bedrooms are very comfortable, with many welcoming touches, such as biscuits, chocolates, fruit and fresh flowers, as well as a fridge with mineral water, fruit juices and fresh milk. All the rooms have full en suite bathrooms, quality toiletries and good fluffy towels. The tiny Garden Room restaurant, also open to non-residents, serves well prepared quality cuisine for dinner, Sunday Luncheon and Full Afternoon Teas. There is a well-stocked bar, and an impressive wine list including 26 half bottles and 13 wines by the glass. In summer, you can enjoy your drink in the pretty garden.

## RECOMMENDED IN THE AREA

**RESTAURANT:**
*Gordleton Mill, Lymington*

**TRADITIONAL PUB:**
*The Chequers Inn, Lymington*

**VISIT:**
*Buckler's Hard Village & Maritime Museum*

# Landguard Lodge

*Cosy, clean and comfortable accommodation in a quiet residential location, handy for amenities*

☎ 023 8063 6904  📠 023 8063 2258
📧 landguard.lodge@mail.com
**Map ref 3 - SU41**

21 Landguard Road, SOUTHAMPTON,
Hampshire, SO15 5DL
north of railway station between Hill Lane &
Shirley Road
10 Rooms, £, No smoking in bedrooms

## RECOMMENDED IN THE AREA

**RESTAURANT:**
*Botleigh Grange, Southammpton*

**TRADITIONAL PUB:**
*Old Horse & Jockey, Romsey*

**VISIT:**
*Southampton Maritime Museum*

*M*r McCowan warmly welcomes guests into this professionally run establishment, which is conveniently located for the city centre, ferry terminals and docks. Bedrooms are neatly laid out and freshly decorated. All bedrooms have en suite shower rooms and are equipped with colour televisions and tea and coffee making facilities. A pretty lounge is also provided for guests' use. The dining room faces east and attracts all the morning sunshine, a tasty breakfast is served here including a good choice of hot items. Children under five years cannot be accommodated, neither can dogs (with the exception of guide dogs). Some car parking is provided.

# May Cottage

*Period house and garden in pretty village*

☎ 01264 771241  📠 01264 771770
**Map ref 3 - SU24**

THRUXTON, Hampshire, SP11 8LZ
from A303 take sign Thruxton (village only),
situated between George Inn and post office
on opposite side
4 Rooms, £, No smoking
Closed Xmas

## RECOMMENDED IN THE AREA

**RESTAURANT:**
*The Vineyard at Stockcross*

**TRADITIONAL PUB:**
*The Mayfly, Stockbridge*

**VISIT:**
*Stonehenge*

*M*ay Cottage, dating back to 1740, is set in a pretty and secluded garden in the heart of Thruxton, yet only two minutes from the A303. This peaceful, picturesque village has a post office and two traditional pubs; 'The George Inn' and 'The White Horse Inn'. The cottage is most comfortably furnished, bedrooms have en suite or private facilities; a TV, radio, hairdryer and tea tray. Guests have their own sitting/dining room. This is a popular place for weekend breaks and overnight stays for visitors to the West Country, with good access to ports and airports. The cathedral cities of Salisbury and Winchester; the towns of Marlborough and Hungerford, and Stonehenge, are all nearby. There are also many stately homes and gardens in the area. Tom and Fiona are happy to help plan your stay and you are assured of a warm welcome. Ample private parking is provided, please note that this is a non smoking establishment.

# $\mathcal{B}$ettmans Oast

*Listed oast house and converted barn in glorious countryside*

☎ 01580 291463   📠 01580 291463

**Map ref 4 - TQ83**

Hareplain Road, BIDDENDEN, Kent,
TN27 8LJ
off A262 at Three Chimneys past telephone
box, house 0.5m on right
2 Rooms, ££, No smoking
Closed 23-30 Dec

$\mathcal{J}$anet Pickup extends a warm welcome to guests at Bettmans Oast, a traditional oast house and converted barn combined to provide the most attractive accommodation in a lovely rural setting. The large oak-beamed bedrooms have en suite facilities, and colour television and tea and coffee making equipment are provided in the rooms.

There is a comfortable guests' lounge, where log fires burn in the inglenook fireplace during the winter months. Full English breakfast is served, prepared from fresh produce including home produced free range eggs, home-made preserves, and honey from the proprietors' own bee hives.

The local pub, the Three Chimneys, is within walking distance, and the house is convenient for Sissinghurst Castle and Gardens.

### RECOMMENDED IN THE AREA

**RESTAURANT:**
*West House Restaurant, Biddenden*

**TRADITIONAL PUB:**
*The Three Chimneys, Biddenden*

**VISIT:**
*Sissinghurst Castle Garden, Sissinghurst*

# $\mathcal{B}$ishopsdale Oast

*Converted oast house in the lovely Weald of Kent*

☎ 01580 291027   📠 01580 292321
✉ bishopdale@pavilion.co.uk

**Map ref 4 - TQ83**

BIDDENDEN, Kent, TN27 8DR
A28, Tenterden-Rowenden rd, 1st right after
Tenterden (Cranbrook Rd), 2.5m, sign for
B&B on left, left and follow signs
4 Rooms, ££, No smoking in bedrooms

$\mathcal{T}$he house is typical of the architecture associated with one of Kent's most enjoyable contributions to society, hop growing. A warm welcome is offered by Mr and Mrs Drysdale, who make their guests feel very much at home.

The bedrooms are decorated with taste and style; all are en suite, and king-size beds, colour television, radio alarms and tea and coffee making facilities are provided.

The house is set in four acres of wild and cultivated gardens and is well located for visits to several nearby castles, houses and gardens. It is within easy reach of the Channel Tunnel, so a trip to France could figure on your itinerary. Dinner, served in the dining room or on the terrace, is a highlight including fresh vegetables from the garden. Guests might relax by a log fire in the sitting room or enjoy croquet on the lawn.

### RECOMMENDED IN THE AREA

**RESTAURANT:**
*West House Restaurant, Biddenden*

**TRADITIONAL PUB:**
*The Three Chimneys, Biddenden*

**VISIT:**
*Sissinghurst Castle, Sissinghurst*

# Magnolia House

*Late Georgian home near Canterbury
centre, with luxury four-poster suite*

☎ 01227 765121   📠 01227 765121
✉ magnolia_house_canterbury@
yahoo.com

**Map ref 4 - TR15**

36 St Dunstan's Terrace, CANTERBURY,
Kent, CT2 8AX
from A2 take turn for Canterbury. Left at 1st
rndbt approaching city (signed University).
3rd turn on right
7 Rooms, £££, No smoking

Ann and John Davies welcome guests to their home, just 10 minutes' stroll from the centre of Canterbury, with tea and biscuits on arrival. It is in a quiet residential street, with parking, and a walled garden that has been beautifully landscaped by John, with fish pond, terraces and shrubberies. Ann uses the garden herbs in her delicious cooking. Breakfast is a generous meal, catering for all diets, and includes home made preserves. Evening meals are available by prior arrangement from November to February.

There is a cosy lounge, and a dining room, overlooking the garden, with separate tables. All the bedrooms have en suite facilities and colour TV; the four-poster suite is perfect for an extra special occasion. Wallpaper with smart vertical stripes in the bedrooms, and fresh flower arrangements throughout the house give the place a bright touch of charm and elegance.

## RECOMMENDED IN THE AREA

**RESTAURANT:**
*The Dove, Dargate*

**TRADITIONAL PUB:**
*Fordwich Arms, Fordwich*

---

# Thanington Hotel

*Georgian house, close to centre, with
swimming pool and snooker*

☎ 01227 453227   📠 01227 453225
✉ thanington_hotel@
compuserve.com

*78 - 85£*

**Map ref 4 - TR15**

140 Wincheap, CANTERBURY, Kent,
CT1 3RY
on A28, just outside city walls
16 Rooms, ££

The Georgian architecture makes for rooms of generous proportions, emphasised by the neat, uncluttered furnishings, with ornate chandeliers and mirrors in the public rooms. Guests have use of a bar, drawing room and elegant breakfast room, where traditional English breakfast, as well as vegetarian and lighter options are served. Some bedrooms are in the main house, with queen size four-poster or antique Victorian bedsteads. Other bedrooms are in the extension, linked to the house by a conservatory; four are on the ground floor; and all have en suite facilities.

It is just 10 minutes' walk to the centre of the city, and plenty of restaurants. There is a secure car park. Guests enjoy the indoor heated swimming pool, with windows opening onto the sunny walled garden, and there is also a snooker room, darts board and other games.

## RECOMMENDED IN THE AREA

**RESTAURANT:**
*Read's, Faversham*

**TRADITIONAL PUB:**
*King William IV, Littlebourne*

**VISIT:**
*Canterbury Tales Visitor Attraction, Canterbury*

# The Oast

*Converted oasthouse with original beams on a working farm*

☎ 01580 712416  📠 01580 712416
✉ hallwoodfm@aol.com

**Map ref 4 - TQ73**

Hallwood Farm, CRANBROOK, Kent,
TN17 2SP
A229 from Cranbrook 1m. Past Duke of Kent
pub on left. Farm turning 400yds on right
2 Rooms, £, No smoking

Parts of the building, originally used for drying hops, date back to the 17th century. It is in a secluded and quiet position, at the end of a private lane.

These days it is the main farmhouse for the Wickham family who run a fruit and sheep farm of some 250 acres. There are excellent walks through the orchards and the pastures of the farm, or into neighbouring Bedgebury Forest. Children under ten, and pets are not allowed. There is ample parking. The bedrooms are light and spacious, both have modern en suite bathroom facilities, tea and coffee, colour TV and many thoughtful extras.

A full and varied farmhouse breakfast is served in the sunny dining room, with free range eggs and home made preserves.

## RECOMMENDED IN THE AREA

**RESTAURANT:**
*Soho South, Cranbrook*

**TRADITIONAL PUB:**
*The Peacock, Iden Green*

**VISIT:**
*Sissinghurst Castle, Sissinghurst*

# The Old Vicarage

*Former vicarage set in rolling countryside outside Dover*

☎ 01304 210668  📠 01304 225118
✉ vicarage@csi.com

**Map ref 4 - TR34**

Chilverton Elms, Hougham, DOVER, Kent,
CT15 7AS
M20/A20 towards Dover, Hougham exit. At
rndbt B2011 (West Hougham), then left. Thro'
Hougham towards Dover, 1m on left
3 Rooms, ££, No smoking in bedrooms

A delightful house ably run by proprietors Bryan and Judy Evison to the very highest standards. The property dates from around 1870 and enjoys a restful country situation, with green fields, woodland and open views, yet it is only two miles from the ferry ports of Dover and nine miles from the Channel Tunnel.

The spacious en suite rooms are decorated with taste and style, and guests are provided with a wealth of extra facilities. Breakfasts are served in the elegant dining room at a polished wooden table set with gleaming silver. There is a cosy lounge and the large gardens are well worth exploring. Secure parking is provided and dinner is available by arrangement.

## RECOMMENDED IN THE AREA

**RESTAURANT:**
*Wallett's Court, St Margaret's, Dover*

**TRADITIONAL PUB:**
*The Griffin's Head, Chillenden*

**VISIT:**
*Dover Castle & Hellfire Corner, Dover*

# Beulah House

*An imposing and elegantly furnished Victorian house close to local amenities*

☎ 01304 824615
🖷 828850
✉ owen@beulah house94.freeeserve. co.uk
**Map ref 4 - TR34**

94 Crabble Hill,
DOVER, Kent,
CT17 0SA
on A256
6 Rooms, £
No smoking

## RECOMMENDED IN THE AREA

**RESTAURANT:**
*Wallett's Court, Dover*

**TRADITIONAL PUB:**
*Griffins Head, Chillenden*

**VISIT:**
*Dover Castle*

*B*eulah House is a charming property set in an acre of magnificent topiary garden, within easy reach of the town centre, railway station, ferry port, cruise terminal and Channel Tunnel. The proprietor, Anita Owen, offers high standards of both accommodation and hospitality and the atmosphere is warm and welcoming. The bedrooms are generally spacious, attractively decorated and comfortably appointed. Three of the rooms have en suite facilities, all have colour television and tea and coffee making equipment. Children are welcome and family rooms are available. A generous breakfast is served in the elegant dining room, and at the end of the day guests can relax in the cosy lounge. There is also a conservatory overlooking the garden. Ample parking space is provided, and garaging if required.

# Ringlestone Inn & Farmhouse Hotel

*16th-century inn and a character farmhouse standing opposite each other in a tranquil rural setting*

☎ 01622 859900
🖷 01622 859966
✉ bookings@ringlestone.com

**Map ref 4 - TQ75**

Ringlestone Hamlet, Harrietsham, MAIDSTONE, Kent, ME17 1NX
M20 junct 8 onto A20. At rndbt opp Great Danes Hotel left to Hollingbourne. Thro' village, right at x-roads at top of hill
4 Rooms, ££
No smoking in bedrooms
Closed 25-Dec

## RECOMMENDED IN THE AREA

**RESTAURANT:**
*Le Soufflé Restaurant, Bearsted*

**TRADITIONAL PUB:**
*The Ringlestone Inn, Maidstone*

**VISIT:**
*Leeds Castle, Maidstone*

Built in 1533, the inn was originally a hospice for monks. It has delightful gardens, open grounds and wonderful old features such as an inglenook fireplace, oak beams and brick and flint walls. The dining room is a later addition, with tables made from the timbers of an 18th-century Thames barge. Traditional English pies and country wines are a feature of the inn, and wherever possible dishes are freshly prepared from local produce for the popular buffet lunches and candlelit suppers. Smart modern bedrooms are housed in the converted farmhouse opposite. These are furnished with quality and comfort in mind, with plenty of individual touches. All the rooms have en suite bathrooms, and one has a canopied four-poster bed. The farmhouse is also a useful venue for private meetings and dinner parties.

**165**

# Merzie Meadows

*A delightful house set in extensive grounds with a swimming pool*

☎ 01622 820500  📠 01622 820500

**Map ref 4 - TQ74**

Hunton Road, MARDEN, Kent, TN12 9SL
A229 Maidstone/Hastings rd, B2079
(Marden), 1st right (Underlyn Lane) 2m. Large
Chainhurst sign, right into drive
2 Rooms, £, No smoking

Merzie Meadows is in a peaceful area of Kent, yet accessible for Maidstone, Tonbridge, the Ashford connection for Eurostar trains to Paris and Brussels and the main routes for the channel ports. The gardens are very well-kept and designed to remain beautiful throughout the year, special features include the large trampoline and outdoor swimming pool (unheated).

The house itself is uniquely designed with two dining rooms and an open plan lounge with polished parquet flooring. Two bedrooms are en suite and

one is suitable for families. All have colour televisions and tea and coffee making facilities. The bedrooms are very tastefully decorated with some lovely furniture. The house is centrally heated and parking is available for guests. Children under 14 years cannot be accommodated.

## RECOMMENDED IN THE AREA

**RESTAURANT:**
*Kennel Holt, Cranbrook*

**TRADITIONAL PUB:**
*Star & Eagle, Goudhurst*

**VISIT:**
*Hop Farm & Country Park, Beltring*

# Danehurst House

*Victorian home with large conservatory breakfast room*

☎ 01892 527739  📠 01892 514804

**Map ref 4 - TQ53**

41 Lower Green Road, Rusthall, ROYAL
TUNBRIDGE WELLS, Kent, TN4 8TW
from Tunbridge Wells A264 W, 1.5m turn right
past Spa Hotel, right at x-rds, Lower Green
Rd 200yds on left
4 Rooms, ££, No smoking

Angela and Michael Godbold manage to provide their guests with the traditional luxuries of a Victorian house, as well as modern home comforts. The conservatory breakfast room is particularly delightful, a full English breakfast is served here with a good choice of dishes. The conservatory is also available for private meetings.

In the garden there is a pond with koi and a waterfall. Light refreshments are available throughout the day, taken on the terrace by the pond in summer. There is also an elegant drawing room with a grand piano and a library. The bedrooms are individually furnished in the style of the house; three have en suite bathrooms. The beds are large and of extremely good quality ensuring a good night's sleep.

## RECOMMENDED IN THE AREA

**RESTAURANT:**
*Hotel du Vin & Bistro, Tunbridge Wells*

**TRADITIONAL PUB:**
*Royal Wells Inn, Tunbridge Wells*

**VISIT:**
*A Day at the Wells, Tunbridge Wells*

# Hempstead House

*Private Victorian country house hotel and restaurant with heated outdoor pool*

☎ 01795 428020
📠 01795 436362
📧 hemphotel@aol.com

**Map ref 4 - TQ96**

London Road,
Bapchild,
SITTINGBOURNE,
Kent, ME9 9PP
on A2, 1.5m E of
Sittingbourne opposite
turning to Tonge
14 Rooms, ££, No
Smoking in bedrooms

*T*his luxurious country house hotel is set in three acres of mature landscaped gardens including a traditional croquet lawn, large outdoor pool surrounded by illuminated terraces, and childrens play area. The reception rooms are elegant and spacious, furnished with antiques and crystal chandeliers. There is a brand new 60 cover restaurant with an optional dance floor for functions and wedding receptions. The beautiful original Victorian dining room, with its huge polished mahogany table, is now used for private parties and conferences. A marquee is available for larger wedding receptions. All bedrooms are fully en suite with baths and separate showers. They also have colour television, direct dial telephones, tea and coffee making facilities, bathrobes and toiletries. An AA rosette award has been made for the quality of the food, which is a mixture of French and English cuisine, using fresh, local and home-grown produce. There is a very extensive wine list to complement the varied menu, the hotel is fully licensed.

## RECOMMENDED IN THE AREA

**RESTAURANT:**
*Reads, Faversham*

**TRADITIONAL PUB:**
*George Inn, Newnham*

**VISIT:**
*Dolphin Sailing Barge Museum, Sittingbourne*

167

# $S$andringham
## Hotel

*A stylish property in a prestigious location a short walk from Hampstead village*

☎ **020 7435 1569**
🖷 **020 7431 5932**
✉ **sandringham. hotel@virgin.net**

**Map 3**

3 Holford Road,
Hampstead, NW3,
London, NW3 1AD
from Hampstead Tube
right into Heath St,
4th right, 1st left into
Holford Rd
17 Rooms, £££, No
smoking in bedrooms

RECOMMENDED
IN THE AREA

**RESTAURANT:**
*Byron's Restaurant*

**TRADITIONAL PUB:**
*The Flask, London NW3*

**VISIT:**
*Fenton House,
London NW3*

*T*his impressive Victorian house is set in a quiet residential area. Manager Sybille de Warren provides a warm welcome and creates a relaxed home-from-home atmosphere. There is a comfortable lounge with an honesty bar, and the breakfast room overlooks a pretty walled garden. The bedrooms vary in size and are all elegantly appointed and equipped with televisions, direct-dial telephones and thoughtful extras such as mineral water and a decanter of sherry. Twenty-four hour room service is also available. Breakfast is not to be missed, with choices such as French toast, eggs Benedict, and smoked salmon with scrambled eggs, in addition to the traditional grill. Fresh juices and home-baked cakes are also a feature. There is a wide and varied choice of places to eat in the vicinity, and plenty to see and do.

# Five Sumner Place Hotel

*Elegant Victorian town house in the heart of South Kensington*

☎ 020 7584 7586
📠 020 7823 9962
✉ reservations@
sumnerplace.com

**Map 3**

5 Sumner Place, South
Kensington,
LONDON,
SW7 3EE
300yds from South
Kensington
underground
13 Rooms, £££

## RECOMMENDED IN THE AREA

**RESTAURANT:**
*Bistro 190, SW7*

**TRADITIONAL PUB:**
*Swag & Tails, SW7*

**VISIT:**
*Victoria & Albert Museum, SW7*

*T*his stylish small hotel forms part of an impressive terrace dating from around 1848. It has recently been completely refurbished to recapture its period atmosphere. Guests are given their own front door key so that they can come and go as they please, and make the most of the central location and all the sight-seeing and shopping opportunities in the vicinity.

The bedrooms are individually designed with an emphasis on traditional furnishings. All the rooms have en suite facilities and are equipped with colour television, radio, ironing board/trouser press, hairdryer and direct dial telephone. Some rooms also have a fridge. A full buffet breakfast is served in the superb Victorian conservatory, and complimentary newspapers are provided. Reception staff are happy to provide information to guests during their stay in the capital, and are able to book tours and theatre tickets, and arrange transfers to and from the airport.

# The Gallery Hotel

*Luxury and tradition in one of London's most exclusive 'town house' hotels, featuring original works of art throughout*

☎ 020 7915 0000
🖷 020 7915 4400
✉ gallery@
eeh.co.uk

**Map 3**

8-10 Queensberry Place, South Kensington, LONDON, SW7 2EA
off Cromwell Rd
opp Natural History Museum, Queensberry Place (S Kensington)
36 Rooms, £££

Originally two Georgian residences, The Gallery Hotel (part of the Elegant English Hotels group), stands in a prime position in South Kensington. The highest level of personal service is provided by a team of butlers 24 hours a day, setting you at ease in the opulent period surroundings. Facilities such as two-line direct dial telephone, with answering and message facility, and private fax lines make it suitable for business guests and leisure travellers. The lounge has the ambience of a private club, with rich mahogany panelling, unique mouldings, cornices and deep colours; there is also a drawing room where you can retire for some peace and quiet, play chess or backgammon, or write letters. The lavish bedrooms are all individually designed, with weave, texture, colour and print of fabrics and furnishings carefully co-ordinated; all have bathrooms, with marble tiling, brass fittings, soft white bath towels and robes.

## RECOMMENDED IN THE AREA

**RESTAURANT:**
*Hilaire, SW7*

**TRADITIONAL PUB:**
*Swag & Tails SW7*

**VISIT:**
*Science Museum, SW7*

*"The Trout" Pub, Godstow, Oxfordshire*

# $\mathcal{D}$inckley Court

*Former farmhouse in mature gardens
fronting the River Thames*

**☎ 01865 407763 📠 01865 407010**
**✉ annette@dinckleycourt.co.uk**

**Map ref 3 - SU49**

Burcot, ABINGDON, Oxfordshire, OX14 3DP
from M40 J7 take A329, right onto A4074
Oxford rd, then A415 to Abingdon
5 Rooms, £, No smoking

## RECOMMENDED IN THE AREA

**RESTAURANT:**
*Springs Hotel, Wallingford*

**TRADITIONAL PUB:**
*The Merry Miller, Abingdon*

**VISIT:**
*Didcot Railway Centre, Didcot*

$\mathcal{D}$inckley Court is a Victorian property set in 12 acres of grounds including a river frontage. The house has been carefully restored to provide comfortable accommodation for the modern business or leisure traveller. It is ideally situated for Oxford, Abingdon, Henley and routes to London. Fishing and boating facilities are available to guests. The cosy bedrooms have en suite bath and shower rooms, remote control televisions, and tea and coffee making equipment. Imaginative snacks and hot dishes are offered by room service, or dinner can be taken, by arrangement, in the homely kitchen at the large family table.

Annette Godfrey is a friendly and caring hostess, justifiably proud to welcome guests to her lovely home. Ample car parking is provided.

# Rafters

*Large modern half-timbered house in a pretty village setting close to major attractions*

☎ 01865 391298
✆ 391173

**Map ref 3 - SU49**

Abingdon Road,
ABINGDON,
Oxfordshire, OX13 6NU
from A34 take A415
towards Witney. Rafters
on right on A415 in
Marcham by 1st street
light on the right
3 Rooms, £
No Smoking

Situated a mile from the A34 with its links to Oxford and the south coast, this imposing detached house offers comfortable accommodation in a convenient and tranquil location. The spacious bedrooms are furnished in a mixture of British and Scandinavian styles. One room, a huge double with its own balcony, has a big en suite bathroom while the other two rooms have private facilities. All the rooms are equipped with colour television, radio alarms, tea and coffee making amenities and bathrobes. Accommodation is also available for children. Guests are warmly welcomed with a cup of tea and a piece of home-made cake on arrival. Farm fresh free range eggs (cooked any way you like) and locally cured bacon are just two of the choices from the breakfast menu, which includes vegetarian alternatives and delicious home-made preserves. Off street parking is provided.

## RECOMMENDED IN THE AREA

**RESTAURANT:**
*The Crazy Bear, Stadhampton*

**TRADITIONAL PUB:**
*Blewbury Inn, Blewbury*

**VISIT:**
*Didcot Railway Centre, Didcot*

# Burford House

*Top quality accommodation in a town house in the heart of the Cotswolds*

☎ 01993 823151
🅵 01993 823240

**Map ref 3 - SP21**

99 High Street,
BURFORD,
Oxfordshire, OX18 4QA
off A40 between
Cheltenham & Oxford,
signs for Burford.
Burford Hse on High St
7 Rooms, £££
No Smoking in
bedrooms

### RECOMMENDED IN THE AREA

**RESTAURANT:**
*The Inn for All Seasons, Burford*

**TRADITIONAL PUB:**
*Golden Pheasant, Burford*

**VISIT:**
*Cotswold Wildlife Park, Burford*

*I*n a wonderful location, right on the High Street of this picturesque town, is Burford House. The tidy exterior is part half-timbered, part mellow Cotswold stone, with hanging baskets full of pretty flowers. The bedrooms have been carefully decorated and furnished in wood to give each one unique characteristics. Some have four-poster beds, all have superb en suite bathrooms. Full English breakfasts are served in the elegant dining room, as well as light meals (also available for non-residents) and homemade cakes with tea. There are two sitting rooms with comfortable sofas and open fires. In fine weather you might want to sit out in the walled flower garden. The resident hosts offer a personal, professional service - they are attentive to every detail, and nothing is too much trouble to ensure that a visit to their lovely home is a happy, memorable one.

# Lenwade

*Attractive Victorian family home in a quiet residential area*

☎ 01491 573468  📠 01491 573468
✉ lenwadeuk@compuserve.com

## Map ref 3 - SU78

3 Western Road, HENLEY-ON-THAMES,
Oxfordshire, RG9 1JL
leaving Henley take Reading Rd, turn right
into St Andrews Rd, over x-rds, left into
Western Rd, premises on left
3 Rooms, ££, No smoking

A hearty breakfast is served around one large table in the attractive dining room, and guests can relax in the comfortable lounge with satellite television and an open fire in cooler weather. Children are welcome and dogs are accepted by prior arrangement. Car parking is provided.

Lenwade is a semi-detached property conveniently located for the area's many attractions and within walking distance of the railway station, river, shops, cinema, pubs and restaurants.

The smartly furnished bedrooms offer many extras for guests' comfort, such as colour televisions, tea and coffee making equipment, clock radios, and hairdryers. All the rooms have either en suite or private facilities.

## RECOMMENDED IN THE AREA

**RESTAURANT:**
*Red Lion Hotel, Henley-on-Thames*

**TRADITIONAL PUB:**
*The Five Horseshoes, Henley-on-Thames*

**VISIT:**
*Greys Court, Henley-on-Thames*

# The Knoll

*Peaceful home with landscaped gardens in the Thames Valley*

☎ 0118 940 2705  📠 0118 940 2705
✉ theknollhenley@aol.com

## Map ref 3 - SU78

Crowsley Road, Shiplake, HENLEY-ON-THAMES, Oxfordshire, RG9 3JT
from Henley take A4155 Reading, 2m, left at war memorial, 1st right (Crowsley Rd), 3rd house on right
2 Rooms, ££, No smoking in bedrooms

The owners take pride in their hospitality at this handsome property, hidden in a residential area in the quiet village of Shiplake. The bedrooms are on the ground floor, with traditional furnishings; both have en suite bath and shower, each with its own hot water supply; one has an adjoining room for children. A hot drinks tray is provided, laid with the finest English bone china and cookies.

Breakfast is made just for you, traditional English or continental, with a luxurious array of muffins, homemade preserves, freshly squeezed juices and English berries in season. This is served in the family dining room, which is decorated in Regency style with a strong Chinese influence.

There is a comfortable lounge, with down-filled upholstery and a wide selection of books, or you can retreat to the summerhouse in the extensive gardens.

## RECOMMENDED IN THE AREA

**RESTAURANT:**
*The Crown, Burchett's Green*

**TRADITIONAL PUB:**
*Bottle & Glass, Binfield Heath*

**VISIT:**
*River & Rowing Museum, Henley-on-Thames*

# Burlington House

*Recently renovated Victorian house in the Summertown area*

☎ 01865 513513 📠 01865 311785
✉ stay@burlington-house.co.uk

**Map ref 3 - SP50**

374 Banbury Road, Summertown, OXFORD, Oxfordshire, OX2 7PP
11 Rooms, ££, No smoking

Burlington House is an impressive Victorian property, which has undergone total renovation by the present owners. It is just five minutes by bus or taxi to Oxford city centre, there are also some good restaurants within walking distance, and the friendly proprietors are happy to assist guests with their choice.

The nine en suite bedrooms are stylishly decorated and well co-ordinated, much thought has been given to guests' comfort. The bathrooms, all of a high standard, have wonderful power showers. The breakfast menu varies from day to day, as well as a traditional breakfast, guests may be offered alternatives such as pecan nut pancakes with maple syrup. Whatever you choose, you are assured of the freshest ingredients in dishes cooked to order.

## RECOMMENDED IN THE AREA

**RESTAURANT:**
*Bath Place Hotel, Oxford*

**TRADITIONAL PUB:**
*The White House, Oxford*

**VISIT:**
*Ashmolean Museum of Arts & Archaeology, Oxford*

---

# Fallowfields Country House Hotel & Restaurant

*Elegant country house with acclaimed restaurant*

☎ 01865 820416 📠 01865 821275
✉ stay@fallowfields.com

**Map ref 3 - SP50**

Kingston Bagpuize with Southmoor, OXFORD, Oxfordshire, OX13 5BH
from A420, 10m SW of Oxford, turn for Kingston Bagpuize. At mini-rbt turn right thro' village to Southmoor
10 Rooms, £££, No smoking in bedrooms

and this is reflected in the character furnishing and decor with sumptuous fabrics and high quality fittings.

The restaurant is a focal point and much of the produce is home grown in the kitchen garden. Weddings and other functions can be catered for and the house is licensed. There is ample parking for guests and the hard tennis court is an added attraction, children over 10 years are welcome. Major credit cards are accepted.

Fallowfield country house, set in its own grounds, provides an excellent base for visitors to Oxford, London and the Cotswolds. All bedrooms have en suite facilities, tea and coffee making facilities and direct dial telephones.

The house was once home to the Begum Aga Khan

## RECOMMENDED IN THE AREA

**VISIT:**
*The Oxford Story, Oxford*
*Museum of Oxford, Oxford*

# Upper Green Farm

## RECOMMENDED IN THE AREA

**RESTAURANT:**
*Sir Charles Napier, Chinnor*

**TRADITIONAL PUB:**
*Abingdon Arms, Thame*

**VISIT:**
*Waterperry Gardens, Waterperry*

*U*pper Green Farm is a delightful 15th-century thatched property in a peaceful rural setting, just an hour from London and conveniently situated for exploring the Cotswolds. Each of the en suite bedrooms has its own theme. The rooms are well appointed and offer a number of thoughtful extras. Two rooms are located in the main house, while the remainder, including four ground floor rooms, are in a separate 18th-century barn conversion. The latter building also offers a lounge. Breakfast is served in the beamed dining room overlooking the Chilterns Hills. Guests can wander around the beautiful grounds, and relax under a shady tree beside the lake. Mind the geese as you drive in, they may be providing the eggs for your breakfast! No credit cards, children under 13, or pets are accepted at the farm.

# The White Horse

*Lovely Elizabethan inn with oak beams and a thatched roof*

☎ 01367 820726  📠 01367 820566

**Map ref 3 - SU28**

WOOLSTONE, Oxfordshire, SN7 7QL

6 Rooms, ££

The White Horse dates from the 16th century and is reputed to be one of the oldest inns in the country. Thomas Hughes of 'Tom Brown's School Days' fame is said to have written his books here. The bedrooms are well equipped with modern facilities, each having an en suite bath and shower, colour television, direct dial telephone, radio, hairdryer, trouser press and hospitality tray. There is also a luxury suite with a lounge and two bedrooms and bathrooms.

Food is carefully prepared from quality fresh produce and served in the intimate restaurant from a carte. A bar menu is also available for light lunches and suppers. The oak beamed bar, with its log fires and old world atmosphere, offers an excellent choice of real ales, wines from around the world, fine cognacs and around 50 malt whiskies.

### RECOMMENDED IN THE AREA

**RESTAURANT:**
*Inglesham Forge Restaurant, Inglesham*

**VISIT:**
*The Uffington White Horse & Ancient Monument*

# The White House

*Antique-furnished period house in a quiet country setting*

☎ 01252 702272  📠 01252 702747
📧 johnhn@globalnet.co.uk

**Map ref 3 - SU94**

Thursley Road, ELSTEAD, Surrey, GU8 6LW from A3, B3001 to Elstead. At village green fork left (signed Churt), cont. 1m. After 40mph sign house short distance on left

3 Rooms, £, No smoking

An attractive property dating from 1800, The White House is just outside the village of Elstead, five miles from Farnham and Godalming. Prue and John Henstridge enjoy welcoming both business and leisure guests to their home. The spacious lounge and cosy dining room afford fine views of the garden with its ornamental fish pond and patio seating area. The well-proportioned bedrooms are individually decorated and have washbasins, hairdryers and tea and coffee making equipment. Guests share a bath and shower room, and a separate WC is provided. Fresh local produce is served at breakfast, there is a choice of pubs and restaurants in the village for evening meals.

Several celebrated houses and gardens, a choice of golf courses and a riding stables are within easy reach. Good walking is available in the Devils Punch Bowl and the surrounding commons. Ample parking is provided.

### RECOMMENDED IN THE AREA

**RESTAURANT:**
*Bishops Table Hotel, Farnham*

**TRADITIONAL PUB:**
*The Woolpack, Elstead*

**VISIT:**
*Loseley Park, Guildford*

# *T*rumbles

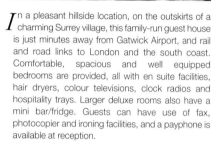

*Victorian house peacefully located close to Gatwick Airport*

☎ 01293 862925

**Map ref 3 - TQ24**

Stan Hill, CHARLWOOD, Surrey, RH6 0EP
6 Rooms, ££, No smoking

## RECOMMENDED IN THE AREA

**RESTAURANT:**
*The Dining Room, Reigate*

**TRADITIONAL PUB:**
*Six Bells, Newdigate*

**VISIT:**
*Hatchlands, East Clandon*

*I*n a pleasant hillside location, on the outskirts of a charming Surrey village, this family-run guest house is just minutes away from Gatwick Airport, and rail and road links to London and the south coast. Comfortable, spacious and well equipped bedrooms are provided, all with en suite facilities, hair dryers, colour televisions, clock radios and hospitality trays. Larger deluxe rooms also have a mini bar/fridge. Guests can have use of fax, photocopier and ironing facilities, and a payphone is available at reception.

An indoor 'koi' pond is the focal point of the public areas, which include a relaxing guest lounge, a sunny conservatory/breakfast room, and an inviting garden patio. A tasty breakfast is served, with vegetarian options available.

Complimentary transport can be provided to Gatwick from 6am.

# *V*ulcan Lodge Guest House

*Period house with lovely grounds in the centre of town*

☎ 01293 771522   ⊕ 01293 786206
✉ reservations@vulcan-lodge.co.uk

**Map ref 3 - TQ24**

27 Massetts Road, HORLEY, Surrey,
RH6 7DQ
exit M23 J9, right exit at 4th rdbt, Massetts
Rd 2nd on right, premises 0.25m on right
4 Rooms, £, No smoking

## RECOMMENDED IN THE AREA

**RESTAURANT:**
*Nutfield Priory, Redhill*

**TRADITIONAL PUB:**
*Ye Olde Six Bells, Horley*

**VISIT:**
*Hathclands, East Clandon*

*G*uests can be assured of a warm welcome from friendly owners Colin and Karen Moon, at this charming, no smoking guest house.

The house dates from the 17th century, and is conveniently situated within walking distance of the town centre and a short drive from Gatwick Airport. Parking is provided, and can also be arranged for guests leaving the country for short periods.

The bedrooms are individually decorated and well equipped to include colour televisions, radio alarms, tea and coffee making facilities, biscuits, mineral water, toiletries and tissues. All the rooms have en suite showers or a private bathroom. Full English breakfast is served in the delightful pine-furnished dining room. There is a comfortable lounge with a television and a good selection of board games.

# *B*onham's Country House

*Luxurious rooms, peaceful gardens and a range of leisure facilities*

☎ 01243 551301  ✆ 01243 551301

**Map ref 3 - TQ90**

Barnham Road, Yapton, ARUNDEL,
West Sussex, BN18 0DX
A27/A29 Bognor Regis, left at first
roundabout, B2233, thro' Barnham. House
after S-bend before Black Dog pub, on left
3 Rooms, £, No smoking in bedrooms

*B*uilt in 1746, this delightful Georgian house is well situated between the historic city of Chichester and charismatic Arundel town. The surrounding coastal area provides a variety of attractions ranging from the horticultural to the recreational. Day trips to London and France are easily accessible, while the natural beauty of the South Downs and the Isle of Wight are on the doorstep.

The spacious bedrooms have been individually designed in quintessential English style. Alongside the south-facing residents' dining room, an oak-panelled lounge makes the most of the afternoon sunshine. There is a marvellous array of activities available at Bonhams House, with an indoor swimming pool, croquet and all-weather tennis and basketball court. Sailing can be arranged on a private 42 foot yacht for the more adventurous.

## RECOMMENDED IN THE AREA

**RESTAURANT:**
*Amberley Castle, Amberley*

**TRADITIONAL PUB:**
*George & Dragon, Burpham*

**VISIT:**
*Arundel Castle, Arundel*

# *K*enwood

*Large Victorian house overlooking Bosham Harbour*

☎ 01243 572727  ✆ 01243 572738

**Map ref 3 - SU80**

Off A259, BOSHAM, West Sussex,
PO18 8PH
400m W of Bosham roundabout on A259
3 Rooms, No smoking in bedrooms

*S*heena Godden's friendly hospitality ensures an enjoyable stay at this fine property, which is set in several acres of well maintained gardens with extensive views over the harbour. The decor and furnishings reflect the period charm, creating a warm, homely atmosphere.

The comfortably appointed bedrooms are all en suite and have many thoughtful extras. A generous breakfast is served in the bright conservatory, which also contains a fridge and microwave oven for guests who wish to cater for themselves in the evening.

The lounge is the ideal setting in which to relax after a busy day, and other amenities include a pool table and solar heated swimming pool covered by a dome.

## RECOMMENDED IN THE AREA

**RESTAURANT:**
*Comme Ça, Chichester*

**VISIT:**
*Fishbourne Roman Palace, Fishbourne*

# *W*ilbury House Bed & Breakfast

*Modern home near Roman palace and Goodwood racing*

☎ 01243 572953  📠 01243 574150
✉ puffin01@globalnet.co.uk

**Map ref 3 - SU80**

Main Road, Fishbourne, CHICHESTER,
West Sussex, PO18 8AT
from A27 Chichester by-pass, take A259
W to Fishbourne and Bosham, 1m on left
from Tesco roundabout
3 Rooms, £, No smoking, Closed Xmas

*J*ackie and Maurice Penfold welcome guests to their family home, a comfortable, modern house of warm brown brick, built in 1994 by Maurice himself. The design and décor of the house reflects the loving care that they have bestowed upon it. It is on the outskirts of Chichester, just a quarter of a mile from the Fishbourne Roman Palace, one of the biggest and best preserved Roman sites in the country.

The rooms look out over farmland towards Goodwood, ten minutes away, where there is horse racing, as well as events at the famous car-racing track. One room has en suite bathroom facilities. A generous breakfast is served.

Guests may use the patio and gardens in the summer, and there is ample off-road parking.

## Recommended in the area

**Restaurant:**
*Comme Ça, Chichester*

**Traditional Pub:**
*Anglesey Arms, Halnaker*

**Visit:**
*Chichester Cathedral, Chichester*

# *S*liders Farm

*A unique 16th-century farmhouse with oak beams and inglenooks*

☎ 01825 790258  📠 01825 790258
✉ jes@slidesfreeserve.co.uk

**Map ref 3 - TQ32**

Furners Green, Danehill, HAYWARDS HEATH,
West Sussex, TN22 3RT
1m S of Danehill village on A275, signposted
at small crossroads
3 Rooms, ££, No smoking in bedrooms
Closed 21-28 Dec

*S*liders Farm is found in a narrow lane surrounded by fields and woodland. The tranquillity of the house and its beautiful grounds provides a welcome countryside retreat.

The 16th-century farmhouse is brightly decorated, and furnished with charming antiques. The spacious lounge has an inglenook fireplace with log fire in winter, a snooker table and a beamed breakfast room. All bedrooms are en suite, one is suitable for family occupation. Television and tea making facilities are provided. Self-catering accommodation is available in a converted barn and separate cottage.

A comprehensive guide to local walks and attractions is provided by the proprietors. Fly fishing is available and there is a swimming pool and tennis court for more active guests. A number of traditional country pubs can be found in the area.

## Recommended in the area

**Restaurant:**
*Gravetye Manor Hotel, East Grinstead*

**Traditional Pub:**
*The Griffin Inn, Fletching*

**Visit:**
*Sheffield Park Gardens*

# *M*izzards Farm

*16th-century stone house, with peaceful gardens and lake*

☎ 01730 821656  📠 01730 821655

**Map ref 3 - SU82**

ROGATE, West Sussex, GU31 5HS
from x-rds in Rogate S for 0.5m, cross river, 300yds then turn right, signed Mizzards Farm
3 Rooms, ££, No smoking
Closed Xmas

The River Rother skirts around the landscaped gardens and the lake, filled with carp. Beyond, there are views of woods and rolling farmland with pedigree Charolais sheep and Bantam chickens. Guests can use the covered swimming pool or the croquet lawn in summer. The owners are very welcoming, and are happy to help with suggestions of activities to enjoy in the area.

Roses climb around the front door, leading into a vaulted hall, where breakfast is served, the traditional range of dishes includes kedgeree and kippers. There is an elegant split-level drawing room with a grand piano, and a log fire in winter. There is also a conservatory furnished with wicker.

The largest of the bedrooms has a four-poster bed on a dais, and a big marble bathroom. All have en suite bathroom, fresh flowers and fine bed linen.

## RECOMMENDED IN THE AREA

**RESTAURANT:**
*Angel Hotel, Midhurst*

**TRADITIONAL PUB:**
*The Three Horseshoes, Elsted*

**VISIT:**
*Uppark, South Harting*

---

# *T*he White Horse Inn

*Village inn at the foot of the South Downs*

☎ 01798 869221  📠 01798 869291

**Map ref 3 - SU91**

SUTTON, West Sussex, RH20 1PS
off A29 at foot of Bury Hill. After 2m pass Roman Villa on right. Follow road 1m to Sutton
5 Rooms, ££, No smoking in bedrooms

The White Horse dates from 1746, since when it has been in continuous service as an ale house to the village. These days it also offers guest accommodation on the carefully renovated first floor. The character of the building has been retained, with the uneven floors, large bathrooms and sash windows, and is reflected in the choice of fabrics and furnishings. A couple of the rooms have balconies overlooking the garden, and there is also a lovely old garden cottage.

Food is a highlight at the White Horse, with traditional country fare served in the dining room, which leads off the bar. Portions are generous and the dishes comprise fresh seasonal produce. Lighter meals are also available by the fireside in the village bar. In the warmer months meals can also be taken in the pretty garden. As there is no residents' lounge, facilities for children are limited.

## RECOMMENDED IN THE AREA

**RESTAURANT:**
*Chequers Hotel, Pulborough*

**VISIT:**
*Uppark, South Harting*

# $\mathcal{M}$oorings

*Double fronted Victorian villa close to the town centre*

☎ 01903 208882

**Map ref 3 - TQ10**

4 Selden Road, WORTHING, West Sussex, BN11 2LL
on A259 towards Brighton, pass indoor swimming pool on right and hotel opposite garage
6 Rooms, £, No smoking
Closed 19 Dec-4 Jan

There is a cosy residents' lounge and a full English breakfast is served in the comfortably furnished dining room. Guests have access to the hotel at all times. Some off-street parking is available and bicycles can be safely stored.

*T*he Moorings is an elegant property set in a quiet residential street to the east of the town centre and just a short walk from the seafront. It is a family run establishment where a warm welcome is assured.

The bedrooms are smart and spacious offering a good range of extras, including en suite showers, direct dial telephones, double glazed windows, colour televisions, shaver points, hairdryers and tea and coffee making facilities.

## RECOMMENDED IN THE AREA

**RESTAURANT:**
*Baliffscourt Hotel, Climping*

**VISIT:**
*Leonardslee Gardens, Lower Beeding*

*Beauclette Marina, Guernsey*

# Midhurst House

*Regency town house
five minutes walk
from the harbour
and the town centre*

☎ 01481 724391
📠 01481 729451
✉ midhurst.house@
virgin.net

**Map ref 14 - GN00**

Candie Road,
ST PETER PORT,
Guernsey, GY1 1UP
adjacent to Candie
Gardens
6 Rooms, ££

**RECOMMENDED
IN THE AREA**

**RESTAURANT:**
*Battens, St Peter Port*

**VISIT:**
*Castle Corner,
St Peter Port*

Midhurst House is an elegant property personally run by Brian and Jan Goodenough, who provide a warm welcome to all their guests. The house enjoys a central location, with the attractions and amenities of St Peter Port within easy reach. A leisurely stroll through the beautiful Candie Gardens will lead you to the harbour and town centre. The house is beautifully appointed throughout, stylish yet comfortable, with period and reproduction furniture. The bedrooms are individually styled, with a good range of equipment and welcoming touches such as fresh flowers and mineral water. All have either en suite bathroom or shower and WC. Day rooms include a comfortable lounge, lit by an unusual octagonal skylight. Pre-dinner drinks may be taken in the pleasant walled garden. Brian's delicious home cooking, based on market-fresh ingredients, is served in the gracious dining room.

**183**

# The Panorama

*Relax and enjoy some of the finest sea views in the Channel Islands from an attractive property in the village of St Aubin*

☎ 01534 742429  📠 01534 745940

**Map ref 14 - JS00**

La Rue du Crocquet, ST AUBIN, Jersey, JE3 8BZ
17 Rooms, ££, No smoking

The Panorama lives up to its name, offering wonderful views over St Aubin Bay from its peaceful, elevated position. Owners John and Jill Squires have been welcoming guests here since 1977 and have been recognised by the AA for almost as long. They are proud recipients of the Jersey Tourism Committee's Gold Merit Award.

Bedrooms are stylishly decorated and many have sea views. Beds are of a high quality and most of them are two metres long. All the rooms have en suite facilities (bath and/or shower), and offer tea and coffee making equipment, clock radios, hairdryers, refrigerators, mini microwave ovens and colour televisions. The televisions receive English and French terrestrial transmissions and satellite on both Astra and Intelsat, which transmit German and Swedish programmes. A full traditional breakfast is served, with a good choice of dishes. It is the only meal (apart from afternoon tea) available in the house. For dinner, the Squires are happy to recommend a number of good restaurants within easy walking distance around the village of St Aubin. Tea is a big event, with a collection of over 500 tea pots and the following 'invitation to tea': "in china cups and silver pots upon a silver tray, tea is served in a quiet corner of St Aubin's Bay". Several times a week Jersey cream teas are served in "The Terrace

## RECOMMENDED IN THE AREA

**RESTAURANT:** *Hotel L'Horizon, St Brelade*

**VISIT:** *Jersey Lavender Farm, St Brelade*

Tea Pot", featuring Jill's home baking. The Panorama is open from Easter to October, and during May to September it operates on a weekly basis from Saturday to Saturday, during this time accounts are due for settlement six weeks before arrival. Children under the age of 14 cannot be accommodated.

# Champ Colin

RECOMMENDED
IN THE AREA

RESTAURANT:
*Longueville Manor,
St Saviour*

VISIT:
*Occupation Tapestry
Gallery, St Helier*

*Traditional old stone
house with original
features in peaceful
surroundings*

☎ 01534 851877
📠 01534 854902

**Map ref 14 - JS00**

Rue du Champ Colin,
ST SAVIOUR, Jersey,
Channel Islands, JE2 7UN
fr airport St Helier
signs, thro' tunnel.
1st L to lights/middle
lane, up Mont Millais.
B28 Hougue Bie,
Rue du Champ Colin
3 Rooms, £
No Smoking
Closed 18 Dec-5 Jan

Champ Colin dates back to 1815. It sits in a quiet rural spot, only 10 minutes from the town centre by car, and 10 minutes from the nearest beach. It has a garden with a luscious long front lawn, and there is plenty of parking space. The bedrooms are lovely and snug, with heavy wooden antique furniture; two of them have half-tester beds. All three have en suite bathrooms, colour TV, tea and coffee making facilities. Beamed ceilings, some exposed stone walls and more antique furniture downstairs make the house feel cosy and rustic. You can take a moment to relax in the drawing room, and you can savour a delicious full English breakfast in front of the imposing granite fireplace in the breakfast room.

*Junction of Bridge Street and Henley Street, Stratford-on-Avon, Warwickshire*

# Central England & East Anglia

This region draws together the central counties of England and the area from Essex to Norfolk. To the west of this region lie Shropshire and Herefordshire (both on the border with Wales) and Worcestershire, West Midlands and Warwickshire. Geographical features include the Malvern Hills, Welsh Marches and the Vale of Evesham.

Towns you may like to visit in this region are Hereford, Leominster, Ross-on-Wye, Shrewsbury, Telford, Stourbridge, Kidderminster and Worcester. Places of particular interest are Malvern, with its famous water, Warwick with its great castle, Coventry with its famous cathedral, and Stratford-on-Avon, best known as Shakespeare's birthplace.

In the centre of this region lie the counties of Northamptonshire, Leicestershire, Lincolnshire, Cambridgeshire and Rutland. The ancient university town of Cambridge is a highlight with many colleges, chapels and historic buildings to explore as well as the town and river. The cathedral cities of Lincoln and Ely are well worth a trip.

In East Anglia, the Norfolk Broads National Park is made up of interconnected waterways. There are many boatyards and companies offering boat trips or boat hire, this is by far the easiest way to see this area. The limited river access to many areas has helped to preserve the wildlife and this is a popular place for birdwatchers.

The city of Norwich in Norfolk has much to offer visitors with its ancient castle, cathedral and museums. Around the coast there are a number of well-known ferry and fishing ports such as Harwich, Felixstowe, Lowestoft and Great Yarmouth.

There are some fine examples of traditional half-timbered buildings in this region. A few of these such as Lavenham Priory and The Great House, Lavenham are AA recommended places to stay so you can admire the architecture at first hand.

# Hill House Farm

*Victorian farmhouse in a delightful village setting*

☎ 01353 778369

**Map ref 4 - TL58**

9 Main Street, Coveney, ELY,
Cambridgeshire, CB6 2DJ
off A142 3m W of Ely
3 Rooms, £, No smoking
Closed Xmas

Public rooms comprise a comfortably furnished sitting room and a separate dining room, where guests are served a freshly cooked breakfast at the highly polished communal table. The house is not suitable for children under twelve or pets.

This charming farmhouse is situated in the village of Coveney, about three miles west of Ely. Guests can expect a warm welcome from the caring proprietor Mrs Nix.

Although the bedrooms are part of the main house, each room has the unique advantage of its own separate entrance. The bedrooms are immaculately kept with a fresh, bright appearance. The pleasant decor and co-ordinated fabrics are enhanced by modern en suite facilities and a range of useful extras.

## RECOMMENDED IN THE AREA

**TRADITIONAL PUB:**
*The Anchor Inn*

**VISIT:**
*Ely Cathedral, Ely*

# Sheene Mill Restaurant

*Restaurant with rooms in a converted 17th-century water mill*

☎ 01763 261393   ☏ 01763 261376

**Map ref 3 - TL34**

Station Road, MELBOURN, Cambridgeshire,
SG8 6DX
off A10
9 Rooms

A delightful old watermill set in three acres of beautiful gardens on the River Mel provides designer accommodation and a celebrity status brasserie. The vibrant, upbeat proprietors are Sally and Steven Saunders. Steven is one of the original media chefs, with many television and radio performances to his credit, plus a number of books and regular columns in the press. The couple's flagship restaurant is the nearby Pink Geranium. Accommodation at the mill is offered in uniquely designed bedrooms, each with its own designer label. Contributors include David Emmanuel, Anna Ryder-Richardson, John Amabile, Anna French, Tracy Wilson and Sally herself, all presenting their own interpretation of these lovely rooms, which have river views. Weekend breaks include dinner at the Pink Geranium and Sunday lunch at Sheene Mill. The Brasserie, open seven days a week, offers an innovative menu, and a live pianist performs every evening except Saturday.

## RECOMMENDED IN THE AREA

**TRADITIONAL PUB:**
*The Queens Head, Newton*

**VISIT:**
*Duxford Airfield*

# $\mathcal{A}$ldhams

*Lutyens-style house a short drive from Manningtree*

☎ 01206 393210 📠 01206 393210
✉ coral.mcewen3@which.net

**Map ref 4 - TM13**

Bromley Road, Lawford, MANNINGTREE,
Essex, CO11 2NE
from S, A12 Colchester N exit, follow sign to
Harwich, A120 for 7.5m, left (Little Bromley),
2.9m, house on right
3 Rooms, £, No smoking
Closed 24-26 Dec

$\mathcal{A}$ldhams is an elegant house situated at the end of a long drive surrounded by three acres of attractive gardens, with peaceful countryside beyond. You are sure of a warm welcome from Mrs McEwen, a cheerful and enthusiastic hostess who offers refreshments to guests on arrival.

The bedrooms are nicely decorated, well maintained and furnished with period-style pieces. The range of useful items includes televisions, clock radios, and tea and coffee making facilities. Two rooms have private bathrooms and the third has a separate bathroom. The comfortable lounge has an open log fire and a selection of books and games. You can enjoy an excellent freshly cooked breakfast at the large dining room table.

## RECOMMENDED IN THE AREA

**RESTAURANT:**
*Pier at Harwich, Harwich*

**TRADITIONAL PUB:**
*Marlborough Head Hotel, Dedham*

**VISIT:**
*Mistley Towers, Mistley*

---

# $\mathcal{D}$airy House Farm

*Victorian farmhouse in a peaceful setting with lovely country views*

☎ 01255 870322 📠 01255 870186

**Map ref 4 - TM12**

Bradfield Road, WIX, Essex, CO11 2SR
between Colchester & Harwich, off A120 into
Wix. At x-rd Bradfield direction, farm is
1m on left
3 Rooms, £, No smoking in bedrooms

$\mathcal{G}$uests are assured of a warm, friendly welcome from Mrs Whitworth at this Victorian farmhouse, which has been sympathetically converted to retain most of its original character.

It is situated at the end of a private road amid 700 acres of arable farmland and offers high quality accommodation throughout. The bedrooms are comfortably furnished with some delightful period pieces and equipped with a range of useful extras. Guests are greeted with a cup of tea and home made cake on arrival, and breakfast is served in the dining room around the large mahogany table.

Guests also have the use of a nicely appointed sitting room. Evening meals are not available, but the village of Bradfield is only a 20-minute walk away and has some good pubs. Constable country, the Suffolk villages and the Port of Harwich are all near by.

## RECOMMENDED IN THE AREA

**RESTAURANT:**
*Pier at Harwich, Harwich*

**TRADITIONAL PUB:**
*Marlborough Head Hotel, Dedham*

**VISIT:**
*Beth Chatto Gardens, Colchester*

# The Hills Farm

*Expect a friendly welcome from the AA Landlady of the Year for 1999, at this attractive Herefordshire farmhouse*

☎ 01568 750205
🖷 01568 750306
✉ conolly@ bigwig.net

**Map ref 2 - SO45**

Leysters,
LEOMINSTER,
Herefordshire, HR6 0HP
exit A4112 Leominster
to Tenbury Wells rd.
On edge of Leysters
5 Rooms, ££, No smoking

Jane and Peter Conolly welcome guests to their lovely farmhouse, which dates back to the 16th century. Many original features are still visible, including exposed beams and flagstone floors. Three spacious bedrooms are found in sympathetically converted barns, these rooms all have modern en suite bathroom facilities. Two further bedrooms are available in the main house, one of these has en suite facilities and the other has a private bathroom. The farm enjoys an idyllic elevated position, with panoramic views across fields and the surrounding hilly countryside from all the rooms. You can enjoy these views while you sample the delicious breakfasts or imaginative dinners in the cosy dining room. There is a comfortable sitting room next door with a wood-burning stove. Information about local beauty spots and leisure walks is provided for guests wishing to explore the area.

### RECOMMENDED IN THE AREA

**RESTAURANT:**
*The Salutation Inn, Weobley*

**TRADITIONAL PUB:**
*Stockton Cross Inn, Kimbolton*

**VISIT:**
*Berrington Hall, Ashton*

# *T*he Bowens Country House

*Country house by the church in a small Herefordshire village*

☎ 01432 860430   📠 01432 860430

**Map ref 2 - SO53**

FOWNHOPE, Herefordshire, HR1 4PS
6m SE of Hereford on B4224. In Fownhope, establishment opposite church
10 Rooms, ££

*T*his 300-year-old stone house has been altered and extended, but it is still small enough to provide a cheerful, friendly atmosphere.

The owners have preserved the original character, rediscovering a magnificent inglenook fireplace in the oak-beamed lounge, and reclaiming the old lawn tennis court, which had been lost to a field for forty years. It is convenient for the Wye Valley, the Brecons and Malverns, and there is ample car parking space. The gardens are beautiful, with mature trees and shrubs. Besides the tennis court, there is a croquet lawn and a putting green.

Bedrooms, overlooking the gardens and countryside, all have modern en suite facilities, TV and telephone, four are on the ground floor. Delicious meals are served in the oak-beamed restaurant from 7pm. The vegetable garden and greenhouse provide much of the produce.

## RECOMMENDED IN THE AREA

**RESTAURANT:**
*Chase Hotel, Ross-on-Wye*

**TRADITIONAL PUB:**
*The Green Man Inn, Fownhope*

**VISIT:**
*Hereford Cathedral*

---

# *L*umleys

*Victorian building with modern comforts in a lovely setting*

☎ 01600 890040
✉ helen@lumleys.force9.co.uk

**Map ref 2 - SO52**

Kern Bridge, Bishopswood, ROSS-ON-WYE, Herefordshire, HR9 5QT
off A40 at Goodrich onto B4229 over Kern Bridge. Right at Inn On The Wye approx 400yds past inn opposite picnic ground
3 Rooms, £, No smoking

*A*n early Victorian roadside hostelry, Lumleys has been transformed into a quality modern guest house while retaining much of its original character. The house is situated south of the historic town, on the banks of the River Wye, in a designated area of outstanding natural beauty. From Lumleys you can see Goodrich Castle, with Symonds Yat and the Royal Forest of Dean not far away.

The comfortable en suite bedrooms offer plenty of thoughtful extras. There are some fine period pieces and ornaments in the public areas, all very much in keeping with the style of the property. Helen Mattis and Judith Hayworth are caring hosts, welcoming guests to their home with justifiable pride. They were 1999 AA Landlady of the Year finalists.

## RECOMMENDED IN THE AREA

**RESTAURANT:**
*Chase Hotel, Ross-on-Wye*

**TRADITIONAL PUB:**
*The Crown, Howle Hill*

**VISIT:**
*Goodrich Castle, Goodrich*

# Church Lane Farm House

*Queen Anne farmhouse in a tranquil rural setting*

☎ 01530 810536  📠 01530 810536
✉ aa.bnb.coalville@talk21.com

**Map ref 3 - SK41**

Ravenstone, COALVILLE, Leicestershire,
LE67 2AE
at A511/A447 junct, follow signs for Ibstock .
Church Lane 1st right
3 Rooms, No smoking
Closed Xmas-New Year

## RECOMMENDED IN THE AREA

**RESTAURANT:**
*Quorn Country Hotel, Quorn*

**TRADITIONAL PUB:**
*Pear Tree Inn, Woodhouse Eaves*

**VISIT:**
*Kirky Muxloe Castle, Kirby Muxloe*

Church Lane Farmhouse is situated in the ancient village of Ravenstone, mentioned in the 11th century Domesday Book. It is peacefully located but with good access to motorways and the East Midlands Airport. This is an ideal location from which to visit the glories of the Heart of England.

The house is furnished with well chosen period furniture, and the rooms are enhanced by the proprietors' artistic flair. The guests' sitting room has an inglenook fireplace, complete with a log-burning stove, as well as a delightful collection of carnival and venetian glassware.

Supper and dinner menus offer an interesting choice of freshly cooked meals with a hint of continental and eastern influences. Meals are served at a highly polished mahogany table in the beamed dining room. Mr Thorne runs a studio at the rear of the house, with art exhibitions world-wide.

# Pipwell Manor

*Georgian manor house in beautiful grounds, with a miniature railway*

☎ 01406 423119  📠 01406 423119

**Map ref 4 - TF32**

Washway Road, Saracens Head,
HOLBEACH, Lincolnshire, PE12 8AL
off A17
4 Rooms, £, No smoking

In the 13th century, when a Cistercian Grange stood on this site, monks were reclaiming the land from the sea. The Wash shore, with its wildlife, lies a little further away now. The house is situated in a small village, surrounded by fields, which are ablaze with daffodils and tulips in the spring. The house itself has extensive flower gardens and a conservatory. There is ample off-street parking and bicycles are available for guests to use.

On arrival, owner Lesley Honnor welcomes you with complimentary afternoon tea and home made cakes. Home grown stewed fruits, fruit salads, home made jams and marmalades, and eggs fresh from the hens outside, are served at breakfast in the elegant dining room. Two of the stylish bedrooms have en suite bathroom facilities. There is a comfortable sitting room with TV, and a log fire in winter.

## RECOMMENDED IN THE AREA

**RESTAURANT:**
*Black Horse Inn, Bourne*

**TRADITIONAL PUB:**
*Chequers, Gedney Dyke*

**VISIT:**
*Spalding Tropical Forest, Spalding*

# Greenfield Farm

*Modern-style farmhouse in a lovely rural setting*

☎ 01507 578457  📠 01507 578457

**Map ref 8 - TF26**

Minting, HORNCASTLE, Lincolnshire,
LN9 5RX
from Lincoln, A158 through Wragby. After 3m
turn right at Midge Pub, farm 1m on right
3 Rooms, £, No smoking
Closed Xmas & New Year

Guests can expect a warm welcome from Mrs Bankes Price at this spacious farmhouse, situated on the edge of the small village of Minting. The farm is within easy striking distance of Lincoln, and nearby Horncastle is an attraction for those with an interest in antiques.

The comfortable bedrooms are nicely furnished. Two rooms have smart en suite facilities while the other has a private bathroom. Public rooms include a cosy dining room where a freshly cooked breakfast is served at one large table. A pleasant lounge is also available to guests, and this overlooks the attractive garden with its wonderful wildlife pond and the added attraction of a grass tennis court. Parking is provided at the front of the house.

## RECOMMENDED IN THE AREA

**RESTAURANT:**
*Magpies Restaurant, Horncastle*

**TRADITIONAL PUB:**
*Black Horse, Donington on Bain*

**VISIT:**
*Tattershall Castle, Tattershall*

---

# Blaven

*Hospitable establishment in a peaceful rural location*

☎ 01673 838352

**Map ref 8 - TF18**

Walesby Hill, Walesby, MARKET RASEN,
Lincolnshire, LN8 3UW
from Market Rasen A46 towards Grimsby,
right at junct with A1103, left at T-junct,
Blaven 100yds on right
2 Rooms, £, No smoking

Guests can expect a warm, friendly welcome and attentive service from Jacqy Braithwaite, the charming owner of this delightful house. It is situated in the village of Walesby at the foot of the Lincolnshire Wolds, and is surrounded by extensive, beautifully tended gardens.

The bedrooms are nicely furnished and equipped with a range of useful extras. Public rooms include a cosy dining room and a comfortably appointed conservatory, which overlooks the garden.

Blaven is conveniently located for visits to the coast and the historic city of Lincoln. It is also on the Viking Way and the Hull-Harwich cycle route. A small parking area is provided at the front of the house.

## RECOMMENDED IN THE AREA

**RESTAURANT:**
*Washingborough Hall, Lincoln*

**TRADITIONAL PUB:**
*Nickerson Arms, Rothwell*

**VISIT:**
*Museum of Lincolnshire Life, Lincoln*

# *M*inster Lodge Hotel

*Unique and unusual Victorian town house, handy for Lincoln's historic city centre*

☎ 📠 01522 513220
📧 minsterlodge@
compuserve.com
**Map Ref 8 – SK96**

3 Church Lane,
LINCOLN, Lincolnshire,
LN21 1QJ
A15, 5 mins walk from
city centre
6 Rooms, ££
No Smoking

## RECOMMENDED IN THE AREA

**RESTAURANT:**
*The Jews House, Lincoln*

**TRADITIONAL PUB:**
*Wig & Mitre, Lincoln*

**VISIT:**
*Lincoln Cathedral, Lincoln*

*M*inster Lodge is ideally situated for discovering the historic sights of Lincoln, just fifty yards from Newport Arch, an ancient gateway to the Roman walled city, that brings you to the cathedral and the castle. It is just four minutes' drive from the Lincoln relief road, with easy access to all outward routes. There is private parking. John and Margaret Baumber strive to delight guests with superlative hospitality. There is a comfortable lounge, and an attractive dining room where full English or continental breakfast is served. The bedrooms, including a family suite, are furnished with handmade natural pine furniture. They all have colour TV, as well as en suite bathrooms, with bath and shower, and beautiful ceramic floor and wall tiles; a licensed bar tray is available at your request.

# Catton Old Hall

*Rest in the sumptuous grandeur of an imposing Jacobean house*

☎ 01603 419379  🖷 01603 400339
✉ enquiries@catton-hall.co.uk

**Map ref 4 - TG20**

Lodge Lane, Old Catton, NORWICH, Norfolk, NR6 7HG

7 Rooms, ££, No smoking in bedrooms
Closed 15 Dec-5 Jan

The approach to this historic house, passing through a modern suburban area, might seem rather plain. Once you step into Catton Old Hall, however, you soon forget about the world outside, because this place is quite delightful. It is full of original features - flint, oak timbers and reclaimed Caen stone. Bold interior design and well chosen antique furnishings show the house off to its magnificent full potential.

The bedrooms are simply wonderful, and the public rooms are so relaxing. The enthusiastic proprietors create an atmosphere of warmth and friendliness from the minute they welcome you on arrival, and their care is felt in all their personal touches throughout the house.

## RECOMMENDED IN THE AREA

**RESTAURANT:**
*Adlards, Norwich*

**TRADITIONAL PUB:**
*The Ribs of Beef, Norwich*

**VISIT:**
*Norwich Cathedral, Norwich*

# The Gables Guest House

*Comfortable accommodation close to the city centre*

☎ 01603 456666  🖷 01603 250320

**Map ref 4 - TG20**

527 Earlham Road, NORWICH, Norfolk, NR4 7HN
off Southern bypass onto B1108, follow signs to Univ of East Anglia, 300yds on left pass Fiveways rdbt, towards city centre

10 Rooms, ££, No smoking
Closed 20 Dec-1 Jan

## RECOMMENDED IN THE AREA

**RESTAURANT:**
*Brummels, Norwich*

**TRADITIONAL PUB:**
*Wildebeest Arms, Stoke Holy Cross*

**VISIT:**
*Sainsbury Centre of Visual Arts, Norwich*

Mr and Mrs Turner offer a warm welcome to guests at this neatly appointed house, conveniently located for Norwich city centre and within easy walking distance of the University of East Anglia.

The bedrooms are warm and comfortable. Effective use has been made of fabrics and delightful pieces of furniture to create a very pleasing environment. All the rooms have spacious modern en suite facilities, colour television with satellite channels, direct dial telephones and tea and coffee making equipment.

The public rooms include a lounge with plush furnishings, a traditional dining room, a conservatory (also acting as a breakfast room), and a first floor snooker room with a full size table. Secure and well lit car parking is provided to the side of the property.

# $H$eath Farmhouse

*Rosy pink farmhouse surrounded by farmland and fishing*

☎ 01986 788417

**Map ref 4 - TM28**

Homersfield, HARLESTON, Norfolk,
IP20 0EX
off A143 onto B1062 Flixton, over bridge
past 'Suffolk' sign, 1st farm entrance on left
2 Rooms, £, No smoking in bedrooms

$T$he Marshes meadow stands between the house and the Waveney River. There is fishing both in the river and in lakes nearby, and owner Julia Hunt is happy to cook any trout you may catch, or freeze them for you to take home! There are lovely walks in the valley, on the route of the Angles Way.

The house dates from the 16th century, and retains extensive unspoilt woodwork and many original features, with log fires in the dining room and both sitting rooms. There is a large garden with flowers, and a kitchen garden. Guests can play croquet on the front lawn, and table tennis in the barn.

Julia is an accomplished cook, using local meat and fish, home grown vegetables and organic produce wherever possible. Special diets can be catered for and sandwich lunches are prepared by arrangement. Guests must provide notice for dinner.

## RECOMMENDED IN THE AREA

**RESTAURANT:**
*Salisbury House, Diss*

**TRADITIONAL PUB:**
*Cornwallis Arms, Brome*

**VISIT:**
*East Anglia's Aviation Heritage Centre, Flixton Suffolk*

---

# $O$ld Thorn Barn

*Converted barn providing appealing accommodation*

☎ 01953 607785   ✆ 01953 607785
✉ oldthornbarn@tinyonline.co.uk

**Map ref 4 - TG20**

Corporation Farm, Wymondham Road,
Hethel, NORWICH, Norfolk, NR14 8EU
6m S of Norwich & 3m E of Wymondham on
B1135. Follow signs for Lotus Cars from A11
or B1113
5 Rooms, £, No smoking

$G$ina Pickwell offers a warm welcome to her delightful bed and breakfast establishment, created with her family, from cattlesheds and outbuildings in the grounds of the original farm. It is peacefully situated in a rural area and offers a high standard of accommodation throughout.

The spacious bedrooms are attractively decorated, well furnished and equipped with many thoughtful extras. Facilities for disabled guests are provided. Breakfast is served in the long barn with its wood-burning stove and inviting dining cum lounge area. Good food is served at nearby pubs and restaurants. In summer guests can relax in the stone courtyard just off the lounge. Pets are not accommodated.

## RECOMMENDED IN THE AREA

**RESTAURANT:**
*Brasted's, Norwich*

**TRADITIONAL PUB:**
*Ribs of Beef, Norwich*

**VISIT:**
*Norwich Castle Museum, Norwich*

# *R*ose Cottage

*Cottage accommodation in a quiet rural location*

☎ 01327 860968  📠 01327 860004

**Map ref 3 - SP64**

Plumpton Road, Woodend, TOWCESTER, Northamptonshire, NN12 8RZ
A43 Towcester, at A5 rndbt follow sign to Blakesley. Left at village green thro' Woodend, right fork past phone box
3 Rooms, £, No smoking

*R*ose Cottage has been carefully renovated by Ann Davey-Turner to provide homely, well equipped accommodation and good food.

Home-produced vegetables and free range eggs are a feature of the meals. Breakfast is served at a family table in the cosy dining room and dinner is available by prior arrangement.

One of the bedrooms offers en suite facilities. The cottage enjoys a quiet location but also provides easy access to the M1 and M40 motorways.

## RECOMMENDED IN THE AREA

**RESTAURANT:**
*Vine House, Towcester*

**TRADITIONAL PUB:**
*Eastcote Arms, Eastcote*

**VISIT:**
*Canal Museum, Stoke Bruerne*

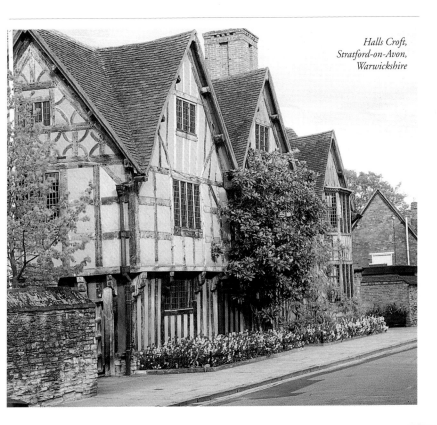

*Halls Croft, Stratford-on-Avon, Warwickshire*

# The Library House

*Grade II listed building at Ironbridge
Gorge World Heritage Site*

☎ 01952 432299 📠 01952 433967
✉ libhouse@enta.net

Map ref 2 - SJ60

11 Severn Bank, IRONBRIDGE, Shropshire,
TF8 7AN
50yds from the Iron Bridge
4 Rooms, ££, No smoking
Closed Xmas

Formerly the village library, this delightful little
guest house dates from the 1750s and is
situated almost opposite the celebrated Iron Bridge.
The house has been sympathetically modernised
to provide comfortable accommodation. One
bedroom has its own private terrace with direct
access to the lovely terraced garden. Other facilities
include a guest lounge and an attractive breakfast
room. The most memorable quality here is the
friendliness and hospitality of Chris and George
Maddocks, who go to great lengths to ensure that
their guests are made to feel at home.

Dinner is not served, but there are several
restaurants and pubs close by which offer good
variety and value. Be careful, however, to keep your
appetite keen for the following morning, as Library
House breakfasts are certainly hearty. Neither credit
nor debit cards are accepted.

## RECOMMENDED IN THE AREA

**TRADITIONAL PUB:**
*The Malthouse, Ironbridge*

**VISIT:**
*Ironbridge Gorge Museums, Ironbridge*

# Line Farm

*Superb bedrooms in a farmhouse with
views from every window*

☎ 01568 780400

Map ref 2 - SO57

Tunnel Lane, Orleton, LUDLOW, Shropshire,
SY8 4HY
signposted from A49 in Ashton. Follow the
B&B signs in Tunnel Lane to Line Farm
3 Rooms, £, No smoking

Sitting five miles south of Ludlow, with glorious
views across the surrounding unspoilt
countryside, this is a perfect place for a peaceful
rural break. The front of the house is decorated with
attractive flowers and shrubs in tubs and hanging
baskets.

Inside, the spacious bedrooms, all with en suite
bathrooms, are furnished with pretty fabrics and
tasteful furniture, with TV, tea and coffee, and other
thoughtful extras to make you feel at home. A
delicious breakfast is served, full English or
continental, with eggs, bacon and sausages fresh
from the farm, and home made preserves.

Local pubs serve food for lunch and dinner. There is
a comfortable sitting room, or you could sit in the
garden and enjoy the panoramic scenery.

## RECOMMENDED IN THE AREA

**RESTAURANT:**
*The Cookhouse, Ludlow*

**TRADITIONAL PUB:**
*Bell Inn, Pensax*

**VISIT:**
*Ludlow Castle, Ludlow*

# Number Twenty Eight

*Unique establishment comprising period houses in the same street*

☎ 01584 876996  ✆ 01584 876860
✉ rossno28@btinternet.com

**Map ref 2 - SO57**

28 Lower Broad Street, LUDLOW,
Shropshire, SY8 1PQ
A49, B4361, premises just off B4361
6 Rooms, ££, No smoking

Situated in the Georgian and early Victorian area of historic Ludlow, this unusual establishment has been created from three separate houses, all retaining original features. The interiors are enhanced by quality period furnishings and decorative schemes.

The bedrooms are all en suite and are well equipped with colour television, tea and coffee making facilities and direct dial telephones. Each of the houses has a comfortable sitting room, in addition to the well equipped bedrooms and pretty gardens. Breakfast is served in the cosy dining room of the main house. Some credit cards are taken and there is a licence to serve alcohol.

## RECOMMENDED IN THE AREA

**RESTAURANT:**
*Dinham Hall, Ludlow*

**TRADITIONAL PUB:**
*The Church Inn, Ludlow*

**VISIT:**
*Stokesay Castle, Stokesay*

# The Day House

*Period farmhouse set in extensive gardens full of wildlife*

☎ 01743 860212  ✆ 01734 860212

**Map ref 2 - SJ41**

Nobold, SHREWSBURY, Shropshire,
SY5 8NL
exit A5 (Shrewsbury) at rdbt with Esso garage, follow Nuffield Hospital signs, 0.5m past hospital, turn right into drive
3 Rooms, £
Closed Xmas & New Year

## RECOMMENDED IN THE AREA

**RESTAURANT:**
*Sol Restaurant, Shrewsbury*

**TRADITIONAL PUB:**
*The Armoury, Shrewsbury*

**VISIT:**
*Shrewsbury Castle, Shrewsbury*

The house, made of mellow brick, is a fascinating combination of 18th-century and mid-Victorian styles, with arches that give the place a cloistered look showing influences of the Gothic Revival. It sits in a secluded location, at the top of a private drive, sheltered by mature trees. There are beautiful gardens, and the farm is home to many wild birds and animals. Access is easy for the medieval town of Shrewsbury, three miles away, and other places of interest.

The bedrooms are spacious, two with en suite shower, all with colour TV, tea and coffee facilities, and refrigerator. The public areas retain many of the building's original features, enhanced by fine period furniture and ornaments.

# Soulton Hall

### RECOMMENDED IN THE AREA

**RESTAURANT:**
*Goldstone Hall, Market Drayton*

**TRADITIONAL PUB:**
*The Raven Inn, Wem*

**VISIT:**
*Hawkstone Historic Park & Follies, Weston-under-Redcastle*

*Elizabethan manor house with a lovely walled garden and fifty acres of oak woodland*

☎ 01939 232786
🖷 01939 234097
✉ j.a.ashton@ farmline.com

**Map ref 6 - SJ52**

Soulton, WEM, Shropshire, SY4 5RS off A49 onto B5065 towards Wem, 2m on left after small bridge
5 Rooms, ££
No smoking

The Ashton family can trace their tenure of this impressive hall back to the 16th century. Much evidence of the building's antiquity remains, notably the sloping floors! The comfortable entrance lounge leads into the bar on one side and a restaurant on the other, offering a good range of freshly prepared dishes. The house has central heating as well as log fires to ensure a warm environment. The bedrooms reflect the character of the house with mullioned windows and exposed timbers, one room also has wood panelling. Five bedrooms have en suite facilities, two of these are located in a converted coach house across the garden. Open farmland surrounds the house and guests are welcome to explore the grounds. These include one and half miles of river and brook where guests can go fishing. Free pony rides and farm walks can also be enjoyed.

# Dearnford Hall

*Fine William and Mary house in a country setting*

☎ 01948 662319 📠 01948 666670
✉ Dearnford_Hall@yahoo.com

**Map ref 6 - SJ54**

Tilstock Road, WHITCHURCH, Shropshire,
SY13 3JJ
at Tilstock rdbt on S Whitchurch by-pass
take B5476 to Tilstock. 0.5m on left. Please
park at front door
2 Rooms, ££, No smoking, Closed Xmas

A delightful combination of 18th-century elegance and 20th-century comfort is offered at this impressive brick-built house. It is surrounded by its own farmland, which includes a 15-acre spring-fed trout pool and many interesting walks. The beauty of the architecture has been further enhanced by Jane Bebbington's stylish selection of antique furniture, rich fabrics and family treasures, which adorn the resplendent sitting and dining rooms. Recommendations can be made for local pubs and restaurants, and guests are welcome to bring back their favourite drink and relax by the fire. Spacious bedrooms, with wonderfully comfortable beds, have been equipped with en suite facilities, and thoughtful extras include reading materials and many useful toiletry items. What makes a stay at Dearnford particularly memorable, however, is the genuine warmth and natural hospitality of Charles and Jane Bebbington. Ample safe parking is available at the front door. Dogs may stay by prior arrangement.

## RECOMMENDED IN THE AREA

**RESTAURANT:**
*Goldstone Hall, Market Drayton*

**TRADITIONAL PUB:**
*Hanmer Arms, Hanmer*

**VISIT:**
*Cholmondley Castle Gardens, Cholmondley*

# Manorhouse

*15th-century Grade II listed Suffolk longhouse*

☎ 01359 270960 📠 01359 271425
✉ manorhouse@beyton1.freeserve.co.uk

**Map ref 4 - TL96**

The Green, BEYTON, Suffolk, IP30 9AF
Beyton is signposted off A14, 4m E of
Bury St Edmunds
4 Rooms, £, No smoking

## RECOMMENDED IN THE AREA

**RESTAURANT:**
*Theobalds Restaurant, Ixworth*

**TRADITIONAL PUB:**
*Brewers Arms, Rattlesden*

**VISIT:**
*Moyse's Hall Museum, Bury St Edmunds*

A warm and friendly welcome is assured from proprietors Kay and Mark Dewsbury at this delightful old farmhouse. It stands in its own large gardens overlooking the village green with its resident geese and local hostelry. There is a combined sitting room and dining room, attractively decorated and furnished with some lovely period pieces. The focal point of the room is a superb inglenook fireplace.

The accommodation is spacious with comfortably appointed rooms offering a choice of king-size, queen-size and twin beds. All the bedrooms have en suite facilities, tea and coffee making equipment, colour television, radio, alarm clock and hairdryer. Guests also have use of washing, drying and ironing facilities, a fridge-freezer and payphone. In addition to a hearty breakfast, freshly prepared and interesting dinners are occasionally available by prior arrangement.

# Twelve Angel Hill

*Handsome house with walled garden in a historic town centre*

☎ 01284 704088  📠 01284 725549

**Map ref 4 - TL86**

12 Angel Hill, BURY ST EDMUNDS, Suffolk, IP33 1UZ
in town centre by Abbey ruins and Cathedral
6 Rooms, ££, No smoking
Closed Jan

Clarke give attention to every detail.

The bedrooms are individually decorated, in sumptuous country house style, each is named after a classic wine-growing region. All have en suite bathrooms or showers, and colour TV, as well as plenty of extra facilities such as a fan, trouser press, books, magazines and mineral water.

Listed for its historical architecture, Twelve Angel Hill owes its façade, and the generous proportions of the dining room, lounge and honeymoon suites to Georgian times. The oldest part of the house, including the bar, painted a warm red, with oak panelling and fireplace, dates back to the 16th century. The property overlooks Angel Hill, with the cathedral and superb Abbey gardens very nearby. At the back there is a colourful courtyard garden, there is also a private car park. The atmosphere is friendly and relaxed, and owners Bernie and John

## RECOMMENDED IN THE AREA

**RESTAURANT:**
*42 Churchgate, Bury St Edmunds*

**TRADITIONAL PUB:**
*The Nutshell, Bury St Edmunds*

**VISIT:**
*Abbey Visitors Centre, Bury St Edmunds*

# Chippenhall Hall

*Candlelit dinners in a Tudor Manor House steeped in history*

☎ 01379 588180  📠 01379 586272

**Map ref 4 - TM27**

FRESSINGFIELD, Suffolk, IP21 5TD
8m E of Diss 1.5m outside Fressingfield on B1116 to Framlingham
4 Rooms, ££

Tucked away in the unspoiled Suffolk countryside, surrounded as it is by seven acres of lawns, trees, ponds and flowers, you can enjoy utter peace and quiet in Chippenhall Hall. This manor house actually originated in the Saxon period, over a thousand years ago, but the leaded windows, the beams and the inglenook fireplace in the sitting room, where log fires burn in winter, are recognisably Tudor.

The bedrooms are spacious and named according to their history: cheese was hung to mature from the high vaulted ceiling of the 'Cheese Room'; pilgrims stayed in the 'Pilgrim Room'. But although they retain their original features, they all have modern en suite bathroom facilities. In summer, guests can use a heated outdoor swimming pool in the rose covered courtyard. Dinner is served by arrangement.

## RECOMMENDED IN THE AREA

**RESTAURANT:**
*Fox & Goose, Fressingfield*

**TRADITIONAL PUB:**
*Kings Head, Laxfield*

**VISIT:**
*Bressingham Steam Museum, Bressingham*

# The Old Guildhall

*15th-century timber-framed guildhall situated in the centre of the village*

☎ 01379 783361

**Map ref 4 - TM07**

Mill Street, GISLINGHAM, Eye,
Suffolk, IP23 8JT
off A140
4 Rooms, ££, No smoking
Closed Jan

Ray and Ethel Tranter extend a warm welcome to guests at this immaculately preserved former guildhall, set in well maintained gardens in the tranquil village of Gislingham. The building has some striking architectural features and offers wonderful accommodation. The character of the building means that there are some low ceilings and a wealth of exposed beams. Colour televisions and tea and coffee making equipment are provided in the rooms.

The open plan public rooms comprise a comfortable lounge and a small combined bar and dining area, with exposed timbers and open fireplaces. A hearty breakfast is served and dinner is available by prior arrangement. Cooking is offered in traditional English style, using fresh local produce.

## RECOMMENDED IN THE AREA

**RESTAURANT:**
*The Bull Auberge, Yaxley*

**TRADITIONAL PUB:**
*Cornwallis Arms, Brome*

**VISIT:**
*Bressingham Steam Museum and Gardens, Bressingham*

# The White House

*Timber-framed house on the banks of the River Stour*

☎ 01440 707731   📠 01440 707731

**Map ref 4 - TL64**

Silver Street, HAVERHILL, Suffolk, CB9 7QG
A143, Haverhill/Bury St Edmunds rd, B1061
into Kedington, 3rd left, King's Hill. House at
bottom of hill opposite pub
3 Rooms, ££, No smoking

An attractive combination of architectural styles, with fine wooden beams, the house dates back to the 17th century. It was extended to serve as a mill, and then a bacon smokery in the Victorian era. The bedrooms are spacious with modern facilities, two with en suite bathrooms. The Blue Room has an antique brass and iron double bed; the Yellow Room overlooks the cobbled yard and herb garden; the Red Room has a king-size half-tester bed, and views over the walled garden and front of the house.

Toby and Chrissy Barclay provide a warm welcome and excellent food, using fresh local produce. They serve a full English breakfast with a wide range of alternatives, including Special White House Porridge and home made fruit bread. Dinners are also available, with game and pastry dishes a speciality. There is a small but carefully selected cellar of wines, beers and spirits.

## RECOMMENDED IN THE AREA

**RESTAURANT:**
*White Hart, Great Yeldham*

**TRADITIONAL PUB:**
*White Horse Inn, Withersfield*

**VISIT:**
*Kentwell Hall, Long Melford*

# The Hatch

*15th-century thatched, timber frame house in a delightful rural setting*

☎ 01284 830226
🖷 01284 830226

**Map ref 4 - TL85**

Pilgrims Lane, Cross Green, HARTEST, Suffolk, IP29 4ED
6m from Bury St Edmunds, A143 (Haverhill), B1066 Glemsford. 1st left on entering village
2 Rooms, ££
No smoking

*T*he Hatch is a lovely medieval house situated in a no through road, formerly the Pilgrims Way to the shrine of Saint Edmund at Bury St Edmunds. It is just outside the village of Hartest, surrounded by rolling countryside. Bridget and Robin Oaten are the charming hosts, greeting their guests with a cup of tea and home-made cakes on arrival. There is an acre of grounds including a wildflower meadow and a wonderful array of rosebushes.

Inside, antique pieces and fine fabrics complement the period architecture and attractive original features. The accommodation comprises a ground floor room, suitable for disabled guests, with separate access, nearby parking and a sunny terrace; and a family suite with a cosy single and double bedroom. Both the drawing room and dining room have splendid inglenook fireplaces where log fires burn on cooler evenings. The breakfast buffet is followed by English or continental choices.

## RECOMMENDED IN THE AREA

**RESTAURANT:**
*Scutchers Restaurant, Long Melford*

**TRADITIONAL PUB:**
*The Crown, Hartest*

**VISIT:**
*Ickworth House, Horringer*

# Lavenham Priory

*Magnificent timber
framed Priory, Grade
I listed, in a celebrated
Suffolk village*

☎ 01787 247404
🖷 01787 248472
✉ tim.pitt@
btinternet.com

**Map ref 4 - TL94**

Water Street,
LAVENHAM, Suffolk,
CO10 9RW
A1141 Lavenham, turn
by Swan (Water St)
right after 50yds into
private drive
4 Rooms, ££
No smoking
Closed 21 Dec-2 Jan

Gilli and Tim Pitt have created a sumptuous haven in the midst of historic Lavenham, one of England's prettiest medieval villages. The Priory dates back to the 13th century and retains many fine historical features, including an oak Jacobean staircase, leading to beautiful bedrooms with crown posts, Elizabethan wall paintings and oak floors. Each room has a spectacular bed, a four-poster, lit bateau or polonaise; and all have en suite facilities, television and tea and coffee making equipment.

Lavenham Priory received the AA Guest Accommodation of the Year Award for 1999-2000.

The house is set in three acres of private grounds, all attractively landscaped and stocked with period herbs, plants and shrubs. Breakfast is taken in the merchants room at an imposing polished table. The great hall with its Tudor inglenook fireplace and an adjoining lounge are comfortable places to relax and are very well stocked with books.

# The Great House

Country house with
a fine restaurant in
a lovely medieval
village

☎ 01787 247431
🖷 01787 248007
🄴 greathouse
@clara.co.uk

**Map ref 4 - TL94**

Market Place,
LAVENHAM, Suffolk,
CO10 9QZ
off A1141 onto Market
Ln, situated just behind
cross on Market Place
5 Rooms, ££
Closed last 3 wks Jan

The Great House is a 15th-century property with a Georgian façade set in Lavenham's magnificent Market Square. The house is run as a 'restaurant with rooms' by owners Regis and Martine Crepy, who provide a little piece of France in this most English of settings. The delightfully furnished restaurant has a large log-burning inglenook fireplace. The menu offers rural French cuisine and features an incredible cheeseboard to finish.

The bedrooms are impressively furnished and include some nice pieces. All the rooms are en suite, but have been sympathetically converted to retain their original character, with beams, and sloping ceilings. Accommodation is spacious; most rooms have separate sitting rooms or a sitting area, and guests can choose between a room with a six-foot wide Jacobean four-poster or a cosier alternative on the top floor. French croissants and petits pains au chocolat are served as part of the English breakfast.

## RECOMMENDED IN THE AREA

**TRADITIONAL PUB:**
*The Angel Hotel,
Lavenham*

**VISIT:**
*Lavenham Guildhall*

# The Angel Inn

*16th-century country village inn, in Constable country*

☎ 01206 263245  📠 01206 263373

**Map ref 4 - TL93**

Polstead Street, STOKE-BY-NAYLAND,
Suffolk, CO6 4SA
off A12 onto B1068 midway between
Colchester and Ipswich
6 Rooms, ££
Closed 25-26 Dec

The landscape artist John Constable was born nearby. He painted extensively in the vale, and the river and villages may seem familiar from his work. The inn itself, with its rustic exterior, and beamed bars with log fires, would be worthy of his painting. The bedrooms are individually furnished, all with en suite bathrooms and colour TV.

Full English breakfast, lunch and supper are served every day in the bar, or in the Well Room. With rough brick walls, a high ceiling with rafters, and a deep well, it makes a unique dining room. Due to local popularity, it is essential to make a dinner reservation when booking accommodation to be sure of a comfortable table at busy times. Fresh local produce is used wherever possible, fresh fish and shellfish from the East Coast, and game from local estates.

## RECOMMENDED IN THE AREA

**RESTAURANT:**
*Hintlesham Hall, Hintlesham*

**VISIT:**
*Colchester Castle Museum, Colchester*

# Comber House

*An impressive Georgian residence in historic Royal Leamington Spa*

☎ 01926 421332  📠 01926 313930

📧 b-b@comberhouse.freeserve.co.uk

**Map ref 3 - SP36**

2 Union Road, ROYAL LEAMINGTON SPA,
Warwickshire, CV32 5LT
from main shopping centre, The Parade,
along Warwick St towards Warwick, pass
fire station on left, 4th right into Union Rd
5 Rooms, ££, No smoking
Closed mid Dec-mid Jan

Situated close to the town centre with ample parking, Comber House makes an ideal base for visiting the surrounding historic sights including Warwick Castle and Stratford-on-Avon. The house has been carefully converted and retains many of its original features making it a fine example of an early 19th-century home. The furniture and fittings throughout the spacious reception rooms are of high quality. Excellent en suite facilities are provided and the bedrooms all have colour televisions and tea and coffee making facilities.

Brian and Roma Shorthouse are friendly and caring hosts, guests are made to feel relaxed and at ease in their charming home and to make use of the private garden. Full English breakfasts are served in the attractive dining room, and a comfortable lounge and snooker room are provided. No dogs are allowed, with the exception of guide dogs; and children must be over 12 years of age.

## RECOMMENDED IN THE AREA

**RESTAURANT:**
*Mallory Court, Leamington Spa*

**TRADITIONAL PUB:**
*Tilted Wig, Warwick*

**VISIT:**
*Baddesley Clinton Hall, Baddesley Clinton*

# *A*shleigh House

*Large Edwardian country residence in spacious grounds, serving splendid breakfasts*

☎ 01564 792315
🖷 01564 794126

**Map ref 3 - SP16**

Whitley Hill,
HENLEY-IN-ARDEN,
Warwickshire, B95 5DL
from Henley-in-Arden
lights, off A3400 onto
A4189 Warwick, house
on left just after
Nurseries
10 Rooms, ££
No smoking

The house stands in a peaceful spot, within two acres of gardens, with well established lawns, borders and shrubs, and big horse-chestnut trees. It is wonderfully handy for trips to Stratford, Warwick or the NEC.

The bedrooms are traditionally furnished, all with modern en suite facilities. Some are on the ground floor in a converted stable building, with parking immediately outside. There is a family room;

however, it is not suitable for children under 12. Dogs are not allowed. A comprehensive English breakfast is served at separate tables in the breakfast room, and dinner is available by arrangement. There are two comfortable sitting rooms, or you can choose to sit in the conservatory overlooking the pretty gardens. Fine period furniture, and memorabilia, enhances the style of the house throughout.

## RECOMMENDED IN THE AREA

**RESTAURANT:**
*Billesley Manor Hotel, Stratford-upon-Avon*

**TRADITIONAL PUB:**
*Bulls Head, Wootton Wawen*

**VISIT:**
*Coughton Court, Coughton*

# Gravelside Barn

*Clever conversion of a lovely old barn set high on a hill overlooking rolling countryside*

☎ 01789 750502
📠 01789 298056
✉ sirguy@gravelside5
.freeserve.co.uk

**Map ref 3 - SP25**

Binton, STRATFORD-UPON-AVON, Warwickshire, CV37 9TU
B439 from Stratford-on-Avon, 3.5m right to Binton. Thro' village & up private drive signposted on left
3 Rooms, ££
No smoking

## RECOMMENDED IN THE AREA

**RESTAURANT:**
*Desports,
Stratford-upon-Avon*

**TRADITIONAL PUB:**
*The Dirty Duck,
Stratford-upon-Avon*

**VISIT:**
*Shakespeare's Birthplace,
Stratford-upon-Avon*

Gravelside is an early 19th-century barn, which has been sympathetically restored by Guy and Denise Belchambers to provide high quality accommodation. It is situated on the outskirts of Binton in an elevated position, offering stunning views over a rural landscape, with the Malvern Hills and the Cotswolds on the horizon. The bedrooms are comfortable, tastefully furnished and well equipped. Extra facilities include mini fridges, televisions and modern en suite shower rooms with power showers. The open plan ground floor includes a very comfortable sitting area and a dining section where home-cooked à la carte breakfasts are served. For dinner there are several pubs and restaurants available locally. This is ideal walking country and the immaculate grounds include the added attraction of an all-weather tennis court. Gravelside makes a superb touring base for visits to Stratford-on-Avon, Warwick Castle and the Cotswolds, with easy access to the M40 motorway.

# Glebe Farm House

**RESTAURANT:**
*Mallory Court,
Leamington Spa*

**TRADITIONAL PUB:**
*Tilted Wig, Warwick*

**VISIT:**
*Warwick Castle, Warwick*

*Country house in a
fabulous location,
with open views and
an exciting organic
menu*

☎ 01789 842501
📠 01789 841194
📧 scorpiolimited
@msn.com

Map ref 3 - SP25

Stratford Road, Loxley,
STRATFORD-UPON-
AVON, Warwickshire,
CV35 9JW

S from Stratford, cross
River Avon, immediate
left B4086 Tiddington
rd, immediate right
(Loxley rd). Farm 2.5m
on left

3 Rooms, £££
No Smoking

*J*ust three miles from Stratford, seven miles from Warwick and five miles from the Cotswolds, the house stands within 30 acres of land, a secluded garden with pristine lawns, trees and flowers, opening onto farmland where you can ramble and look out for wildlife. From all the rooms there are panoramic views of the unspoilt countryside. Kate McGovern, the owner makes excellent use of organic meat and produce from the farm and the kitchen garden to create thrilling dishes, served in the conservatory overlooking the garden. She is also a talented watercolour artist, and some of her paintings can be seen around the house. The pretty bedrooms, all with en suite bathrooms, have oak furniture, four-poster beds, TV, and tea and coffee facilities. The lounge has big comfy sofas and a fireplace, and the subtle warmth of the colours throughout the house makes you feel very much at home.

# $\mathcal{M}$ill Hay House

*Elegant Queen Anne country house located in extensive gardens*

☎ 01386 852498
📠 01386 858038
✉ broadway-tower@clara.net

**Map ref 3 - SP03**

Snowshill Road,
BROADWAY,
Worcestershire,
WR12 7JS
off A44 at Broadway
Main Green towards
Snowshill. House
0.75m on right
3 Rooms, ££
No Smoking in
bedrooms

$\mathcal{M}$ill Hay is a handsome country house set in three acres of landscaped gardens including a medieval pond and moat. Adjacent to the house is the site of a water mill dating from the 12th century. Built of red brick and mellow Cotswold stone, Mill Hay has been lovingly restored to provide quality accommodation in a peaceful rural location. The bedrooms are comfortably furnished and all have en suite facilities. Direct dial telephones, colour televisions, and tea and coffee making equipment are also provided. Original features including floors and panelling are enhanced by fine period pieces in the public areas. Children under 12 are not accommodated, neither are dogs (except guide dogs).

## RECOMMENDED IN THE AREA

**RESTAURANT:**
*Lygon Arms, Broadway*

**TRADITIONAL PUB:**
*Fleece Inn, Bretforton*

**VISIT:**
*The Almonry Heritage Centre, Evesham*

211

# The Old Rectory

## RECOMMENDED IN THE AREA

**RESTAURANT:**
*Marsh Goose, Moreton in Marsh*

**TRADITIONAL PUB:**
*Churchill Arms, Chipping Campden*

**VISIT:**
*Hidcote Manor Garden, Mickleton*

*Mellow Cotswold stone house in a peaceful location opposite the church*

☎ 01386 853729
📠 01386 858061
📧 beauvoisin@ btinternet.com
Map ref 3 - SO75

Church Street, Willersey, BROADWAY, Worcestershire, WR12 7PN
from Broadway B4632 Stratford rd 1.5m, at Bell Inn turn right into Church St
8 Rooms, £££
No smoking
Closed 23-27 Dec

Situated at the end of a quiet lane opposite the 11th-century village church, this former rectory has been carefully restored to provide quality accommodation. The six bedrooms have modern en suite facilities and are all equipped with direct dial telephones, colour televisions, radio alarms, hairdryers and hospitality trays. Period furniture is a feature of the elegant breakfast room, which also has a small sitting area in front of the log fire. A mulberry tree in the walled garden is centuries old and still produces fruit for breakfast in the summer months. The garden is beautiful, and will prove of great interest to the informed plantsman or woman. There are wonderful walks to be had and the Cotswold Way passes nearby the house. The proprietor, Liz Beauvoisin, is happy to advise on a range of local eating places for dinner.

# Leasow House

*Early 17th-century Cotswold stone farmhouse*

☎ 01386 584526 📠 01386 584596
✉ leasow@clara.net

**Map ref 3 - SP03**

Laverton Meadows, BROADWAY,
Worcestershire, WR12 7NA
B4632 from Broadway to Winchcombe for
2m & right to Wormington, 1st on right
7 Rooms, ££, No smoking

Leasow House is situated south of the town in a peaceful rural setting. Parts of the building date from the early 1600s and renovation has been carried out sympathetically to ensure that much of the original charm and character is retained. Bedrooms are comfortable and well equipped with en suite facilities, central heating, colour television, direct dial telephones and hospitality trays. Some have low beams set off by pretty decorative schemes. Two bedrooms are located in a former barn and one has been adapted for disabled guests. Delicious breakfasts are taken in the attractive dining room, which overlooks the gardens. The library lounge is a comfortable and relaxing room where smoking is permitted.

Barbara and Gordon Meekings are friendly and caring hosts who delight in welcoming guests to their lovely home.

## RECOMMENDED IN THE AREA

**RESTAURANT:**
*Dormy House Hotel, Broadway*

**TRADITIONAL PUB:**
*Crown Inn, Blockley*

**VISIT:**
*Broadway Tower Country Park*

---

# The Dell House

*Moulded cornices, marble fireplaces and views to the Cotswolds*

☎ 01684 564448 📠 01684 893974
✉ diana@dellhouse.co.uk

**Map ref 2 - SO74**

Green Lane, Malvern Wells, MALVERN,
Worcestershire, WR14 4HU
2m S of Gt Malvern on A449. left off A449
into Green Ln & premises at top of this road
3 Rooms, £, No smoking

The elegant Regency and early Victorian architecture features in the beautiful ceiling mouldings and chandeliers, finely moulded wall panelling, heavy panelled doors, and sweeping staircase. The house enjoys a wonderfully relaxing location, in two acres of mature private grounds, studded with specimen trees, with a footpath nearby leading into the hills. There is ample guest parking.

A full English, or continental breakfast is served in the lovely morning room, around an antique Victorian table, with stunning views through the French windows to the distant Cotswolds.

Two of the bedrooms have en suite bathroom facilities, all have colour TV and hospitality tray. 'Bredon' has a canopied king-size double bed, easy chairs and coffee table, and views for thirty miles. There is also a very spacious guest lounge.

## RECOMMENDED IN THE AREA

**RESTAURANT:**
*Croque-en-Bouche, Malvern*

**TRADITIONAL PUB:**
*The Talbot Inn, Ledbury*

**VISIT:**
*Museum of Local Life, Worcester*

# *L*ink Lodge

*Beautiful house connected with Edward Elgar*

☎ 01684 572345  🖷 01684 572345
✉ linklodge@aol.com
**Map ref 2 - SO74**

3 Pickersleigh Road, MALVERN,
Worcestershire, WR14 2RP
A449 from Worcester, thro' main traffic lights
in Malvern Link. 1st left. 1st house on left
3 Rooms, £, No smoking

*E*lgar, the famous English composer, once taught music within the walls of this elegant listed building. It was originally built around 1700 and was extended during the Georgian period, in the Palladian style. It features curved walls and a curved staircase. En suite facilities are available, as well as an extensive library of local information.

An excellent four-course traditional or vegetarian breakfast is cooked on the Aga, and served around one table, the large bright kitchen is decorated with dried flowers in farmhouse style. Restaurants for dinner are found close by. The house is near the station and buses, with plenty of private parking.

The acre of landscaped gardens around the house includes a variety of large and unusual trees. Croquet can be played on the lawn. There are views and walks across a tree-lined common to the Malvern Hills.

## RECOMMENDED IN THE AREA

**RESTAURANT:**
*Colwall Park Hotel, Malvern*

**TRADITIONAL PUB:**
*Farmers Arms, Malvern*

**VISIT:**
*Worcester Cathedral, Worcester*

*Dan Yr Ogof Caves, Powys*

*Harlech Castle, Gwynedd*

*The Octagonal Room,*
*Castle Coch,*
*South Glamorgan*

# Wales

Wales has much to offer with mountain ranges such as the Brecon Beacons and Snowdonia National Parks and its coastline stretching from Flintshire to Newport. The Isle of Anglesey is reached via the Menai Bridge and the AA recommends places to stay here at Cemaes Bay, and Holyhead (the port for ferries to Ireland).

Llandudno and Colwyn Bay are popular centres on the north coast of Wales. The Llandudno Junction RSPB nature reserve overlooks the estuary and Conwy Castle. There are a number of AA recommended places to stay in this area, including a Lighthouse!

There are many historic castles to visit in Wales, these include Beaumaris, Cardiff, Caernarfon, Caerphilly, Conwy and Harlech. St David's is worth a visit for its cathedral alone, found in a quiet valley it houses the tomb of St David. Bishop Gower's ruined palace is found next door to the cathedral.

The National Botanic Garden of Wales can be found at Llanarthne and is the first 'national' botanic garden created in the UK this century. It is set in the 18th-century parkland of Middleton Hall, in a 568-acre estate on the edge of the beautiful Towy Valley. The centrepiece is one of the largest single span glasshouses in the world.

# Cwmtwrch, Four Seasons Restaurant with rooms

*Georgian farmhouse in massive grounds with leisure centre and restaurant*

☎ 01267 290238  📠 01267 290808

**Map ref 2 - SN42**

Nantgaredig, CARMARTHEN,
Carmarthenshire, SA32 7NY
5m E of Carmarthen, take B4310 at
Nantgaredig crossroads towards Brechfa,
premises 0.25m N off A40 on right
6 Rooms, ££
Closed 23 Dec-28 Dec

This small family run hotel is part of a development that started with a 200 year old farmhouse and outbuildings. It is set in 30 acres of beautiful landscaped countryside, with trees and shrubs, and garden seats for guests to enjoy the views. A heated swimming pool, jacuzzi and gym are also housed on the grounds.

All the bedrooms are en suite, furnished to match the period of the house: three are at ground level in the converted Georgian barn; three are in the farmhouse itself, where breakfast is served; all have tea and coffee facilities, and colour TV. There is also a large comfortable lounge, and the licensed restaurant, with conservatory and an outdoor deck, offers a choice of delicious dishes, cooked with flair using only the best fresh ingredients.

## RECOMMENDED IN THE AREA

**TRADITIONAL PUB:**
*The Salutation Inn, Pont-ar-Gothi*

**VISIT:**
*National Botanic Gardens of Wales, Llanarthe*

*Snowdon reflected in Llynnau Mymbry, Snowdonia*

# *A*berconwy House

## RECOMMENDED IN THE AREA

**RESTAURANT:**
*Tan-y-Foel Hotel,
Betws-y-Coed*

**TRADITIONAL PUB:**
*Ty Gwyn Hotel*

**VISIT:**
*Dolwyddelan Castle*

*A*berconwy House is a large Victorian property just ten minutes walk from Betws-y-Coed, affording lovely views over the Llugwy and Conwy valleys. It is an ideal location from which to explore the glories of Snowdonia. Bedrooms are attractively decorated and comfortably furnished, all with en suite facilities.

Colour televisions, tea and coffee making equipment, trouser presses and ironing facilities are provided. One bedroom is suitable for family occupation. Guests are welcome to send and receive e-mails. Public rooms comprise a relaxing residents' lounge and a separate breakfast room. Car parking is provided for guests.

# Plas Rhos Hotel

*An impressive hotel located on the promenade offering superb hospitality and wonderful views out to sea*

**☎ 01492 543698 📠 01492 540088**
**✉ enquiries@destination-wales.co.uk**

**Map ref 5 - SH87**

Cayley Promenade, Rhos-on-Sea, COLWYN BAY, Conwy, LL28 4EP
11 Rooms, ££

This imposing property, built in the late 19th century, is situated on the promenade at Rhos-on-Sea, where it commands panoramic views over the bay, beach and coast. It has been extensively and tastefully renovated by Gillian Ponton, to provide high quality, well equipped modern accommodation.

The eleven guest bedrooms are individually styled and beautifully decorated, all have en suite facilities. Remote control television, central heating, hairdryer, luxury bathrobes and toiletries are provided. An extra welcome touch is the hospitality tray, offering a variety of hot beverages, cookies and mineral water. The hotel is decorated with extraordinary arrays of floral art, 19th century 'objets d'art' and Victoriana. The public areas include a bright and welcoming dining room where a generous cooked breakfast is served, along with a tempting breakfast buffet. Dinner is available by

## RECOMMENDED IN THE AREA

**RESTAURANT:**
*Café Niçoise, Colwyn Bay*

**TRADITIONAL PUB:**
*Kinmel Arms, Abergele*

**VISIT:**
*RSPB Nature Reserve, Llandudno Junction*

arrangement. Guests have a choice of two comfortable lounges, one with a small bar and the other with lovely views over the bay. There is also a secluded tea arbour in the pretty rear garden. The car park is a great advantage here. Guide dogs only can be accommodated.

# Gwern Borter Manor

*Horseride across the Snowdonia National Park from a country manor house, lying at the foot of the TalyFan mountain*

☎ 01492 650360
📠 01492 650360
✉ mail@snowdonia holidays.co.uk

**Map ref 5 - SH77**

Barkers Lane, CONWY, Conwy, LL32 8YL from Conwy B5106 2.25m, right onto unclass rd (Rowen) 0.5m, right to Gwern Borter approx 0.5m on left

3 Rooms, ££

Surrounded by woodland, lakes, rivers and mountains, steeped in Celtic history, the Manor stands in 12 acres of landscaped grounds, with beautiful ornamental and medicinal herb gardens, a pond with ducks and geese, and pets' corner, with lots of farm animals. Guests can go riding from the manor's own riding stables. Other facilities include a gym and sauna, games room and cycle hire. The house is full of historic character, with an oak entrance hall and staircase, a magnificent oak fireplace in the dining room, and a cosy lounge. All these rooms have antique furniture, there is also an intriguing collection of oil paintings and limited edition prints. The bedrooms all have a Victorian theme, one has a genuine Victorian four-poster bed. All the bedrooms have private facilities, colour TV, radio alarm and hairdryer. There is a wide choice of breakfasts, although no evening meal is provided the proprietors are happy to supply a list of personally tested and recommended restaurants. There is also cottage accommodation in the farm's converted outbuildings.

## RECOMMENDED IN THE AREA

**RESTAURANT:**
*Café Niçoise, Colwyn Bay*

**TRADITIONAL PUB:**
*Queens Head, Llandudno Junction*

**VISIT:**
*Bodnant Gardens, Tal-y-Cafn*

# Abbey Lodge

*Former gentleman's residence built in 1870, close to town centre and beaches*

☎ **01492 878042**
📠 **01492 878042**

**Map ref 5 - SH78**

14 Abbey Road,
LLANDUDNO, Conwy,
LL30 2EA
from prom (sea on right)
last left before pier.
Straight on at rdbt,
3rd right Clarence Rd,
at top into Abbey Rd
turn right, Lodge on left
4 Rooms, £
No smoking
Closed Xmas/New Year

AA ★★★★

## RECOMMENDED IN THE AREA

**RESTAURANT:**
*Empire Hotel, Llandudno*

**TRADITIONAL PUB:**
*Groes Inn, Conwy*

**VISIT:**
*RSPB Nature Reserve,
Llandudno Junction*

Abbey Lodge has been carefully restored over recent years by Trish and Geoffrey Howard. The atmosphere is welcoming and the luxurious bedrooms are attractively decorated, all have bath and shower, with bathrobes. Hospitality trays, bottled mineral water, colour television, hairdryer, new beds and furnishings all contribute to a very comfortable stay. The charming drawing room with its open fire and elegant furniture is the ideal place to relax. Afternoon tea is served in the lounge, or in summer months on the patio. The country house style dining room is used for breakfast, a choice of continental or traditional cooked breakfast is offered and individual requirements are willingly catered for. The emphasis is very much on relaxation and pampering, and the proprietors will be happy to assist you in planning a tailor-made holiday or just finding your feet in the area. You can board a Victorian tram nearby which will take you to the summit of the Great Orme. Sights and activities include the country park, ancient copper mines ski slope, tobbogan run and cable car.

**221**

# Bryn Derwen Hotel

*Classy Victorian home serving fresh, imaginative cuisine with a reputation for excellence*

☎ 01492 876804
📠 01492 876804
✉ brynderwen@
m.s.n.com

**Map ref 5 - SH78**

34 Abbey Road,
LLANDUDNO,
Conwy, LL30 2EE
from A55, A470, left at
promenade to cenotaph,
turn left, straight on at
rdbt, 4th right (York Rd),
hotel at top
10 Rooms ££, No
smoking, Closed Nov-Feb

### RECOMMENDED IN THE AREA

**RESTAURANT:**
*Bodysgallen Hall, Llandudno*

**TRADITIONAL PUB:**
*The Queen's Head, Llandudno Junction*

**VISIT:**
*RSPB Nature Reserve, Llandudno Junction*

Built in 1878 as a private home for a wealthy merchant and his family, The Bryn Derwen has been restored by owners Stuart and Valerie Langfield to make it an elegant hotel with an atmosphere of easy tranquillity, and the added luxuries of a beauty salon and sauna. It is located in a residential area, a short walk from the shops and the beach. There is off street parking. Stuart was awarded Welsh Chef of the Year, and he creates a series of exciting dishes. Dinner is served in the elegant, candlelit dining room.

An original pine staircase leads to the en suite bedrooms, all with colour TV, tea and coffee, and luxury toiletries, and more evidence of the heritage of the house is seen in the stained glass windows in the garden lounge. There is another room at the front of the house for reading and quiet relaxing.

# Bryn-y-Bia Lodge

## RECOMMENDED IN THE AREA

**RESTAURANT:**
*Bodysgallen Hall, Llandudno*

**TRADITIONAL PUB:**
*The Queen's Head, Llandudno Junction*

**VISIT:**
*RSPB Nature Reserve, Llandudno Junction*

*Victorian house with large walled gardens overlooking Llandudno and the sea*

☎ 01492 549644
📠 01492 549644
✉ carol@brynybia.demon.co.uk

**Map ref 5 - SH78**

Craigside,
LLANDUDNO, Conwy,
LL30 3AS
from Promenade
(with sea on left &
facing Little Orme),
as road rises Lodge
200yds on right
12 Rooms, ££

This gracious house, built as a gentleman's residence in the middle of the 19th century, stands back from the main road, on the descent into Llandudno from the Little Orme. There is parking for all guests within the grounds. Inside, the rooms are light and airy, with a harmonious blend of colours and styles. All the bedrooms are en suite with colour TV, beverage tray and telephone. A delightfully restful lounge and cocktail bar are available for residents use, both have bay windows looking over the garden. In the spacious dining room, cream clad tables and warm terracotta panelled walls provide a fitting setting for breakfast, including freshly squeezed orange juice, home made muesli and preserves and usually home made bread. Dinner is available by arrangement.

# Cranberry House Guest House

*A Victorian townhouse in a quiet residential area*

☎ **01492 879760**  📠 **01492 879760**

**Map ref 5 - SH78**

12 Abbey Road, LLANDUDNO, Conwy,
LL30 2EA
from A470, down Conway Rd to Mostyn St,
turn left at bottom rdbt, 1st right up Arvon
Ave, 1st left, 5th house on right
5 Rooms, £, No smoking
Closed Dec-Jan

## RECOMMENDED IN THE AREA

**RESTAURANT:**
*Bodysgallen Hall, Llandudno*

**TRADITIONAL PUB:**
*Groes Inn, Conwy*

**VISIT:**
*RSPB Nature Reserve, Llandudno Junction*

This elegant house was built in 1880. It has pretty gardens at the front and at the back, and lies just a few minutes' walk away from the shopping area and the pier. It also makes a convenient base for visits to Bodnant Gardens, Conwy Castle and Snowdonia. The landlady was selected for Wales in the AA Landlady of the Year awards, so rest assured that you will be well looked after. Pets are not admitted.

The bedrooms, decorated with patterned wallpaper and fabrics, all have en suite bathrooms, colour TV, tea and coffee, hairdryer and a lock-up safe. Furniture has been chosen to match the style of the house. In the dining room, where a varied breakfast menu is served, there are fine dark wooden chairs and an antique wooden sideboard, as well as a collection of red glassware. There is also a sitting room.

# The Lighthouse

*Distinctly different accommodation in Grade II listed building*

☎ **01492 876819**  📠 **01492 876668**
✉ **enquiries@llandudno-lighthouse.co.uk**

**Map ref 5 - SH78**

Marine Drive, Great Ormes Head
LLANDUDNO, Conwy, LL30 2XD
from promenade towards pier, enter Marine
Drive just past The Grand Hotel. The
Lighthouse 2m on right
3 Rooms, £££, No smoking

## RECOMMENDED IN THE AREA

**RESTAURANT:**
*Martins Hotel & Restaurant, Llandudno*

**TRADITIONAL PUB:**
*Queen's Head, Llandudno Junction*

**VISIT:**
*RSPB Nature Reserve, Llandudno Junction*

Built in the style of a small fortress by the Mersey Docks and Harbour Board in 1862, The Lighthouse stands proudly at the northern edge of the famous Great Orme's Head, Llandudno's spectacular headland. It was fully operational until 1985. Many of the original features have been carefully preserved, such as the panelling in the impressive entrance hall. The comfortable en suite bedrooms are furnished with quality period and antique pieces. Two have their own lounge areas, one of these is the actual glazed dome which contained the optic. Needless to say, all the bedrooms enjoy stunning views of the Irish Sea and Liverpool Bay and each is equipped with a pair of binoculars. On the ground floor is a spacious lounge where a solid fuel stove burns during colder weather. Sumptuous breakfasts are served in the beautifully furnished breakfast room.

# Martins
# Restaurant With Rooms

*Edwardian villa in
the Craig-y-Don area
providing comfortable
accommodation and
award-winning
cuisine*

☎ 01492 870070
📠 01492 876661

**Map ref 5 - SH78**

11 Mostyn Avenue,
Craig-y-Don,
LLANDUDNO, Conwy,
LL30 1YS
exit A55 or A5 at
Colwyn Bay or Conwy
for Llandudno. Martins
is around corner from N
Wales Theatre on prom
4 Rooms, £, No
smoking in bedrooms

Formerly the home of the Arch Druid of Wales, this town house has been tastefully converted to provide comfortable accommodation with en suite facilities. It is conveniently located near the seafront and the North Wales Theatre (theatre breaks are available to guests). The bedrooms are individually styled, and their names, including Walnut, Mahogany and Pine, reflect the furnishings within. A hospitality tray, remote control television, and hairdryer are provided in each room along with welcoming extras such as fresh flowers, fruit and home-made biscuits. Martins is run by professional proprietors Jan and Martin James. Martin is a talented chef and the restaurant has been awarded two AA rosettes for Martin's excellent British cooking, using the best of fresh local produce. Medallions of Welsh black beef, roast rack of Welsh lamb and fillets of wild Conwy salmon are among the specialities of the house, followed by deliciously wicked desserts.

# Eyarth Station

*Elegant accommodation provided in a former railway station*

☎ 01824 703643  📠 01824 707464

**Map ref 5 - SJ15**

Llanfair Dyffryn Clwyd, RUTHIN,
Denbighshire, LL15 2EE
off A525
7 Rooms, £, No smoking in bedrooms

twin rooms, including some rooms on the ground floor, all have en suite facilities and tea and coffee making equipment. Breakfast and supper are served in the dining room, which offers great views of the surrounding countryside.

An old railway station has been converted by Jen and Bert Spencer to create this fine country house providing comfortable accommodation. The line closed in 1964, but the platform remains, and the ticket office has been retained as an interesting and nostalgic feature. The house is set in secluded gardens with magnificent views of the hills surrounding the Vale of Clwyd. Beamed ceilings, antique furniture and log fires characterise the interior of the house.

The bedrooms offer a choice of family, double or

## RECOMMENDED IN THE AREA

**RESTAURANT:**
*Bodidris Hall, Llandegla*

**TRADITIONAL PUB:**
*Cerrigllwydion Arms, Llanynys*

**VISIT:**
*Denbigh Castle, Denbigh*

# Borthwnog Hall Hotel

*Grade II listed 17th-century house overlooking the Mawddach Estuary*

☎ 01341 430271  📠 01341 430682
✉ borthwnoghall@enterprise.net

**Map ref 5 - SH61**

BONTDDU, Gwynedd, LL40 2TT
2m on left from junct A470/A496
3 Rooms, £££
Closed Nov-27 Dec

Borthwnog Hall enjoys a quiet location in Snowdonia National Park surrounded by magnificent Welsh mountain scenery and adjoining the Garth Gell nature reserve. The Georgian style hall has its own Library Art Gallery containing many original watercolours, oil paintings, pottery and sculpture for sale.

The bedrooms and public rooms afford spectacular views towards Cader Idris and the Arran mountains. An elegant sitting room opens out onto the gardens in summer and a log fire burns in colder weather, the house is centrally heated. The bedrooms are comfortable and spacious, one with its own sitting room and all with tea and coffee making facilities. Table d'hote and carte menus are available, last orders for dinner are taken at 8 pm and the premises are licensed.

## RECOMMENDED IN THE AREA

**RESTAURANT:**
*Penmaenuchaf Hall, Dolgellau*

**TRADITIONAL PUB:**
*The Halfway House, Bontddu*

**VISIT:**
*Cymer Abbey, Nr. Dolgellau*

# Hafoty

*Snowdonian farmhouse with stunning
views of Caernarfon Castle*

☎ 01286 830144  📠 01286 830441

**Map ref 5 - SH46**

Rhostryfan, CAERNARFON, Gwynedd,
LL54 7PH
off A487 Caernarfon/Porthmadog rd, 2.5m
from Caernarfon B rd signed Rhostryfan. 1st
left after 30mph sign in village, pass school
5 Rooms, £, No smoking in bedrooms

From its rural situation, just outside the pretty
village of Rhostryfan in Snowdonia, the farm
enjoys spectacular views of the Menai Straits and
Caernarfon Castle. Hafoty has been created over
several years from converted farm buildings and
now provides well-equipped modern
accommodation. Mari and Wil Davies are the
friendly owners, who create a peaceful and relaxing
atmosphere.

Bedrooms are spacious and children are especially
welcome. There is a play area for children, and a cot
and highchair are available. The main house has
comfortably furnished and attractively decorated
public areas, where cheery log fires burn in cooler
weather. One bedroom is located in nearby
outbuildings and several self-catering cottages are
also available.

There are two pubs within a mile and a half serving
reasonably priced meals, and a very good fish and
chip shop five minutes' drive away. All the facilities of
Caernarfon are within 10 minutes' drive.

## RECOMMENDED IN THE AREA

**RESTAURANT:**
*T'yn Rhos, Caernarfon*

**TRADITIONAL PUB:**
*Harp Inn, Llandwrog*

**VISIT:**
*Caernarfon Castle*

# Pengwern Farm

*Victorian house with unobstructed views
of Snowdonia*

☎ 01286 831500  📠 01286 830741
📧 jhjgr@enterprise.net

**Map ref 5 - SH46**

Saron, CAERNARFON, Gwynedd, LL54 5UH
from Caernarfon A487 S, pass supermarket
on right, 1st right after bridge 2m to Saron,
thro' x-rds, farm is 1st drive on right
3 Rooms, £, No smoking
Closed Dec & Jan

Pengwern is a delightful farmhouse surrounded
by 130 acres of beef and sheep farmland
running down to Foryd Bay, noted for its bird life.
There are fine views from many bedrooms over to
Anglesey, and the top of Snowdon can also be seen
on clear days.

Bedrooms are generally spacious and all are well
equipped with modern facilities, including en suite
bath and shower rooms, colour televisions, and tea
and coffee making equipment. A comfortable
lounge is provided for guests and good home
cooking is served.

The farmhouse is a good base from which to explore
the Snowdonia National Park and the historic town
of Caernarfon.

## RECOMMENDED IN THE AREA

**RESTAURANT:**
*T'yn Rhos, Caernarfon*

**TRADITIONAL PUB:**
*Harp Inn, Llandwrog*

**VISIT:**
*Snowdon Mountain Railway, Llanberis*

# Tyddynmawr Farmhouse

*Farmhouse at the foot of the mountain of Cader Idris*

☎ 01341 422331

**Map ref 3 - SH71**

Islawrdref, DOLGELLAU, Gwynedd, LL40 1TL
from town centre branch left at top of square, left at garage into Cader Rd approx 3m. 1st farm on left after Gwernan Lake
2 Rooms, £, No smoking
Closed Nov-17 Mar

About three miles from the historic market town of Dolgellau, behind a neat white fence, with the mountain rising behind it, you find this cosy 18th-century stone farmhouse. Oak beams, log fires and brasses above the fireplace give it plenty of character, and there are spectacular views of the mountain scenery from the windows. The bedrooms, one with a shower, the other with bath and shower en suite, are decorated with trim wallpaper, and pretty patterned curtains and bedspreads. The magnificent surroundings make this a paradise for birdwatchers, ramblers, photographers and artists. The owners, Alun and Olwen (AA Landlady of the Year Finalist in 1999), farm Cader Idris itself. Guests are welcome to watch the day-to-day activities of a working farm, and to explore the land, a disused slate mine, a cave, spectacular hidden waterfalls, and mountain lakes with private fishing, or even climb to the summit.

## RECOMMENDED IN THE AREA

**RESTAURANT:**
*Penmaenuchaf Hall, Dolgellau*

**TRADITIONAL PUB:**
*George III Hotel, Dolgellau*

**VISIT:**
*Cymer Abbey, Nr. Dolgellau*

# Gwrach Ynys Country Guest House

*Country house close to the mountains and sea*

☎ 01766 780742  📠 01766 781199
✉ gwynfor@talk21.com

**Map ref 5 - SH53**

Ynys, Talsarnau, HARLECH, Gwynedd, LL47 6TS
2m N of Harlech on A496
7 Rooms, £, No smoking

Billed as the ideal house for nature lovers, this impeccably maintained Edwardian property is situated on reclaimed marshland, in a lowland area between Harlech Castle and Cardigan Bay. A National Nature Reserve is close by and Snowdonia is within easy reach. Gwrach Ynys is surrounded by lawns and gardens and the family's ponies graze in the adjoining paddock.

Bedrooms are decorated with pretty wallpapers and six of them are equipped with en suite facilities. Some rooms are suitable for families, and children are especially welcome. Two comfortably furnished lounges are provided for residents, and hospitality from Deborah and Gwynfor Williams is warm and welcoming. Deborah is an accomplished cook and provides hearty breakfasts. Gwynfor looks after front of house matters and is always happy to offer advice on local attractions.

## RECOMMENDED IN THE AREA

**RESTAURANT:**
*Castle Cottage, Harlech*

**TRADITIONAL PUB:**
*Grapes Hotel, Maentwrog*

**VISIT:**
*Harlech Castle, Harlech*

# Tyddyn Du Farm

*Delightful 17th-century farmhouse in the heart of Snowdonia, with luxury barn and stable suites*

☎ 01766 590281
🖷 01766 590281
✉ info@tyddyndu.co.uk

**Map ref 5 - SH53**

Gellilydan, Ffestiniog,
PORTHMADOG,
Gwynedd, LL41 4RB
1st farmhouse on left
after junct of A487/
A470 near Gellilydan
4 Rooms, £
No smoking inside

## RECOMMENDED IN THE AREA

**RESTAURANT:**
*Hotel Portmeirion, Portmeirion*

**TRADITIONAL PUB:**
*The Grapes, Maentwrog*

**VISIT:**
*Ffestiniog Railway, Porthmadog*

Set against the spectacular backdrop of the Moelwyn mountain range, the stone farmhouse is warm and cosy, with wooden beams, and a large inglenook fireplace in the lounge. It is a working farm, with sheep and lambs, as well as some hens, ducks on the mill pond, and Welsh mountain ponies. Guests are welcome to observe the farm at work and help to collect eggs or feed the chickens ducks and ponies. Bedrooms in the house look out towards the hills and mountains, one is en suite.

There are luxury ground-floor suites in the converted stable and barn, with private access. These are equipped with fridge, microwave, shower and jacuzzi bath, French windows open onto slate patios with open views of the countryside. Traditional farmhouse cooking is served at separate tables in the dining room. Besides breakfast, you can arrange to have a three-course candlelit dinner (not on Sundays and Thursdays).

# Ty Isaf Farmhouse

*Traditional longhouse with meadow and stream in a sleepy hamlet*

☎ 01341 423261
✉ raygear@tyisaf78.freeserve.co.uk
Map ref 5 - SH72

LLANFACHRETH, Gwynedd, LL40 2EA
from Dolgellau, cross river & turn right onto
A494 (Bala), pass Kwiksave store on right,
next left signed Llanfachreth & up hill
3 Rooms, £, No smoking
Closed Xmas & New Year

*I*n idyllic surroundings, opposite the church in the centre of the village, this beautiful former farmhouse has its own meadow with hens and pet llamas, garden and rushing mountain stream. It is built with thick stone walls, a slate roof, and oak rafters.

The Hay Loft, Straw Store and Stable bedrooms, all with en suite facilities, are simply decorated and fitted with stripped pine furniture and comfortable beds. The lounge has books, games and TV, or you can retreat to the 'Brewis' with its ancient butter churn, and mountain views.

Delicious, fresh home-cooked food is served, using local produce, and eggs from the farm's own hens. There is a choice at breakfast and a set four-course meal is available in the evening.

## RECOMMENDED IN THE AREA

**RESTAURANT:**
*Bontddu Hall, Bontddu*

**TRADITIONAL PUB:**
*George III Hotel, Dolgellau*

**VISIT:**
*Cymer Abbey, Nr. Dolgellau*

# Dolffanog Fawr

*Former farmhouse idyllically situated in Snowdonia National Park*

☎ 01654 761247
Map ref 2 - SH70

TAL-Y-LLYN, Gwynedd, LL36 9AJ
A487 midway between Machynlleth &
Dolgellau, turn left onto B4405,
establishment 1m on right
4 Rooms, ££, No smoking

*A* 17th-century farmhouse has been lovingly restored by Pam and Alan Coulter to create this small haven of a guest house in one of Snowdonia's most beautiful spots.

The house lies at the foot of Cader Idris and there are superb views towards this and across Tal-y-Llyn lake. It is the perfect setting for naturalists, anglers and walkers. Bedrooms (four en suite) are attractively furnished and include colour television, tea and coffee making equipment and other thoughtful extras. The comfortable lounge has patio doors leading out to the garden.

Pam is responsible for the imaginative home cooking. Hospitality is warm and friendly, and a welcoming glass of sherry is offered before dinner, which is served dinner party style. Children and pets are not accommodated.

## RECOMMENDED IN THE AREA

**RESTAURANT:**
*Bontddu Hall, Bontddu*

**TRADITIONAL PUB:**
*Penhelig Arms Hotel, Aberdyfi*

**VISIT:**
*Castell-Y-Bere, Llanfihangel-Y-Pennant*

# Hafod Country House

*Handsome Edwardian house set in an acre of gardens*

☎ 01407 710500  📠 01407 710055
✉ hirst.hafod@tesco.net

**Map ref 5 - SH39**

CEMAES BAY, Isle of Anglesey, LL67 0DS
off A5025, turning for Llanfechell, opposite
renovated windmill
3 Rooms, £, No smoking

This fine country house is situated on the outskirts of the lovely fishing village of Cemaes Bay, within easy walking distance of the village and the beach. It is set amid pretty lawns and gardens, where croquet can be played in the summer months. There is a wildlife pond that is a haven for a variety of wild birds. The bedrooms are smart, modern and attractively decorated. En suite facilities are provided along with colour television, clock radios, tea and coffee trays, and hairdryers.

Antique pieces and a collection of books to browse through are features of the elegant drawing room. There is a separate dining room where a substantial breakfast is served, including home made apple and pear juice in the autumn, wild mushrooms in season, and delicious home-made preserves. Ample private parking is available.

## RECOMMENDED IN THE AREA

**RESTAURANT:**
*Ye Olde Bulls Head Inn, Beaumaris*

**TRADITIONAL PUB:**
*Ship Inn, Red Wharf Bay*

**VISIT:**
*Din Llugwy Ancient Village, Llanallgo*

# Yr Hendre

*A warm welcome to Holyhead, off the West coast of the Isle of Anglesey*

☎ 01407 762929  📠 01407 762929
✉ rita@yr-hendre.freeserve.co.uk

**Map ref 5 - SH28**

Porth-y-Felin Road, HOLYHEAD, Isle of
Anglesey, LL65 1AH
from A5 in town centre, left at War Memorial,
next left, over crossroads, house on right
facing park
3 Rooms, £, No smoking in bedrooms

## RECOMMENDED IN THE AREA

**RESTAURANT:**
*Ye Olde Bulls Head Inn, Beaumaris*

**TRADITIONAL PUB:**
*Ye Olde Bulls Head Inn, Beaumaris*

**VISIT:**
*Bryn Celli Ddu Burial Chamber, Bryncelli Ddu*

The house and grounds are opposite a park yet are only a few minutes from the Holyhead town centre and ferry terminals. There are many lovely walks to enjoy in the area as well as sandy beaches, a sailing school, watersports, pony trekking and a championship golf course. Boat trips can also be arranged locally giving opportunities for bird watching.

The house itself has been tastefully restored to provide high standards of guest accommodation. The bedrooms are individually designed and furnished, all with en suite bathrooms. Facilities include colour TV, tea and coffee, radio alarms, hairdryers and many extras. The lounge has TV, video and a selection of books. Wonderful views of the sea and gardens can be appreciated from the dining room.

# Llanwenarth House

*Property of historical and architectural interest peacefully located in the Brecon Beacons National Park*

### RECOMMENDED IN THE AREA

**RESTAURANT:**
*Walnut Tree Inn,
Llandewi Skirrid*

**TRADITIONAL PUB:**
*Clytha Arms,
Abergavenny*

**VISIT:**
*Big Pit Mining Museum,
Blaenavon*

☎ 01873 830289
🖷 01873 832199

**Map ref 2 - SO21**

Govilon,
ABERGAVENNY,
Monmouthshire, NP7 9SF
from roundabout E of
Abergavenny A465
towards Merthyr Tydfil
for 3.5m to next rdbt.
1st exit Govilon, drive
150yds on right
5 Rooms, ££
No smoking in
bedrooms or dining
room

This fine country house is set against the beautiful backdrop of the Brecon Beacons National Park and was built prior to 1600 by the ancestors of Sir Henry Morgan, infamous privateer and Governor of Jamaica. Personally run by Bruce and Amanda Weatherill, the house provides easy comfort in elegantly appointed accommodation, with fine period furnishings. The spacious bedrooms, including one on the ground floor, all have en suite bath or shower room and all the expected amenities. Dinner, served in the attractive dining room, makes extensive use of quality home-grown and local produce, including organically grown vegetables and fruit from the large kitchen garden. Aperitifs are served in the drawing room before dinner, where a log fire burns cheerfully in cooler months. There is adequate parking, young children cannot be accommodated.

# Highfield House

## Stone-built house affording wonderful country views

☎ 01291 689286 📠 01291 689286

**Map ref 2 - SO50**

Chapel Hill, TINTERN, Monmouthshire, NP6 6TF
pass Tintern Abbey, next left at Royal George Hotel, bear left at fork & uphill for 0.25m into forest. Signed on left
3 Rooms, £, No smoking in bedrooms

Perched on the hillside above Tintern Abbey and surrounded by forest, this remarkable stone-built house offers glorious views of the surrounding countryside.

The bedrooms and public rooms have been imaginatively decorated. All the bedrooms have en suite facilities, and log fires enhance the welcoming atmosphere of the public rooms in cooler weather. Dinner is lovingly prepared by the proprietor Mr McCaffery, with an emphasis on Mediterranean cuisine.

The six acres of land around the house include woodland areas with plenty of scope for lovely walks. There is also a variety of farm animals, including chickens to ensure fresh free range eggs for your breakfast. For the more adventurous, mountain biking, canoeing and badminton can be arranged.

### RECOMMENDED IN THE AREA

**RESTAURANT:**
*Cwyrt Bleddyn, Llangybi*

**TRADITIONAL PUB:**
*Lion Inn, Trelleck*

**VISIT:**
*Tintern Abbey, Tintern*

# Green Lanterns Guest House

## 18th-century farmhouse in a hillside setting

☎ 01639 631884
✉ stuart.brown7@virgin.net

**Map ref 2 - SS79**

Hawdref Ganol Farm, Cimla, NEATH, Neath Port Talbot, SA12 9SL
exit M4 J43 (Neath). Take B4287 (Cimla) & right at x-rds 300yds past comprehensive school, look for AA sign
4 Rooms, £, No smoking in bedrooms

Peacefully situated in open countryside, this beautifully restored property is part of a 46-acre equestrian and pony trekking centre. From its hillside location it offers panoramic views over the Vale of Neath. On the ground floor guests can relax in the welcoming lounge where real fires burn in the enormous inglenook fireplace, and meals are taken in the attractive dining room.

The spacious bedrooms are furnished and decorated in a style appropriate to the house, but modern facilities are provided, including en suites in two of the rooms. Margaret Brown extends a warm welcome to her guests, while the family connection is maintained by her daughter Caren, who runs the equestrian side of the business.

### RECOMMENDED IN THE AREA

**RESTAURANT:**
*Aberavon Beach Hotel, Port Talbot*

**TRADITIONAL PUB:**
*Prince of Wales Inn, Kenfig*

**VISIT:**
*Glyn Vivian Art Gallery, Swansea*

# Poyerston Farm

*Traditional Victorian farmhouse, and working farm, with sandy beaches and scenic walks nearby*

☎ 01646 651347
📠 01646 651347

**Map ref 1 - SM90**

Cosheston,
PEMBROKE,
Pembrokeshire,
SA72 4SJ
from Carmarthen A477
Pembroke rd, approx
0.5m past sign for
Milton, farm on left just
before Vauxhall garage
5 Rooms, £
No smoking
Closed 20 Dec-10 Jan

The farm is found at the end of a private drive, nestling between the medieval town of Pembroke and the historic village of Carew. It is only minutes away from the beautiful South Pembrokeshire coastline with its many wonderful beaches and the scenery of the famous National Park. The bedrooms, some on the ground floor, are all en suite, offering comfort and style. There are two comfortable lounges where guests can relax, and a lovely Victorian conservatory overlooking the attractive gardens. Superb, traditional home cooking is offered from the Aga, using fresh local produce. A hearty breakfast is served, preparing guests for a day exploring the area. Dinner is available by prior arrangement. Please note that this is a completely non smoking establishment.

## RECOMMENDED IN THE AREA

**TRADITIONAL PUB:**
*Dial Inn, Lamphey*

**VISIT:**
*Pembroke Castle, Pembroke*

# $\mathcal{E}$rw-Lon Farm

*Working farm in the Pembrokeshire Coast National Park*

 **01348 881297**

**Map ref 1 - SM93**

Pontfaen, FISHGUARD, Pembrokeshire, SA65 9TS
on B4313 between Fishguard and Maenclochog
3 Rooms, £, No smoking

*T*raditional Welsh hospitality is offered by the friendly McAllister family at their comfortable farmhouse. It is a beef and sheep farm looking over the lovely wooded Gwaun Valley at the foot of the Preseli Hills, with some superb views to be enjoyed. There are three thoughtfully furnished and well equipped bedrooms, two doubles and one twin, all with en suite facilities, colour television, clock radios, hairdryers, shaving points and tea and coffee-making equipment. A relaxing lounge is also provided for residents.

Maintenance standards are high throughout and a homely atmosphere prevails. Mrs McAllister serves up some of the finest examples of traditional farmhouse cooking, where the size of the portions matches the warmth of the welcome!

## RECOMMENDED IN THE AREA

**RESTAURANT:**
*Warpool Court Hotel, St David's*

**TRADITIONAL PUB:**
*Harp Inn, Letterston*

**VISIT:**
*Oceanlab, Fishguard*

# $\mathcal{Y}$-Gorlan Guest House

*Comfortable family-run house near the cathedral and coast*

**01437 720837** **01437 721148**

**Map ref 1 - SM72**

77 Nun Street, ST DAVID'S, Pembrokeshire, SA62 6NU
in centre of St David's
5 Rooms, £, No smoking in bedrooms

*J*ust a short walk from the centre and the cathedral, this establishment is ideally situated for exploring the picturesque little city. There are sandy beaches, boat trips and golf nearby, or you could take a walk along the coastal path and see the craggy cliffs and headlands, and the wild open countryside.

The cream exterior is decorated with hanging baskets, and inside, on the first floor, there is a lounge with TV and video, and stunning panoramic views across open fields to Whitesands Bay. The neat, modern bedrooms all have en suite bathrooms with showers, as well as colour TV, tea and coffee facilities, clock radio and hairdryer, some bedrooms enjoy same aspect as the lounge. There is a restaurant with a bar, and a varied menu with a vegetarian selection is served at dinner.

## RECOMMENDED IN THE AREA

**RESTAURANT:**
*Warpool Court Hotel, St David's*

**TRADITIONAL PUB:**
*Cambrian Inn, Solva*

**VISIT:**
*St David's Cathedral & Bishops Palace, St David's*

# *G*langrwyney
## court

*A splendid Georgian house on the edge of the Brecon Beacons National Park*

☎ 01873 811288
🖷 01873 810317

**Map Ref 2 – SO21**

CRICKHOWELL, Powys, NP8 1ES
3m from Abergavenny on A40 towards Brecon, 1st right after Powys county change on left
5 Rooms, ££, No smoking in bedrooms

*G*langrwyney Court is a welcoming family home set in beautiful gardens and parkland. The Brecon Beacons National Park and the Black Mountains nearby offer a vast expanse for walkers to explore.

*T*he house has spacious public rooms and log fires burn in the main sitting rooms during the winter months. All the bedrooms are beautifully furnished and have en suite or private facilities. Double, twin, single and family rooms are available, as well as the master suite with en suite steam shower and a luxuriously deep bath. The twin room has its own private jacuzzi bathroom. The Master Suite and West Wing rooms have king-size beds. Colour televisions and tea and coffee making facilities are provided in all the rooms, and there are superb views of the gardens and surrounding

## RECOMMENDED
IN THE AREA

**RESTAURANT:**
*Gliffaes Hotel,
Crickhowell*

**TRADITIONAL PUB:**
*The Bear, Crickhowell*

**VISIT:**
*Tretower Court & Castle,
Tretower*

scenery. Dogs may be permitted by prior arrangement and smoking is permitted in one of the lounges. Evening meals are available by prior arrangement and the premises have a residential license. Short breaks holidays are offered here, child discounts may apply for children under 10 years, and children of all ages may be accepted.

A tennis court, crouqet and boules are available to guests, while pony trekking, fishing and shooting can be arranged nearby. Abergavenny and Brecon offer excellent golf courses with teaching professionals.

# York House Guest House

*Late Victorian residence with mountain views and country house atmosphere*

☎ 01497 820705

**Map ref 2 - SO24**

Hardwick Road, Cusop, HAY-ON-WYE, Powys, HR3 5QX
on B4348 0.5m from main car park in Hay-on-Wye
4 Rooms, ££, No smoking

This beautifully preserved and refurbished house, with its bay windows and tall chimneys, displays all the elegance of a house of its period in a distinctive Welsh style. It is in a quiet position, less than ten minutes' walk from the centre of Hay-on-Wye.

The bedrooms all face south, away from the road, across the beautiful, large garden, and towards the peaks of the Black Mountains. They are all en suite, individually decorated and furnished in period style, with easy chairs, colour TV, books, dried flowers and potted plants. Meals, using fresh produce from the garden and other local sources, are served at separate tables in the dining room. A full English or lighter breakfast is offered, with cereals, yoghurt and brown bread always available. A traditional dinner menu is offered, with home made fudge, and coffee or tea in the lounge afterwards. Packed lunches are available on request.

## RECOMMENDED IN THE AREA

**RESTAURANT:**
*Old Black Lion Hotel, Hay-on-Wye*

**TRADITIONAL PUB:**
*The Famous Old Black Lion, Hay-on-Wye*

**VISIT:**
*South Wales Borderers (24th Regiment) Museum, Brecon*

*Dan Yr Ogof Caves, Powys*

# Guidfa House

*An elegant setting for Cordon Bleu cooking in the heart of Wales*

☎ 01597 851241
📠 01597 851875
✉ guidfa@
globalnet.co.uk

**Map ref 2 - SO06**

Crossgates,
LLANDRINDOD
WELLS, Powys,
LD1 6RF
3m N, at junct of
A483/A44
6 Rooms, £
No smoking in
bedrooms

*T*ony and Anne Millan are the welcoming proprietors of this long established country guest house in a fine Georgian property. In 1999 Tony's front of house qualities were recognised when he reached the finals of the AA Landlady of the Year award. Bedrooms, including one located at ground floor level, are individually designed and all have en suite facilities. Central heating, colour television, tea and coffee making equipment are provided along with various thoughtful extras. In the comfortable sitting room a cheerful log fire burns in the cooler months, and in the evenings Tony serves drinks to guests at the bar. In fine weather guests may wish to take their drinks out onto the front lawn, or enjoy a stroll in the garden. Food at Guidfa House is rather special. Anne is a qualified chef and serves imaginative dishes using fresh local produce whenever possible.

## RECOMMENDED IN THE AREA

**RESTAURANT:**
*Carlton House,
Llanwrtyd Wells*

**TRADITIONAL PUB:**
*The Bell Country Inn,
Llandrindod Wells*

**VISIT:**
*The Judge's Lodging,
Presteigne*

# Yr Hen Felin

*'The Old Mill' set on the banks of the River Gwydol*

☎ **01650 511868**

**Map ref 2 - SH70**

Abercegir, MACHYNLLETH, Powys,
SY20 8NR
off A489 approx 4m E of Machynlleth signed
Abercegir. On entering village, right onto
unmade rd after telephone kiosk, cross
bridge
3 Rooms, £, No smoking
Closed Xmas/New Year

## Recommended in the Area

**Restaurant:**
*Ynyshir Hall, Eglwysfach*

**Traditional Pub:**
*Dolbrodmaeth Inn, Machynlleth*

**Visit:**
*Centre of Alternative Technology, Machynlleth*

*D*ating from the early 19th century, this lovely house was originally a water mill. It is located on the banks of the River Gwydol and offers superb views over the surrounding countryside. Two bedrooms overlook the river where trout and herons can often be seen. The mill has been carefully restored over recent years but exposed beams and timbers still remain and the rooms are laid throughout with the original stripped pine floorboards. An inglenook fireplace, with a wood-burning stove, features in the very comfortable lounge. The bedrooms are attractively furnished and decorated, all have en suite showers. The house is owned and run by the very hospitable Jill and Barry Stevens, who create a peaceful and relaxing atmosphere. At breakfast guests can choose between the traditional, vegetarian or continental breakfast, all served with orange juice, cereals, fruit, toast, preserves and honey.

# Dyffryn Farmhouse

*Restored 17th-century half-timbered barn*

☎ **01686 688817** 📠 **01686 688324**
📧 **daveandsue@clara.net**

**Map ref 2 - SO19**

Dyffryn, Aberhafesp, NEWTOWN, Powys,
SY16 3JD
B4568 to Aberhafesp, right to Bwlchyffridd,
bear left at next junct, then left twice. Right
at x-rds and farm is down hill
3 Rooms, ££, No smoking

## Recommended in the Area

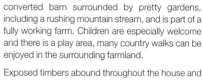

**Traditional Pub:**
*Lion Hotel, Llandinam*

**Visit:**
*Montgomery Castle, Montgomery*

*D*ave and Sue Jones have lovingly restored this fine old building over the last few years. It is a converted barn surrounded by pretty gardens, including a rushing mountain stream, and is part of a fully working farm. Children are especially welcome and there is a play area, many country walks can be enjoyed in the surrounding farmland.

Exposed timbers abound throughout the house and three well-equipped bedrooms are provided, all with en suite facilities. Residents have the use of a comfortable sitting room and meals are served family style. Dave and Sue, together with their young family, are exceptionally friendly and hospitable, and a peaceful and relaxing atmosphere prevails. Restaurants and pubs can be recommended, and places to visit include Powis Castle, the ancient border town of Montgomery, the Cambrian mountains and a nearby nature reserve.

# The Old Vicarage

*Tranquil 18th-century property surrounded by stunning countryside*

☎ 01691 791345  🖷 01691 791345
✉ oldvicarage@breathemail.net

**Map ref 5 - SJ22**

LLANSILIN, Powys, SY10 7PX
centre of village, follow B4580 from
Oswestry, entrance near red telephone
box by Give Way sign
3 Rooms, £, No smoking

Located in the little village of Llansilin, six miles west of Oswestry, this former vicarage is set in its own extensive lawns and gardens. The house is ideally placed for walking, or visiting the numerous attractions in the area, including mountains, gardens and castles. The friendly hosts, Pam and Rick Johnson, have wide ranging interests and enjoy welcoming guests into their home.

Accommodation is provided in pretty bedrooms, two of which have en suite facilities, and a third which has a private shower room. Tea, coffee and chocolate is provided in the rooms. Everywhere is fresh in appearance and attractively decorated.

A hearty breakfast is served in the dining room, and guests can relax in the lounge in the evenings, watching television, reading or chatting. The house is warmed by oil fired central heating, with relaxing log fires in cooler weather. Pets and children under 12 are not accommodated.

## RECOMMENDED IN THE AREA

**RESTAURANT:**
*Pen-y-Dyffryn Hotel, Oswestry*

**TRADITIONAL PUB:**
*Bradford Arms, Oswestry*

**VISIT:**
*Old Oswestry Hill Fort, Oswestry*

# Woodside Guest House

*A former cottage only two hundred metres from the beach*

☎ 01792 390791

**Map ref 3 - SS48**

OXWICH, Swansea, SA3 1LS
from A4118 from Penmaen after 1m turn
left for Oxwich and Slade, premises at
crossroads
5 Rooms, £
Closed Dec-Jan

The beach, with safe bathing and watersports, coastal path for picturesque walks, and a nature reserve with rare orchids, other plants and birds are all an easy walk away. There is a patio area outside the house, and off-street parking. An original inglenook fireplace in the bar, and wooden beams give the building traditional character.

There are bedrooms on the ground floor with easy access, a room with its own small lounge, and a family suite comprising two bedrooms. They are simply decorated and furnished in pine, all but one have en suite bathrooms.

Meals are taken in the conservatory extension at separate tables; the first course at breakfast is served buffet style.

## RECOMMENDED IN THE AREA

**RESTAURANT:**
*Fairyhill, Reynoldston*

**TRADITIONAL PUB:**
*King Arthur Hotel, Reynoldston*

**VISIT:**
*Oxwich Castle, Oxwich*

*Grasmere in the Lake District, Cumbria*

# Northern England

This region in the guide covers a large area of England from the Midlands to the Scottish border. A number of distinct areas fall within this region, including the Potteries, the Derbyshire Dales, the Peak District, the Yorkshire Dales National Park, North York Moors National Park, The Lake District National Park, The Pennine Way, Hadrians Wall, Kielder Water and the Northumberland National Park.

Chester was a major Roman fortress and is still an important town in Cheshire with a number of attractions. The cathedral here was founded as a Benedictine monastery in 1092 on the site of earlier churches. In 1541 it became the cathedral church of the Diocese of Chester and is an unusually well-preserved example of a medieval monastic complex. A summer music festival is held here during the last two weeks of July and a flower festival in

early September. Chester also has a visitor centre offering information and guided tours. Nearby Chester Zoo boasts the largest zoological gardens in the UK with 5000 animals in 500 species.

York is another ancient city well worth a visit. Constantine was made Emperor here in 306 and the modern name for the town is derived from the Norse, Jorvik, as the Vikings named the town when they took over for about a century in 866. The Jorvik Viking Centre opened in 1984 to display archaeological discoveries found between 1976 and 1981 which shed new light on the Viking way of life. York Minster, the largest medieval structure in the UK, is the fourth building on its site and took some 250 years to build. York Castle and the National Railway Museum are other highlights.

County Durham boasts the ancient city of Durham, founded in 995 when a Saxon church was built on the rock in the River Wear's hairpin bend. Less than a century later Bishop William of Calais began building Durham Cathedral which like the Saxon church before it, was built to house the shrine of St Cuthbert. Durham Castle was built by William the Conqueror, the entrance to the main hall is the most extravagant piece of

Norman work remaining in Britain. Much of the castle was later renewed and it is now used by the university.

Cumbria is most famous for the Lake District National Park, the visitor centre can be found at Windermere and was England's first National Park Visitor Centre. Windermere Steamboat Museum houses a unique collection of Victorian and Edwardian steamboats and vintage motorboats, many still in working order.

There are some interesting literary connections to the Lake District. Beatrix Potter wrote many of her books in a little 17th-century house, Hill Top, at Near Sawrey. You can visit the house which contains her furniture and china. William Wordsworth lived at Dove Cottage, Grasmere, from 1799 to 1808. The house is kept in its original condition and houses The Wordsworth Museum.

Hadrians Wall runs across England from Carlisle in Cumbria to the coast of Northumberland. The Roman fort of Housesteads is one of the best preserved Roman forts, found on the wall at Bardon Mills it covers five acres and houses the only known Roman hospital in Britain.

*ievaulx Abbey,*
*Helmsley,*
*North Yorkshire*

# Redland Private Hotel

*Elegant Victorian villa with original features*

☎ 01244 671024  📠 01244 681309
**Map ref 5 - SJ46**

64 Hough Green, CHESTER, Cheshire,
CH4 8JY
from Chester on A483 Wrexham rd, 1m &
take A5104 Saltney rd for 200yds, opp
Westminster Park
13 Rooms, ££

The Redland Hotel, a handsome property dating from 1850, has been beautifully restored by the resident proprietors. Rich wood panelling, suits of armour and antique four-poster beds all contribute to the general atmosphere of period splendour.

The bedrooms, including four honeymoon suites, have been individually designed and equipped with thoughtful extras. All the rooms have luxurious en suite facilities and feature some fine pieces of antique and period furniture. There is a delightful drawing room, and for further enjoyment and relaxation there is a solarium, sauna and honesty bar. An additional convenience is the guests' laundry.

The hotel is located just a mile from Chester city centre and provides ample parking.

## RECOMMENDED IN THE AREA

**RESTAURANT:**
*The Chester Grosvenor, Chester*

**TRADITIONAL PUB:**
*The Grosvenor Arms, Aldford*

**VISIT:**
*Chester Visitor's Centre*

*Street Musician at the Cross, Chester, Cheshire*

# *B*elle Epoque

*Lavishly decorated town centre brasserie, family-owned for 25 years*

☎ 01565 633060 📠 01565 634150

**Map ref 6 - SJ77**

60 King Street, KNUTSFORD, Cheshire, WA16 6DT
2miles from M6 J19
7 Rooms, ££

*T*his restaurant with rooms boasts some unique architectural features including marble pillars and a Venetian glass floor. Lunch and dinner menus offer a tempting range of dishes. Renowned chef David Mooney can be seen out and about sourcing top produce on his 1500cc Honda Goldwing. The seven bedrooms all have en suite facilities, direct dial telephones, colour television and tea and coffee making facilities. Some of the bedrooms overlook the Italianate terrace and are surrounded by the Kitchen herb garden. There are conference, banqueting and function facilities to suit different occasions.

## RECOMMENDED IN THE AREA

**TRADITIONAL PUB:**
*The Dog Inn, Knutsford*

**VISIT:**
*Tatton Park, Knutsford*

---

# *T*he Old Vicarage

*Former vicarage set in two acres of wooded gardens*

☎ 01565 652221 📠 01565 755918

**Map ref 6 - SJ77**

Moss Lane, Over Tabley, KNUTSFORD, Cheshire, WA16 0PL
exit M6 junct 19 onto A556 signposted Manchester Airport. Turn right after Little Chef into Moss Lane
4 Rooms, ££, No smoking
Closed 2 Jan-18 Jan

*T*his beautifully restored 19th-century property is in a delightful setting of natural woodland, landscaped grounds and gardens, surrounded by Cheshire countryside, just four miles from Knutsford. The bedrooms are attractively furnished in pine; one is located at ground floor level and another is suitable for families. Trouser presses and hairdryers are provided for guests' convenience, and additional comforts include en suite facilities in all rooms, plus colour television and a teasmade. The pretty dining room is open throughout the day for teas and snacks. Light lunches and suppers are also served by arrangement. Ample parking is available, and there is a croquet lawn and golf nets with a practice area.

## RECOMMENDED IN THE AREA

**RESTAURANT:**
*Belle Epoque, Knutsford*

**TRADITIONAL PUB:**
*The Dog Inn, Knutsford*

**VISIT:**
*Tatton Park, Knutsford*

# Oakland House

*A genuinely hospitable household with easy access*

☎ 01270 567134
📠 01270 651752

**Map ref 6 - SJ65**

252 Newcastle Road, Blakelow, Shavington, NANTWICH, Cheshire, CW5 7ET
on A500 5m from M6 junct 16, and 2m from Nantwich
5 Rooms, £
No Smoking in bedrooms

## RECOMMENDED IN THE AREA

**RESTAURANT:** *Rookery Hall, Nantwich*

**TRADITIONAL PUB:** *The Swan, Wybunbury*

**VISIT:** *Cholmondeley Castle Gardens, Cholmondeley*

*A* peaceful and relaxing atmosphere prevails at Oakland House, which is run by warm and welcoming proprietors Sandra and Malcolm Groom. The house is conveniently situated alongside the A500 and near junction 16 of the M6. The bedrooms, all of which have en suite showers, are well equipped, attractively furnished and offer many thoughtful extras. Six rooms are located in an adjacent building and two of these are suitable for family occupation. Guests have use of a spacious and comfortably furnished sitting room, there is also a modern conservatory that overlooks the pretty garden to the rear. Whatever your plans, business or leisure, a hearty Oakland breakfast will set you up for the day ahead.

# $\mathcal{T}$he Limes

*An elegant period property, convenient for the M6*

☎ 01270 624081  📠 01270 624081

**Map ref 6 - SJ65**

5 Park Road, NANTWICH, Cheshire, CW5 7AQ

M6 junct 16 follow signs for Nantwich & Stapeley Water Gdns, continue into Nantwich, then follow signs for A530 Whitchurch

3 Rooms, £, No smoking

Closed Nov, Dec & Jan

*A*n impressive Victorian house, The Limes is set in a quiet residential area of Nantwich, just a short walk from the centre of town. It is well located for exploring the many and varied centres of interest in the area.

The house is impeccably maintained and the owners, Judy and Keith Chesters, extend a warm and friendly welcome to their guests. Three spacious and well equipped bedrooms are available. All have en suite facilities and one has a four-poster bed, ideal for special occasions. The lounge is elegantly furnished, and there is a delightful dining room where breakfast is served. The house has pleasant lawns and gardens to the rear, and private parking is provided at the front.

## RECOMMENDED IN THE AREA

**RESTAURANT:**
*Rookery Hall, Nantwich*

**TRADITIONAL PUB:**
*The Swan, Wynbunbury*

**VISIT:**
*Beeston Castle, Beeston*

*The River Wear and Durham Castle, County Durham*

# Clow-Beck House

*Luxurious rooms with superb furnishings in the beautiful gardens of a working farm*

☎ 01325 721075
🖷 01325 720419
✉ clow.beck.house
@pipex.dial.com
**Map ref 7 - NZ21**

Monk End Farm, Croft on Tees,
DARLINGTON,
Co Durham, DL2 2SW
A167 from Darlington
2m, over bridge,
follow brown signs
14 Rooms, ££

Clow-Beck House gets its name from the Beck which winds its way through the grounds of the farm to meet the River Tees, providing a perfect opportunity for some trout fishing.

The bedrooms are in a cottage and in separate chalets in the gardens. Each one has been decorated with great expertise to give a real sense of period style. The beamed dining room is light and airy. There is a good wine list, and à la carte menu that is imaginative in its diversity. The inviting lounge with its attractive blue upholstery is in the house itself. Heather and David Armstrong are dedicated to making you feel at home, and they are keen to help you plan your route for an outing through the rolling North Yorkshire countryside.

## RECOMMENDED IN THE AREA

**RESTAURANT:**
*Hall Garth Hotel, Darlington*

**TRADITIONAL PUB:**
*Black Bull Inn, Moulton*

**VISIT:**
*Darlington Railway Centre & Museum*

# Greenhead Country House Hotel

*Converted traditional Dales longhouse and blacksmith's workshop*

☎ 01388 763143  📠 01388 763143

**Map ref 7 - NZ13**

FIR TREE, Co Durham, DL15 8BL
on A68, turn right at Fir Tree Inn
8 Rooms, ££

Greenhead is an extended early 18th-century property, just 500 yards from the A68, set in well tended gardens at the foot of the Weardale Valley. The location is convenient for visiting Durham, the Beamish Open Air Museum, and the Durham Dales. It is a smartly presented establishment with spacious modern en suite bedrooms. One room has a four-poster bed, all have colour television, tea and coffee making facilities, and clock radios. Accommodation is provided in a quiet and reserved atmosphere.

The central stone arched lounge provides a relaxed centre for planning future outings. There are three restaurants in Fir Trees, all serving dinner from 7 to 9pm, two are within easy walking distance. Menus are available to view in the house, no advance booking is required.

## RECOMMENDED IN THE AREA

**RESTAURANT:**
*Rose & Crown, Romaldkirk*

**TRADITIONAL PUB:**
*The Morritt Arms Hotel, Barnard Castle*

**VISIT:**
*Durham Cathedral, Durham*

# Grey Friar Lodge Country House Hotel

*Victorian vicarage looking across the river to the mountains beyond*

☎ 015394 33158  📠 015394 33158
✉ greyfriar@veen.freeserve.co.uk

**Map ref 5 - NY30**

Clappersgate, AMBLESIDE, Cumbria,
LA22 9NE
1.5 miles West off A593
8 Rooms, ££, No smoking

In the centre of the Lake District, one mile from Lake Windermere, this small hotel was built as the Bishop's House in 1869. There are breathtaking views of the River Brathay, the wooded fells and mountains, from the public rooms, the veranda, terrace, and most of the bedrooms. The cuisine and décor reflect a keen eye for detail. The evening set menu makes skilful use of local produce: fresh vegetables complement the finest cuts of Westmorland beef, Cumbria lamb, game, poultry, salmon and trout.

The house is richly furnished with antique pictures and porcelain. It is also beautifully decorated, shades of pink echoing the blooms of the rhododendrons in the garden. Most of the bedrooms have antique or four-poster beds and patchwork quilts, all but one have en suite bathroom facilities.

## RECOMMENDED IN THE AREA

**RESTAURANT:**
*The Glass House, Ambleside*

**TRADITIONAL PUB:**
*Drunken Duck Inn, Ambleside*

**VISIT:**
*Rydal Mount, Rydal*

# Riverside Lodge Country House

*Period property at the foot of Loughrigg Fell*

☎ 015394 34208  📠 015394 31884
✉ alanrhone@riversidelodge.co.uk
**Map ref 5 - NY30**

Rothay Bridge, AMBLESIDE, Cumbria,
LA22 0EH
follow A593 from Ambleside, turning right
after crossing Rothay Bridge
5 Rooms, ££

### RECOMMENDED IN THE AREA

**RESTAURANT:**
*The Glass House, Ambleside*

**TRADITIONAL PUB:**
*Queen's Head, Troutbeck*

**VISIT:**
*Dove Cottage & Wordsworth Museum, Grasmere*

Riverside Lodge is an impressive stone-built property beautifully situated on the river bank a short walk from the centre of Ambleside and the head of Lake Windermere. The house is close to Loughrigg Fell, which offers excellent walks and fine views. A private footbridge connects the car park to the house.

The Lodge has many historical associations and Bonnie Prince Charlie is believed to have rested here. Inside, the rooms have the charm and character of a cottage, with low beamed ceilings in the cosy lounge and pretty dining room. There is a stone fireplace in the lounge, and the dining room offers river views. Bedrooms vary in size and style, most overlook the river, and all have en suite facilities, television, radio, hairdryers, and tea and coffee making equipment.

There is also a self-catering cottage for two, in a part of the building that projects out over the river.

# Rowanfield Country House

*Lakeland house with lake and mountain views*

☎ 015394 33686  📠 015394 31569
**Map ref 5 - NY30**

Kirkstone Road, AMBLESIDE, Cumbria,
LA22 9ET
off A591 at Bridge House, signed Kirkstone
7 Rooms, ££, No smoking

Rowanfield is a period property set high behind Ambleside, with stunning views sweeping across Windermere to the peaks beyond. Proprietors Jane and Philip Butcher have restored the house in a simple farmhouse style with effective use of colour and quality Laura Ashley and Liberty fabrics. The bedrooms are individual in style and are thoughtfully equipped with colour television, radio alarms, hairdryers and tea and coffee making facilities. All the rooms have en suite showers, some have baths too. The cosy lounge, with the advantage of the fantastic view, has a wood-burning stove and a selection of books and magazines. Philip's excellent cooking is served in the homely dining room; candlelit dinners by night and a substantial breakfast in the morning, with plenty of options from pancakes to the full cooked Cumberland feast. Guests are invited to bring their own choice of drinks, as the premises are unlicensed.

### RECOMMENDED IN THE AREA

**RESTAURANT:**
*Queen's Head Hotel, Troutbeck*

**TRADITIONAL PUB:**
*Travellers Rest Inn, Grasmere*

**VISIT:**
*Dove Cottage & Wordsworth Museum, Grasmere*

# Willowfield

RECOMMENDED
IN THE AREA

**RESTAURANT:**
*Crooklands Hotel,
Crooklands*

**TRADITIONAL PUB:**
*Wheatsheaf, Beetham*

**VISIT:**
*RSPB Nature Reserve,
Silverdale, Lancs*

*Magnificent views of
the River Kent
estuary with the
Lakeland hills on the
horizon*

☎ 01524 761354
✉ kerr@willow
field.net1.co.uk
Map ref 6 - SD47

The Promenade,
ARNSIDE, Cumbria,
LA5 0AD
off A6 at Milnthorpe
traffic lights onto
B5282, right at T-
junction & right again at
Albion public house
10 Rooms, £
No smoking

*W*illowfield enjoys a superb position in the picturesque village of Arnside, just over seven miles from Junction 36 of the M6, thirty minutes drive from the Lake District and close to the Yorkshire Dales. The hotel is on the Promenade, a quiet cul-de-sac along the waterfront that becomes the coastal path. Leighton Moss RSPB nature reserve is close by. Wonderful views of the estuary can be enjoyed from the lounge, most of the bedrooms, and from the fine new conservatory extension to the dining room. Breakfast and four-course dinners of traditional English cooking are served here and the hotel has a table licence. There is ample parking including a private car park. Guests should note that the house is completely non smoking. The bedrooms vary in size and are individually and attractively decorated, seven have en suite shower rooms. All the bedrooms are equipped with colour TV, electric blankets, hot drinks facilities and comfortable dressing gowns.

# Greenbank

*Victorian property peacefully located in the heart of Borrowdale*

☎ 017687 77215  📠 017687 77215

**Map ref 5 - NY21**

BORROWDALE, Cumbria, CA12 5UY
3 miles South of Keswick on B5289
10 Rooms, ££, No smoking in bedrooms

lovely views, and one with a television.

Guests are greeted with a tray of tea on arrival, and a four-course dinner of imaginatively presented dishes can be taken in the tastefully appointed dining room. Here too a substantial Cumbrian breakfast is served.

Greenbank is a delightful establishment, set in its own grounds, affording breathtaking views across the valley to Derwentwater and northwards towards Skiddaw. It is the perfect place from which to enjoy some excellent walking.

Jean Wood offers a warm welcome to all her guests, and provides comfortable accommodation in thoughtfully equipped bedrooms, with full en suite facilities, hospitality trays, hairdryers and clock radios. Two lounges and an honesty bar are available for guests' use, both with log fires and

### Recommended in the Area

**Restaurant:**
*Borrowdale Gates, Borrowdale*

**Traditional Pub:**
*Bridge Hotel, Buttermere*

**Visit:**
*Keswick Museum & Gallery, Keswick*

# Hazel Bank

*Imposing Victorian residence in the beautiful Borrowdale Valley*

☎ 017687 77248  📠 017687 77373
✉ enquires@hazelbankhotel.
demon.co.uk

**Map ref 5 - NY21**

Rosthwaite, BORROWDALE, Cumbria, CA12 5XB
6 miles from Keswick on B5289 Seatoller road, turn left at sign just before Rosthwaite village
9 Rooms, £££, No smoking

### Recommended in the Area

**Restaurant:**
*Rothay Garden Hotel, Grasmere*

**Traditional Pub:**
*Swan Hotel, Thornthwaite*

**Visit:**
*Mirehouse, Keswick*

Hazel Bank stands in four acres of grounds in the Borrowdale Valley, one of the Lake District's loveliest spots. From its elevated position, the house commands magnificent views of the central Lakeland peaks, including Great Gable. Many of the peaks are within walking distance.

The house has been carefully renovated to provide modern facilities and high quality furnishings, while retaining its Victorian character. Bedrooms, including two with four-poster beds, are well proportioned, individually furnished and thoughtfully equipped. All have en suite facilities, colour television, hospitality trays, hairdryers, and, of course, wonderful views. The room price includes a full breakfast freshly cooked to your taste, and a set four-course dinner of excellent cuisine using the best of local produce. Meals are served in the attractive dining room, and the house has a restaurant and residential licence.

# Augill Castle

*An extraordinary Victorian extravagance of neo-gothic castle, set in picture-book pastoral scenery*

☎ **017683 41937**
📠 **017683 41936**
✉ **augill@aol.com**

**Map ref 6 - NY71**

BROUGH, Cumbria,
CA17 4DE
M6 J38, A685 thro'
Kirkby Stephen &
Brough Sowerby, right
to South Stainmore.
Castle 1m on left
6 Rooms, ££
No smoking in bedrooms

## RECOMMENDED IN THE AREA

**RESTAURANT:**
*Black Swan Hotel, Ravenstonedale*

**TRADITIONAL PUB:**
*Royal Oak, Appleby-in-Westmorland*

**VISIT:**
*Brough Castle, Brough*

*T*he castle had been left to crumble, but Simon and Wendy Bennett have taken care of it and restored it to its original beauty. It is not only the outside that impresses; the interior is fabulous too, and the owners have made the most of it, with plenty of stylish touches.

The bedrooms all face south, with fantastic views across surrounding farmland, as far as the Pennines and Cumbrian mountains. All of them have en suite bathrooms; all have period furniture; and in some, the castle's turrets have been converted into walk-in wardrobes. The flamboyant magic of this place is manifest in the opulent lounges, and in the dining room, where great food is served for dinner around a huge oak table, in the style of a 'House Party'. A traditional set menu includes treats such as roasted rack of minted Dales lamb or baked chocolate custard for dessert.

# Swaledale Watch Farm House

*Friendly atmosphere on a working sheep farm by a stream*

☎ 016974 78409  📠 016974 78409

**Map ref 5 - NY34**

Whelpo, CALDBECK, Cumbria, CA7 8HQ
1mile South West on B5299
4 Rooms, £, No smoking
Closed Xmas

## RECOMMENDED IN THE AREA

**RESTAURANT:**
*Armathwaite Hall, Bassenthwaite*

**TRADITIONAL PUB:**
*The Pheasant, Bassenthwaite*

**VISIT:**
*Hutton-in-the-Forest, Skelton*

*T*his busy farm is set in idyllic surroundings, with open views of the fells and mountains. Guests are welcome to look round, a very special treat at lambing time. Just a mile away is the picturesque village of Caldbeck, once renowned for its milling and mining. Take a memorable walk through 'The Howk', a beautiful wooded limestone gorge with waterfalls. Nan and Arnold Savage work hard to make their hospitality seem effortless and to put their guests at ease.

The recently converted farmhouse, is enhanced by open stonework and has log fires for colder evenings. The lounges have TV, books and games. The bedrooms are tastefully furnished in pine, beautifully decorated and have bath and shower en suite. Two bedrooms and a lounge are in the converted cowshed, ideal for a group of four. Nan's homecooked dinners and hearty Cumbrian breakfasts are delicious.

*Housesteads Crag, Hadrian's Wall, Northumberland*

# *B*essietown Farm
## Country Guest House

*A traditional
farmhouse welcome
with delicious home
cooking*

**☎ 01228 577219**
**✆ 01228 577219**

**Map ref 5 - NY35**

Catlowdy, Longtown,
CARLISLE, Cumbria,
CA6 5QP
from Bush Hotel
Longtown, 6.5m to
Bridge Inn, right onto
B6318, 1.5m to
Catlowdy, farm
1st on left
4 Rooms, £
No smoking

### RECOMMENDED IN THE AREA

**RESTAURANT:**
*Magenta's Carlisle*

**TRADITIONAL PUB:**
*Riverside Inn, Canonbie*

**VISIT:**
*Carlisle Castle & Border
Regiments Museum,
Carlisle*

Open all year, Bessietown is situated north of Carlisle and offers country house style hospitality. The delightfully decorated dining room, lounge bar and TV lounge provide a comfortable, relaxing environment for guests. The warm, cosy bedrooms offer tea and coffee making facilities and an en suite bath or shower. The luxury Dove Cote suite offers extremely elegant, spacious accommodation with a king-size four-poster bed. There is a separate lounge area with TV and hospitality tray, as well as a twin bedroom/dressing room. A splendid spa corner bath with shower is also part of the suite. The secluded grounds house a courtyard development including a heated indoor swimming pool (open mid-May-mid-September). Bessietown is renowned for its hearty breakfasts, setting you up for a day exploring the Border country or Hadrians Wall and the City of Carlisle. Delicious home-cooked evening meals are available by prior arrangement, served at 7pm, the mouthwatering desserts are a speciality.

# *H*igh Side Farm

*17th-century farmhouse 650ft up Ling Fell*

☎ 017687 76893
✉ marshall@highsidehols.
freeserve.co.uk

**Map ref 5 - NY13**

Embleton, COCKERMOUTH, Cumbria,
CA13 9TN
A66 Keswick-Cockermouth, left at sign to
Lorton/Buttermere, left at T-junction. After
300 mtrs, right opp church, Farm at top of hill
2 Rooms, £, No smoking in bedrooms
Closed 24 Dec-1 Jan

## RECOMMENDED IN THE AREA

**TRADITIONAL PUB:**
*Kirkstile Inn, Loweswater*

**VISIT:**
*Wordworth House, Cockermouth*

*H*ighside Farm is a lovely old house with striking views over the Embleton Valley and Solway Firth to the Scottish peaks. While it is certainly off the beaten track, it's only 20 minutes from six of the famous lakes and the valleys of Borrowdale and Buttermere. It is also ideally placed for walking, as nearly all of the High Fells are within easy reach. The spacious open-plan lounge and dining room is sumptuously furnished with deep sofas and fine antique furniture. One piece is a 10-foot mahogany table, at which a substantial breakfast is served, with an emphasis on local produce. On cooler days you can also expect welcoming log fires. The equally opulent en suite bedrooms are west facing, with panoramic views. Colour televisions are provided, along with comfortable chairs, hairdryers, tea making equipment, central heating, and drying facilities. Packed lunches are available by arrangement. Dogs are welcome.

---

# *T*oddell Cottage

*Cumbrian longhouse with beamed rooms in an idyllic setting*

☎ 01900 828696  📠 01900 828696

**Map ref 5 - NY13**

Brandlingill, COCKERMOUTH, Cumbria,
CA13 0RB
from A66 take A5086 towards Egremont. Left
at Paddle School towards Lorton & Embleton
then first right for 0.75m
3 Rooms, £, No smoking

## RECOMMENDED IN THE AREA

**RESTAURANT:**
*Dale Head Hall, Keswick*

**TRADITIONAL PUB:**
*Kirkstile Inn, Loweswater*

**VISIT:**
*Wordworth House, Cockermouth*

*T*he cottage is found in the tiny hamlet of Brandlingill, in unspoilt countryside three miles from the market town of Cockermouth. Janet and Mike Wright have sympathetically refurbished the listed building, which is over 300 years old, and welcome guests with genuine warmth and hospitality. Superb food is served in the bright dining room. Breakfast is a real feast, with a menu that ranges from a traditional full English breakfast, to more extravagant dishes such as ricotta pancakes with caramelised fruit. Dinner is no less a treat, with three courses, vegetarian alternatives and a specially selected wine list. Besides being an accomplished cook, Janet is a qualified aromatherapist and reflexologist, handy if you get too carried away with the local walking! The bedrooms are thoughtfully furnished, both with showers en suite. There is an open fire in the lounge, comfortable seating, and books to read.

# $\mathcal{A}$rrowfield Country Guest House

*A Victorian house with beautiful views of the surrounding countryside*

☎ 015394 41741

**Map ref 5 - SD39**

Little Arrow, Torver, CONISTON, Cumbria, LA21 8AU

1.5 miles from Coniston on A593

5 Rooms, £, No smoking

*T*he house is set back from the road in its own attractive gardens, in a quiet and peaceful location outside Coniston village. There is access to the fells, with walks to suit all tastes in the immediate vicinity. Other activities - riding, sailing, windsurfing - are not much further away. There is ample private parking. The bedrooms are bright and well equipped, four have en suite bathroom facilities. There is a spacious, luxurious guest lounge with deep, comfortable sofas and an open fire. The dining room has a fireplace made of local stone, and always a fire in cold weather it is a cosy place to sample the delicious breakfast, which includes an extensive buffet. Packed lunches can also be provided on request. With some help from the hens and the bees, eggs and honey, as well as bread, preserves, chutney and cakes are home produced.

## RECOMMENDED IN THE AREA

**RESTAURANT:**
*Nanny Brow, Ambleside*

**TRADITIONAL PUB:**
*Black Bull Inn, Coniston*

**VISIT:**
*Ruskin Museum, Coniston*

# $\mathcal{C}$oniston Lodge Hotel

*Excellent accommodation in a beautiful lakeland setting*

☎ 015394 41201  📠 015394 41201

**Map ref 5 - SD39**

Station Road, CONISTON, Cumbria, LA21 8HH

at crossroads on A593 (close to filling station), turn up hill at crossroads - Station Rd

6 Rooms, ££, No smoking

*T*his small private hotel, reminiscent of a Swiss chalet has stunning views. It makes an ideal base for touring the southern lakes and lakeland towns. Visitors will receive a warm welcome from hosts Anthony and Elizabeth Robinson. A special feature in the lounge is the commissioned relief in local slate depicting former guest Donald Campbell, with his famous Bluebird racing boat. Bedrooms are all en suite and furnished in modern style, they are well equipped with direct dial telephones, tea and coffee making facilities and colour television. Dinner can be taken in the co-ordinated dining room, the adventurous home cooking features local game and fresh fish. Children under ten can be accommodated by arrangement. No dogs, (with the exception of guide dogs).

## RECOMMENDED IN THE AREA

**RESTAURANT:**
*The Glass House, Ambleside*

**TRADITIONAL PUB:**
*Outgate Inn, Outgate*

**VISIT:**
*Braunwood, Coniston*

# The Old Rectory Hotel

*Victorian rectory set in three acres of garden and woodland*

☎ 015394 41353  📠 015394 41156

**Map ref 5 - SD39**

Torver, CONISTON, Cumbria, LA21 8AX
A593, 2.5m S of Coniston, turn left by green railings and over railway bridge, 0.25m N of Torver village
8 Rooms, ££, No smoking

Bedrooms vary in size but all are well equipped with mini bars and other thoughtful touches. Public rooms include a cosy lounge with a selection of games and books, and a stylish conservatory restaurant. In summer, guests can enjoy an aperitif out on the garden terrace.

The Old Rectory is a smartly presented establishment set amid open pasture on the Torver side of the town, under the peak of Coniston Old Man and close to the shores of Coniston Water. Hospitality is excellent, as is the attentive and personal service provided by the thoughtful team of staff. Dinner is taken by candlelight and the simple set menu is expertly prepared and includes a delicious course of local cheeses and home made puddings. A short wine list is available offering an informed choice.

## RECOMMENDED IN THE AREA

**RESTAURANT:**
*Gilpin Lodge, Windermere*

**TRADITIONAL PUB:**
*Queen's Head Hotel, Hawkshead*

**VISIT:**
*Brantwood, Coniston*

# Wheelgate Country House

*Old farmhouse surrounded by fells and lakes*

☎ 015394 41418  📠 015394 41114
📧 wheelgate@conistoncottages.co.uk

**Map ref 5 - SD39**

Little Arrow, CONISTON, Cumbria, LA21 8AU
1.5 miles South of Coniston, on West side of road
5 Rooms, ££, No smoking in bedrooms
Closed Dec-8 Feb

## RECOMMENDED IN THE AREA

**RESTAURANT:**
*Jericho's, Windermere*

**TRADITIONAL PUB:**
*Drunken Duck Inn, Ambleside*

**VISIT:**
*Ruskin Museum, Coniston*

Converted from a 17th-century farmhouse, the award-winning gardens with mature hedges and bushes, and the wisteria on the outside set the Wheelgate back into a world of its own. Through the front door, there are oak beams and panelling, low ceilings, high-quality antique furniture and ornaments, and a complimentary sherry to welcome you. There is an intimate, friendly bar for a peaceful drink, where smoking is permitted. The oak-beamed lounge has deep comfortable sofas, a crackling log fire and fresh flowers. One bedroom has an opulent four-poster; all are en suite, with colour TV. A hearty breakfast can be taken in the dining room.

The Lake District is all around; many pleasant walks can be started from the house, with the shore of Coniston Water not far away. An added attraction is that guests are free to use weekday membership of a leisure club.

# Crosthwaite House

*Peace and quiet in unspoilt corner of the Lake District*

☎ 015395 68264  📠 015395 68264
📧 crosthwaite.house@kencomp.net

**Map ref 6 - SD49**

CROSTHWAITE, Cumbria, LA8 8BP
exit M6 J36, A591 (Kendal), A590 (Barrow),
right onto A5074, 4m small thro' rd for
Crosthwaite, 0.5m turn left
6 Rooms, £, No smoking

*I*n a sturdy house from the middle of the 18th century, this establishment stands in the village of Crosthwaite, at the northern end of the Lyth Valley, famous for its damson orchards. You can see across the valley from the spacious lounge, and from the light and airy dining room, where an imaginative menu of traditional home cooking is served, all freshly prepared on the Aga. There is plenty of room in the bedrooms, and all have en suite showers and toilets, colour TV, and tea and coffee making facilities.

The owners have been looking after guests in Lakeland for many years now, and they create a relaxed atmosphere in which it is easy to feel at home. They know the local surroundings extremely well, and will be happy to provide you with any information.

## RECOMMENDED IN THE AREA

**RESTAURANT:**
*The Punchbowl, Crosthwaite*

**TRADITIONAL PUB:**
*The Punch Bowl Inn, Crosthwaite*

**VISIT:**
*Sizergh Castle, Sizergh*

# Rough Close Country House

*Charming country hotel close to Esthwaite Water*

☎ 015394 36370  📠 015394 36002

**Map ref 5 - SD39**

HAWKSHEAD, Cumbria, LA22 0QF
1.25 miles South of Hawkshead, on Newby
Bridge road
5 Rooms, ££, No smoking in bedrooms

*R*ough Close is a delightful small hotel and home to Anthony and Marilyn Gibson, who set great store on hospitality, traditional values and good home cooking. The daily changing five-course evening meals are a delight, as are the substantial breakfasts.

Reception rooms extend to a light and airy dining room next to the traditionally furnished lounge, where log fires burn in cooler weather. There is also a cosy bar looking out onto the surrounding mature gardens. Four of the bedrooms are en suite, one double room has a private bathroom. All are comfortably furnished and thoughtfully equipped with central heating, colour television, hairdryers, clock radios and hospitality trays. The house is situated in lovely countryside overlooking the lake, and the atmosphere is peaceful and relaxed.

## RECOMMENDED IN THE AREA

**RESTAURANT:**
*Miller Howe Hotel, Windermere*

**TRADITIONAL PUB:**
*Queen's Head Hotel, Hawkshead*

**VISIT:**
*Beatrix Potter Gallery, Hawkshead*

# Higher House Farm

*17th-century beamed farmhouse in a village setting*

☎ 015395 61177  📠 015395 61520
Map ref 5 - SD59

Oxenholme Lane, Natland, KENDAL, Cumbria, LA9 7QH
exit M6 at junct 36, A65 to Kendal, at 2nd sign for Natland. Left onto Oxenholme Lane, premises at bottom of lane on right
3 Rooms, ££, No smoking

## RECOMMENDED IN THE AREA

**RESTAURANT:**
*Jericho's, Windermere*

**TRADITIONAL PUB:**
*Gateway Inn, Kendal*

**VISIT:**
*Abbot Hall Art Gallery, Kendal*

This lovely old farmhouse, retaining much of its original character, is set in a peaceful village south of Kendal. There are stunning views of nearby fells from the well-kept orchards and gardens. On colder days a log fire warms the cosy lounge, where guests will find books on the local area. The snug dining room has a communal table where delicious breakfasts are served, featuring local produce and home made jams.

The comfortable bedrooms are individual in style and include one with a delightful four-poster bed. All the rooms have en suite facilities and are provided with colour televisions and tea and coffee making facilities. The house is easily reached from the M6, and is ideally located for visiting the Lake District and the Yorkshire Dales. Great hospitality and service are key features, and landlady Valerie Sunter was a 1999 AA Landlady of the Year finalist.

# Low Jock Scar

*Small, friendly country guest house with gardens*

☎ 015398 23259  📠 015398 23259
✉ philip@low-jock-scar.freeserve.co.uk
Map ref 5 - SD59

Selside, KENDAL, Cumbria, LA8 9LE
6 miles north of Kendal on A6 left down a small side road signposted to Low Jock Scar
5 Rooms, ££, No smoking

Philip and Alison Midwinter are the proud owners of this small riverside country guest house, built in Lakeland Stone and surrounded by six acres of garden and woodland. On the Eastern edge of the Lake District National Park, it offers excellent access to the Lakes and Yorkshire Dales. The historic market town of Kendal is 6 miles away, Windermere is 10 miles away and Ullswater 20 miles away.

There are five double or twin bedrooms with good views of the garden. All individual in style, three have en suite bathroom facilities and two are on the ground floor. The comfortable guest lounge is full of interesting books and maps of the area for walkers and motorists. Good home cooked dinners are available by prior arrangement, using fresh local produce. Vegetarians can be catered for and dinner is served at 7:30pm. The house has a residential licence and picnic lunches are available on request.

## RECOMMENDED IN THE AREA

**RESTAURANT:**
*Linthwaite House, Bowness on Windermere*

**TRADITIONAL PUB:**
*Blue Bell Hotel, Heversham*

# *A*vondale

*Comfortable accommodation handy for the town centre and Derwentwater*

☎ **Freephone 0800 028 6831**
📠 **017687 75431**

**Map ref 5 - NY22**

20 Southey Street, KESWICK, Cumbria, CA12 4EF
take 1st left at Cenotaph into Southey St. Avondale 100yds on right
6 Rooms, £, No smoking, Closed Xmas

*T*his grand Victorian terrace house is less than five minutes' level walk from the town centre and parks, with Derwentwater a pleasant 10 minute stroll away. In the light and airy dining room you can make a great start to the day with fruit juice, fruit and cereals, a choice of hearty full English or vegetarian breakfast, kippers, eggs, omelette. The bedrooms vary in size and style, all are warm, clean and well-equipped, with modern en suite showers and colour TV. An iron and ironing board are always available. There is a cosy lounge with deep armchairs and a collection of games and books. Guests have their own keys to come and go as they please. Hospitality, provided by Sandra and John Williams, is first class, borne out by the many guests who choose to return here.

## RECOMMENDED IN THE AREA

**RESTAURANT:**
*Underscar Manor, Keswick*

**TRADITIONAL PUB:**
*White Horse, Scales*

**VISIT:**
*Mire House, Keswick*

# *D*alegarth House Country Hotel

*Super views of lakes and fells, with a great choice at dinner*

☎ **017687 72817** 📠 **017687 72817**
✉ **john@dalegarthhousehotel. freeserve.co.uk**

**Map ref 5 - NY22**

Portinscale, KESWICK, Cumbria, CA12 5RQ
approach Portinscale from A66 pass Farmers Arms approx 100yds on left to hotel
10 Rooms, ££, No smoking

*I*n the small lakeside village of Portinscale, just one mile from Keswick, this roomy Edwardian house sits in a sunny elevated position. It has landscaped gardens and superb views towards Derwentwater and the surrounding mountains. There is a private car park. Children under five and dogs cannot be accommodated. Fresh, traditional food, carefully prepared, is served in the restaurant: full English breakfast, and a six-course table d'hôte dinner menu that changes daily, accompanied by an extensive wine list. Packed lunches are available on request.

Bedrooms vary in size but all have en suite bathrooms and colour TV. There are two spacious lounges, one with a small bar in the corner. The house is kept very neat and tidy, lightly furnished in a modern style, decorated with simple patterned wallpaper and soft furnishings. You can expect good value for money.

## RECOMMENDED IN THE AREA

**RESTAURANT:**
*Underscar Manor, Keswick*

**TRADITIONAL PUB:**
*Horse & Farrier Inn, Keswick*

**VISIT:**
*Mire House, Keswick*

# Derwent Cottage

*Quietly located property with mature Lakeland gardens*

☎ 017687 74838
✉ Dercott@btinternet.com

**Map ref 5 - NY22**

Portinscale, KESWICK, Cumbria, CA12 5RF
A66 to Portinscale, pass Farmers Arms,
200mtrs turn right after left bend
6 Rooms, ££, No smoking

Derwent Cottage is set in idyllic grounds set back from the village road. Enthusiastically run by Mr and Mrs Newman, the house is comfortably furnished and offers cosy lounges and a small, well-stocked bar. The dining room is the venue for freshly prepared, home-cooked meals in traditional English style, and hearty Cumbrian breakfasts to set you up for the day.

Bedrooms are spacious and well furnished with many personal touches. All the rooms have en suite facilities, colour televisions, and tea and coffee making equipment. Car parking is provided, and this is an excellent location for easy access to the whole of the northern, central and eastern Lake District. Children under 12 years cannot be accommodated, neither can dogs (except guide dogs).

## RECOMMENDED IN THE AREA

**RESTAURANT:**
*Underscar Manor, Keswick*

**TRADITIONAL PUB:**
*White Horse Inn, Scales*

**VISIT:**
*Keswick Museum & Gallery, Keswick*

# The Grange Country House

*Stylish Victorian residence overlooking the town and the surrounding fells*

☎ 017687 72500

**Map ref 5 - NY22**

Manor Brow, Ambleside Road, KESWICK,
Cumbria, CA12 4BA
leave M6 at J40, take A66 into Keswick, left
on A591 towards Windermere 0.5m. 1st right
& house 200mtrs on right
10 Rooms, ££, No smoking

Set in its own tidy gardens, and just a leisurely stroll from the town centre, this elegant Lakeland house boasts fabulous panoramic views of the countryside and mountains. Built in the 1840s, the high ceilings, large windows and doors create a sense of space and grandeur. There are two lounges, one with a beautiful ceiling rose, cream walls and long velvet curtains. The other has an open log fire, and tables and chairs where you can enjoy a drink from the bar. The five-course dinner menu is highly recommended, as is the full English breakfast, served at separate tables in the dining room. There is a carefully selected wine list and an extensive range of malt whiskies. The bedrooms are light and cheery, with traditional wooden furniture. Those at the top of the house feature exposed beams. They are all en suite, and one has a half-tester bed.

## RECOMMENDED IN THE AREA

**RESTAURANT:**
*Dale Head Hall, Keswick*

**TRADITIONAL PUB:**
*The Horse & Farrier Inn, Keswick*

**VISIT:**
*Mire House, Keswick*

# Bridge End Farm

*18th-century farmhouse on a pedigree Holstein dairy farm*

☎ 017683 61362

**Map ref 6 - NY62**

KIRKBY THORE, Cumbria, CA10 1UZ
on A66 at Kirkby Thore
3 Rooms, £, No smoking
Closed Xmas

Yvonne Dent offers a warm and friendly welcome to her comfortable farmhouse, which is conveniently situated for exploring the Lake District and Eden Valley. Spacious bedrooms are individually designed, with Yvonne's hand-made cushions and patchwork quilts adding a homely touch.

The rooms are stylishly furnished and thoughtfully equipped, with tea and coffee making facilities, hairdryers, clock radios and televisions. Comforting extras such as fruit, biscuits and reading material are also provided. Two rooms are en suite and the third has a private bathroom. Substantial home made meals are served at one large table in the dining room, and the deep, comfortable seating in the lounge makes it the ideal place in which to relax. Dogs can be accommodated by prior arrangement, and private fishing is available on the River Eden.

## RECOMMENDED IN THE AREA

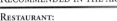

**RESTAURANT:**
*Rampsbeck Hotel, Watermillock*

**TRADITIONAL PUB:**
*Tufton Arms, Appleby-in-Westmorland*

**VISIT:**
*Acorn Bank Garden, Temple Sowerby*

# New House Farm

*17th-century Lakeland farmhouse with warm hospitality and good cuisine*

☎ 01900 85404  ✆ 01900 85404

**Map ref 5 - NY12**

LORTON, Cumbria, CA13 9UU
6 miles South of Cockermouth, on B5289
between Lorton and Loweswater
5 Rooms, ££, No smoking

Despite its name, the farmhouse dates back to 1650. The old oak beams and rafters, flagged floors and stone open fireplaces remain unspoilt. These features and the bold decorative colour schemes create a cosy, traditional atmosphere. The property lies in 15 acres of open fields, woods, streams and ponds, in the picturesque Lorton Vale, with lakes and fells all around. There are spectacular views of the countryside from every window. The bedrooms, with large beds, pine furniture and thoughtful extras such as fresh fruit, biscuits and flowers, all have en suite bathroom facilities. There are two separate sitting rooms on the ground floor, with deep sofas, books and magazines, one with log fire on colder days. Breakfast makes extensive use of local produce, and is served in the cosy dining room. Traditional five-course English dinners are also served, main courses are usually roasts, and puddings are a speciality.

## RECOMMENDED IN THE AREA

**RESTAURANT:**
*Dale Head Hall, Keswick*

**TRADITIONAL PUB:**
*Kirkstile Inn, Loweswater*

**VISIT:**
*Wordsworth House, Cockermouth*

# Winder Hall

*Historic manor house serving fine food and wine, on the River Cocker in a peaceful Lakeland village*

☎ 01900 85107
🖷 01900 85107
📧 winderhall@
lowlorton.freeserve.
co.uk

**Map ref 5 - NY12**

LORTON, Cumbria,
CA13 9UP
from Keswick A66 W, at
Braithwaite B5292
Whinlatter Pass
(Lorton). 6m to B5289,
turn left, Winder Hall
0.5m on right
6 Rooms, ££, No
smoking, Closed Xmas

## RECOMMENDED IN THE AREA

**RESTAURANT:**
*Underscar Manor, Keswick*

**TRADITIONAL PUB:**
*The Pheasant, Bassenthwaite*

**VISIT:**
*Wordsworth House, Cockermouth*

Winder Hall is named after the family who built the Hall between 1400 and 1700. Additions in Victorian times retained the style of the stone mullioned windows with lattice leaded lights. The luxurious guest rooms, all en suite, are brightened with fresh flowers. Fine antique or pine furniture gives character to the rooms, whilst comfortable chairs and TV are among the modern comforts. The two largest rooms have four-poster beds, one Tudor-style in carved oak, the other Georgian-style in mahogany. Views of the fells can be enjoyed from all the rooms. Meals are served in the oak-panelled dining room, looking out over the formal walled garden to the Lorton fells. A full Cumbrian breakfast, smoked haddock, egg dishes and a cold buffet are served, with wonderful homemade preserves. A skilfully prepared four-course dinner is available, accompanied by a quality wine list. There is a comfortable lounge with open fire and window seats for relaxation. In the afternoon complimentary tea or coffee is served in the lounge or garden.

# *E*es Wyke Country House

*Georgian country house set in the Esthwaite valley*

☎ 015394 36393  📠 015394 36393

**Map ref 5 - SD39**

NEAR SAWREY, Cumbria, LA22 0JZ
1.5 miles outside Hawkshead on B5285.
On the road to the ferry across Windermere
8 Rooms, £££
Closed Jan-Feb

*A* handsome property with lovely views over Esthwaite, Ees Wyke was once the holiday home of Lakeland writer Beatrix Potter. The garden provides colour all year round, and the terrace is a pleasant place to relax after a day's activities. Owners John and Margaret Williams create a friendly, relaxed atmosphere in the comfortable lounges and the spacious dining room, which overlooks the lake. Delightful five-course dinners are served, featuring the finest local produce. Breakfast offers a choice of a full English breakfast, smoked fish, or a lighter continental selection with porridge, cereals, fresh fruits and yoghurts, plus a wide range of preserves. Bedrooms are attractively furnished and comfortable. All of them have either en suite or private facilities, televisions, hairdryers, and tea and coffee making equipment.

## RECOMMENDED IN THE AREA

**RESTAURANT:**
*Old Vicarage, Witherslack*

**TRADITIONAL PUB:**
*Queens Head Hotel, Hawkshead*

**VISIT:**
*Hill Top, Near Sawrey*

*Rydal Water in the Lake District, Cumbria*

# Sawrey House
## Country Hotel

*Victorian house, full of character, with wonderful lake and forest views*

☎ 015394 36387
🖷 015394 36010
✉ enquiries@
sawrey-house.com

Map ref 5 - SD39

NEAR SAWREY,
Cumbria, LA22 0LF
in village on B5285
11 Rooms, £££
No smoking in
bedrooms
Closed Jan

Shirley and Colin Whiteside extend a friendly welcome to guests at their splendid house, which is built of slate hewn from the fells it overlooks. It stands just a few minute's walk from 'Hilltop', the former home of Lakeland writer Beatrix Potter, at Near Sawrey in the heart of the Southern Lakeside National Park.

The comfortable, stylish and individually designed bedrooms offer superb views of Esthwaite Water. All the rooms have en suite facilities, colour television, radio, and tea and coffee making equipment. There is a charming lounge with deep sofas and a log fire, and the spacious restaurant also affords marvellous views. A full English breakfast is served, with alternatives available for vegetarians and small children. The restaurant has achieved two AA rosettes for fine dining. The house is set in three acres of mature grounds, just a few minutes from the Windermere Ferry.

### RECOMMENDED IN THE AREA

**VISIT:**
*Windermere Steamboat Museum, Windermere*

# *H*ill Crest

*Traditional Lakeland stone house on the fringes of Lake Windermere*

☎ 015395 31766  **F** 015395 31986

**Map ref 5 - SD38**

Brow Edge, NEWBY BRIDGE, Cumbria, LA12 8QX

1mile after Newby Bridge on A590 turn left into Brow Edge Rd, premises 0.75m on right

3 Rooms, £, No smoking

As its name suggests, this lovely family home is located in an elevated position offering fine south Lakeland views. It is an ideal base from which to explore the Lake District, for a touring or walking holiday.

The bedrooms are furnished in pine and are thoughtfully equipped, with en suite shower rooms, tea and coffee making facilities, colour television and full central heating. The comfortable lounge doubles as a breakfast room, which opens out onto a patio where guests can sit and admire the view. Throughout the atmosphere is warm and friendly. The breakfast menu features local produce. The food is carefully prepared by proprietor Jane Jenkinson, who has professional catering training. Children are welcome, and car parking is provided.

## RECOMMENDED IN THE AREA

**RESTAURANT:**
*Lakeside Hotel, Newby Bridge*

**TRADITIONAL PUB:**
*Rusland Pool, Haverthwaite*

**VISIT:**
*Levens Hall, Levens*

# *C*ross Keys Temperance Inn

*Coaching inn turned to temperance in the Yorkshire Dales*

☎ 015396 20284  **F** 015396 21966

**Map ref 6 - SD69**

Cautley, SEDBERGH, Cumbria, LA10 5NE

M6 junct 37 to A683 through Sedbergh. Hotel 4m north of Sedbergh on left

2 Rooms, ££, No smoking

Nestling beneath the Howgill Fells, The Cross Keys was a coaching inn in the 1700s, and it is rich with character. The parlour has flagstones on the floor and a low beamed ceiling, 18th-century settle, old copper scales, lots of books, comfy chairs and a wind-up gramophone. The dining room has wooden floors and a glassed veranda, with spectacular views of the Cautley Spout waterfall. Dinner is served here (also for non-residents) Wednesday to Friday. Superb traditional and modern British cooking is the norm, using only the finest local produce. The property was left to the National Trust by Edith Bunney in 1948, on the condition that alcohol never be sold here again, but you can bring your own drinks! Meals and snacks are available all day including Sunday lunch, and packed lunches can be provided. A library and sitting room adjoin the two bedrooms each have en suite facilities; the double room also has a bed-settee useful for families.

## RECOMMENDED IN THE AREA

**RESTAURANT:**
*Black Swan Hotel, Ravenstonedale*

**TRADITIONAL PUB:**
*Sun Inn, Dent*

**VISIT:**
*National Park Centre, Sedburgh*

# The Beaumont

*Stylish Victorian house a short walk from the town centre*

☎ 01539 447075
🖷 01539 447075
✉ thebeaumont
hotel@btinternet.
com

**Map ref 6 - SD49**

Holly Rd,
WINDERMERE,
Cumbria, LA23 2AF
follow town centre
signs thro' one-way
system, 2nd left & 1st
left into Holly Rd
10 Rooms, ££
No smoking, Closed
mid Dec-mid Jan

*T*his lovely Lakeland house is home to the Casey family, who are renowned for their warm hospitality. The elegant interior retains period atmosphere while providing comfortable modern convenience. The beautifully presented lounge offers deep sofas where guests can relax and enjoy the collection of books, magazines and games. A full English breakfast is served in the bright dining room. The Beaumont has a special arrangement with the nearby marina village, where guests can use the facilities of the sport and leisure complex, including the swimming pool, gym, steam room, sauna, bar and restaurant. The house provides well appointed bedrooms, some with four-poster beds, including a romantic honeymoon suite. A choice of 'romantic welcomes' is also available, in the form of flowers, wine and chocolates. All the rooms have en suite facilities, quality linens, colour television, hairdryers, and hospitality trays. Children over 10 can be accommodated.

## RECOMMENDED IN THE AREA

**RESTAURANT:**
*Holbeck Ghyll, Windermere*

**TRADITIONAL PUB:**
*Queens Head, Troutbeck*

**VISIT:**
*Windermere Steamboat Museum*

# Dene House

*Quietly situated Victorian Lakeland stone house*

☎ 015394 48236  📠 015394 45986
✉ jdene@globalnet.co.uk

**Map ref 6 - SD49**

Kendal Road, WINDERMERE, Cumbria,
LA23 3EW
0.5m from Bowness on A5074 next to
Burnside Hotel
6 Rooms, ££

## RECOMMENDED IN THE AREA

**RESTAURANT:**
*Linthwaite House, Bowness on Windermere*

**TRADITIONAL PUB:**
*Tower Bank Arms, Near Sawrey*

**VISIT:**
*Lake District National Park Visitor Centre,
Windermere*

*T*his stylish house is set back from the main road in a small copse just a short walk from the lake and the village. A warm welcome is provided to all, and in summer, afternoon teas are served on the secluded terrace. Leaflets and maps are available for guests' use, and the proprietors are happy to advise on places to visit in the area. The bedrooms vary in size but all are furnished to a high standard to include en suite showers. Remote control colour television, tea and coffee making facilities and central heating are provided in every room. The comfortable dining room is the setting for a hearty breakfast, including Cumberland sausages. For dinner, there are plenty of eating places to

choose from in Bowness or Windermere, including pubs, bistros and restaurants with international cuisine. Private car parking is available, and guests have access to their rooms at all times.

# Howbeck

*Professionally run establishment where customer care comes first*

☎ 015394 44739  📠 015394 44739
✉ enquiries@howbeck.com

**Map ref 6 - SD49**

New Road, WINDERMERE, Cumbria,
LA23 2LA
left off A591 through Windermere town centre
300yds on left. Main road to Bowness
10 Rooms, ££, No smoking

## RECOMMENDED IN THE AREA

**RESTAURANT:**
*Miller Howe, Windermere*

**TRADITIONAL PUB:**
*Punchbowl Inn, Crosthwaite*

**VISIT:**
*Windermere Steamboat Museum*

*H*owbeck is conveniently situated on the main road close to the town centre and within easy reach of the lake. The proprietors are professional hoteliers and are proudly committed to providing caring service to their guests. They also have a wealth of local knowledge to assist guests with the planning of their itineraries.

Bedrooms are spacious and smartly appointed with quality fabrics and furniture. Some rooms offer four-poster beds, which are popular for special occasions. A good range of facilities is provided, including full en suites in each room. A full English or vegetarian breakfast is served in the relaxed atmosphere of the charming dining room. Howbeck also holds a residential licence.

# Newstead

*Handsome Victorian property located between Windermere and Bowness*

☎ 015394 44485

**Map ref 6 - SD49**

New Road, WINDERMERE, Cumbria,
LA23 2EE
0.5m from A591 between
Windermere/Bowness
7 Rooms, ££, No smoking

Sue and Bill Jackson provide a warm welcome to guests at their stylish home, which is a leisurely stroll from the town centre. The Jacksons are also happy to help guests make the most of their stay by advising on places to visit and activities available. The comfortable bedrooms retain their original features and are tastefully furnished in pine. All the rooms are en suite and offer a host of thoughtful extras and homely touches to ensure a memorable stay. The light and airy reception rooms include a comfortable lounge, which looks out over the neat garden. Sue's freshly prepared breakfasts are served in the attractive dining room. Vegetarians are willingly catered for and special diets can be accommodated by arrangement. For dinner, a good variety of pubs and restaurants is available nearby. Children under seven and pets cannot be accommodated. There is a private car park.

## RECOMMENDED IN THE AREA

**RESTAURANT:**
*Gilpin Lodge, Windermere*

**TRADITIONAL PUB:**
*Travellers Rest Inn, Grasmere*

**VISIT:**
*Lake District National Park Visitor Centre, Windermere*

# The Outpost

*Welcoming guest house peacefully located in the Peak District National Park*

☎ 01433 651400

**Map ref 7 - SK28**

Shatton Lane, BAMFORD, Derbyshire,
S33 0BG
turn off A625 between Bamford & Hope
opposite High Peak Garden Centre, then
200yds on right
3 Rooms, £, No smoking
Closed 24 Dec-2 Jan

Located in a quiet lane in the small hamlet of Shatton, this friendly establishment offers good levels of hospitality and service, creating a very relaxing environment. The owner's skills as a wood craftsman are evident around the house, in the attractive furniture and the superb oak wall panelling in the guests' lounge, enhanced by the log fire and beamed ceilings. Many comforting extras are included in the comfortable bedrooms. One double room looks out over the garden, and another can be combined with a single room to create a family suite. The rooms have either en suite or private facilities. Dinner is available by arrangement in the beamed dining room, and breakfast is served in the conservatory.

## RECOMMENDED IN THE AREA

**RESTAURANT:**
*Milano, Sheffield*

**TRADITIONAL PUB:**
*Yorkshire Bridge Inn, Bamford*

**VISIT:**
*Bluejohn Cave & Mine, Castleton*

# Coningsby

*Noble late-Victorian residence kept in immaculate condition*

☎ 01298 26735  📠 01298 26735
📧 coningsby@btinternet.com

**Map ref 7 - SK07**

6 Macclesfield Road, BUXTON, Derbyshire,
SK17 9AH
between A515 and A53 on B5059
3 Rooms, ££, No smoking

The house stands in tidy gardens in one of Buxton's conservation areas, just a short walk from the town centre and the Pavilion gardens. The owners pride themselves on their warm welcome and friendly service, Coningsby's motto is 'Every guest is a guest of honour' and their attention to detail is faultless. Children and pets are not catered for. For the very reasonable prices, the bedrooms provide a wealth of luxury, all with en suite shower or bathrooms. The Ivory Room has a power shower and an air bath; The Green Room is prettily decorated in Laura Ashley's 'Winter Lily'; The Blue Room has an original blue Victorian fireplace; The Pink Room has a large shower room with a sauna and power shower. Breakfast is served in the Red Dining Room. Dinner is available by arrangement on four days a week, with candlelight to make the silver and crystal sparkle. Please note, this is a no-smoking establishment.

## RECOMMENDED IN THE AREA

**RESTAURANT:**
*Best Western Lee Wood, Buxton*

**TRADITIONAL PUB:**
*Red Lion Inn, Litton*

**VISIT:**
*Chatsworth, Chatsworth*

# Grendon Guest House

*Detached Edwardian house in lovely gardens with fine views*

☎ 01298 78831

**Map ref 7 - SK07**

Bishops Lane, BUXTON, Derbyshire,
SK17 6UN
0.5m from Buxton centre, just off A53, St John's Rd, behind Burbage Parish Church
3 Rooms, £, No smoking

Grendon is a large Edwardian house standing in an acre of well tended grounds overlooking the Cavendish Golf Course to the hills of the Peak District. It is located in a quiet country lane, yet is within easy walking distance of the town centre. The en suite bedrooms are particularly spacious and include one room with a four-poster bed. Colour television, easy chairs, and tea and coffee making equipment are all provided, along with very comfortable beds and excellent goose down duvets.

Public rooms are comfortable and relaxing. The lounge/dining room offers hill views, and opens onto a balcony where guests can sit and relax. Good home cooking is served, with carefully prepared dishes made on request using quality produce. The breakfast menu offers a wide variety, with fresh fruit salad, home made bread, and free-range eggs. Ample driveway parking is available.

## RECOMMENDED IN THE AREA

**RESTAURANT:**
*Callow Hall, Ashbourne*

**TRADITIONAL PUB:**
*Bulls Head, Wardlow*

**VISIT:**
*Chatsworth, Chatsworth*

# Dannah Farm
## Country House

*Beautifully furnished 18th-century farmhouse set in peaceful countryside just below Alport Heights, which stand at 1,034 feet offering superb views of five counties*

☎ 01773 550273 📠 01773 550590 ✉ dannah@demon.co.uk

**Map ref 8 - SK34**

Bowmans Lane, Shottle, BELPER, Derbyshire, DE56 2DR

fr Belper A517 Ashbourne rd c 1.5m, right to Shottle. 1m to village over x-rds turn right

8 Rooms, ££, No smoking in bedrooms, Closed 25-26 Dec

Dannah Farm is a beautiful Georgian farmhouse on the Chatsworth Estates at Shottle. It is still a working farm of 128 acres producing arable crops and naturally reared beef cattle. There are other animals about the place, the usual cats and hens, a naughty nanny goat and a pig.

Visitors are encouraged to walk the surrounding footpaths and admire the superb views across rolling countryside. The house is full of character and beautifully furnished. Single, double and twin rooms are offered, all with en suite facilities and some with whirlpool baths or Japanese tubs. Colour televisions, direct dial telephones, radios, and hospitality trays are all provided. Two of the bedrooms are split-level, offering a private lounge on the ground floor leading via a spiral staircase to the

## RECOMMENDED IN THE AREA

**RESTAURANT:**
*Riber Hall, Matlock*

**TRADITIONAL PUB:**
*Red Lion Inn, Hognaston*

**VISIT:**
*Kedleston Hall, nr Kedleston*

upper floor with its canopied four-poster bed. There are two guests' sitting rooms and large gardens for peaceful relaxation. Good farmhouse cooking is served in The Mixing Place, a licensed dining room converted from the building where feed for the stock was stored and prepared. Fresh local produce is a feature of the menu, and at breakfast you can expect home-made bread, home-produced organic sausages, and free range eggs.

Vegetarian and other special diets can also be catered for. Dannah is located midway between Wirksworth and Belper, and is convenient for Dovedale. There are plenty of places of interest in the vicinity, from Alton Towers to Chatsworth House, and some good shopping opportunities in the local factory shops. Ample safe car parking is provided, and while smoking is not permitted in the bedrooms or restaurant, guests may smoke in one of the sitting rooms.

# Beeches Farmhouse & Restaurant

*Enjoy superb food and warm hospitality at this traditional 18th-century farmhouse*

☎ 01889 590288
📠 01889 590559
✉ beechesfa
@aol.com

**Map ref 3 - SK13**

Waldley, DOVERIDGE,
Derbyshire DE6 5LR
A50 W, right at
Doveridge & N down
Marston Lane.
At Waldley 1st right,
1st left
10 Rooms, ££
No Smoking
Closed 24-26 Dec

## RECOMMENDED IN THE AREA

**TRADITIONAL PUB:**
*Ye Olde Dog & Partridge, Tutbury*

**VISIT:**
*Alton Towers*

Superb British food is served in the restaurant here, which has the AA's two rosette award for fine food. Barbara Tunnicliffe researches old country recipes and makes the most of fresh produce, served in a number of charming dining areas. The small bar, roaring log fire and rough hewn tables add to the welcoming atmosphere. The spacious en suite bedrooms are tastefully decorated and spotlessly clean. Direct dial telephones and tea and coffee making facilities are provided, home made biscuits and fresh flowers are among the thoughtful extras. The farmhouse is set in peaceful gardens and 60 acres of farmland. The Derbyshire Dales area easily accessed and for visitors to Alton Towers this is an ideal place to stay. Some credit cards are taken and there is ample parking. Dogs cannot be accommodated (except for guide dogs).

# $O$ld Barn

*Converted barn with magnificent views across the Hope Valley*

☎ 01433 650667  📠 01433 650667

**Map ref 7 - SK28**

Sheffield Road, HATHERSAGE, Derbyshire, S32 1DA
on A6187 1m E of Hathersage, 100yds below Millstone Inn, on same side of road, with white B&B sign
3 Rooms, ££, No smoking

The Old Barn is thought to date back to the 16th century, the original beams and flagstone floors can still be enjoyed. The large entrance hall has floor to ceiling glass windows and a staircase leading to the gallery landing. Guests can relax in the beautiful 24ft lounge with its coal effect gas stove. A traditional English breakfast is served in a pleasant country-style dining room. The four-poster bedroom is furnished in pine and has a small sitting area, en suite bathroom and video TV. The twin bedded room is attractively furnished in rosewood and has video TV, a sitting area and en suite. The third bedroom has a large double bed, TV and en suite shower room. All the bedrooms have tea and coffee making facilities. There is a large patio area outside, with a seating area, ample secure parking is available away from the main road. The owners' accommodation is in a separate building

## RECOMMENDED IN THE AREA

**RESTAURANT:**
*Cavendish Hotel, Baslow*

**TRADITIONAL PUB:**
*Maynard Arms, Grindleford*

**VISIT:**
*Peveril Castle, nr Castleton*

# $T$he Redhouse

*Fine red-brick house with luxury bedrooms and four-posters*

☎ 0115 932 2965  📠 0115 932 1253
✉ fourposter@redhouse5diamonds.freeserve.co.uk

**Map ref 8 - SK44**

Wharncliffe Road, ILKESTON, Derbyshire, DE7 5HL
from A6007 follow signs for Market Place
7 Rooms, ££

All the bedrooms are named after artists, with prints of their work on the walls. 'Cezanne' and 'Hopper' are on the ground floor. They are decorated and carpeted in appealing colours, with views over the gardens. As well as four-poster beds, they all have en suite shower rooms, remote control colour TV with fast-text and video recorder, telephones and other luxury facilities. The house is close to the town centre, two miles from American Adventure Theme Park and six miles from the centre of Nottingham. It was built in 1899 and retains interesting architectural features. There is an entrance hall with oak panelling, wooden staircase and green-tiled inglenook fireplace. An inviting lounge and conservatory lead through to the restaurant, overlooking the gardens and lawns, where full English breakfast is served. There is a large car park and a mini exercise suite for guests.

## RECOMMENDED IN THE AREA

**RESTAURANT:**
*Hart's Restaurant, Nottingham.*

**TRADITIONAL PUB:**
*The Abbey, Darley Abbey*

**VISIT:**
*Denby Pottery Visitors Centre*

# Robertswood Guest House

*A handsome Victorian family house*

☎ 01629 55642  📠 01629 55642

**Map ref 7 - SK35**

Farley Hill, MATLOCK, Derbyshire, DE4 3LL
exit M1 J28, A615 to Matlock. In Matlock
take last exit at rdbt, up steep hill, left into
Smedley St, 1m right, 1st right
8 Rooms, £, No smoking in bedrooms

On the edge of the Peak District, the stone-built house stands proudly in neat gardens, in a quiet, elevated position to the north of Matlock. There are spectacular views across the Derwent Valley, with its pastures lined with trees and hedges. There is a convenient small car park.

The friendly young owners offer a relaxed atmosphere and traditional values of service and hospitality in their comfortable, elegant home. There are chandeliers to set off the high ceilings, and marble fireplaces, both in the spacious lounge, decorated in pink, and in the dining room. Freshly cooked breakfast is served at separate tables here. The bedrooms all have remote control colour TV, radio alarm, hospitality tray, hairdryer, and en suite bathrooms with bath and shower.

## RECOMMENDED IN THE AREA

**RESTAURANT:**
*Riber Hall, Matlock*

**TRADITIONAL PUB:**
*The White Lion Inn, Matlock*

**VISIT:**
*Heights of Abraham Country Park & Caverns, Matlock Bath*

# The Dower House

*16th-century mellow limestone country house*

☎ 01629 650931  📠 01629 650932
✉ fosterbig@aol.com

**Map ref 7 - SK26**

Main Street, WINSTER, Derbyshire,
DE4 2DH
from A6 turn onto B5057 to Winster, The
Dower House is large house at end of main
street
3 Rooms, ££, No smoking

The Dower House is set in a south facing walled garden at the heart of the historic village. It is a Grade II listed Elizabethan property furnished in complete harmony with its period. Dinner and breakfast are taken at oak tables in the elegant dining room. The food is skilfully prepared by proprietor Marsha Foster-Biggin, using quality local produce. The sitting room has a part stone-flagged and oak floor, and an unusually low stone fireplace where a wood fire burns in winter. Bedrooms are particularly spacious, comfortably appointed, and individually decorated, with delightful views of the village or garden. One room has en suite facilities and the other two have private bathrooms across the landing. All rooms have their own washbasin, colour television, hospitality tray and hairdryer. An iron and ironing board is accessible from the 'priest hole', and car parking is provided in the courtyard.

## RECOMMENDED IN THE AREA

**RESTAURANT:**
*Riber Hall, Matlock*

**TRADITIONAL PUB:**
*Druid Inn, Birchover*

**VISIT:**
*Haddon Hall & Chatsworth House*

# Park View Farm

*Attractive Victorian farmhouse on a 370-acre farm surrounded by beautiful countryside*

☎ 01335 360352
📠 01335 360352

**Map ref 7 - SK24**

WESTON UNDERWOOD, Derbyshire, DE6 4PA
6m NW of Derby off A38 1.5m Kedleston Hall National Trust property
3 Rooms, ££
No smoking
Closed 24-25 Dec

## RECOMMENDED IN THE AREA

**RESTAURANT:**
*Darleys Restaurant, Darley Abbey*

**TRADITIONAL PUB:**
*Red Lion, Hognaston*

**VISIT:**
*Royal Crown Derby Visitors Centre, Derby*

*T*his delightful early Victorian farmhouse is surrounded by its own beautiful gardens and 370 acres of arable farmland. The house overlooks extensive parkland where the National Trust's Kedleston Hall is located. Linda and Michael Adams have furnished their home with great thought and care to provide comfortable accommodation throughout. Each double bedroom has an antique four-poster bed and period furniture which perfectly suits the style of the house. Two rooms are en suite while the others have private facilities, every room has tea and coffee making equipment.

The public areas feature a comfortable sitting room where guests can relax and watch television, and a nicely presented dining room where breakfast is served. For dinner there are several hotels and inns nearby. Children under six cannot be accommodated.

# The Wold Cottage

*Georgian farmhouse in a beautiful location with fine views*

☎ 01262 470696  📠 01262 470696
✉ woldcott@wold-newton.
freeserve.co.uk

**Map ref 8 - TA07**

WOLD NEWTON, East Riding of Yorkshire,
YO25 0HL
from B1249 towards Wold Newton, turn right
by pond, round double bend, 1st right, past
bungalow, 200yds to farmhouse
3 Rooms, £, No smoking

## RECOMMENDED IN THE AREA

**TRADITIONAL PUB:**
*Seabirds Inn, Flamborough*

**VISIT:**
*RSPB Nature Reserve, Bempton*

Built as a city gentleman's country retreat in the 18th century, Wold Cottage is set in its own grounds surrounded by open Wold countryside. A nearby monument marks the spot where a meteorite landed in 1795. The house is delightfully furnished and offers very comfortable and spacious bedrooms, including one with a four-poster bed and spa bath. All three rooms have en suite facilities and tea and coffee making equipment along with a welcoming cake or biscuit. A friendly atmosphere prevails in the elegant dining room, where quality home cooking is served. An evening meal is available on request, and guests are invited to bring their own wine. The traditional English breakfast includes fresh fruit, yoghurt and local free-range eggs. The proprietor, Mrs Gray, prides herself on the cleanliness of her house, no smoking is permitted and pets cannot be accommodated.

# Ash Farm Country Guest House

*A relaxing retreat deep in the Cheshire Countryside near Manchester*

☎ 0161 929 9290  📠 0161 928 5002

**Map ref 6 - SJ78**

Park Lane, Little Bollington, ALTRINCHAM,
Greater Manchester, WA14 4TJ
turn off A56 beside Stamford Arms
3 Rooms, ££, No smoking in bedrooms
Closed 22 Dec-5 Jan

## RECOMMENDED IN THE AREA

**RESTAURANT:**
*Juniper, Altrincham*

**TRADITIONAL PUB:**
*Green Dragon, Lymm*

**VISIT:**
*Dunham Massey Hall, Altrincham*

Ash Farm is the home of international snooker player, David Taylor, and his wife, Janice. Dunham Hall and Park, formerly the home of the Earl of Stamford, is close by. The luxury double bedrooms offer en suite facilities, telephone, colour television and video. Thoughtful extras include fresh fruit, tea and coffee-making facilities and towelling robes.

Meals are a special feature with an extensive menu of traditionally cooked food, using fresh local produce, complemented by a carefully chosen wine list. Guests can enjoy exploring the surrounding National Trust countryside, and come home to a welcoming open fire.

Access is easy with Manchester International Airport only six miles away and Manchester City Centre with theatres, shops and entertainment only ten miles away.

# The Old Coach House

*Historic building close to the beach and pier*

☎ 01253 349195 📠 01253 344330
📧 blackpool@theoldcoachhouse.
freeserve.co.uk

**Map ref 5 - SD33**

50 Dean Street, BLACKPOOL, Lancashire,
FY4 1BP
at end of M55 follow signs for main car park,
at Go-Karts turn right, at lights turn left, next
lights left, Dean St 2nd on right
7 Rooms, ££, No smoking in bedrooms

Claire and Mark Smith are charming hosts, offering a warm and friendly welcome to their lovely home. The Old Coach House is just a few minutes walk from Blackpool's famous Pleasure Beach and South Pier.

The bedrooms are attractively decorated and furnished, including two rooms with four-poster beds, and two rooms suitable for family occupation. All the rooms have en suite facilities and offer many thoughtful extras, such as colour televisions, direct dial telephones, and tea and coffee making equipment. Guests enjoy their meals in the period-style dining room, while the delightful conservatory is a comfortable place to sit at the end of the day. For those seeking total relaxation, a huge open air jacuzzi is located in the pretty water garden and is popular with guests throughout the year.

## RECOMMENDED IN THE AREA

**RESTAURANT:**
*Paul Heathcote's Restaurant, Longridge*

**TRADITIONAL PUB:**
*Grapes Hotel, Wrea Green*

**VISIT:**
*Harris Museum & Art Gallery, Preston*

# New Capernwray Farm

*Old farmhouse in beautiful countryside conveniently close to the M6*

☎ 01524 734284 📠 01524 734284
📧 newcapfarm@aol.com

**Map ref 6 - SD47**

Capernwray, CARNFORTH, Lancashire,
LA6 1AD
from M6 J35 follow signs for Over
Kellet/Kirkby Lonsdale. Left at village green in
Over Kellett, house on left after 2m
3 Rooms, ££, No smoking

This is no longer a working farm, but the farmhouse stands in two acres of grounds in a delightful rural location, five minutes from the M6, between the Lake District and the Yorkshire Dales. Guests are given the warmest of welcomes, greeted on arrival and offered tea or coffee.

Built in 1697, the lounge has exposed stone wall and oak beams. One bedroom has a private bathroom, the other two have facilities en suite; they are fresh and airy with lovely views over the countryside. The full English breakfast, served in the intimate green dining room, includes home baked bread, local free range eggs, traditionally cured bacon and sausages. Dinner is served in informal house-party style, with the table lit by candles, set with silver, porcelain, and crystal. Guests are invited to bring their own wine.

## RECOMMENDED IN THE AREA

**TRADITIONAL PUB:**
*Dutton Arms, Carnforth*

**VISIT:**
*RSPB Nature Reserve, Silverdale*

# The Inn at Whitewell

*Delightful old inn with a riverside setting*

☎ **01200 448222** 🖷 **01200 448298**

**Map ref 6 - SD64**

WHITEWELL, Lancashire, BB7 3AT
from Clitheroe take B6243 and follow signs
for Whitewell
17 Rooms, ££

For centuries visitors have been welcomed at this dramatically located establishment in the beautiful Forest of Bowland. Log fires, exposed timbers and flagstone floors have been retained and many fine antiques and pictures are placed about the inn, not least in the bedrooms. The guest rooms all have en suite facilities and other modern comforts, and some of them are suitable for family occupation.

Staff are friendly and helpful, and the quality of the cooking is excellent. A range of bar food is supplemented by an extensive carte menu and blackboard extras. Dishes are interesting, wholesome and uncomplicated, and are prepared from fresh ingredients.

## RECOMMENDED IN THE AREA

**RESTAURANT:**
*Spread Eagle, Sawley*

**VISIT:**
*Clitheroe Castle Museum, Clitheroe*

# The Bower

*Georgian country house with lovely country views*

☎ **01524 734585** 🖷 **01524 730710**
✉ **info@thebower.co.uk**

**Map ref 6 - SD57**

YEALAND CONYERS, Carnforth,
Lancashire, LA5 9SF
leave M6 junct 35, follow A6 towards
Milnthorpe for 0.75m, under narrow bridge,
take next left & bear left at end
2 Rooms, ££, No smoking

The Bower is an elegant 18th-century property set in attractive grounds in this small village. There is a croquet lawn at the front, while behind the house the grounds rise up to woodland. A short walk from here is a spot with marvellous views of Leighton Hall and Morecambe Bay. The two spacious bedrooms are attractively furnished and equipped with tea and coffee making facilities, colour television, clock radios, hairdryers, and electric blankets. One room has an en suite bathroom and a double and single bed, while the smaller room has a double bed and a private bathroom. There is a lovely drawing room where a log fire burns in the cooler months. The dining room, which has french windows onto the garden, is the setting for some excellent home-cooked dinners. Breakfast is served in the delightful kitchen. Dogs are welcome by prior arrangement.

## RECOMMENDED IN THE AREA

**RESTAURANT:**
*Linthwaite House, Bowness on Windermere*

**TRADITIONAL PUB:**
*New Inn, Yealand Conyers*

**VISIT:**
*Levens Hall, Levens*

# Shallowdale House

*1960's property in the Hambleton Hills affording spectacular views*

☎ 01439 788325  📠 01439 788885

**Map ref 8 - SE57**

West End, AMPLEFORTH, North Yorkshire, YO62 4DY
from Thirsk A19, thro' Coxwold & Wass. Or B1363 from York, left at Brandsby. Or A170 (Thirsk-Helmsley) turn 4m from Sutton Bank
3 Rooms, ££, No smoking
Closed Xmas/New Year

Anton van der Horst and Phillip Gill's charming house sits high up on the fringes of Ampleforth village, set in over two acres of hillside garden with lawns and terraced shrubberies. The villa-style property has huge windows to take advantage of the magnificent country views.

The vibrant yet simple interior design is a major attraction. There is a downstairs drawing room with an open fire in winter, the upstairs sitting room houses a collection of books and local information. Two bedrooms have en suite bathrooms, one has an adjacent private bathroom. Televisions, hairdryers and tea and coffee making facilities are provided. Food is a highlight, with delicious home baking at tea time, and a memorable four-course dinner featuring the best regional produce in simple but appealing dishes. The house is licensed, so guests can enjoy wine with their meal.

## RECOMMENDED IN THE AREA

**RESTAURANT:**
*Star Inn, Helmsley*

**TRADITIONAL PUB:**
*Wombwell Arms, Wass*

**VISIT:**
*Rievaulx Abbey, Rievaulx*

# Elmfield Country House

*Extended and fully modernised former gamekeeper's cottage*

☎ 01677 450558  📠 01677 450557
✉ bed@elmfieldhouse.
freeserve.co.uk

**Map ref 7 - SE28**

Arrathorne, BEDALE, North Yorkshire, DL8 1NE
from A1, A684 thro' Bedale towards Leyburn. After Patrick Brompton, right towards Richmond. Premises 1.5m on right
9 Rooms, ££

This country house is set in lovely rolling countryside at the gateway to the Yorkshire Dales. Bedrooms are spacious and comfortable, and one has a delightful four-poster bed. All the rooms have en suite showers or baths, and other facilities include direct dial telephones, colour television with a separate movie channel, radio alarms, and Teasmades. Two rooms are designed specifically for disabled guests.

There is a stylish lounge with a small corner bar, an additional large conservatory lounge, plus a games room and solarium. Also on site is a private fishing lake, four-wheel drive, and paintball game. Full English breakfast is served, featuring home made preserves, and in the evening a home-cooked set dinner is offered.

## RECOMMENDED IN THE AREA

**RESTAURANT:**
*McCoys (Tontine Inn), Staddlebridge*

**TRADITIONAL PUB:**
*Freemasons Arms, Bedale*

**VISIT:**
*Bedale Hall, Bedale*

**281**

# *U*psland Farm

*A beautiful house in a peaceful, rural location*

☎ **01845 567709** 🖷 **01845 567709**

**Map ref 7 - SE28**

Kirklington, BEDALE, North Yorkshire, DL8 2PA
from A1 take B6267 towards Masham, farm 2.2m from A1 on B6267 on left. Set back from road by a field
3 Rooms, £, No smoking

*T*his lovely farmhouse makes a good base for visitors exploring the North Yorkshire moors, the Yorkshire Dales and National Parks. It is conveniently situated for access to the A1 motorway (Great North Road) and for visits to nearby castles, abbeys and stately homes. The house is set in 45 acres of farmland and surrounded by the remains of an ancient moat, the land was once owned by Katherine Parr, the last wife of Henry VIII.

The three bedrooms are stylishly furnished and enjoy wonderful countryside views. All have en suite bath or shower, colour television and tea and coffee making facilities. The lounge and dining room are warm and welcoming with open fires and generous hospitality. Breakfast and dinner can be enjoyed around one large table, dinner-party style, or served in the conservatory. Golf, riding, fishing, walking, gliding and birdwatching can all be enjoyed in the local area.

## RECOMMENDED IN THE AREA

**RESTAURANT:**
*Star Inn, Helmsley*

**TRADITIONAL PUB:**
*Buck Inn, Thornton Watlass*

**VISIT:**
*Middleham Castle, Middleham*

# *A*shfield House Hotel

*17th-century house in the limestone countryside of the Dales*

☎ **01756 752584** 🖷 **01756 752584**
✉ **keilin@talk21.com**

**Map ref 7 - SE06**

Summers Fold, GRASSINGTON, North Yorkshire, BD23 5AE
take B6265 to village centre then turn off Main St into Summers Fold
7 Rooms, ££, No smoking
Closed Jan & early Feb

*I*n a quiet, secluded position, just off Grassington village square, is Ashfield House, a listed building of rough, weathered local stone, with neat little windows and doorways. At the front of the house there is a cobbled drive leading to a private car park. At the back there is a walled garden with a lovely lawn; inside there are beamed ceilings, window seats and big stone fireplaces.

A full English breakfast is served each morning, and in the evening a freshly prepared three-course dinner is available using local produce wherever possible. The bedrooms are pleasantly simple in style, six have en suite bathrooms and all have colour TV. Downstairs there are two lounges with big comfy sofas.

## RECOMMENDED IN THE AREA

**RESTAURANT:**
*Devonsire Arms, Skipton*

**TRADITIONAL PUB:**
*Old Hall Inn, Threshfield*

**VISIT:**
*National Park, Grassington*

# *A*cacia Lodge

*Victorian house in a conservation area of Harrogate*

☎ 01423 560752  📠 01423 503725

**Map ref 8 - SE35**

21 Ripon Road, HARROGATE, North
Yorkshire, HG1 2JL
on A61, 600yds N of town centre
6 Rooms, ££ No smoking

*A* carefully restored house, built of local stone, Acacia Lodge is now a small family-run hotel, conveniently located for the conference centre and the town. Original features have been retained, including the wonderfully ornate ceilings. The house features some fine furnishings, interesting antiques, and paintings. The friendly atmosphere reflects the care and enthusiasm of resident owners Dee and Peter Bateson.

Comfortable bedrooms, all en suite, are thoughtfully furnished and equipped. Reception rooms extend to a period-style lounge, with its open fire and library of books. In the oak-furnished dining room, guests are served a hearty, freshly prepared breakfast. The house is set in pretty gardens and has a private floodlit car park. A good choice of restaurants is available locally. The house is entirely non smoking.

## RECOMMENDED IN THE AREA

**RESTAURANT:**
*The Bistro, Harrogate*

**TRADITIONAL PUB:**
*Pine Marten, Harrogate*

**VISIT:**
*Harlow Carr Botanical Gardens, Harrogate*

---

# *A*lexa House & Stable Cottages

*Splendid Georgian house close to town centre*

☎ 01423 501988  📠 01423 504086
📧 alexahouse@msn.com

**Map ref 8 - SE35**

26 Ripon Road, HARROGATE, North
Yorkshire, HG1 2JJ
on A61, 0.25m from junction of A59/A61
13 Rooms, ££, No smoking in bedrooms

## RECOMMENDED IN THE AREA

**RESTAURANT:**
*Olivers 24, Harrogate*

**TRADITIONAL PUB:**
*General Tarleton Inn, Knaresborough*

**VISIT:**
*The Royal Pump Room Museum, Harrogate*

*T* he hotel, built in 1830, is just five minutes' walk from the centre, in a great spot for exploring the Yorkshire Dales and Moors, and touring the area. The large private car park is useful for guests. There is superb choice at breakfast, with full English breakfast, fresh fish, fruit and continental options, served in the spacious dining room. A daily set dinner menu is also served. You can relax in the lounge and enjoy a drink from the well-stocked bar, or take advantage of the corporate membership of a nearby health and leisure club, with swimming, tennis, gym, sauna and health spa.

The bedrooms, comfortably furnished and prettily decorated, all have en suite bathroom facilities. There are ground floor bedrooms in converted stable cottages, and some rooms have a four-poster bed. John and Roberta Black are friendly, attentive hosts.

# Britannia Lodge Hotel

*Fine town house in pretty, mature gardens, a few minutes from the town centre*

☎ 01423 508482
📠 01423 526840

**Map ref 8 - SE35**

16 Swan Road,
HARROGATE, North
Yorkshire, HG1 2SA
from S follow signs for
Town Centre, down hill,
through lights and
1st left to Swan Rd
12 Rooms, ££
No smoking in
bedrooms

This is a fine Grade II listed town house on a corner site in the most elegant part of Harrogate. It is conveniently located within easy walking distance of the centre and town attraction. The bedrooms have been very smartly refurbished, many with beautiful antique furniture. They all have modern comforts, including en suite facilities, colour TV, radio alarm, direct dial telephone and hot drinks tray. Hairdryers, ironing, shoe cleaning facilities and laundry service are also available. The bar and the lounge, with brass fireplace and rich green sofas, are warm and welcoming. In summer you can sit on the terrace overlooking some of Harrogate's finest architecture. Good breakfasts, using fresh local eggs, bacon and sausages, with vegetarian alternatives, are served in the bright dining room. There is an award-winning garden at the front of the hotel and a private car park to the rear.

## RECOMMENDED IN THE AREA

**RESTAURANT:**
*Boar's Head Hotel, Harrogate*

**TRADITIONAL PUB:**
*Malt Shovel, Brearton*

**VISIT:**
*Ripley Castle, Ripley*

# *R*uskin Hotel

*Victorian property with a mature gardens in a central location*

☎ 01423 502045  📠 01423 506131
✉ ruskin.hotel@virgin.net

**Map ref 8 - SE35**

1 Swan Road, HARROGATE, North Yorkshire,
HG1 2SS
off A61, Ripon road
6 Rooms, £££, No smoking in bedrooms

*T*his delightful small hotel has its own private car park and is just a five minute stroll from the Valley Gardens and the Royal Baths. The house was visited by the eminent artist, writer amd art critic, John Ruskin, in the late 19th century, and a feature is made of this connection with Pre-Raphaelite pictures and the use of William Morris and Arts & Crafts fabrics in the bedrooms. There is also a collection of books on the period and on Ruskin himself.

The en suite bedrooms have been individually designed and offer many useful facilities. The furnishings are Victorian pine, and one room has a four-poster bed. There is an elegant drawing room and bar, in fine weather guests can take their drinks out on the terrace. Candlelit dinners and freshly cooked breakfasts using local produce are served in the handsome dining room.

## RECOMMENDED IN THE AREA

**RESTAURANT:**
*The White House, Harrogate*

**TRADITIONAL PUB:**
*The Boars Head Hotel, Harrogate*

**VISIT:**
*Knaresborough Castle, Knaresborough*

# *P*lumpton Court

*Charming 17th-century stone-built house*

☎ 01439 771223

**Map ref 8 - SE68**

High Street, Nawton, HELMSLEY, North Yorkshire, YO62 7TT
entering Beadlam & Newton from Helmsley on A170, take 3rd turn on left. Plumpton Court 60yds on left
7 Rooms, £, No smoking

*T*he Braithwaites' delightful guest house is peacefully situated in the little village of Nawton. It is an attractive period property offering modern bedrooms, each with en suite facilities, colour television, clock radios, and tea and coffee making equipment. One of the bedrooms is conveniently located on the ground floor.

There is a cosy lounge with a real fire, and drinks are available from the bar. Good home cooking is served in the pleasant dining room, and special diets can be catered for by prior arrangement. Private, secure residents' parking is provided at the back of the house, where there is also a secluded garden. The house makes a good base for visiting the North Yorkshire Moors National Park, and the steam railway which runs from Pickering to Grosmont.

## RECOMMENDED IN THE AREA

**RESTAURANT:**
*Milburn Arms, Rosedale Abbey*

**TRADITIONAL PUB:**
*The Feversham Arms Hotel, Helmsley*

**VISIT:**
*Duncombe Park, Helmsley*
*Castle Howard, Malton*

# Manor House Farm

*Yorkshire stone house at the foot of the Cleveland Hills*

☎ 01642 722384

✉ mbloom@globalnet.co.uk

**Map ref 8 - NZ50**

INGLEBY GREENHOW, North Yorkshire, TS9 6RB

entrance to farm drive opposite church

3 Rooms, ££, No smoking

Closed 21-29 Dec

Located on its own farm at the end of a leafy lane, this lovely old sandstone house is surrounded by woodland and parkland in the North York Moors National Park. It dates in part from 1760 and offers excellent accommodation with exposed beams and interior stonework.

Guests have their own separate entrance, and a lounge and dining room with wood-burning fires. The lounge offers a fine selection of reading material and colour television. Delicious home cooking can be sampled in the pretty dining room. The appealing bedrooms are fresh in appearance and all are equipped with full central heating, tea-making facilities and radios. Each room has a beautiful separate bathroom, one is en suite. Dr and Mrs Bloom are devoted to animals and they keep some interesting pets, including wallabies and peacocks. There is also a collection of waterfowl on the 300-year-old pond. Stabling is available for guests who wish to bring their own horses.

## RECOMMENDED IN THE AREA

**RESTAURANT:**
*McCoys (Tontine Inn), Staddlebridge*

**TRADITIONAL PUB:**
*Three Tuns, Osmotherley*

**VISIT:**
*Mount Grace Priory, Osmotherley*

# Langcliffe Country House

*Detached stone-built house in Upper Wharfedale*

☎ 01756 760243

**Map ref 7 - SD97**

KETTLEWELL, North Yorkshire, BD23 5RJ

off B6160, at 'Kings Head' take road marked Access Only

6 Rooms, £, No smoking

Closed Xmas

Richard and Jane Elliot are the hospitable and friendly hosts at this attractive house in the picturesque valley of Upper Wharfedale. Jane's four-course home-cooked dinners are a special feature. The daily changing menu, which relies heavily on local produce, offers a choice of dishes for the starter and main course followed by a set dessert then cheese. Vegetarians are willingly catered for. The house is licensed, so guests can enjoy a drink at dinner.

The pine-furnished bedrooms are very well equipped and include a two-bedroom family suite. All the rooms have en suite facilities, direct dial telephones and hospitality trays, and all rooms have colour televisions. The house is adorned with an abundance of interesting collectables and lovely floral arrangements. Parking space is provided.

## RECOMMENDED IN THE AREA

**RESTAURANT:**
*Devonshire Arms, Skipton*

**TRADITIONAL PUB:**
*Angel Inn, Hetton*

**VISIT:**
*Yorkshire Dales National Park Centre, Malham*

# Newton House Hotel

*Carefully restored 17th-century coaching inn*

☎ 01423 863539　🖷 01423 869748

**Map ref 8 - SE35**

5-7 York Place, KNARESBOROUGH, North Yorkshire, HG5 0AD
on A59, 2.5m from A1 turn off
12 Rooms, ££
Closed Feb

Newton House is a delightful old property, just two minutes from the river, the castle and the market square. The hotel is entered through its own archway into a courtyard. The attractively decorated bedrooms include rooms with four-poster and king size beds, family rooms, and a family suite comprising inter-connecting double and twin rooms. There is also a ground floor room (double or twin), which can accommodate a wheelchair. All rooms have en suite facilities, except one with a private bathroom, and are equipped with central heating,

colour television, radios, telephones, mini-bars and complimentary tea and coffee. There is a spacious lounge incorporating a small dispense bar. Traditional English breakfast is served in the elegant dining room, and home-cooked meals are available by prior arrangement. Children and pets are welcome, and hosts Barry and Stella Elliott are confident German speakers. Private parking is provided to the rear of the hotel.

## RECOMMENDED IN THE AREA

**RESTAURANT:**
*General Tarleton Inn, Knaresborough*

**TRADITIONAL PUB:**
*The General Tarleton Inn, Knaresborough*

**VISIT:**
*Knaresborough Castle, Knaresborough*

# Park Gate House

*Smartly presented accommodation full of old world charm*

☎ 01677 450466

**Map ref 7 - SE19**

Constable Burton, LEYBURN, North Yorkshire, DL8 2RG
on A684 opposite Constable Burton Hall
4 Rooms, ££, No smoking

Terry and Linda Marshall provide a genuine and friendly welcome at their lovely period property, situated on the edge of Constable Burton. The house is full of character with oak beams and open log fires, and creative use is made of plants and home grown flowers to produce impressive displays. Both the lounge and dining room are furnished in a traditional style, and guests are encouraged to relax in the lovely walled garden in the warmer months.

The bedrooms all have en suite facilities and are fitted out to a high standard, featuring antique pine. Delicious home made breakfasts include local produce, home baking, fruit compotes and fish.

## RECOMMENDED IN THE AREA

**RESTAURANT:**
*Waterford House, Middleham*

**TRADITIONAL PUB:**
*Sandpiper Inn, Leyburn*

**VISIT:**
*Middleham Castle, Middleham*

# *B*ank Villa Guest House

*Grade II listed house with a wealth of antique furniture*

☎ 01765 689605  📠 01765 689605

**Map ref 7 - SE28**

MASHAM, North Yorkshire, HG4 4DB
on A6108 from Ripon, premises just after
30mph sign on entering Masham
6 Rooms, £, No smoking in bedrooms

*B*ank Villa is charming Georgian house featuring old beams and antique pine furniture in the bedrooms. Three of the rooms have en suite facilities, one has a private bathroom and the remaining two have their own shower and basin. Two comfortable and inviting lounges are provided, where guests can relax after a day out, perhaps exploring the Yorkshire Dales National Park and James Herriot country.

Good home cooking is served in the delightful dining room, using fresh local produce where possible. Service, from the proprietors Bobby and Lucy Thomson, is attentive and friendly. Children under five cannot be accommodated, neither can dogs (except guide dogs). Guest parking is available.

## RECOMMENDED IN THE AREA

**RESTAURANT:**
*Waterford House, Middleham*

**TRADITIONAL PUB:**
*Fox & Hounds, Carthorpe*

**VISIT:**
*Norton Conyers Hall, Ripon*

---

# *T*he Grey House Hotel

*A quiet Edwardian house set in attractive gardens*

☎ 01642 817485  📠 01642 817485

**Map ref 8 - NZ41**

79 Cambridge Road, Linthorpe,
MIDDLESBROUGH, North Yorkshire,
TS5 5NL
9 Rooms, ££, No smoking in bedrooms

*B*uilt in 1910, this charming property is now a small and friendly private hotel. The veranda and big bay windows preside over neat gardens, including some conifers, shrubs, roses and herbaceous borders. The house is situated in a quiet residential area of Linthorpe, convenient for the town centre, as well as the North Yorkshire moors and dales, York and Durham. There is off-street parking. The house is furnished with antiques and quality fittings in keeping with its character.

The bedrooms are spacious, all with en suite bathroom facilities. Nine rooms have showers, one has bath and shower; while all are equipped with TV, hairdryers and hot drinks tray. There is a comfortable guest lounge.

## RECOMMENDED IN THE AREA

**RESTAURANT:**
*The Purple Onion, Middlesborough*

**TRADITIONAL PUB:**
*Kingshead, Newton under Roseberry*

**VISIT:**
*Captain Cook Birthplace Museum*

# *B*urr Bank

*Recently built stone house set in attractive natural gardens*

☎ 01751 417777  📠 01751 417789
✉ bb@burrbank.com

**Map ref 8 - SE88**

Cropton, PICKERING, North Yorkshire,
YO18 8HL
from A170 take rd to Wrelton/Cropton, right
after New Inn. Thro' village, house on left
500yds past post office
3 Rooms, £, No smoking

*D*esigned to fit sympathetically into the surrounding countryside, this stone-built cottage enjoys fine views over Rosedale and the moors, and is surrounded by 70 acres of farmland. The comfortable bedrooms are delightfully furnished and equipped to a high standard. All the rooms have en suite bathrooms, and two have corner baths and walk-in showers. Hospitality trays are provided, with tea, coffee, chocolate, spring water, biscuits and sweets, and additional facilities include a pay phone, iron and ironing board, trouser press and hairdryer.

A full English breakfast is served and a four-course dinner is available every evening except Sunday and Wednesday. Most special diets can be catered for with prior notice. The house has a beer and wine license for dinner. Pets are not accommodated and bookings cannot be accepted for children under 12.

## RECOMMENDED IN THE AREA

**RESTAURANT:**
*Milburn Arms, Rosedale Abbey*

**TRADITIONAL PUB:**
*Fox & Hounds Country Inn, Pickering*

**VISIT:**
*North Yorkshire Moors Railway, Pickering*

# *T*he Old Manse

*Conveniently and quietly situated former manse*

☎ 01751 476484  📠 01751 477124

**Map ref 8 - SE88**

19 Middleton Road, PICKERING, North
Yorkshire, YO18 8AL
from A169, left at roundabout, thro' traffic
lights, 1st right (Potter Hill) follow rd to left.
From A170 left at local traffic only sign
8 Rooms, £, No smoking
Closed mid Dec-Jan

*W*hat was once a Methodist minister's home is now a comfortable and very well furnished guest house. The Old Manse is peacefully located within easy walking distance of the town and the North Yorkshire Moors Steam Railway (which runs from Pickering to Grosmont), and makes an ideal base from which to explore the moors, the Yorkshire coast and the historical city of York.

The comfortable bedrooms all have en suite facilities. A cosy lounge is available for guests' use, and excellent hospitality is assured from the resident owners. There is a private car park and a large secluded garden where guests can wander and relax.

## RECOMMENDED IN THE AREA

**RESTAURANT:**
*Star Inn, Helmsley*

**TRADITIONAL PUB:**
*The White Swan, Pickering*

**VISIT:**
*Pickering Castle, Pickering*

# *W*hashton Springs Farm

*Georgian farmhouse and busy working farm high in the hills*

☎ 01748 822884  ℻ 01748 826285
**Map ref 7 - NZ10**

RICHMOND, North Yorkshire, DL11 7JS
in Richmond turn right at traffic lights
towards Ravensworth, 3m down steep hill
farm at bottom on left
8 Rooms, £
Closed late Dec-Jan

*I*n the heart of James Herriot country, the house faces south, with unusual bay windows overlooking lawns which slope down to a stream. The Turnbull family farm corn, potatoes, cows and sheep on 600 acres of land. Guests are free to explore, and enjoy the peace and quiet. There is a range of good pubs and restaurants nearby. Children over five are welcome, but no pets. All the bedrooms are well equipped with en suite bathrooms or showers, colour TV and direct dial telephone. Rooms in the farmhouse are traditional in style, one with a four-poster, those in the courtyard are more modern. A delicious Yorkshire breakfast is served at separate tables in the dining room, fitted with plush red velvet curtains. Evening coffee is served in the drawing room, with a cosy log fire in winter.

## RECOMMENDED IN THE AREA

**RESTAURANT:**
*Hall Garth Hotel, Darlington*

**TRADITIONAL PUB:**
*Charles Bathurst Inn, Richmond*

**VISIT:**
*Green Howards Museum, Richmond*

# *B*ay Tree Farm

*A delightful working farm close to Fountains Abbey*

☎ 01765 620394  ℻ 01765 620394
**Map ref 8 - SE37**

Aldfield, RIPON, North Yorkshire, HG4 3BE
approx 4m W, take unclass road S off B6265
6 Rooms, £, No smoking

*B*ay Tree Farm covers 400 acres of land with beef and arable farming. Situated between the Yorkshire Dales and the North York Moors, there is ample opportunity to explore the countryside or to visit Fountains Abbey nearby. The farmhouse itself is in the quiet village of Aldfield, near Ripon, with spacious accommodation in a converted barn. Family and ground floor rooms are available, all are en suite with colour television and tea and coffee making facilities. Dinner is available and the wholesome farm fare uses fresh local produce.

A comfortable lounge is available for guests to relax in, a wood-burning stove is lit here in colder weather. Proprietors Valerie and Andrew Leeming are attentive hosts. Visa and Mastercard are accepted.

## RECOMMENDED IN THE AREA

**RESTAURANT:**
*Crab & Lobster, Asenby*

**TRADITIONAL PUB:**
*Bruce Arms, West Tanfield*

**VISIT:**
*Fountains Abbey & Studley Royal, Ripon*

# Spital Hill

*Victorian country house set in extensive grounds*

☎ 01845 522273 ✆ 01845 524970
✉ wolsey@wolseylo.demon.co.uk

**Map ref 8 - SE48**

York Road, THIRSK, North Yorkshire, YO7 3AE
from A1(M) take A168, then A170, at rdbt take A19 (York) 1m. House set back 600yds from rd on right, drive marked by 2 white posts
5 Rooms, ££, No smoking

## RECOMMENDED IN THE AREA

**RESTAURANT:**
*Crab & Lobster, Asenby*

**TRADITIONAL PUB:**
*Nags Head Inn, Pickhill*

**VISIT:**
*Rievaulx Abbey, Rievaulx*

*R*obin and Ann Clough welcome guests warmly to their beautiful home, a fine country house set in its own gardens and parkland surrounded by open countryside. The atmosphere is very relaxing; there is a lovely lounge and meals are taken house-party style at one large table in the dining room. Ann produces a set dinner each evening, using good fresh produce, much of which comes from the garden. The well-prepared breakfast is also a highlight.

Bedrooms are furnished with quality and style, and thoughtfully equipped to include items such as bathrobes, fresh fruit, shortbread, mineral water, books, alarm clocks and hairdryers. There is no tea making equipment in the rooms as Ann prefers to offer tea as a service. The excellent dinner is an optional extra.

# Four Seasons Hotel

*Attractive house in a cul-de-sac minutes from York Minster*

☎ 01904 622621 ✆ 01904 620976
✉ roe@fourseasons.netline.uk.net

**Map ref 8 - SE65**

7 St Peters Grove, Bootham, YORK, North Yorkshire, YO30 6AQ
leave ring rd (A1237) at A19 signed York Centre. After 2m St Peter's Grove on left by pedestrian bridge
5 Rooms, ££, No smoking
Closed 24-26 Dec-Jan

## RECOMMENDED IN THE AREA

**RESTAURANT:**
*The Grange, York*

**TRADITIONAL PUB:**
*Dormouse, York*

**VISIT:**
*Jorvik Viking Centre, York*

*B*ernice and Steve Roe are the hospitable resident proprietors at this spacious house, which is located in a leafy side road within easy walking distance of the city centre and its many attractions. Bedrooms are spacious and well equipped, with a choice of double, twin or family rooms. All have en suite facilities, colour television, hospitality trays, trouser presses, and hairdryers. A hearty four-course breakfast sets guests up for the day. Continental breakfast is available as an alternative, and special diets can be catered for. In the evening, guests can relax in the large comfortable lounge and bar. There are several good places to eat within walking distance of the hotel, and ample private parking is provided.

# The Hazelwood

*Elegant Victorian
town house quietly
situated in the very
heart of York*

☎ 01904 626548
📠 01904 628032
📧 reservations@
thehazelwoodyork.
com

**Map ref 8 - SE65**

24-25 Portland Street,
YORK, North Yorkshire,
YO31 7EH
approach York via
A1237 then N on A19,
left before City Gate,
1st turning left
14 Rooms, ££
No smoking

*A*n attractive property, retaining many original features, The Hazelwood is set in a peaceful residential area in the centre of the ancient city, just 400 yards from York Minster. It has its own car park, a great advantage in such a central location, and is an ideal base from, which to explore the historic city and its shops and restaurants. The bedrooms are individually styled and tastefully fitted to the highest standard using designer fabrics. All the rooms have en suite bathrooms, which are well equipped and imaginatively lit. The breakfast room is graced with stylish fabrics and smart linen, and the walls hung with an interesting collection of floral prints. Enjoy a hearty Yorkshire breakfast or vegetarian alternative, or for those with lighter tastes croissants and Danish pastries. The cosy lounge offers plenty of reading material and features a small kitchen where tea and coffee are always available.

# Holmwood House Hotel

*Luxury bedrooms and breakfast feasts in an early Victorian town house within walking distance of the city centre*

☎ 01904 626183
🖷 01904 670899
📧 holmwood.house
@dial.pipex.com
**Map ref 8 - SE65**

114 Holgate Road,
YORK, North Yorkshire,
YO24 4BB
on A59 Harrogate road
on right 300yds past
traffic lights at The Fox
pub
12 Rooms, ££
No smoking

uilt as two private houses in the middle of a mid 19th-century terrace, and backing on to one of the prettiest squares in York, these listed buildings have been stylishly restored. The bedrooms all have en suite facilities, some have especially large baths, and one has a super spa bath. The bedrooms are decorated with beautiful printed wallpaper, a variety of antiques, four-poster, king or queen-size beds. Three rooms are at ground level and one is at garden level. The comfortable lounge has an open fire, and plenty of books and information on the area. There is a very wide choice at breakfast, including cereals, a fresh fruit platter, hot croissants, traditional oak-smoked Craster kippers, and full English breakfast, all served to soothing classical music in the pleasant dining room. The city walls are only five minutes' walk away. Guests are given keys to their room and to the front door. There is a private car park.

## RECOMMENDED
### IN THE AREA

**RESTAURANT:**
*The Grange Hotel, York*

**TRADITIONAL PUB:**
*Rose & Crown,
Sutton on the Forest*

**VISIT:**
*York Minster, York*

293

# High Buston Hall

*Country house accommodation with stunning coastal views*

☎ 01665 830606  📠 01665 830707
✉ highbuston@aol.com

**Map ref 10 - NU21**

High Buston, ALNMOUTH, Northumberland, NE66 3QH
off A1068 between Alnmouth & Warkworth
3 Rooms, ££, No smoking

Lying between Alnmouth and Warkworth, in a peaceful village, this five-bay, Grade II listed Georgian Villa stands in attractive gardens with mature trees, on a rocky promontory overlooking Northumberland's beautiful Heritage Coastline. The grandeur of the house and the antiques with which it has been tastefully furnished are impressive. Owners, Ian and Therese Atherton, are keen antiques collectors and are delighted to recommend dealers, auctions and fairs in the area to interested guests. This is a welcoming family home where guests can use the sumptuous drawing room as their own. Breakfasts are served around one large table in the elegant dining room. Evening meals are also served here, in dinner party style, by arrangement, on Friday, Saturday and Sunday. The bedrooms are huge, with superb beds and period pieces; all have either en suite or private bathroom facilities.

## RECOMMENDED IN THE AREA

**RESTAURANT:**
*Fisherman's Lodge, Newcastle upon Tyne*

**TRADITIONAL PUB:**
*Cook & Barker, Newton-on-the-Moor*

**VISIT:**
*Alnwick Castle, Alnwick*

# The Courtyard

*Country house with stunning views of the Tyne Valley*

☎ 01434 606850  📠 01434 607962

**Map ref 7 - NY96**

Mount Pleasant, Sandhoe, CORBRIDGE, Northumberland, NE46 4LX
off A68 for Sandhoe, 200yds N of A68/A69 junct at Corbridge, over x-rds into narrow lane to T-junct, then right. Courtyard 0.5m on left
3 Rooms, ££, No smoking

The house represents a truly magnificent transformation, from old farm buildings to stylish country house. Bill and Margaret Weightmans's delightful home is in an elevated position affording splendid views of the Upper Tyne Valley,

Corbridge and Corstopitum, a fort on Hadrian's Wall. The ancient oak beams and flagstone floors in the spacious lounge and dining room are enhanced by Margaret's stylish interior design. The bedrooms are equally impressive, all with luxury bathrooms, central heating and tea and coffee making equipment. Two rooms are particularly well proportioned and one has an antique ebony four-poster bed. Locally produced food is served for breakfast, from the award-winning farm shop. Children and pets cannot be accommodated, and credit cards are not accepted.

## RECOMMENDED IN THE AREA

**RESTAURANT:**
*Swallow George Hotel, Chollerford*

**TRADITIONAL PUB:**
*The Angel Inn, Corbridge*

**VISIT:**
*Chesters Roman Fort & Museum, Walwick*

# The Pheasant Inn

*Traditional country inn with a superb Northumberland location*

☎ 01434 240382
📠 01434 240382
✉ thepheasantinn
@kielderwater.
demon.co.uk

**Map ref 6 - NY78**

Stannersburn,
FALSTONE,
Northumberland,
NE48 1DD
from A68 onto B6320,
from A69, B6079,
B6320, follow signs to
Kielder Water
8 Rooms, ££
No smoking
Closed 25-26 Dec

Set in the beautiful Northumberland National Park, just a mile away from the Kielder Water reservoir, this charming inn retains the character of a quaint country pub while providing comfortable modern accommodation. Originally a farmhouse, the building dates from the 1620s and features stone walls and low beamed ceilings.

The courtyard bedrooms are bright and well maintained, and all have en suite facilities. Each of the rooms can be accessed from the outside, five of them are at ground floor level and three are upstairs. Delicious home-cooked meals are served in the bar or in the pine furnished dining room. Bar meals are available at lunchtime and in the evening, and the restaurant is open for dinner. A traditional roast is served on Sundays. There are two beamed bars with open fires, adorned with a collection of old farm implements, pictures and antique brass and copper ware.

# Dene House

*Former farmhouse in a delightful rural location*

☎ 01434 673413  📠 01434 673413
✉ margaret@dene-house.
freeserve.co.uk

**Map ref 7 - NY96**

Juniper, HEXHAM, Northumberland,
NE46 1SJ
from town take B6306, 1st right fork, then 1st
left, both signed Dye House. Follow road for
3.5m, Dene House 100yds past Juniper sign
3 Rooms, £, No smoking

## RECOMMENDED IN THE AREA

**RESTAURANT:**
*Lovelady Shield Hotel, Alston*

**TRADITIONAL PUB:**
*Dipton Mill Inn, Hexham*

**VISIT:**
*Vindolanda (Chesterholm), Bardon Mill*

*F*riendly proprietors Margaret and Brian Massey have converted this former farmhouse into a lovely family home. Set in the small village of Juniper, it is backed by attractive gardens and nine acres of meadow. A beamed ceiling is a feature of the lounge, where on cooler days an open fire is lit. For the warmer weather a sun lounge offers the perfect place to relax.

Aga-cooked breakfasts are served in the farmhouse kitchen, and home made bread, cakes and preserves are an enjoyable aspect of a stay here. The well-proportioned bedrooms are charmingly decorated and furnished in pine. One room offers en suite facilities. Thoughtful extras such as hot water bottles, hairdryers and bookshelves full of reading material are provided.

# Browns

*A rural retreat in Robin Hood country*

☎ 01909 720659  📠 01909 720659

**Map ref 8 - SK57**

The Old Orchard Cottage, Holbeck,
HOLBECK, Nottinghamshire, S80 3NF
6m from M1 junct 30, 0.5m off A616
Sheffield/Newark road
2 Rooms, £
Closed Xmas wk

## RECOMMENDED IN THE AREA

**RESTAURANT:**
*Goff's Restaurant, Nether Langwith*

**TRADITIONAL PUB:**
*Hardwick Inn, Doe Lea*

**VISIT:**
*Clumber Park, Worksop*

*U*p a winding lane in a quiet hamlet near Sherwood Forest, you come to an iron gate. On up the drive, across a shallow ford, and you arrive at a stone country cottage dating back to 1730. It stands in one acre of colourful gardens, and there are two lodges for guests to stay in, each with its own private terrace and en suite bathroom - the larger one sleeps up to four, the other just for two. Breakfast is very enticing, including a choice of a traditional full English menu, or a taste of New England (bacon, French Toast and maple syrup), or smoked haddock, kippers, or eggs anyway you like them. This feast is served in a Regency-style dining room with mahogany tables and fresh flowers. There is a choice of local pubs, and the Browns will provide a chauffeur service to the Country House Restaurant nearby.

# $\mathcal{W}$estbourne House Hotel

*Located in a conservation area, close to the city and university*

☎ 0114 266 0109 📠 0114 266 7778
📧 mike.chris@
westbournehousehotel.co.uk

**Map ref 8 - SK38**

25 Westbourne Road, Broomhill, SHEFFIELD,
South Yorkshire, S10 2QQ
11 Rooms, ££

*T*his impressive house dates from 1860 and is a former Gentleman's residence. Michael and Christine, the friendly owners, previously owned a hotel on the Isle of Mull and also spent some years overseas in the yacht charter business. With their chef and personal assistant, they offer a caring and efficient service. The bedrooms are individually styled and decorated to a high standard with a range of thoughtful extras. All rooms have en suite or private facilities. Two rooms are suitable for family occupation and one has a four-poster bed. The comfortable guest lounge looks out over lovely gardens and a patio area. An excellent breakfast is served in the dining room, choices include smoked haddock, Scottish kippers or oatcakes and croissants. For an evening meal there are many options nearby or towards the city. There is off-street parking and a reliable taxi firm in the area.

## RECOMMENDED IN THE AREA

**RESTAURANT:**
*Milano, Sheffield*

**TRADITIONAL PUB:**
*Strines Inn, Bradfield*

**VISIT:**
*Kelham Island Museum, Sheffield*

# $\mathcal{C}$hoir Cottage and Choir House

*Four-poster beds and an excellent breakfast in a 17th-Century stone cottage*

📧 01538 360561

**Map ref 7 - SJ95**

Ostlers Lane, CHEDDLETON, Staffordshire,
ST13 7HS
off A520 opposite Red Lion into Hollow Ln
pass church & left into Ostlers Ln. Cottage on
right at top of hill
2 Rooms, ££, No smoking
Closed Xmas

*C*hoir Cottage is found in a quiet village near Leek, conveniently located between The Potteries, the Peak District and Alton Towers. There is private parking. Inside the 300-year-old cottage there are two double bedrooms, which have been delicately decorated and furnished with care to match the original style of the building, making the most of its exposed beams. They have en suite bathrooms, colour TV, and tea and coffee making facilities. Guests have complete freedom of access. The larger Pine Suite also has its own small sitting room and two more rooms with single beds.

There is the choice of a cooked or continental breakfast, and evening meals are available by prior arrangement. The dining room and lounges are in the owners' house (Choir House) next door, which is fairly modern. The Sutcliffe family extend a warm and friendly welcome to their guests.

## RECOMMENDED IN THE AREA

**RESTAURANT:**
*Callow Hall, Ashbourne*

**VISIT:**
*Cheddleton Flint Mill, Cheddleton*

# Bank House

*Delightful former farmhouse in a scenic location*

☎ 01538 702810  📠 01538 702810
✉ john.orme@dial.pipex.com

**Map ref 7 - SK04**

Farley Lane, OAKAMOOR, Staffordshire,
ST10 3BD
from Cheadle take B5417. In Oakamoor pass
church, then pub (both on left), 80yds turn
right. Bank House on right in 0.3m
3 Rooms, ££, No smoking
Closed Xmas week

## RECOMMENDED IN THE AREA

**RESTAURANT:**
*Callow Hall, Ashbourne*

**TRADITIONAL PUB:**
*The Green Man, Ashbourne*

**VISIT:**
*Gladstone Pottery Museum, Stoke-on-Trent*

Originally a farmhouse, this delightful property has been lovingly restored by John and Muriel Orme over many years. Bedrooms are spacious and well equipped, and one has a four-poster bed. Every conceivable luxury is provided and the comfort and well-being of guests is the prime objective.

An elegant drawing room is available, where a cheerful log fire burns in cooler weather, and guests dine family-style with Muriel and John in the dining room. There is an abundance of reading material throughout the house and leaflets on local walks are created to order by Muriel.

Hospitality is a major strength and there is a relaxing and peaceful atmosphere. Excellent meals are provided and the gardens are a joy to behold. Muriel is a recent winner of the AA's prestigious Landlady of the Year award.

# Ribden Farm

*18th-century stone-built farmhouse in beautiful open countryside*

☎ 01538 702830  📠 01538 702830

**Map ref 7 - SK04**

Three Lows, Oakamoor, OAKAMOOR,
Staffordshire, ST10 3BW
on B5417 Cheadle/Ashbourne road, on right
0.5m before junction with A52
5 Rooms, £, No smoking in bedrooms

This Grade II listed farmhouse dates back to 1748. It is peacefully set amid the picturesque scenery of the Staffordshire Moorlands, between Oakamoor and Ashbourne, just two miles from the popular Alton Towers theme park. The house has been extensively and sympathetically modernised by friendly proprietors, Chris and Peter Shaw.

The well equipped, high quality accommodation offers a choice of en suite or private facilities. The range of bedrooms includes rooms with four-poster beds and rooms suitable for family occupation. Two bedrooms are located on the ground floor of a separate former farm building. Guests also have use of a pine-furnished breakfast room and a choice of cosy lounges. The large garden includes a play area for children.

## RECOMMENDED IN THE AREA

**RESTAURANT:**
*The Beeches Farmhouse Hotel, Doveridge*

**TRADITIONAL PUB:**
*The Green Man, Ashbourne*

**VISIT:**
*Ceramica, Stoke-on-Trent*

# *O*ak Tree Farm

*Comfortable accommodation in a lovely country house with a river frontage*

☎ 01827 56807
📠 01827 56807

**Map ref 3 - SK20**

Hints Road, Hopwas,
TAMWORTH,
Staffordshire, B78 3AA
A51 Lichfield/Tamworth
rd, into Hints Rd at pub.
Last house on left
where rd divides
7 Rooms, ££
No smoking in
bedrooms

*T*his beautifully renovated farmhouse is situated on the edge of the village of Hopwas, north west of Tamworth. It is surrounded by spacious gardens and overlooks the River Thame. The well equipped bedrooms are comfortably furnished and offer many thoughtful extras. Two rooms are located in the main house and the others are on the first and ground floors of a cleverly converted former grain store and farm building. All of them have en suite facilities.

There is a spacious lounge and an attractively appointed breakfast room, where separate tables are provided. Other facilities include an indoor swimming pool. The Purkis family create a friendly and relaxing atmosphere and really enjoy welcoming guests into their home. Despite the peace and tranquillity assured by its rural location, the house is a convenient base for visitors to Tamworth, Lichfield and the National Exhibition Centre.

## RECOMMENDED IN THE AREA

**RESTAURANT:**
*New Hall, Sutton Coldfield*

**TRADITIONAL PUB:**
*Bulls Head, Shenstone*

**VISIT:**
*Drayton Manor Theme Park & Zoo*

**299**

*Laxey Wheel, Isle of Man*

*Ramsey, Isle of Man*

# Engelwood Lodge

*Detached modern house overlooking Douglas Bay*

☎ 01624 616050   📠 01624 616051

**Map ref 5 - SC37**

105 King Edward Road, ONCHAN,
Isle of Man, IM3 2AS
1m N from Promenade. In King Edward Rd
on left after Churchill of India Restaurant.
Private rd parallel to main rd over railway line
3 Rooms, ££, No smoking

Engelwood Lodge is a large detached house built in 1996. It is situated at Onchan, just north of Douglas, from where it commands superb views of Douglas Bay and the harbour.

The bedrooms are luxuriously appointed. All are en suite and have their own television, radio and tea making facilities.

Linda and Martyn Lister are caring hosts, and in 1999 Linda was an AA Landlady of the Year finalist. The house has three separate lounges, one with a pool table and another in the form of a conservatory, which opens onto the sun terrace. Afternoon tea, served either on the terrace or in the conservatory, is available on request, and includes home-baked scones with cream and strawberry jam. In the morning you can expect a feast in the attractive breakfast room, with Manx kippers providing a local flavour.

## RECOMMENDED IN THE AREA

**RESTAURANT:**
*The Chablis Cellar, Castletown*

**VISIT:**
*Manx Museum, Douglas*

# The River House

*Top breakfasts in a Georgian house overlooking the river*

☎ 01624 816412   📠 01624 816412

**Map ref 5 - SC49**

RAMSEY, Isle of Man, IM8 3DA
3 Rooms, ££

Built in about 1820, with Victorian additions, the house is five minutes' walk from the town centre. It is found in a private lane and has large mature gardens and a river passing nearby. All the spacious bedrooms have views across the river. The rooms are furnished with pretty chintzes, and have luxury bathrooms en suite, and colour TV. You can also see the river from the Garden Room, where breakfast is served from 7.30am to 9.30am, featuring an ample full breakfast, home made bread and preserves. All food is cooked on the traditional Aga, using fresh produce from the vegetable garden. Cordon Bleu dinners can be arranged from Sunday to Thursday, around the table in the elegant dining room, with its beautiful antique furniture and pictures. There is no licence but guests can bring their own wine.

## RECOMMENDED IN THE AREA

**RESTAURANT:**
*The Chablis Cellar, Castletown*

**VISIT:**
*'The Grove' Rural Life Museum, Ramsey*

# Scotland & Northern Ireland

Edinburgh's old town centres on the large rock where the castle stands. The Scottish crown and other royal regalia are displayed in the Crown Room, the Scottish National War Museum is worth a visit. The National Gallery of Scotland, just off Princes Street, is home to Scotland's greatest collection of European paintings and sculpture. It contains notable collections of works by Old Master, Impressionists and Scottish Artists. The Palace of Holyroodhouse, still used by the Royal Family, can be visited when they are not in residence. There are fine 17th-century state rooms and the picture gallery houses a series of Scottish monarchs, starting in 330BC with Fergus I. The Former Royal Yacht Britannia can be toured in Leith.

Glasgow has undergone a revival in recent years and has much to offer visitors. The Burrell Collection, housed in a specially designed gallery, holds around 8000 items from Ancient Egyptian alabaster to medieval European Art and illuminated manuscripts. Glasgow Cathedral, founded in the 6th century, is the most complete medieval

*Kilchurn Castle, view east towards Ben Lui, Loch Awe*

cathedral surviving on the Scottish mainland. The Glasgow Gallery of Modern Art and Glasgow Art Gallery and Museum have a range of paintings and sculptures, part of the Museum is devoted to the 'Glasgow Style' with furniture by Charles Rennie Macintosh among others. Glasgow Botanic Gardens, established in 1817, includes the 23,000 sq ft Kibble Palace. This spectacular glasshouse contains enormous tree ferns and Victorian sculptures. The People's Palace museum in Glasgow Green looks at work and leisure of the ordinary people of Glasgow with exhibits from Roman times to modern football momentoes.

*Edinburgh Castle, Edinburgh*

# Arbor Lodge

*Large luxury home with landscaped gardens and woodland*

☎ 01339 886951  📠 01339 886951
📧 arborlodge@aol.com

**Map ref 10 - NO59**

Ballater Road, ABOYNE, Aberdeenshire,
AB34 5HY
on A93 0.5m W of village centre
3 Rooms, ££, No smoking in bedrooms

Arbor Lodge stands in over an acre of grounds: the formal garden is at the front of the house, the woodland at the back. It is ideally situated for touring Royal Deeside and visiting the many castles in the area - it has a private car park. There are also plenty of activities on offer in the village of Aboyne, ranging from golf to gliding, water-skiing to squash.

The bedrooms are big and luxurious: not only do they all have en suite bathrooms, they also have walk-in dressing rooms, not to mention tea making facilities and colour TV. There is a reading room as well as a sitting room, with access to the patio at the back of the house. Breakfast is freshly prepared, and served at tables for two in the dining room.

## RECOMMENDED IN THE AREA

**RESTAURANT:**
*White Cottage, Aboyne*

**TRADITIONAL PUB:**
*Gordon Arms, Kincardine O'Neil*

**VISIT:**
*Banchory Museum, Banchory*

# Kirkton House

*Quiet location 25 minutes from Glasgow Airport*

☎ 01389 841951  📠 01389 841868
📧 info@kirktonhouse.co.uk

**Map ref 9 - NS37**

Darleith Road, CARDROSS, Argyll & Bute,
G82 5EZ
0.5m N of village, turn N off A814 into
Darleith Rd at W end of village. Kirkton House
0.5m on right
6 Rooms, ££
Closed Dec-Jan

Kirkton House is a converted traditional 17th-18th century farmhouse in a peaceful country location, enjoying panoramic views of the River Clyde. Loch Lomond is only ten minutes' drive away. As a member of the 'Taste of Scotland' good food scheme and licensed to sell alcohol, guests may wine and dine to good home cooking, from an extensive daily menu, at individual oil lamplit tables. The farmhouse retains a rustic style and cosy ambience (with real open fire on chilly evenings), yet has modern amenities and comforts. All bedrooms have en suite bathrooms and all the facilities of a hotel, such as an ironing board, tea/coffee making facilities, direct dial phones, modem plugs, TV and hairdryer. Two downstairs rooms are suitable for those with mobility or respiratory problems (one has wheelchair access, with grab rails in the bathroom). Four rooms are suitable for family occupation. Loch Lomond Golf Club (members only) is fifteen minutes' drive away, and there are excellent local courses (open to visitors on weekdays).

## RECOMMENDED IN THE AREA

**RESTAURANT:**
*Cameron House Hotel, Balloch*

**TRADITIONAL PUB:**
*Fox & Hounds, Houston*

**VISIT:**
*Dumbarton Castle, Dumbarton*

# Dunvalanree Guest House

*A welcoming family atmosphere and great home baking*

☎ 01583 431226  📠 01583 431339
✉ house@milstead.demon.co.uk

Map ref 9 - NR83

Port Righ Bay, CARRADALE, Argyll & Bute, PA28 6SE
in Carradale centre turn left at sign for Portrigh Bay & follow road to end
7 Rooms, ££, No smoking

This detached home is peacefully situated beside a small bay with a sheltered beach. There are glorious views from the house over the water, with the hills of Arran on the horizon. There is a lounge and an attractive dining room, both with superb views over the well-tended gardens to the beach beyond. In the dining room you can enjoy good home cooking and baking, using fresh local produce. Five of the smart bedrooms have en suite facilities, one room is suitable for families. Tea and coffee making facilities are provided in the rooms but there is television only in the lounge. The premises are licensed and parking is available for guests (no coaches). Nearby amenities include a nine-hole golf course and fishing.

## RECOMMENDED IN THE AREA

**TRADITIONAL PUB:**
*Kilberry Inn, Kilberry*

**VISIT:**
*Dumbarton Castle, Dumbarton*

*Whiting Bay, Arran and Holy Isle*

# Ards House

*Victorian villa with glorious views of the Firth of Lorn and the Morvern Hills*

☎ ✆ **01631 710255**
✉ **jb@ardshouse. demon.co.uk**

**Map ref 9 - NM93**

CONNEL, Argyll & Bute, PA37 1PT
on A85, 4m N of Oban
7 Rooms, £££
No smoking
Closed Dec-Jan

## RECOMMENDED IN THE AREA

**RESTAURANT:**
*Airds Hotel, Port Appin*

**TRADITIONAL PUB:**
*Polfearn Hotel, Taynuilt*

**VISIT:**
*Bonawe Iron Furnace, Taynuilt*

Guests return time and again to Jean and John Bowman's welcoming small hotel. It is beautifully located, affording superb sea and sunset views. The bedrooms are individually designed and six have en suite facilities. All the rooms are equipped with central heating, radio alarms and hospitality trays, and a new ground floor single has recently been created. The house is licensed to sell wine and spirits, and drinks are served in the drawing room from 6.30pm. Here a real fire burns in the cooler months, providing a warm and relaxing environment. Books and board games are provided and there is even a grand piano.

The Bowmans have been members of Taste of Scotland since 1993, and every evening they serve a five-course dinner using fresh local produce. The dinner menu is displayed each afternoon, and alternatives provided should any of the components be unsuitable. Children and pets cannot be accommodated.

# Lethamhill

*Spacious bedrooms and tasty cuisine, five miles from Loch Lomond*

☎ 01436 676016  📠 01436 676016

**Map ref 9 - NS28**

West Dhuhill Drive, HELENSBURGH,
Argyll & Bute, G84 9AW
off A82 onto B831, left onto B832, follow
sign for Hillhouse. Take 2nd right after
30mph sign
3 Rooms, ££, No smoking

Lethamhill is a large, listed detached villa, designed by John Burnett and built in 1911. It is set in large secluded grounds, with ample parking and fine views of the Clyde Estuary and the Arran Peaks beyond. Helensburgh was the home of John Logie Baird, the inventor of television, and Hillhouse, the home of Charles Rennie McIntosh (now owned by the National Trust) is nearby. The famous West Highland Railway line is also in close proximity. Glasgow is 40 minutes away by train, with a half-hourly service, Glasgow Airport is a half hour drive by car. From the red telephone box in the garden to old typewriters and slot machines inside, Douglas and Jane Johnston's house is an Aladdin's Cave of interesting collectibles and memorabilia. Beyond this unique nostalgia trip, the house offers spacious comfortable bedrooms, all with en suite bathrooms, individual in style and thoughtfully equipped. Jane is a qualified chef, and her cooking and baking is highly recommended.

## RECOMMENDED IN THE AREA

**RESTAURANT:**
*Cameron House Hotel, Balloch*

**TRADITIONAL PUB:**
*Clachan Inn, Drymen*

**VISIT:**
*Balloch Castle Country Park, Balloch*

# Glenburnie Private Hotel

*Elegant Victorian villa situated on the seafront*

☎ 01631 562089  📠 01631 562089
✉ graeme.strachan@btinternet.com

**Map ref 9 - NM83**

The Esplanade, OBAN, Argyll & Bute,
PA34 5AQ
directly on Oban seafront, follow signs for
Ganavan
14 Rooms, ££, No smoking

## RECOMMENDED IN THE AREA

**RESTAURANT:**
*Manor House Hotel, Oban*

**TRADITIONAL PUB:**
*Tigh an Truish Inn, Clachan-seil*

**VISIT:**
*Caithness Glass Visitors Centre, Oban*

From its prime position on the esplanade, this handsome establishment offers dazzling views over the bay to the Isle of Mull. The house has been lovingly restored and refurbished by its dedicated owners, the Strachan family. The bedrooms, which include a superior four-poster room and mini suite, are beautifully decorated, comfortably furnished and equipped with modern facilities, including en suites in every room. There is a lovely sitting room with a fire for the cooler evenings. Guests are greeted with tea and shortbread on arrival, and delicious breakfasts, featuring the best of local produce and home made preserves, are served in the attractive dining room. For dinner, the Strachans are happy to advise guests on the many local restaurants located in the town centre, which is just a leisurely five-minute stroll away. Private car parking is provided.

# Dunstane House

*Historic mansion in a city centre location*

☎ 0131 337 6169
🖷 0131 337 6169
✉ smowat@
compuserve.com

**Map ref 10 - NT27**

4 West Coates,
Haymarket,
EDINBURGH,
EH12 5JQ
A8 between Murrayfield
and Haymarket. 5 mins
from city centre opp
church
15 Rooms, ££
No smoking in
bedrooms

Shirley and Derek Mowat are the friendly owners of this listed period property, which is easily found on the main Glasgow road, and is conveniently located for the city centre. The house has been lavishly refurbished with quality appointments, including a four-poster bed in the master bedroom. Delightful original features include stained glass windows, wood panelling, fireplaces, and ornate cornices. The well proportioned bedrooms are equipped with colour television, radios, and tea and coffee making equipment, and 15 have en suite facilities. Public areas comprise a relaxing lounge with a corner bar, where a selection of malt whiskies is offered, and the dining room where breakfast and dinners are served. Both of these rooms overlook the lovely mature garden, where guests are welcome to wander and relax. Private car parking is provided to the rear of the building.

## RECOMMENDED IN THE AREA

**RESTAURANT:**
*The Witchery by the Castle, Edinburgh*

**TRADITIONAL PUB:**
*Royal Ettrick Hotel, Edinburgh*

**VISIT:**
*Royal Observatory Visitors Centre*

# $\mathcal{E}$lmview

*Fine Victorian terraced house in a central location*

☎ 0131 228 1973  📠 0131 229 7296
✉ marny@elmview.co.uk

**Map ref 10 - NT27**

15 Glengyle Terrace, EDINBURGH, EH3 9LN
take A702 S up Lothian Rd, 1st left past
Kings Theatre into Valleyfield St, one-way
system leading to Glengyle Terrace
3 Rooms, ££
No smoking

---

## RECOMMENDED IN THE AREA

**RESTAURANT:**
*Atrium, Edinburgh*

**TRADITIONAL PUB:**
*Royal Eltrick Hotel, Edinburgh*

**VISIT:**
*National Gallery of Scotland, Edinburgh*

Occupying the lower ground level of a substantial Victorian property, Elmview offers superior bed and breakfast accommodation, with constantly upgraded decoration and facilities, which appeals to both tourist and business travellers.

The tastefully furnished bedrooms have stylish en suite bathrooms and a good level of comfort, which compensates for the absence of a lounge. The rooms are exceptionally well equipped, including thoughtful extras such as wine glasses and a fridge with fresh milk.

Marny and Richard Hill are caring and attentive hosts who are always on hand when needed. The highlight of one's stay will be their excellent breakfasts taken at one large, elegantly appointed table.

---

# $\mathcal{T}$he International Guest House

*Luxurious modern facilities in a 19th-century setting*

☎ 0131 667 2511  📠 0131 667 1112
✉ intergh@easynet.co.uk

**Map ref 10 - NT27**

37 Mayfield Gardens, EDINBURGH,
EH9 2BX
1.5m S of Princes St on A701 (4m from
Straiton Junction on Edinburgh City by-pass)
9 Rooms, ££

---

## RECOMMENDED IN THE AREA

**RESTAURANT:**
*Number One, Balmoral Hotel, Edinburgh*

**TRADITIONAL PUB:**
*Ship on the Shore, Leith*

**VISIT:**
*Scotch Whisky Heritage Centre, Edinburgh*

This attractive stone-built terrace house lies on the south side of the city. There is ample private parking, and it is on a main bus route, giving easy access to the town centre. The high ceilings and large windows, wooden staircase, and  décor, with ornate plasterwork on the ceilings, embody the splendour of the Victorian era. All the bedrooms, decorated and fitted in matching period floral prints, and brightened with fresh flowers, have modern en suite facilities and colour TV. Some rooms enjoy magnificent views across to the extinct volcano known as Arthur's Seat.

A hearty Scottish breakfast is served, on the finest bone china, at separate tables in the dining room; the marble fireplace with mirror above it is a lovely feature in this room. The International has received top accolades for quality and hospitality.

# Inveresk House

*Historic house in a tranquil setting close to Edinburgh*

☎ 0131 665 5855  📠 0131 665 0578
✉ chute.inveresk@btinternet.com
**Map ref 10 - NT27**

3 Inveresk Village, Musselburgh,
EDINBURGH, EH21 7UA
from Musselburgh sharp right off A6124
towards St Michaels Church. 2nd driveway
on right, pass cottage and fork right
3 Rooms, ££, No smoking
Closed 22-27 Dec

Once used as a base by Cromwell at the Battle of Dunbar, this lovely old house is situated in three and a half acres of woodland and gardens on the outskirts of Musselburgh. Public areas include a large sitting room on the first floor, which has been furnished in keeping with the character of the house. Downstairs, an enjoyable Scottish breakfast is served in the dining room, which boasts an ornate ceiling and a fine carved fireplace. The bedrooms vary in size, but are well proportioned, very comfortable, and offer many thoughtful extras such as fresh flowers and a superbly stocked hospitality tray. All rooms have private bathrooms adjacent. There is a good choice of pubs and restaurants in Musselburgh and all the facilities of Edinburgh are within easy reach. The proprietors are happy to give advice on the best places to eat. This is a family friendly establishment.

### RECOMMENDED IN THE AREA

**RESTAURANT:**
*Caledonian Hotel, Edinburgh*

**TRADITIONAL PUB:**
*Bridge Inn, Ratho*

**VISIT:**
*Palace of Holyroodhouse, Edinburgh*

# Kew House

*Centrally located Victorian guest house with secure private parking*

☎ 0131 313 0700  📠 0131 313 0747
✉ kewhouse@worldsites.net
**Map ref 10 - NT27**

1 Kew Terrace, Murrayfield, EDINBURGH,
EH12 5JE
on A8 Glasgow rd, 1mile West of city centre,
close to Murrayfield Rugby Stadium
6 Rooms, ££, No smoking

Situated to the west of the city, this immaculately maintained establishment is convenient for the Murrayfield Rugby Stadium and the Edinburgh International Conference Centre, and is less than a mile from Princes Street. The stone-built house forms part of a listed terrace dating from around 1860. It has recently been converted to offer guest house accommodation and two self-contained apartments. The bedrooms come in a variety of sizes, but all have been designed and equipped for the comfort of both business and leisure guests. En suite facilities are provided along with remote control colour television, hospitality trays, direct dial telephones, hairdryers and trouser presses. Full Scottish breakfast is included in the tariff, and there is a guest bar and lounge offering a supper and snack menu. The house has a private secure car park.

### RECOMMENDED IN THE AREA

**RESTAURANT:**
*Channings, Edinburgh*

**TRADITIONAL PUB:**
*Hawes Inn, South Queensferry*

**VISIT:**
*Royal Botanic Garden, Edinburgh*

# The Lodge Hotel

*An attractive period property conveniently located in Edinburgh's west end*

☎ 0131 3373682
🖶 0131 3131700
📧 thelodgehotel
@btconnect.com
Map ref 10 - NT27

6 Hampton Terrace,
West Coates,
EDINBURGH,
EH12 5JD
on A8, 1 mile West of
city centre
10 Rooms, ££,
No Smoking,
Closed 24 & 25 Dec

A warm welcome awaits you at Linda and George Jarron's handsome Georgian home. It is ideally located in the west end of Edinburgh, providing a convenient base for seeing the sights of the city and beyond. Following a good day out, guests will enjoy relaxing in the beautiful lounge or the cosy bar. The bedrooms at The Lodge are beautifully presented and all of them have en suite facilities. A high standard of housekeeping and cleanliness is maintained throughout, and guests are made to feel very much at home. For new arrivals, fresh fruit and a small decanter of port are thoughtfully provided. The Jarrons pride themselves on their cuisine and freshly prepared breakfasts and evening meals are served in the elegant dining room.

## RECOMMENDED IN THE AREA

**RESTAURANT:**
*Haldanes, Edinburgh*

**TRADITIONAL PUB:**
*Hawes Inn,
South Queensferry*

**VISIT:**
*Scottish National Portrait
Gallery, Edinburgh*

# The Witchery by the Castle

*A restaurant with rooms in a stunning location at the heart of the ancient city of Edinburgh*

☎ 0131 225 5613
📠 0131 220 4392

**Map ref 10 - NT27**

Castlehill, Royal Mile,
EDINBURGH, City of
Edinburgh, EH1 2NE
2 Rooms, £££
Closed Xmas/
Boxing Day

*T*his restaurant with rooms lives up to its very unusual name and address, it is found in an ancient 16th-century building right at the gates of Edinburgh Castle. There are two historic and atmospheric restaurants to choose from, both on the ground floor and open for lunch and dinner. The dining rooms are most elegantly decorated with gilded heraldic ceilings, tapestry hangings and panelled walls, taking diners back to a bygone age.

The accommodation is no less theatrical and much in demand. Two suites of rooms are decorated in decadent, gothic style with four-poster beds. Acclaimed as a romantic hideaway, these rooms offer every luxury and are ideal for honeymoons or a celebration.

## RECOMMENDED IN THE AREA

**TRADITIONAL PUB:**
*The Ensign Ewart, Edinburgh*

**VISIT:**
*Edinburgh Castle, Edinburgh*

# Priory Lodge

*Purpose built guest house attractively situated close to Edinburgh*

☎ 0131 331 4345   📠 0131 331 4345
✉ calmyn@aol.com

**Map ref 10 - NT27**

The Loan, SOUTH QUEENSFERRY, near
Edinburgh, EH30 9NS
just off High St
5 Rooms, ££, No smoking

*F*riendly owners Calmyn and Gordon Lamb enjoy welcoming people to their delightful guest house. It is located just off the quaint cobbled High Street in South Queensferry, which sits between the two famous bridges on the south side of the Firth of Forth. The town offers a good choice of pubs and restaurants and the City of Edinburgh is just 20 minutes away. The attractive bedrooms are maintained to a high standard and are comfortably furnished in antique pine. Each room has a remote control colour television, hospitality tray and en suite shower and WC.

A small lounge is provided, and guests are welcome to use the kitchen facilities. Tartan has been used to good effect in the attractive dining room where hearty Scottish breakfasts are served at individual tables, with a vegetarian option. Pets are not accommodated.

## RECOMMENDED IN THE AREA

**RESTAURANT:**
*Champany Inn, Linlithgow*

**TRADITIONAL PUB:**
*Hawes Inn, Edinburgh*

**VISIT:**
*Hopetoun House, South Queensferry*

---

# The Stuarts

*Central location in Edinburgh, close to the Kings Theatre*

☎ 0131 229 9559   📠 0131 229 2226
✉ reservations@the-stuarts.com

**Map ref 10 - NT27**

17 Glengyle Terrace, EDINBURGH, EH3 9LN
East of A702, between the Kings Theatre
and Bruntsfield Links
3 Rooms, ££, No smoking
Closed Xmas

*T*he highest levels of comfort and facilities are provided here. Spacious, comfortable centrally-heated bedrooms are furnished with easy chairs. Extra items include a fridge with chilled wine; trouser press and ironing centre, direct dial telephone, hi-fi and video with music and entertainment to choose from.

The dining room is made available during the day for guests and breakfast is served at one table here in the mornings. No dogs can be accommodated.

Mastercard, American Express and Visa credit cards may be accepted.

## RECOMMENDED IN THE AREA

**RESTAURANT:**
*The Marque, Edinburgh*

**TRADITIONAL PUB:**
*Royal Ettrick Hotel, Edinburgh*

**VISIT:**
*Royal Museum of Scotland, Edinburgh*

# Auchenskeoch Lodge

*Victorian shooting lodge in twenty acres of grounds surrounded by lovely countryside*

☎ 01387 780277
📠 01387 780277

**Map ref 5 - NX86**

DALBEATTIE,
Dumfries & Galloway,
DG5 4PG
5m SE off B793
3 Rooms, ££
Closed Nov-Mar

Situated to the south east of the town, this fine house enjoys a peaceful setting with extensive grounds including woodland walks, a vegetable garden, croquet lawn, a maze and a small fishing loch. Christopher and Mary Broom-Smith have carefully retained the original character of the house, which is full of charm, graced with antiques, period furniture, books, painting and sculptures. Two of the well proportioned bedrooms have a lounge area and one of these can also be used as an additional single bedroom. The spacious ground floor room is ideally suited for disabled or elderly guests. A set four-course dinner is served house party style at 8pm and features Mary's home-cooked dishes, which include vegetables picked from the garden. There is a good wine list and guests are invited to help themselves to drinks in the billiard room, where they will also find a full size billiard table.

## RECOMMENDED IN THE AREA

**RESTAURANT:**
*Plumed Horse Restaurant, Castle Douglas*

**TRADITIONAL PUB:**
*Criffel Inn, New Abbey*

**VISIT:**
*Threave Gardens & Castle, Castle Donglas*

# $\mathcal{B}$aytree House

*Georgian townhouse with walled garden, near the picturesque harbour*

☎ 01557 330824  📠 01557 330824

**Map ref 5 - NX65**

110 High Street, KIRKCUDBRIGHT, Dumfries & Galloway, DG6 4JQ
from A75 take A711 into town, turn right 200yds past St Cuthberts Church into High St. House at junction with Castle St
3 Rooms, ££, No smoking

The house is found right on the High Street, in the old part of an area well-known for its artists colony. The beautiful garden features two ponds, a sun deck, and other places to sit in seclusion. There is accessible parking.

The large bedrooms are all en suite, attractively furnished, with many original features and paintings by local artists. One has a four-poster bed, one is on the ground floor. Twin and double rooms are on the first floor. The house has a huge drawing room on the first floor with an open fire for cold winter nights.

Fine Scottish cuisine is served using vegetables and herbs from the garden and fish straight from the local harbour: at breakfast, you could try scrambled eggs with Creetown smoked salmon and fennel, or traditional 'Clootie Dumpling'; dinner is also available.

## RECOMMENDED IN THE AREA

**RESTAURANT:**
*Plumed Horse Restaurant, Castle Douglas*

**TRADITIONAL PUB:**
*Anchor Inn, Kippford*

**VISIT:**
*Broughton House & Garden, Kircudbright*

---

# $\mathcal{H}$artfell House

*Conveniently located Victorian country house with lovely views*

☎ 01683 220153
✉ robert.white@virgin.net

**Map ref 10 - NT00**

Hartfell Crescent, MOFFAT, Dumfries & Galloway, DG10 9AL
exit A74(M) J15, A701, to town centre. At clock tower turn right up Well St. Into Old Well Rd. 1st right (Hartfell Crescent)
8 Rooms, £

Hartfell House is located in a peaceful rural setting yet is only a few minutes' walk from the centre of Moffat. Built of local stone, it is a listed building of architectural interest, and from its elevated position, high above the town, the house enjoys superb views of the surrounding countryside.

The bedrooms are mostly spacious and all offer a high degree of comfort. Seven have en suite facilities, and televisions, radio alarms, hairdryers and tea and coffee making facilities are provided in every room. There is a large guest lounge on the first floor, and delicious home-cooked meals are served in the elegant dining room. The house has a residential licence and presents its own carefully chosen wine list.

Dogs are allowed to stay by prior arrangement, and there is ample car parking space.

## RECOMMENDED IN THE AREA

**RESTAURANT:**
*Well View Hotel, Moffat*

**TRADITIONAL PUB:**
*Black Bull Inn*

**VISIT:**
*Broughton House & Garden, Kircudbright*

# Scoretulloch House

## 500-year-old country house in a hillside setting

☎ 01560 323331 📠 01560 323441
✉ mail@scoretulloch.com
**Map ref 9 - NS53**

DARVEL, East Ayrshire, KA17 0LR
turn off A71 just East of Darvel & follow
signs for 1 mile
4 Rooms, £££, No smoking in bedrooms

*D*onald and Annie Smith have restored a former ruin and created a dream house. Set high on a hillside, sheltered by landscaped gardens, it enjoys fine views across valley and moorland. The original walls date back 500 years, otherwise everything is new, but the style is that of a Scottish shooting lodge and country home. The personal service and relaxed atmosphere is very much in keeping with this style. Scoretulloch is first and foremost a restaurant with rooms. The elegant dining room is the setting for excellent cooking which has earned the AA's two

rosette award. Oscar's Brasserie, located in the conservatory, serves simpler food all day.

There is a cosy library bar with masses of wildlife books - Donald is a naturalist, author and photographer. Dark wood panelling and huge ceiling beams characterise the public rooms, while the bedrooms, each with en suite facilities, are quietly gracious.

## RECOMMENDED IN THE AREA

**VISIT:**
*Dean Castle Country Park, Kilmarnock*

---

# Kippielaw Farmhouse

## Superb breakfasts and wonderful views from the farmhouse

☎ 01620 860368 📠 01620 860368
**Map ref 10 - NT57**

EAST LINTON, East Lothian, EH41 4PY
leave A1 at E Linton, follow Traprain sign
0.75m, take single track rd on right after
farm. Establishment 0.5m on left opposite CP
3 Rooms, £, No smoking

*S*et in an elevated position but sheltered by gardens, Kippielaw Farmhouse enjoys magnificent views of the Tyne Valley. The Firth of Forth and east coast are nearby, and Edinburgh is easily accessible by car, about half an hour's drive away. Guests receive a warm welcome here from Liz and Bill Campbell.

The country-style en suite bedrooms are thoughtfully equipped with tea and coffee making facilities, hairdryers and radios but no televisions. Dinner is available by prior arrangement, served

around a cherry wood dining table. The breakfasts are particularly highly recommended. There is a cosy guest lounge with open staircase, and a traditional log fire. Parking space is available for guests. Dogs cannot be accommodated.

## RECOMMENDED IN THE AREA

**RESTAURANT:**
*The Marque, Edinburgh*

**TRADITIONAL PUB:**
*Drovers Inn, East Linton*

**VISIT:**
*Hailes Castle, East Linton*

# *F*aussetthill House

*Edwardian house in a peaceful coastal village*

☎ 01620 842396  📠 01620 842396

**Map ref 10 - NT48**

20 Main Street, GULLANE, East Lothian,
EH31 2DR
on A198, from A1 follow A198 to Gullane
4 Rooms, ££, No smoking

George and Dorothy Nisbet welcome you to their delightful home, which stands in well tended gardens in the picturesque village of Gullane. Spotlessly clean and immaculately maintained, the house is both comfortable and inviting. Bedrooms are well proportioned and attractively decorated. Three rooms are en suite, and all have tea and coffee making equipment. There is a first-floor lounge with well filled bookshelves, and breakfast is served at one table in the elegant dining room.

From Gullane, North Berwick is just 10 minutes away, and Edinburgh 30 minutes by car; there are many places of interest to visit in the area. Keen golfers will be pleased to note that there are 19 golf courses within easy reach, with five in the village itself, including Muirfield. Children under 10 are not accepted at Faussetthill House, and dogs are not permitted in the rooms.

## RECOMMENDED IN THE AREA

**RESTAURANT:**
*La Potiniere, Gullane*

**TRADITIONAL PUB:**
*Drovers Inn, East Linton*

**VISIT:**
*Dirleton Castle, Dirleton*

# *B*eaumont Lodge Guest House

*Family-run guest house in the coastal village of Anstruther*

☎ 01333 310315  📠 01333 310315
✉ reservations@beau-lodge.
demon.co.uk

**Map ref 10 - NO50**

43 Pittenweem Road, ANSTRUTHER, Fife,
KY10 3DT
take B9131 from St Andrews to Anstruther,
turn right at crossroads, Beaumont Lodge
on left past hotel
5 Rooms, ££, No smoking

## RECOMMENDED IN THE AREA

**RESTAURANT:**
*Cellar Restaurant, Anstruther*

**TRADITIONAL PUB:**
*The Dreel Tavern, Anstruther*

**VISIT:**
*Scottish Fisheries Museum, Anstruther*

Beaumont Lodge is close to the university and historical town of St Andrews, home to the Royal and Ancient Golf Club and world famous Old Course. Anstruther has a nine-hole golf course by the shoreline only two minutes' walk from the guest house. There are a number of other parkland and links courses nearby making the area a golfing mecca. Two of the luxury en suite bedrooms have interconnecting doors, ideal for families (children must be over 10 years old). Some rooms have sea views, one has a splendid four-poster bed and one is located on the ground floor. Dinner is available here and the breakfast and dinner menus offer a wide choice including 'Taste of Scotland' delicacies and high quality local produce. Major credit cards and switch cards are accepted here.

# The Spindrift

*Attractive detached Victorian house 10 minutes' drive from St Andrews*

☎ 01333 310573  📠 01333 310573
✉ spindrift@east-neuk.co.uk

**Map ref 10 - NO50**

Pittenweem Road, ANSTRUTHER, Fife,
KY10 3DT
from W, 1st building on left on entering town.
From E last building on right when leaving
8 Rooms, ££, No smoking
Closed 17 Nov-10 Dec & Xmas

## RECOMMENDED IN THE AREA

**RESTAURANT:**
*The Cellar Restaurant, Anstruther*

**TRADITIONAL PUB:**
*Ship Inn, Elie*

**VISIT:**
*Kellie Castle & Gardens, nr Anstruther*

The house was built in 1872 by Captain John Smith, a tea clipper captain. A special feature here is the unique Captain's Room, a replica of a ship's cabin. The rest of the house is brightly decorated and the atmosphere is friendly and welcoming. The en suite bedrooms are individually furnished and two are suitable for family occupation. All bedrooms have colour television, tea and coffee making facilities and direct dial telephones. An attractive lounge is available to guests, the house is licensed and an honesty bar is provided here. The dining room has individual tables where enjoyable home-cooking is served at breakfast. Spindrift is run as a home where the proprietors welcome guests as friends, offering very high standards of comfort, cleanliness and service. Please note that this is a completely non-smoking house, and that children and dogs cannot be accommodated.

# Hillview House

Italian and English are spoken at this delightful house. The location makes it an ideal base for visitors touring Scotland; with Edinburgh, Perth, St Andrews, Glasgow and Stirling all within an hour's drive. Your hosts can help you plan an itinerary and offer local information.

The attractively decorated en suite bedrooms all have video, colour television and tea and coffee making facilities.

Dinner is available here by prior arrangement, assistance can also be given in choosing a local restaurant or pub.

*Close to Dunfermline town centre, M90 and Pitreavie Business Park*

☎ 01383 726278  📠 01383 726278
✉ hillviewhousedunfermline@
tinyonline.co.uk

**Map ref 10 - NT08**

9 Aberdour Road, DUNFERMLINE, Fife,
KY11 4PB
from Edinburgh exit M90 J2, take A823
(Dunfermline), right at T-junct by Cottage Inn
pub into Aberdour Rd. House 100yds on right
3 Rooms, £, No smoking

## RECOMMENDED IN THE AREA

**RESTAURANT:**
*Atrium, Edinburgh*

**TRADITIONAL PUB:**
*Nivington House, Cleish*

**VISIT:**
*Andrew Carnegie Birthplace Museum,
Dunfermline*

# *P*itreavie Guest House

*Easy atmosphere and professional care in a comfortable home*

📞 01383 724244 📠 01383 724244
📧 pitreavie@aol.com

**Map ref 10 - NT08**

3 Aberdour Road, DUNFERMLINE, Fife, KY11 4PB
at west end of Aberdour Rd at junct with A823. 0.5m S of Dunfermline town centre
5 Rooms, ££, No smoking

## RECOMMENDED IN THE AREA

**RESTAURANT:**
*Martin's Restaurant, Edinburgh*

**TRADITIONAL PUB:**
*Gartwhinzean Hotel, Powmill*

**VISIT:**
*Dunfermline Abbey*

Anne and John Walker have been running this guest house for five years, and it has belonged to the family since it first opened in 1980. The atmosphere is unhurried and relaxed, and the Walkers are well practised and skilled at attending to their guests' needs. They pride themselves on their high standards at affordable prices. It is a semi-detached house conveniently located on the bus route for Edinburgh and the Fife coast, within easy reach of the centre of town. The bedrooms, with attractive fabrics and pine furniture, are equipped with colour TV, hospitality trays, hairdryers, radio alarms and luxury bathrobes. None have bathrooms en suite, but there are three WCs, two showers and a bathroom shared by the five rooms. One room serves as lounge and dining room, where impressive breakfasts are served, evening meals are available by arrangement.

# *F*ossil House Bed & Breakfast

*Victorian house and cottage in a pretty village setting*

📞 01334 850639 📠 01334 850639
📧 the.fossil@virgin.net

**Map ref 10 - NO51**

12-14 Main Street, Strathkinness, ST ANDREWS, Fife, KY16 9RU
follow A91 towards St Andrews, Strathkinness signed. Fossil House at top end of village close to pub
4 Rooms, £, No smoking

## RECOMMENDED IN THE AREA

**RESTAURANT:**
*The Old Course Hotel, St Andrews*

**VISIT:**
*British Golf Museum, St Andrews*

Fossil House is located in the village of Strathkinness two miles west of St Andrews. The en suite bedrooms are divided between the main house and a converted cottage to the rear. They are all at ground floor level with direct access to the courtyard, garden and car park, and guests have their own keys for easy access at any hour. Each room has been carefully designed to make the best use of available space, and is equipped with remote control colour television, trouser press, central heating, fridge, radio alarm, hairdryer, shaver point, and tea and coffee making facilities. One room is suitable for family occupation, and a cot and highchair are also available.

There is a choice of comfortable lounges in the cottage, including a conservatory, and both have an ample supply of books, board games and videos. An imaginative breakfast menu offers something to suit everyone.

# Glenderran

*Attractive house near the Old Course and the sea*

☎ 01334 477951  ✆ 01334 477908
✉ glenderran@telinco.co.uk

**Map ref 10 - NO51**

9 Murray Park, ST ANDREWS, Fife,
KY16 9AW
enter St Andrews on A91 straight over rdbt
2nd left into Murray Place, right into Murray
Park. Glenderran on left
5 Rooms, ££, No smoking

Claire and Chris Toll ensure a warm welcome and a friendly stay at their lovely, late Victorian terraced house, which is located just a short walk from the famous Old Course and the beach. Attractive public areas are enhanced by fresh flowers and soft background music. Bedrooms come in a variety of sizes, from cosy singles to a massive mini suite, all with en suite or private facilities. The rooms are beautifully decorated and provide many thoughtful extras including CD players, remote control televisions, tea and coffee making equipment, and bottles of mineral water.

Breakfast is a highlight of a stay at Glenderran, with its impressive selection of dishes, including a cooked vegetarian option. The dining room also serves as a lounge to relax in and meet with friends, play cards and have a drink. The honesty bar features a range of classic Scottish malt whiskies.

## RECOMMENDED IN THE AREA

**RESTAURANT:**
*Rufflets Country House, St Andrews*

**VISIT:**
*Castle & Visitors Centre, St Andrews*

---

# Glenavon House

*Central location for golf, fishing, walking or skiing*

☎ 01479 831213  ✆ 01479 831213
✉ glenavonhouse@aol.com

**Map ref 12 - NH91**

Kinchurdy Road, BOAT OF GARTEN,
Highland, PH24 3BP
off A9, follow Grantown-on-Spey signs until
Boat of Garten sign. At Boat of Garten P.O.
right into Kinchurdy Rd, on right
5 Rooms, ££, No smoking in bedrooms

Elegant, family-run and Victorian, Glenavon House offers the discerning holiday maker the very highest standards of comfort and care. It is situated in the idyllic Highland village of Boat of Garten, making it the perfect base for a Scottish holiday. Golf, fishing, walking and wildlife are almost on the doorstep. Glenavon House is world renowned for its cuisine and wine cellar, the cuisine is described as 'Auld Alliance', Scotland's finest produce cooked with a French influence. Every evening a gourmet dinner is served in the traditional candle-lit dining room. The bedrooms are decorated to a high standard, with en suite shower facilities. Colour televisions and tea and coffee making facilities are provided. Guests can enjoy a pre and post dinner drink in the elegant sitting room with open fire.

## RECOMMENDED IN THE AREA

**RESTAURANT:**
*Culloden House Hotel, Inverness*

**TRADITIONAL PUB:**
*The Old Bridge Inn, Aviemore*

**VISIT:**
*RSPB Nature Reserve, Boat of Garten*

# Glenaveron

*Quietly situated old stone house convenient for beach and golf course*

☎ 01408 621601  📠 01408 621601

**Map ref 12 - NC90**

Golf Road, BRORA, Highland, KW9 6QS
from S cross bridge in middle of Brora, then
right into Golf Rd. 2nd house on right
3 Rooms, ££, No smoking

Glenaveron is the elegant home of Alistair, Mary and Tom Fortune. It stands in a mature garden just a short walk from Brora Golf Course, in a peaceful part of town.

The house has recently been completely renovated, and is decorated and furnished to a high standard. The bedrooms are both spacious and comfortable, and all have en suite facilities. A specially fitted ground floor room is suitable for disabled guests.

There is an attractive lounge where a fire burns on colder evenings. Alistair's traditional Scottish breakfasts, featuring the best of local produce, are served in the charming dining room. A good choice of restaurants is available in the locality.

## RECOMMENDED IN THE AREA

**RESTAURANT:**
*Royal Marine Hotel, Brora*

**TRADITIONAL PUB:**
*Mallin House Hotel, Dornoch*

**VISIT:**
*Dunrobin Castle, Golspie*

---

# Mansefield House

*Victorian splendour on the 'Road to the Isles'*

☎ 01397 772262  📠 01397 772262
✉ mansefield@aol.com

**Map ref 12 - NN17**

Corpach, FORT WILLIAM, Highland,
PH33 7LT
turn off A82 onto A830 , establishment 2m
from junct on left on corner of Hill View Drive
6 Rooms, £, No smoking in bedrooms
Closed 24-28 Dec

The exterior walls of this former Victorian manse are over two feet thick; combine this with a roaring log fire and you can imagine the warm and cosy atmosphere. The house enjoys a prime location on the famous Road to the Isles, with excellent access to the Highlands and Islands.

Doug and Sue Pearse are friendly, welcoming hosts who will make you feel at home. Five rooms have en suite facilities and two are suitable for family occupation. All bedrooms have colour television and tea and coffee making facilities. The attractive dining room is the setting for delicious breakfasts and classic British cuisine at dinner, all expertly cooked.

Dogs cannot be accommodated (except Guide Dogs). There is ample parking for guests.

## RECOMMENDED IN THE AREA

**RESTAURANT:**
*Inverlochy Castle, Fort William*

**TRADITIONAL PUB:**
*Loch Leven Hotel, Ballachulish*

**VISIT:**
*Glencoe Visitor Centre, Glencoe*

# Ashburn House

*Victorian home in a stunning location, close to the centre of Fort William, overlooking Loch Linnhe*

☎ 01397 706000
📠 01397 702024
✉ ashburn@
scotland2000.com
**Map ref 12 - NN17**

8 Achintore Road,
FORT WILLIAM,
Highland, PH33 6RQ
JA82 and Ashburn Ln
500yds from rbt at S
end of High St or
400yds on right after
30mph zone from S
7 Rooms, ££
No smoking

The Hendersons have restored their elegant home with love and care to provide their guests with top standards of quality and comfort. The pretty flowers in the front garden, and the cheerful white and yellow painted exterior make for a happy welcome, and the big bay windows make the rooms light and airy. The bedrooms are charming and spacious, all with en suite bathrooms and a wide range of amenities including colour TV, and tea and coffee making facilities, and each with its own look - some have the added luxury of super king-size beds. Breakfast is highly commended. It is served at separate tables in the dining room. There is also a conservatory lounge for a peaceful moment of relaxation. Throughout their home the Hendersons instil a friendly atmosphere with their unique Highland charm.

## RECOMMENDED IN THE AREA

**RESTAURANT:**
*No 4 Cameron Square,
Fort William*

**TRADITIONAL PUB:**
*Moorings Hotel,
Fort William*

**VISIT:**
*Old Inverlochy Castle,
Fort William*

# The Grange

*Victorian villa with lovely loch views*

☎ 01397 705516  📠 01397 701595

**Map ref 12 - NN17**

Grange Road, FORT WILLIAM, Highland,
PH33 6JF
leave Fort William on A82 S-300yds from
rdbt take left onto Ashburn Ln. The Grange
is at top on left
4 Rooms, ££, No smoking
Closed Nov-Mar

Over the years, a lot of careful planning and hard work has gone into the restoration of this lovely property, to ensure that only the highest standards are offered to guests. Meticulous attention to detail is evident throughout the house, and warm Highland hospitality is assured.

Attractive decor and pretty fabrics have been used to stunning effect in the charming bedrooms, all of which enjoy beautiful views over Loch Linnhe. All the rooms have quality en suite facilities.

There is an abundance of books and fresh flowers in the comfortable lounge, and the dining room provides a lovely setting for the extensive breakfast, which gives guests a really good start to the day.

## RECOMMENDED IN THE AREA

**RESTAURANT:**
*No 4 Cameron Square, Fort William*

**TRADITIONAL PUB:**
*Onich Hotel, Onich*

**VISIT:**
*Old Inverlochy Castle, Fort William*

# Ardconnel House

*Victorian villa with many original features*

☎ 01479 872104  📠 01479 872104
✉ ardconnel.grantown@virgin-net

**Map ref 12 - NJ02**

Woodlands Terrace, GRANTOWN-ON-SPEY,
Highland, PH26 3JU
from SW & A95 to town, premises on left
near Craislynne Hotel
6 Rooms, ££, No smoking

Visitors to the area will find this house an ideal base for mountain walking, golf, the whisky trails and castle tours. The antique furnishings and paintings enhance the original features of the interior. Bedrooms are tastefully decorated and all have en suite facilities, colour television, a welcome tray and a hairdryer. One room has a superb four-poster. Children over 8 are welcome. Hearty breakfasts and delicious home-cooked evening meals are served in the spacious dining room at separate tables. Menus have a strong French influence and are freshly prepared from good local produce. There is a carefully selected, reasonably priced wine list and a variety of malt whiskies. Visa and Mastercard are accepted here.

## RECOMMENDED IN THE AREA

**RESTAURANT:**
*The Boath House, Nairn*

**VISIT:**
*RSPB Nature Reserve, Boat of Garten*

# The Pines

*19th-century country house backing directly onto beautiful woodland*

☎ 01479 872092  📠 01479 872092
✉ enquiry@pinesgrantown.
freeserve.co.uk

**Map ref 12 - NJ02**

Woodside Avenue, GRANTOWN-ON-SPEY,
Highland, PH26 3JR
at traffic lights follow Elgin signs then take
1st right
8 Rooms, ££, No smoking

The house has a particularly lovely garden, with interesting plants and flowers, a pond and stream. A gate leads from the garden to the pine woods, where deer and rare birds can be seen, and to the famous River Spey. Fishing and golf can be arranged nearby, with a wide range of golf courses to choose from. The town centre is five minutes away on foot. In the house, family portraits, paintings and antiques give a strong sense of heritage. There are two elegantly refurbished lounges where you can read books, magazines and maps from the library, or just enjoy a drink in the glow of the log and peat fire. The dining room and conservatory provide a warm ambience for candlelit dinners, an exciting blend of traditional and modern Scottish cooking. Seven of the bedrooms have en suite facilities, one has an adjacent private bathroom; all are equipped with colour TV, refreshment tray, luxury toiletries and hairdryer.

## RECOMMENDED IN THE AREA

**RESTAURANT:**
*The Boath House, Nairn*

**TRADITIONAL PUB:**
*Dalrachney Lodge Hotel, Carrbridge*

**VISIT:**
*RSPB Nature Reserve, Boat of Garten*

# Ballifeary House Hotel

*A lovely, imposing house with a beautiful, neat garden*

☎ 01463 235572  📠 01463 717583
✉ ballifhotel@btinternet.com

**Map ref 12 - NH64**

10 Ballifeary Road, INVERNESS, Highland,
IV3 5PJ
off A82, 0.5m from town centre, turn left into
Bishops Rd & sharp right into Ballifeary Rd
5 Rooms, ££, No smoking
Closed mid Oct-Easter

Built in the early Victorian era, the house is situated in a quiet, residential area, an easy walk away from some excellent restaurants, and 10 minutes' walk from the town centre, along the banks of the River Ness. It is not suitable for young families, as the minimum age for guests is 15 years. There is ample parking. The house is immaculately kept. The pretty bedrooms are decorated in soft colours with simple floral prints on the fabrics. All have their own en suite bath and shower, colour TV, hairdryer and radio alarm.

There is a charming sitting room with potted plants, and an elegant dining room with deep burgundy curtains and tablecloths, where excellent Scottish breakfasts are served at separate tables. Malt whiskies and wines are available from the list of refreshments.

## RECOMMENDED IN THE AREA

**RESTAURANT:**
*Culloden House, Hotel, Inverness*

**TRADITIONAL PUB:**
*Cawdor Tavern, Cawdor*

**VISIT:**
*Castle Stuart, Inverness*

# Moyness House

*Gracious Victorian villa with a pretty walled garden*

☎ 01463 233836  📠 01463 233836
✉ kayjonesmoyness@msn.com

**Map ref 12 - NH64**

6 Bruce Gardens, INVERNESS, Highland,
IV3 5EN
off A82 Fort William road, almost opposite
Highland Regional Council headquarters
7 Rooms, ££, No smoking in bedrooms
Closed 24 Dec-3 Jan

*J*enny and Richard Jones' elegant villa is located in a quiet residential area just minutes from the town centre. Car parking is provided, and the house makes an ideal base from which to explore the beautiful Highlands.

Inviting public rooms overlook the garden to the front, and guests are welcome to use the secluded and well-maintained back garden. The bedrooms are attractively decorated and are all fitted with en suite bath or shower rooms. Facilities in the bedrooms include colour televisions and tea and coffee making equipment.

## RECOMMENDED IN THE AREA

**RESTAURANT:**
*Culloden House Hotel, Inverness*

**TRADITIONAL PUB:**
*Cawdor Tavern, Cawdor*

**VISIT:**
*Culloden Battlefield, Culloden Moor*

---

# Avondale House

*An elegant Edwardian house in a peaceful village setting*

☎ 01540 661731  📠 01540 661731

**Map ref 12 - NH70**

Newtonmore Road, KINGUSSIE, Highland,
PH21 1HF
7 Rooms, £, No smoking

*A*vondale House enjoys an excellent location in the heart of Scotland, making it an ideal base for touring. Fort William and Inverness are within an hour's drive, while Aviemore is in easy reach with plenty of scope for walking, fishing or golf.

The house has one room with en suite bathroom and four with shower rooms. All the bedrooms have colour television and tea and coffee making facilities. One room is suitable for families, children over 8 years are welcome.

Attractively decorated throughout, the house has a bright, airy dining room and a comfortable lounge. Good home cooking is offered at breakfast and dinner in traditional Scottish style. There is ample parking.

## RECOMMENDED IN THE AREA

**RESTAURANT:**
*The Cross, Kingussie*

**TRADITIONAL PUB:**
*Royal Hotel, Kingussie*

**VISIT:**
*Highland Folk Museum, Kingussie*

# Columba House Hotel & Restaurant

*A former Manse with an excellent restaurant*

☎ 01540 661402  📠 01540 661652
✉ reservations@columba-hotel.co.uk

**Map ref 12 - NH70**

Manse Road, KINGUSSIE, Highland,
PH21 1JF
from A9 at Kincraig/Kingussie take B9152
towards Kingussie, telephone box on corner
of Manse Rd, Hotel drive 2nd on left
8 Rooms, ££

## RECOMMENDED IN THE AREA

**RESTAURANT:**
*The Cross, Kingussie*

**TRADITIONAL PUB:**
*Royal Hotel, Kingussie*

**VISIT:**
*Highland Folk Museum, Kingussie*

This imposing stone house is in a peaceful spot, hidden behind tall Scots pines, just two minutes from the centre of the small picturesque village of Kingussie. It dates back to the 19th century, some of it is even older, and it has been carefully restored. It boasts large grounds, with a car park, and a secluded walled garden with putting and croquet. There is no lack of beautiful scenery and plenty of opportunity for sport in this area.

Some of the bedrooms have romantic four-poster beds; all are en suite, with colour TV, direct dial telephones, mini bar and hospitality tray, and views of the surrounding mountains.

Staff are always willing to serve refreshments in the lounge, where a coal fire burns in winter, and superb traditional Scottish cuisine is served in the restaurant which overlooks the garden.

# The Old Smiddy Guest House

*AA Best British Breakfast National Award Winner*

☎ 01445 731425  📠 01445 731425
✉ oldsmiddy@aol.com

**Map ref 11 - NG89**

The Old Smiddy, LAIDE, Highland, IV22 2NB
from Inverness A835 towards Ullapool. At
Braemore Junct take A832. In Laide, last
house on left opposite church
3 Rooms, ££, No smoking

## RECOMMENDED IN THE AREA

**TRADITIONAL PUB:**
*Old Inn, Gairloch*

**VISIT:**
*Inverewe Gardens, Poolewe*

You need no better excuse to visit the Old Smiddy than to sample the award-winning breakfast, not to mention the superb home-baking and delicious dinners. This fantastic food is complemented with an equally superb setting. The Old Smiddy is a charming whitewashed cottage with stunning loch and mountain views. To add to these superlatives, Kate MacDonald was a top twenty finalist in the AA Landlady of the Year Award for 1999, so genuine hospitality is part of the experience.

The cottage has three delightful bedrooms with en suite facilities, colour television and tea and coffee making equipment. The cosy lounge leads to a dining room where meals are served. Children over 12 years are welcome, and there is ample parking. Mastercard and Visa are accepted here.

# Craigvar

*Fine detached Georgian house on town square*

☎ 01997 421622  📠 01997 421796
✉ craigvar@talk21.com

**Map ref 12 - NH45**

The Square, STRATHPEFFER, Highland,
IV14 9DL
3 Rooms, ££, No smoking
Closed Xmas & New Year

*C*raigvar stands in a prime location in the centre of this Highland spa town. It has been lovingly restored, by dedicated and enthusiastic owner Margaret Scott. You can expect all the best of Scottish hospitality here.

All of the bedrooms are furnished to match the Georgian style of the house. They all have en suite bathrooms, colour TV, tea and coffee making facilities and direct dial phones. Two are on the first floor - one with a four-poster bed, the other with twin beds and a private dressing room. The third bedroom is on the ground floor.

The lounge overlooks The Square, and features a modern doll's house. The breakfast room is spacious, with a large central table. The food is quite fabulous, especially the local black pudding.

## RECOMMENDED IN THE AREA

**RESTAURANT:**
*The Dower House, Muir of Ord*

**TRADITIONAL PUB:**
*Achilty Hotel, Contin*

**VISIT:**
*Moniack Castle, (Highland Winery), Kirkhill*

---

# Aldie House

*Victorian house and gardens surrounded by magnificent Highland scenery*

☎ 01862 893787  📠 01892 893787

**Map ref 12 - NH78**

TAIN, Highland, IV19 1LZ
from Inverness, 500yds before Tain on A9,
turn left and follow private road
3 Rooms, £, No smoking

*T*his proud house has four acres of woods and beautiful gardens, full of rare and exotic plants. The surrounding area is rich in flora and fauna, with spectacular hills and lochs, and possibilities for a range of sporting activities. Guests are free to use the private car park.

The house has been beautifully decorated, and filled with elegant Victorian antiques, to preserve the feel of a Scottish country home, and the Belgian owners make you feel very pleased you came - on arrival, guests are welcomed with tea in the drawing room. The bedrooms are grand and spacious, each with individual features and design; all have en suite bathrooms.

English or continental breakfast is served in the dining room, on delicately patterned china. It is lovely to sit in the sun lounge overlooking the gardens.

## RECOMMENDED IN THE AREA

**RESTAURANT:**
*Mansfield House, Tain*

**TRADITIONAL PUB:**
*Mallin House Hotel, Dornoch*

**VISIT:**
*Dunrobin Castle, Golspie*

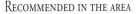

# Golf View House

*Former manse with lovely views of the Dornoch Firth*

☎ 01862 892856  🖷 01862 892172
✉ golfview@btinternet.com

**Map ref 12 - NH78**

13 Knockbreck Road, TAIN, Highland,
IV19 1BN
1st right off A9 at Tain (B9174), follow for
0.5m, house signposted on right
5 Rooms, £, No smoking
Closed Dec-Jan

Ian and Ray Ross take great delight in welcoming guests to their delightful Victorian home, set in two acres of secluded gardens where hens and ducks are kept. There are splendid views from the front lawn across the nearby golf course to the Dornoch Firth. The bedrooms are attractively decorated and comfortably appointed in both modern and traditional styles, including one suitable for family occupation. Three of the rooms have en suite facilities and all of them offer colour televisions and tea and coffee making equipment. The elegant lounge with its stunning outlook is the ideal place in which to relax, and the dining room with its individual tables provides an appropriate setting for Ray's hearty breakfasts. The Ross' own free-range eggs are a feature of the meal.

## RECOMMENDED IN THE AREA

**RESTAURANT:**
*Mansfield House, Tain*

**TRADITIONAL PUB:**
*Mallin House Hotel, Dornoch*

**VISIT:**
*Dunrobin Castle, Golspie*

# Gruline Home Farm

Dedicated owners Angela and Colin Boocock look forward to welcoming guests old and new to their charming island home. The house has been sympathetically converted and restored, and is peacefully set amid five acres of land just two and a half miles west of Salen. The two beautifully appointed first floor twin bedrooms are comfortably furnished with antiques and are serviced by luxurious en suite bathrooms. The cosy lounge invites relaxation, while the elegant dining room provides the appropriate setting for Colin's carefully prepared five-course dinners. Everything is made on the premises and Colin's menus will satisfy the most discerning palate and heartiest appetite.

*Former farmhouse located in the centre of the Isle of Mull*

☎ 01680 300581  🖷 01680 300573
✉ gruline@ukonline.co.uk

**Map ref 11 - NM54**

Gruline, SALEN, Argyll & Bute, PA71 6HR
from Craignure ferry turn right, go 10m to
Salen. In village turn left (B8035) for 2m,
keep left at fork, past church, farm on left
2 Rooms, ££, No smoking

## RECOMMENDED IN THE AREA

**VISIT:**
*Torosay Castle & Gardens*

# The Croft

*Victorian town house in peaceful location close to town centre*

☎ 01343 546004  📠 01343 546004
**Map ref 12 - NJ26**

10 Institution Road, ELGIN, Moray, IV30 1QX
turn off A96 at Safeway and down Queen St
turn right at bottom
3 Rooms, £, No smoking

The house was built in 1848, and it stands within mature formal gardens, carefully restored and replanted. It is situated in a quiet area in the historic east end of Elgin, just a five minute walk from the centre. The railway and bus stations are also an easy walk away. There is private off-street parking.

The rooms benefit from the generous proportions of the architecture, enhanced by period furnishings, and the stripped woodwork of the doors and window frames. The Nautical Bedroom, with handsome blue and white striped bedspreads, can serve as a family or twin room, the Country Diary Bedroom is a double room with a deep bay window. These two rooms have spacious en suite bathrooms. There is an elegant lounge overlooking the garden, and breakfast, featuring the best of local produce, is served at one table in the dining room.

## RECOMMENDED IN THE AREA

**RESTAURANT:**
*Knockomie Hotel, Forres*

**TRADITIONAL PUB:**
*Gordon Arms Hotel, Fochabers*

**VISIT:**
*Biblical Gardens, Elgin*

# Knockomie Lodge

*Traditional Scottish lodge providing superior en suite accommodation*

☎ 01309 676785
✉ knockomi@globalnet.co.uk
**Map ref 12 - NJ05**

FORRES, Moray, IV36 2SG
A940, Forres to Grantown-on-Spey road,
1m from Forres on right
3 Rooms, £, No smoking

Knockomie Lodge is a former gate house set in well tended grounds a mile outside the garden town of Forres. Each of the attractively decorated en suite bedrooms is equipped with television, radio and hospitality tray. The Lodge is ideally situated for touring Inverness and the Grampians, and there are plenty of opportunities for leisure activities, with four golf courses within a 12-mile radius and both loch and sea fishing close by. The area has many attractions, among these are Dallas Dhu Distillery, a few minutes' pleasant walk away, and Brodie Castle just four miles distant.

A warm welcome is assured, with tea and home made cakes offered to guests on arrival. The bright lounge/dining room provides a comfortable setting for a hearty Scottish breakfast, with home made jams and pancakes as a welcome addition to the options available.

## RECOMMENDED IN THE AREA

**RESTAURANT:**
*Knockomie Hotel, Forres*

**TRADITIONAL PUB:**
*Gordon Arms Hotel, Fochabers*

**VISIT:**
*Dallas Dhu Distillery, Forres*

# South Whittlieburn Farm

*Only 5 minutes' drive from Largs, near the island ferries, and 40 minutes from Glasgow/Prestwick airports*

☎ 01475 675881  📠 01475 675080

**Map ref 9 - NS25**

Brisbane Glen, LARGS, North Ayrshire, KA30 8SN

2m NE of Largs town centre, off road signed Brisbane Glen, just past leisure complex

3 Rooms, £, No smoking in bedrooms

*A* warm welcome is assured from Mary Watson at this superb farmhouse, on a working sheep farm, in peaceful Brisbane Glen (where Sir Thomas MacDougall Brisbane, founder of Brisbane Australia, came from). All the bright, cheerful bedrooms have en suite facilities. A two-room suite is suitable for families. Televisions, hospitality trays, hairdryers and radio alarms are among the useful items provided. The enormous and delicious breakfast here is highly recommended. There is a comfortable TV lounge for guests to relax in. Ample parking is provided, dogs cannot be accommodated (except for guide dogs). There are many activities nearby making this a great holiday destination. Hill-walking, golf, horseriding, fishing, diving, sailing, a cinema, theatre, swimming pool and putting green are among the local attractions. The Largs Viking festival takes place in the 1st week in September and Vikingar (story of the Vikings) is another local attraction.

## RECOMMENDED IN THE AREA

**RESTAURANT:**
*Braidwoods, Dalry*

**VISIT:**
*Vikingar, Largs*

*Whiting Bay, Arran and Holy Isle*

# *M*yfarcclan
# Guest House

### RECOMMENDED IN THE AREA

**RESTAURANT:**
*Yes, Glasgow*

**TRADITIONAL PUB:**
*Fox & Hounds, Houston*

**VISIT:**
*Paisley Museum & Art Gallery, Paisley*

*Convenient for Glasgow Airport and a central base for touring Scotland*

☎ 0141 884 8285
🖷 0141 581 1566
📧 myfarrclan_qwest
@compuserve.com

**Map ref 9 - NS56**

146 Corsebar Road,
PAISLEY, Renfrewshire,
PA2 9NA
pass Royal Alexandra
Hospital on left, house
0.5m up hill on right,
tall evergreen hedge
3 Rooms, ££
No smoking

*M*yfarrclan is convenient for Glasgow Airport and an ideal central base for touring Stirling, Loch Lomond, Ayrshire, Edinburgh and the Isles. Brenda and Keith offer genuine, friendly hospitality and a welcoming atmosphere.

Situated in a leafy suburb, the charming bungalow has a warm, homely interior with traditional guest lounge and a garden conservatory lounge overlooking the 'decked' rear garden. Bedrooms have en suite showers and quality fittings. There are colour satellite TVs and well stocked beverage trays in all the rooms and guests will find a wide range of thoughtful extras including trouser press/ironing suite, hairdryers and toiletries.

A substantial choice of breakfasts are served in the dining room, and in the evening, fresh salmon fillet dinners are the speciality, followed by single malt tasting for whisky lovers. Your hosts will be happy to assist in planning your Scottish itinerary, as well as conducting tours.

# East Lochhead

*Renovated 100-year-old farmhouse with loch views*

☎ 01505 842610   📠 01505 842610
📧 winnoch@aol.com

**Map ref 9 - NS35**

Largs Road, LOCHWINNOCH, Renfrewshire,
PA12 4DX
from Glasgow take M8 J28a for A737 Irvine.
At Roadhead rdbt turn right on A760.
Premises 2m on left
2 Rooms, ££, No smoking

## RECOMMENDED IN THE AREA

**RESTAURANT:**
*Braidwoods, Dalry*

**TRADITIONAL PUB:**
*Fox & Hounds, Houston*

**VISIT:**
*RSPB Nature Reserve, Lochwinnoch*

*E*nthusiastic owner Janet Anderson has made a superb job of renovating this former farmhouse, which is well situated one mile west of the village. The location is convenient for Glasgow airport - ideal for before or after a long flight - and a good base for visiting Glasgow, Ayrshire, the Clyde Coast, the Trossachs and Loch Lomond.

There is a relaxed country house atmosphere, and accommodation is offered in an en suite ground floor room, suitable for double/family occupation, and an upstairs twin room with its own private bathroom. Guests can relax in the combined lounge/dining room, which has magnificent views of Barr Loch.

Janet is an enthusiastic cook and her enjoyable home cooking is served at the communal table. Vegetarian and other diets are catered for. Pets can be brought by prior arrangement.

# The Glenholm Centre

*Peace and quiet on an upland farm with superb views*

☎ 01899 830408   📠 01899 830408
📧 glenholm@dircon.co.uk

**Map ref 10 - NT13**

BROUGHTON, Scottish Borders, ML12 6JF
on A701, 1m S of Broughton, turn right
signed Glenholm/Glenholm Centre. Continue
1m, centre on right, before cattlegrid
4 Rooms, £, No smoking
Closed Jan

## RECOMMENDED IN THE AREA

**RESTAURANT:**
*Shieldhill Hotel, Biggar*

**TRADITIONAL PUB:**
*Crook Inn, Tweedsmuir*

**VISIT:**
*Broughton Palace, Broughton*

*T*he Glenholm Centre is a converted school house set in a peaceful valley, visitors can explore 1,000 acres of farmland in the area. Situated just 30 miles south of Edinburgh, it makes an excellent stopover on your journey through Scotland, or a base for exploring the upper Tweed Valley.

Wholesome cooking is a special feature here and all tastes can be catered for. Home cooked breakfasts and baking are the highlight of any stay. The en suite bedrooms are bright and airy, a family suite is available in an adjacent cottage, sleeping up to four people. In addition to colour televisions, the rooms are equipped with extras such as a fridge, direct dial telephone and video. The centre is licensed and there is plenty of parking.

A small computer training centre adjoins the guest house and computing activity holidays are available.

# Dunlaverock Country House

*A house with a spectacular setting affording amazing seascape views*

☎ 018907 71450  📠 018907 71450
✉ dunlaverock@lineone.net

**Map ref 10 - NT96**

EYEMOUTH, Scottish Borders, TD14 5PA
6 Rooms, £££
Closed 1 Dec-31 Jan

Dunlaverock is a private country house hotel with six en suite bedrooms. Perched on a small cliff, it has a large garden reaching down to the stunning bay of Coldingham Sands. The hotel is situated between St Abbs, famous for bird-watching, and the small fishing town of Eyemouth, which is only 15 minutes from historic Berwick-Upon-Tweed.

The marvellous 'Taste of Scotland' menu has a strong local theme and uses the best produce available. Guests are invited to relax in the drawing room and sample some of the world's best malt whiskies, in front of a welcoming log fire.

The area is a walker's paradise with great coastal paths. There is good trout and sea fishing and an excellent 18-hole golf course.

## RECOMMENDED IN THE AREA

**RESTAURANT:**
*Marshall Meddows, Berwick-upon-Tweed*

**TRADITIONAL PUB:**
*The Rob Roy, Berwick-upon-Tweed*

**VISIT:**
*Paxton House, Berwick-upon-Tweed*

# Maplehurst Guest House

*Early 20th-century house with art deco features*

☎ 01896 754700  📠 01896 754700

**Map ref 10 - NT43**

42 Abbotsford Road, GALASHIELS, Scottish Borders, TD1 3HP
on A7, South side of town
3 Rooms, ££, No smoking
Closed Xmas & New Year

## RECOMMENDED IN THE AREA

**RESTAURANT:**
*Burt's Hotel, Melrose*

**TRADITIONAL PUB:**
*Abbotsford Arms, Galashiels*

**VISIT:**
*Lochcarron Cashmere & Wool Centre, Galashiels*

Built for a mill owner and his Canadian wife in 1907, this magnificent detached house retains many of its original features, including art deco stained glass, wood panelling, hardwood floors, a tapestry wall covering, and recessed dresser.

The guest bedrooms are located on the first floor and are very individual in character. The turret suite has a cast iron bath from which views of the surrounding Border hills can be enjoyed. There is also a twin room, and a family room with double and twin beds. An attractive first floor sitting area is provided, with a balcony and payphone. Dinner is available by prior request, Janice Richardson's home cooking is well worth sampling. The house is peacefully situated in a mature garden, with lots of trees and shrubs, yet the centre of Galashiels is within easy walking distance.

# The Spinney

*An attractive home set in beautiful grounds and gardens*

☎ 01835 863525  📠 01835 864883
✉ thespinney@btinternet.com
**Map ref 10 - NT62**

Langlee, JEDBURGH, Scottish Borders,
TD8 6PB
2 miles South of Jedburgh on A68
3 Rooms, £, No smoking

Ten miles north of the border, nestling in the foothills of the Cheviots, lies the historic Royal Burgh of Jedburgh. The Spinney is located two miles south of the town on one of the most scenic routes into Scotland, and is set in mature landscaped gardens bordering woodland and open countryside. The house is well maintained and provides extensive facilities for guests. The spacious bedrooms are furnished to a very high standard and include a television in each, tea-making facilities and private or en suite bathrooms. For the comfort and well being of guests there is a no smoking policy in the house. A wide variety of breakfast choices are available in the luxurious dining room, providing guests with the perfect start to the day and an experience to remember.

## RECOMMENDED IN THE AREA

**RESTAURANT:**
*Jedforest Hotel, Jedburgh*

**TRADITIONAL PUB:**
*Buccleugh Arms Hotel, St Boswells*

**VISIT:**
*Jedburgh Abbey, Jedburgh*

*Nethermill, Galashiels in the Scottish Borders*

# Toftcombs House & Country Restaurant

*Beautifully restored property only 26 miles from Edinburgh, with an award-winning restaurant*

☎ 01899 220142
🖷 01899 221771
✉ toftcombs@aol.com

**Map ref 10 - NT03**

Peebles Road, BIGGAR, South Lanarkshire, ML12 6QX
A702 from Biggar towards Edinburgh, A72 Peebles turning on right, house 50yds from junction
4 Rooms, ££, No smoking in bedrooms

*C*harles and Vivian Little have recently completed a magnificent restoration job on this fine red sandstone building. The house has an interesting history and was owned by the ancestors of William Gladstone for four generations from 1832. The impressive turret was added in 1874 and the coat of arms remains over what was then the main entrance. Toftcombs combines the comfort and elegance of a country house with the convivial atmosphere of a country restaurant, which has an AA rosette award for fine food and a "Taste of Scotland" recommendation. The same menu can also be enjoyed in the bar-lounge, and there are other lounges in which to relax with a magazine or a coffee. The impressive wine cellar offers fine wines from around the world at affordable prices. Upstairs, the character of the property is retained in the tastefully appointed bedrooms, one of which is suitable for family occupation. All the rooms have en suite bath or shower, colour televisions, and tea and coffee making facilities.

## RECOMMENDED IN THE AREA

**TRADITIONAL PUB:**
*The Crook Inn, Tweedsmuir*

**VISIT:**
*Broughton Palace, Broughton*

# *A*rden House

*Dr Finlay's house in the well loved BBC TV series*

☎ **01877 330235** 📠 **01877 330235**

**Map ref 9 - NN60**

Bracklinn Road, CALLANDER, Stirling, FK17 8EQ
from A84 in Callander, right into Bracklinn Rd, sign for golf course & Bracklinn Falls. House 200yds on left

6 Rooms, ££, No smoking

*I*n a quiet position, with panoramic views and its own gardens, this large Victorian family home is located just a few minutes' walk up the hill from the village centre. It is an ideal base for exploring the Highlands, within easy reach of the main Scottish cities. It is also just two minutes from the first tee of Callander's golf course. Arden House is not suitable for children under 14, or for pets.

The bedrooms are elegant, all individually refurbished, with en suite bathrooms, colour TV and many thoughtful touches. There is a very comfortable and stylish lounge. Breakfast is substantial and includes fresh produce from the local bakery. The owners assure their guests a warm and hospitable welcome.

## RECOMMENDED IN THE AREA

**RESTAURANT:**
*Roman Camp, Callander*

**TRADITIONAL PUB:**
*Byre Inn, Brig O'Turk*

**VISIT:**
*Doune Castle, Doune*

# *B*rook Linn Country House

*Victorian country house on the edge of Callander*

☎ **01877 330103** 📠 **01877 330103**
✉ **derek@blinn.freeserve.co.uk**

**Map ref 9 - NN60**

Leny Feus, CALLANDER, Stirling, FK17 8AU
take A84 thro' Callander from Stirling, right at Pinewood Nursing Home into Leny Feus. Right again & up hill at 'Brook Linn' sign

7 Rooms, £, No smoking

*F*iona and Derek House have sympathetically restored their elegant home to provide guests with a comfortable, relaxing and friendly place to stay. Bedrooms are bright and airy with big windows showing off the super views. All rooms are now either en suite or have private facilities and are equipped with televisions, radios, hospitality trays, hairdryers and electric blankets. Attractive decor, pretty fabrics and thick duvets are a home from home touch.

Public areas include an inviting sitting room and pleasantly appointed dining room. The house stands in an elevated position ten minutes' walk from town and is set in two acres of mature grounds, with terraced lawns, flowers, shrubs and a kitchen garden.

## RECOMMENDED IN THE AREA

**RESTAURANT:**
*Creagan House, Strathyre*

**TRADITIONAL PUB:**
*Byre Inn, Brig O'Turk*

**VISIT:**
*Blair Drummond Safari & Leisure Park*

# Rokeby House

*Edwardian villa in the heart of Perthshire*

**☎ 01786 824447**
**🖷 01786 821399**
**✉ rokeby.house@btconnect.com**

**Map ref 10 - NN70**

Doune Road,
DUNBLANE, Stirling,
FK15 9AT
M9 N, Dunblane exit,
next turn to Doune,
along Doune Road
0.5m on left
3 Rooms, ££
No smoking

*B*uilt in 1907, this delightful property has been sympathetically restored to its former glory by enthusiastic proprietor Richard Beatts. A combination of high standards of accommodation, warm hospitality and gracious surroundings make this a wonderful place to rest and relax. Antique pieces and original paintings are a feature of many of the rooms, and the lovely grounds include a secret garden and an Italian garden with a rustic pergola. All the bedrooms have either en suite or private facilities and look out onto the gardens. They are decorated in period style and are equipped with central heating, colour television and clock radios. Tea and coffee making facilities are provided in the elegant guests' lounge. Breakfast is served in the stylish dining room and evening meals are available by prior arrangement. For golfing enthusiasts, Gleneagles is just a few minutes away, and St Andrews and Carnoustie are within easy reach.

## RECOMMENDED
### IN THE AREA

**RESTAURANT:**
*Cromlix House,*
*Dunblane*

**TRADITIONAL PUB:**
*Lion & Unicorn,*
*Thornhill*

**VISIT:**
*Stirling Castle, Stirling*

# Ashcroft Farmhouse

*Special care from your hosts in a modern farmhouse with ground floor bedrooms*

☎ 01506 881810
📠 01506 884327
📧 ashcroftfa
@aol.com

**Map ref 10 - NT06**

EAST CALDER, West
Lothian, EH53 0ET
on B7015, off A71
6 Rooms, ££
No smoking

Derek and Elizabeth will ensure that your stay at their lovely home is so memorable you will want to return time and time again, Elizabeth was chosen as a finalist in the AA's Landlady of the Year competition. The farmhouse is in the country but conveniently close for Edinburgh, it has its own flocks of sheep and landscaped gardens. There is parking for guests. In the bedrooms, pretty fabrics complement the smart pine furnishings, and all have en suite bathrooms with showers. One room has a four-poster bed. After early morning tea in your room, there is a choice of breakfasts - one of the highlights is Derek's home-made sausages. The residents' lounge has a library, and there is a bright and comfortable dining room, adorned with fascinating golf bric-a-brac.

## RECOMMENDED IN THE AREA

**RESTAURANT:**
*Houston House Hotel, Uphall*

**TRADITIONAL PUB:**
*Bridge Inn, Ratho*

**VISIT:**
*Malleny Garden, Balerno*

# Northern Ireland

Belfast's baronial-style castle on the lower slopes of Cave Hill has a square six-storey tower and baroque staircase. There is a visitor centre and the surrounding area is popular for picnics and walks. The Botanic Gardens in Belfast has a palm house pre-dating the one in Kew Gardens, making it one of the earliest curved-glass and iron structures in the world. There is also a tropical ravine full of exotic plants.

There are two particularly popular attractions in County Antrim, the Old Bushmills Distillery at Bushmills, and two miles north, the Giant's Causeway Centre with an exhibition and guided walks.

*Rope Bridge at Carrick A Rede, County Antrim*

## Craig Park

*Exceptional service in a country house with panoramic views*

☎ 028 20732496  📠 028 20732479
✉ jan@craigpark.co.uk

**Map ref 13 - B5**

24 Carnbore Road, BUSHMILLS, Antrim, BT57 8YF
3 Rooms, £, No smoking
Closed Xmas & New Year

*T*his lovely old farmhouse sits in quiet surroundings, at the head of a long lawn. It is close to the Causeway Coast, with dramatic scenery for cliff-top walks and magnificent beaches nearby. There are also good opportunities for golf and for bird-watching. From its elevated position you can see across to the mountains of Donegal and the Antrim Hills in the distance.

The large, light, airy bedrooms, furnished in a style appropriate to the character of the house, all have en suite bathrooms with superb power showers, and colour TV. Guests are invited to share the owners' spacious sitting room, and carefully prepared breakfasts are served around the table in the attractive dining room.

## RECOMMENDED IN THE AREA

**RESTAURANT:**
*Ramore, Portrush*

**VISIT:**
*Old Bushmills Distillery, Bushmills*

# Rayanne Country House & Restaurant

RECOMMENDED
IN THE AREA

VISIT:
*Belfast Castle,*
*Belfast & The Botanic*
*Gardens, Belfast*

*19th-century country house serving an award-winning breakfast*

☎ 028 90425859
📠 028 90423364

Map ref 13 - C4

60 Desmesne Road, HOLYWOOD, Down, BT18 9EX
A2 Belfast-Bangor, past airport & Holywood Palace turn right opp Esso garage, 0.75m past golf club
9 Rooms, ££, No Smoking in bedrooms
Closed 24 Dec-3 Jan

*G*enuine Irish hospitality and excellent food at both dinner and breakfast are part of the appeal at this fine house located in Holywood. Public rooms include two charming lounges, but the focal point is the elegant restaurant. Here, the innovative menu combined with technical skills in the kitchen, have won wide acclaim, including a two rosette award from the AA. Breakfast is also a memorable experience, indeed Rayanne House won the AA's National Breakfast Award in 1999. Options from an extensive list include compote of marinated spiced fruits, chilled fresh raspberry porridge, delicious breads, smoked haddock frittata, and the Rayanne House grill. The lovely en suite bedrooms have been equipped with a wide range of thoughtful extras, such as hospitality trays, home-made shortbread, fresh fruit, spring water, toiletries, electric blankets, colour television, alarm clock, hairdryer, reading materials, sewing kit and stationery.

# Pheasants' Hill Country House

*Modern farmhouse on a seven-acre rare breeds smallholding*

☎ 028 44617246   🖷 028 44617246
✉ pheasants.hill@dnet.co.uk

**Map ref 13 - C3**

37 Killyleagh Road, DOWNPATRICK, Down,
BT30 9BL
on A22
3 Rooms, £, No smoking

Pheasants' Hill is situated just north of the town, on the borders of the Quoile Pondage and close to Strangford Lough. The farmhouse was built in 1994, and is surrounded by fields where rare breed pigs and ponies roam, and vegetables, fruit and herbs are grown using organic methods.

Inside the house, the bedrooms are well appointed with country furniture, and many thoughtful extras are provided, including fresh flowers, colour televisions, tea and coffee trays and hairdryers. Two rooms have en suite facilities and one has an adjacent private bathroom. Guests have exclusive use of a comfortable lounge and a cosy dining room, and are welcomed with tea served by the turf fire or in the orchard. Wholesome Irish breakfasts are a highlight, winning the AA's National Breakfast Award for 2000. Janis Bailey's splendid dinners are available by arrangement, including vegetarian dishes if required.

## RECOMMENDED IN THE AREA

**RESTAURANT:**
*Portaferry Hotel, Portaferry*

**VISIT:**
*Down County Museum, Downpatrick*

# Grange Lodge

*Hospitable Georgian retreat set in three and a half acres*

☎ 028 87784212   🖷 028 87784313

**Map ref 13 - B4**

7 Grange Road, DUNGANNON, Tyrone,
BT71 7EJ
1mile from M1 J15 on A29 Armagh, take sign for 'Grange' then 1st right & 1st house on right
5 Rooms, ££, No smoking in bedrooms
Closed 21 Dec-9 Jan

Norah and Ralph Brown are enthusiastic and sincere hosts who maintain their charming home in immaculate condition. The splendid drawing room, with its period pieces and paintings, is the ideal place to relax, along with the comfortable den, the only room where smoking is permitted.

All of the guest bedrooms are provided with en suite facilities. During the summer guests can dine in the bright and airy extension overlooking the gardens - the perfect setting for Norah's award-winning cooking. Her imaginative dishes have won her a reputation as a talented cook, and her eye for detail is demonstrated in the fine glassware, crisp linen, and even wild flowers to decorate the plates.

## RECOMMENDED IN THE AREA

**VISIT:**
*Argory, Moy, County Armagh*

# Greenhill House

*Georgian country house in quiet wooded surroundings*

☎ 028 70868241   🖷 028 70868365
✉ greenhill.house@btinternet.com

**Map ref 13 - B5**

24 Greenhill Road, Aghadowey, COLERAINE,
Londonderry, BT51 4EU
from Coleraine take A29 for 7m, turn left
onto B66 Greenhill Rd for approx 300yds.
House on right, AA sign at front gate
6 Rooms, £

Friendly family hospitality is extended to guests at Greenhill House. It is a fine property situated in the Bann Valley overlooking the Antrim Hills, and has its own lovely gardens, the daffodil display in spring is particularly stunning. Public rooms are very comfortable and traditional in style. They include a relaxing lounge where a real fire burns in the winter months, and a tastefully appointed dining room, where enjoyable home cooking is served, featuring Taste of Ulster dishes.

The bedrooms all have en suite facilities, two with a bath, two with a shower and two with a bath and shower. The rooms are bright and airy, and equipped with many thoughtful extras.

## RECOMMENDED IN THE AREA

**RESTAURANT:**
*Ramore, Portrush*

**VISIT:**
*Hezlett House, Coleraine*

*Donaghadee, County Down*

# *I*NDEX

## How to use the Index

Town names are listed alphabetically in the index. Establishments are listed under the nearest town or village, which may be up to five miles away. After the town name the county name appears in brackets, followed by the region number. Establishments are listed in alphabetical order under the town name.

Please note that establishments appear in alphabetical order as far as possible within each town throughout the guide. The page number for each establishment is shown last.

e.g.

**Town name (County name)** Region number

    Establishment name      page number

## Reminder of region numbers:

**Region 1:** The West Country

**Region 2:** South & South East England

**Region 3:** Central England & East Anglia

**Region 4:** Wales

**Region 5:** The North of England

**Region 6:** Scotland & Northern Ireland

# CREDITS

## Photograph Credits

*Permission for the use of photographs in the preliminary pages of this guide was kindly given by the following establishments:*

At The Sign of The Angel, Lacock
Augill Castle, Brough
Ballifeary House Hotel, Inverness
Bettmans Oast, Biddenden
Dannah Farm Country House, Shottle, Nr Belper
King Charles II Guest House, Rye
Lavenham Priory, Lavenham
Magnolia house, Canterbury
Martins Restaurant with Rooms, Llandudno
Sawrey House Country Hotel, Near Sawrey
The Gallery Hotel, London SW7

*Other photographs used with the kind permission of the AA Photo Library are as follows:*

All main pictures are held in the Automobile Association's own library (AA PHOTOLIBRARY) and were taken by
AA PHOTOLIBRARY Front Cover (c) and (g), 15b, 100, 171, 215, 242/3; M ALEXANDER 305; PETER BAKER 32/3, 113, 187; VIC BATES 300 (a) and (b); JEFF BEAZLEY 247, 254; LIAM BLAKE Front Cover (d), 1; IAN BURGUM 215; DOUGLAS CORRANCE 202/3, 334; STEVE DAY 9a, 202/3, 242/3, 265; M DIGGIN 342; ERIC ELLINGTON 13a; PHILIP ENTICKNAP 139; DEREK FORSS 138; R HAYMAN 50; CAROLINE JONES 216; ANDREW LAWSON 45, 55, 72; S & O MATHEWS Front Cover (b), 3, 94; JOHN MILLAR 8b; C & A MOLYNEUX 238; JOHN MORRISON 5a; ROGER MOSS 59; JOHN MOTTISHAW 14a; GEORGE MUNDAY 339; RICH NEWTON 5c, 113; KEN PATERSON 330; M SIEBERT 10a; RICK STRANGE 14b; TOM TEEGAN 114; JAMES TIMS 15a; JONATHON WELSH 197; HARRY WILLIAMS 32/3; STEPHEN WHITEHORN 4a; LINDA WHITEMAN 244; WYN VOYSEY 32/3, 182